Sport in the Global Society

General Editor: J.A. Mangan

THE POLITICS OF SOUTH AFRICAN CRICKET

SPORT IN THE GLOBAL SOCIETY

General Editor: J.A. Mangan

The interest in sports studies around the world is growing and will continue to do so. This unique series combines aspects of the expanding study of *sport in the global society*, providing comprehensiveness and comparison under one editorial umbrella. It is particularly timely, with studies in the political, cultural, anthropological, ethnographic, social, economic, geographical and aesthetic elements of sport proliferating in institutions of higher education.

Eric Hobsbawm once called sport one of the most significant practices of the late nineteenth century. Its significance was even more marked in the late twentieth century and will continue to grow in importance into the new millennium as the world develops into a 'global village' sharing the English language, technology and sport.

Other Titles in the Series

THE POLITICS OF SOUTH AFRICAN CRICKET

JON GEMMELL

Routledge
Taylor & Francis Group

LONDON AND NEW YORK

First published in 2004
by Routledge
11 New Fetter Lane, London EC4P 4EE

Simultaneously published in the USA and Canada
by Routledge
29 West 35th Street, New York, NY 10001

Routledge is an imprint of the Taylor & Francis Group

Typeset in Times by Taylor & Francis Books Ltd

British Library Cataloguing in Publication Data
A catalogue record for this book is available from the British Library

Library of Congress Cataloging-in-Publication Data
A catalog record for this book has been requested

ISBN 0-7146-5346-2 (HB)
ISBN 0-7146-8284-5 (PB)
ISSN 1368-9789

To:

Mike — *the inspiration*
Stephen — *the encouragement*
James — *the coaching*

Contents

Acknowledgements

Without the influence of three people, this book would not have been possible: Mike Marqusee, Stephen Wagg and James Hamill. In your various ways you have proved invaluable and it is to you that I dedicate this work.

A lot of the research was carried out in various libraries. I would like to thank the library authorities and staff at the University of Leicester, the University of Reading, Roehampton Institute and the British Library. Special thanks go to Jeff Hancock at the Oval for not only the use of the Surrey County Cricket Club library (and the lock-ins) but also the enlightening conversation; Jeff is a man who appreciates both his cricket and its relationship with the outside world.

My experience at the University of Leicester was nothing less than fantastic, and I would like to single out Dr Clive Dewey for suggesting at an early stage of my undergraduate life that I consider postgraduate research. His confidence in me was greatly appreciated. I would also like to thank Professor John Hoffman, a fascinating individual who I wish I could have got to know better.

I am really grateful to Professor Mangan and the staff at Frank Cass for providing an outlet for my work. Special thanks to Douglas Booth for reading the early draft and making a number of suggestions. It goes without saying, of course, that many have influenced the work, but the final opinions are mine, as are any mistakes or misinterpretations. I should also mention Paul Dick, his staff and my colleagues at Kennet School, Thatcham.

Finally, I am grateful to my mother for her support and my father for sitting me in front of the cricket at an early age. A special mention must also go to Martin Hughes for the top-quality sports-chat, and Bukharin and Rachael, my life companions.

Abbreviations

ACB	Australian Cricket Board
ANC	African National Party
COSATU	Confederation of South African Trade Unions
FIS	Freedom in Sport
HNP	Herstigte Nasionale Party (Restored National Party)
ICC	Imperial Cricket Council (became International Cricket Council in 1965)
IOC	International Olympic Committee
MCC	Marylebone Cricket Club
MDM	Mass Democratic Movement
NP	National Party
NSC	National Sports Congress
PAC	Pan African Congress
SACA	South African Cricket Association
SACB	South African Cricket Board
SACBOC	South African Cricket Board of Control
SACOS	South African Council on Sport
SACTU	South African Council of Trade Unions
SACU	South African Cricket Union
SADF	South African Defence Force
SASA	South African Sports Association
STST	Stop the Seventies Tour
TCCB	Test and County Cricket Board
UCBSA	Union Cricket Board of South Africa (also known as UCB)
UDF	United Democratic Front
UNESCO	United Nations Education, Scientific & Cultural Organisation

Series Editor's Foreword

The opening sentence of Jon Gemmell's Introduction sets the tone for *The Politics of South African Cricket*: 'It should be stressed from the outset that this book is not about cricket – at least not in the conventional sense.'[1] This old tune played on a new whistle brings a loud cheer from this Series Editor, who shares the same approach to the general study of sport. In my preface to *The Games Ethic and Imperialism*, I expressed the wish that 'I would not like this study of cultural diffusion to be naively and erroneously catalogued under "Games". It is concerned with much more: with ethnocentricity, hegemony and patronage, with ideals and idealism, with educational values and aspirations, with cultural assimilation and adaptation and, most fascinating of all, with the dissemination throughout the Empire of a hugely influential moralistic ideology.'[2] To indulge in one further metaphor, from his 'South African Pulpit' Jon Gemmell preaches to at least one of the converted.

Gemmell remarks that *The Politics of South African Cricket* is about the game as it has reflected South African society. It is concerned with what lies 'beyond the boundary'. He makes two further unequivocal points: recent (South African) sport has been political and sports policies in Apartheid South Africa were designed specifically to ensure its perpetuity.

These observations are hardly original but his concentration on South African cricket as a case-study, is. Here is the value of *The Politics of South African Cricket*.

Gemmell's concern with more general analysis 'in the round' is equally praiseworthy. One illustration of this is his interest in economics, which he argues with some truth, 'ultimately determines the politics of individual states'.[3]

Finally, Gemmell suggests convincingly that the term 'interdependence' is the password allowing access to an understanding of the politics of South African cricket which requires a consideration, as he repeatedly states, of more than just the game. The interdependence forged between racism, a *laager* mentality and economics, created a gross inequality which, as he frankly admits, still exists. This, in turn, determined (and determines) access, participation and opportunity in South African sport. Now, however, there is an inexpungable desire for change. Thus Gemmell points out that cricket, as in the Apartheid era, still has a political role – albeit very different now. It has been assigned a part in the construction of a democratic, non-racial South Africa. South African sport, which has always 'known politics', still 'knows' politics!

To paraphrase a great English writer,[4] *The Politics of South African Cricket* reveals an independent mind, freed from convention and committed to originality, and it is an admirable companion volume to the earlier *The Race Game: Sport and Politics in South Africa* by Douglas Booth, also published in the series Sport in the Global Society.

J. A. Mangan
Director, IRCSSS,
De Montford (Bedford) University

Introduction

It should be stressed from the outset that this book is not about cricket – at least not in the conventional sense. The contest between bat and ball, with all its complexities, intrigue and insights into character, serves no purpose to the political scientist beyond mere aesthetics. My primary concern is with what the game represents and its place in a model of society. This assumes that sports are subject to the extensive dynamics that shape our social and political environment. In this sense, I follow in the tradition of C.L.R. James, Rowland Bowen, Mike Marqusee and Hilary Beckles (to name a few), who set out to explore what exactly lay 'beyond the boundary'.[1]

There are two principal aims to this exercise:

- to demonstrate that the development of sport is inextricably linked with that of politics;
- to show that sporting policy in South Africa was an important element within the 'reform process' and constituted a group of measures purposely designed to prolong the existence of apartheid.

The project is divided into three distinct sections, each adopting a different approach to the examination of the material. The first section provides the philosophical foundations for the subject matter. The instruments of the political theorist are deployed to examine what is meant when we discuss terms such as 'politics', 'sport' and 'cricket'. Are they simply value-free phenomena, or does an individual's perception of them dictate his or her insight into their interdependence, thus colouring his or her judgement on questions devolved from such interpretations? For example, it is often argued that politics and sport should not mix. From the perspective of the political scientist, an examination of such a statement can only accurately be made once it is clear what is meant by such terms. My reasons for adopting such an approach at the outset are threefold:

- Whilst there has been a considerable literature on the question of politics and sport, I feel that it has largely failed to establish a strong theoretical grounding in that it assumes the reader is aware of what is meant by 'politics'.[2] 'What is politics?' is a question that has intrigued political scientists throughout the history of the discipline. The answer to this, for me, will determine the individual's outlook on the relationship between politics and sport.

- To show that politics is about more than the analysis of institutions, the functions of the executive and the history of government. I have set out to construct a model that places politics in relation to the other social sciences, and then examines how this affects other channels and avenues of social life. I intend to show that, because of the interrelatedness between the subject matter, sport is part of this wider structure.
- To examine the 'ethos' of cricket, and to assess its contribution and influence to the world game. I am concerned with issues such as: Are differentials in class and race common throughout the history of the Test-playing nations? Does politics have a role in the shaping of the game? Has cricket been exploited for political gain? Has cricket, itself, influenced the development of politics? The reason for raising such issues is that they are comprehensively intertwined in South Africa's history. What I am interested in is whether 'cricket' can be analysed as a distinct variable, or can we simply dismiss the development of the sport in South Africa as unique to that country. To do this I examine the role of the sport in a number of countries other than South Africa.

The second section is concerned with a number of themes relevant to the political and social history of racially segregated South African cricket. It begins, as does the analysis of 'politics', with an examination of the executive and how it has formally legislated on the issue of sport. The enquiry ventures beyond the descriptive and seeks to determine external trends that may have pre-empted government initiatives. I am particularly concerned with economic developments as I hold that these ultimately determine the politics of individual states. Chapter 4, therefore, seeks to outline the processes or developments behind actual policy.

From this platform, the next two chapters of the section take up the arguments between the protagonists and sympathisers of white-led South African cricket. In this vein, Chapter 5 examines the history of racial cricket in South Africa. Nationalist politicians argued that any racial division in South African sport was principally a consequence of tradition; cricket, for example, had always been segregated into as many as four distinct racial groups. 'Tradition' is a key term for conservative theorists, and what interests me is from where and when such 'traditions' emerge: Are they politically manufactured? How are they maintained? Whose interests do they serve?

The official stance of the International Cricket Council (ICC) had been that South Africa had to create the conditions for genuine multiracial cricket to be recognised as the norm before the international community would re-engage in sporting relations with it. It was then argued that the steps taken by the government had slowly created an environment in which racial sport was no longer enforced, hence South Africa should be welcomed back into the international fold from which it was excluded in 1961. The counter argument to this stance is that apartheid had penetrated every area of society, and – even if legislation enabled mixed sport at the highest level – the wider framework of legislation had created such a society that equality of opportunity was certainly an illusion. Therefore, merit selection would still result in all-white teams.

'No normal sport in an abnormal society' became the rallying cry of the opposition to white-led cricket. Pressure was to be maintained, both at home – by directly challenging the white authorities within the overall political opposition – and overseas – by maintaining a sporting boycott on South Africa. In general, those who wanted to play against South Africa argued that the two variables – sport and politics – should not be mixed, whereas those intent on isolating the Republic did so on an appreciation of the intimate association between them. Thus, Chapters 5 and 6 are crucial in demonstrating the interrelatedness of sport and politics.

The seventh chapter, on the sports boycott of South Africa, concludes the thematic section by attempting to draw conclusions from the preceding chapters and placing them within an international context. Isolating South Africa from normal sporting relations was an important psychological weapon in the campaign for liberation. This body blow to the regime was increasingly supported by governments, both European and African, though perhaps not by all sporting organisations. This chapter is concerned with the nature and the strengths of the debate, and considers the argument of 'bridge-builders' who claimed that links with South Africa needed to be maintained in order to influence and assist reform. This was an extension of the classical liberal position which insisted that capitalism would eventually corrode apartheid.[3] Furthermore, Chapter 7 analyses the political influence of countries from Africa and the Caribbean who found themselves with a voice and a newly discovered influence on the world stage. What effect did that have on 'white' nations such as Britain, Australia and New Zealand? Why was the boycott of South African cricket so solid?[4] I am also interested in the role isolating South African sport played within the whole context of the struggle for sanctions. Were governments willing to pressurise sporting bodies against playing with South Africa in order to provide a smokescreen to disguise their maintenance of economic relations? In other words, were they prepared to condemn apartheid through one illuminating action, but not at the cost of economic well-being?

Section three explores the politics of South African cricket. It focuses on the role of the government and the state in the development of the sport. Analysis centres on four case-studies, each being a pivotal moment in the evolution of cricket in South Africa. Starting from the Springboks departure from the ICC – due to South Africa declaring itself a Republic, then considering the infamous 'Basil D'Oliveira Affair', the abandoned 1970 Springbok tour to England and South Africa's subsequent isolation from international cricket, and finally the 1980s 'rebel tours' – the last of which ran parallel to the formal abolition of apartheid – I intend to highlight the defining role of politics in cricket. This is scrutinised in an 'institutional' form that observes the functions of the government and counterbalances their strategy with the reaction of the opposition, both at home and overseas. Theoretical concerns are thrust into the forefront by the evaluation of reactions to these events. The cancellation of the 1970 South African tour to England, for example, had a seismic effect among conservatives in both Britain and South Africa as authority and law and order were perceived to be undermined. What ultimately interests this study, then, is how sport became such an important component of the struggle between opposing camps in South Africa, each striving to become the dominant hegemonic power.

I conclude by turning the initial theme of the book – the impact of politics on cricket – on its head by analysing the impact of the game on apartheid and the part that 'multiracial' sport played in undermining that system, thus leading to its demise. Protagonists of the 'bridge-building' argument claimed that by encouraging South African cricket you would, in effect, be destabilising the social fabric because of the advances made towards multiracialism, and thus forcing the regime into reform. This is a comparative study in that psychological assaults against the ruling order have to be weighted in relation to other contributing phenomena, permitting the political scientist to examine the elements that ultimately determine a country's political direction. The reversal of themes also allows for a more thorough review of the place of sport in the social structure.

A short examination of conservatism clarifies the notion that a definition of 'politics' is subject to certain ideological constraints. The argument that the two variables are independent of each other and so should not be considered in an academic context is by its very nature a political statement. Political science is not like the study of biology and chemistry, whereby 'maps' determine what is in the sphere of interest. If we are studying politics in order to gauge an understanding of the political process that is central to most of our lives, then we have to consider the effects of policy. A study of the civil service or of the qualities that make a minister tell us nothing about the society in which we live; the influences behind government, the forces that mould a counter-force to the dominant hegemony and an examination of legislation in a social and economic context do. Although disjointed, there are a number of features that allow an assessment of a conservative philosophy. Disdain for extra-parliamentary activities, an emphasis on law and order and respect for authority (core beliefs which were promoted in cricket) are all central components, and are exposed to scrutiny in the study of South African cricket. While it is difficult to show that the Conservative Party in Britain supported apartheid, the evidence suggests that many conservatives were sympathetic to South Africa. Sport provided an indicator of this support, especially when considering the reaction to the 1980 Moscow Olympics, when suddenly it was deemed acceptable by many conservatives to locate sport within a political context.

Ferdinand de Saussure argued that language constitutes a system in which no element can be defined independently of others.[5] This interdependency is certainly true of the politics of South African cricket, which requires an understanding of much more than simply cricket: racism, economics and a laager mentality all combined to create immense and substantial inequality, which, in turn, determined access to and participation in sport. Having already remarked on the interpretation of 'politics', 'sport' and 'cricket', a theoretical understanding of 'apartheid' and 'segregation' in the period before 1948 is required in order to apply the original concepts to the social and political entity that is South Africa. Thus, this book is influenced by the techniques of investigation advocated by discourse theorists. Academic texts on South African cricket are limited as most studies relate to South African sport in general – and cricket has probably played 'second-fiddle' to rugby, the game associated with Afrikaners. The data for this study stems largely from the actors themselves: newspapers for assessments of both political developments and reports on cricket; specialist cricketing publications such as *The Cricketer, Wisden Cricket Monthly* and *Playfair*; biographies of individual cricketers; as well as an exploration into the vast literature on cricket. Of course, there is a wealth of knowledge available on the South African political economy, as well as theoretical studies on matters such as political philosophy. These have all been consulted, as have an extensive number of articles in academic journals. However, I claim originality on three fronts:

- an examination of sport in society has, in the main, been attempted through the disciplines of sociology and sports studies, rather than that of political science;
- there has been no academic study of cricket in South Africa;[6]
- academic texts on sport that include cricket are written in the interests of politics;[7] reference to specialist cricketing material such as magazines, histories and biographies have enabled an analysis of cricket's role in the political process.

1

The Problems of Defining 'Political Science'

'Problem' is not always a negative term; rather, it should be seen as a puzzle or an investigation. It is not necessary that the problem be solved, more that it be thoroughly examined. Any examination requires prioritisation, and the first priority of any academic discipline is that of definition. A definition ties a word to a concise and accepted meaning. This is difficult with political terms because they are contested. Consider the question 'Is politics a science?' British Universities have tended to refer to courses of study as 'government', 'politics', 'international relations' and 'political theory', shying away from a term that would endow politics with a stature and authority reserved for the 'natural' sciences. Disagreement and debate are the very essence of all political activity; a definition of 'politics' is no exception. There is no objective perspective on what constitutes politics, and, as a result, the stance that an individual adopts will determine his or her world-view.

David Easton proclaims at the outset of his 1971 study that 'from the days of Aristotle, political science has been known as the master science'.[1] The claim that politics can be treated as a science is a contentious one as all studies should be 'scientific' to the extent that they are based on facts. Mathematical formulae, though, cannot be prescribed to prove statements of a political nature.

The word 'science' derives from the Latin *scientia* and has come to mean a body of systematic knowledge about a well-defined area of enquiry.[2] It is applied to politics to show that there exists an academic tradition in the study of the subject. Of course, politics cannot be considered alongside physics and biology, the 'exact' sciences; in almost every aspect of politics, for example, there are at least two different views. It does, though, allow us an insight into human behaviour and the wealth of historical data enables the student to analyse and formulate general principles, aiding an understanding of the world. The debate relating politics' relevance to science is arduous and technical, and – as it will not enhance our comprehension of a society – anything beyond a reference to its existence is beyond the scope of this work.

Politics is all around us, influencing our lives, whether or not we choose to participate in it. What, though, are the characteristics that determine 'politics'? We know that it evolves from interaction between individuals, that it is usually associated with diversity of opinion, that this often leads to conflict, and that the role of politics is that of decision: it is how conflict is resolved. Yet, which individuals are engaged in politics? Whose decision is all-powerful and therefore adjudged to be political? Can these generalisations be applied to all areas of conflict?

Whilst these initial characteristics would be accepted by most students of the subject, theorists have traditionally been divided into two camps. For some theorists, the definition of politics is seen as a study of Government and its functions, associated organisations and institutions. Employing this institutional definition enables a 'text-book' approach to be made towards the subject. In contrast, other theorists see politics as part of a greater whole that embraces the social sciences; hence, the subject is seen in a broad sense, and one that overlaps other areas of traditional study. In essence, politics is a study of society, because it is a crucial component in the day-to-day activities of all social units.

The purpose of this chapter is to explore these different strands of thought and to investigate the various analyses made by commentators who have contributed to our understanding of politics. Conscious that this thesis is related to sport and the South African political environment, I am anxious to evaluate the context of the different approaches in order to assess how they would relate to the two areas. What emerges is a journey through the process of political thought, dealing initially with politics in its most restrictive form and concluding by considering the belief that it is all powerful and embraces everyday life.

Politics as a study of institutions

A popular notion is that 'politics' is what politicians do; hence, politics is about Government. Go to the politics section of a bookshop and it is usually stocked with the memoirs and diaries of politicians, alongside biographies and details of parties' programmes. Academic texts are almost uniformly concerned with Government – executive and party, the legislature as a whole, the functions of political parties and outlines of what makes a constitution, etc. This convergence on Government is known as the 'institutional approach' to politics, which draws its emphasis from a tradition steeped in history and concentrated on the mechanisms of legislation. This approach allows a study of politics within a certain restrictive boundary, establishing clear lines of demarcation between the 'political' and the supposedly 'non-political'. It is primarily concerned with Government and the State, drawing on normative influences in a manner which suggests that this is what politics is and this is how it should be conducted.

Political theory evolved in the fifth century BC among the Hellenes. It was here that Europeans came into contact with the ancient Middle East and were introduced to science, philosophy and crude political theory – an introduction of such importance that George Sabine and Thomas Thorson equate it with that of the evolution of mammals.[3] Early philosophers, such as Plato and Aristotle, discussed the polis, by which they referred to a small, self-supporting community organised to govern itself. They used the term 'politics' to refer to the affairs of the polis and contemplated a preferred manner in which to make decisions, to train rulers, to trade and to better the lives of the participants; that is, they contemplated Government. In its widest sense, the term 'government' relates to 'the organisation of a group of men in a given community for survival'.[4]

Jean Bodin (1530–96), the French political philosopher, coined the phrase 'political science'. Bodin was also a lawyer, and this background ensured that politics' primary concerns lay with the organisation of institutions related to law. This approach was later developed from the wider influence of not just law, but of philosophy and history as well.[5] The traditional 'British School' of political study has been determined by three interrelated elements: a constitutional doctrine, a conception of the State, and an emphasis on history.[6] This allows for

> studies which systematically describe and analyse phenomena that have occurred in the past and which explain contemporary political phenomena with reference to past events. The emphasis is on explanation and understanding, not on formulating laws.[7]

These defined boundaries enable the student to identify the study of politics as an examination of the legislative process. It purports a distaste for theory, preferring to detail and record and work at a less abstract level. Early political scientists were concerned that change should be evolutionary and gradual because there were limits on what could be achieved through political action.[8]

Within the institutional approach emphasis is placed on the study of public law and of governmental organisations because political science is concerned with power – who has it and how it is used. The legitimisation of authority involves the application of law. We focus on the institution of Government because order is the first necessity of political life. It is difficult for the community to thrive without an established order. We live in a world where resources are scarce and diversity of opinion rife. Only governments can claim authority to establish and enforce priorities and policies. Politics is about arriving at these decisions. It takes place within organisations solely concerned with the machinery of Government, including the civil service, lobbyists, advisers and even the media. Most people outside of these institutions are considered to be excluded from politics.

As well as providing a resolution to the concepts of power and authority, a study of Government provides the political scientist with defined boundaries within which s/he can operate. Such details are considered as a 'matter of common sense, an obvious starting point for studying a country'.[9] A study of apartheid, for example, would normally begin with the 1948 general election and the victory of the National Party (NP), then logically progress to an analysis of the various acts of legislation that combined marked a departure from informal segregation to a policy of 'separateness'.

Institutions also provide the political scientist with a rare area of autonomous study, distinct from matter that intrudes onto related fields. An understanding of politics is greatly enhanced if we can locate the settings in which it takes place. Political experience is expressed by the creation and maintenance of institutions; political activity is such because it is carried out within institutional constraints.[10] This 'somewhere' of political activity we call a 'political system'.

Normative theory is a branch of political philosophy that considers how moral questions affect political life. It concerns itself with what 'ought to be', as opposed to 'what is'. What are the purposes of political organisation and what are the best means of achieving them? How is the virtue of Government related to virtue in general? On what conditions do I owe allegiance to the authority of Government? What is the relation between political rights and duties? What are the limitations of the State? It will, of course, overlap into practically all schools of political thought as all political actors are so because of a chosen ethical stance. Nevil Johnson draws on Michael Oakeshott to justify this normative approach to institutional studies:

> political institutions express particular choices about how political relationships ought to be shaped; they are in the nature of continuing injunctions to members of a society that they should try to conduct themselves in specific ways when engaged in the pursuit of political ends. This is to define political institutions as necessarily containing a normative element.[11]

Thus, ideas – as opposed to influences – are treated as key components of political action. The substantive questions given prominence by normative theorists relate to the State and obligation and the concepts of freedom and equality.[12] They each have implications for this study.

The public affairs of the State

A broader definition, though still within the institutional structure, has been presented by other commentators. Raphael, for example, defines politics as that which 'concerns the behaviour of groups and individuals in matters that are likely to affect the course of government.'[13] Politicians do not make decisions in a vacuum. Political parties and interest groups seek to influence the sources of power, as do the media and business. Raphael still holds that the political is whatever concerns the State. However, he is concerned less with the institution of Government and more with the actual institutions that comprise the State.

The 'State' is often identified as an organisation in which the governing power exercises sovereign authority; all other associations are subordinate to this sovereignty. Its bodies include the courts, the police, the army, the social security system, etc, which are organised in the public sector and are responsible (theoretically) for and to the community. Individual citizens – for their own private interests – fund other organisations such as clubs, trade unions and families. These are not political because they do not directly affect the State.

The public/private distinction is central to liberal political thought. It is assumed that the coercive ability of the State is undesirable. Liberals argue that the rights and preferences of the individual should always outweigh those of the State. Therefore, politics should be excluded from affairs that can be left to individuals. It should be taken out of, for example, schools, the Church and sport. Some might even argue that party politics should be removed from Parliament and that representatives should vote not according to party allegiances but to their consciences.

Power, authority and force

We have established that, according to the 'institutional' stance, politics is concerned with the role and function of the State. We focus on the Government because it has the ultimate authority to regulate: it is sovereign. Sovereignty stems from a unique position in society in being the sole legitimate source of power and having the coercive means to enforce it. In this position it is able to mobilise human resources in the pursuit of a desired policy or programme.

In the 1950s and 60s this specific line of enquiry became contested. Institutional studies of Parliament and the Civil Service were challenged to broaden their areas of interest in order to include examinations of elections, political parties and pressure groups. W.J.M. Mackenzie noted a further emphasis away from the traditional study of institutions toward a more diverse assessment of politics, thereby taking on board the contribution of Marxism, systems theory and the economic approach to the study of politics.[14]

Yet, power remained an all-important concept for examination by all political theorists. In economics, how an individual disposes of his or her income is the central element of study; Peter Harris claims that power plays this role in the examination of political science. This is not to say that it signalled a break from either institutional or normative enquiries. If anything, it reinforced them: ultimate authority lay with the Government, a further reason to limit the scope of the subject to the machinery of the State. Moreover, questions such as legitimacy and responsibility are central to the normative approach. Politics, then, is often seen as a struggle over these concepts between the State and its citizens, with one attempting to extend its power and authority and the other trying to diminish it.

In order to successfully legislate, a Government has to secure the cooperation of the members of the necessary groups within society. What distinguishes Government from other associations is that its decisions can be enforced; the rules of other associations can only be applied if permitted by the central power. The trade unions, for example, despite their potential economic muscle have to subordinate campaigns and disputes (even to the extent of choosing key personnel) to the 'rule of law' or else face financial sequestration, and the Federation of International Football Association's (FIFA) policy of only allowing three foreign players per team in European competitions was contrary to the European Union's policy regarding the free movement of labour within the Union. Thus, it is only by authority, derived from the threat of coercion, that the few can rule the mass. Hobbes argued that supreme authority was a necessity, without which society would be in a state of chaos.[15] An association such as the Church, for example, could challenge the State's claim as the final authority by claiming that political decisions are subordinate to the issue of religion. Indeed, this attitude was adopted by the Pope in the Middle Ages, and again by the Catholic Church in Poland during the unrest in the late 1980s. Ultimately, the Church would either lose out because of the State's superior power – the force of arms – or become the authority, as in Iran and Afghanistan.

The use of force is central to Peter Nicholson's definition of politics. He argues that the use and control of force by some members, and the resulting process of influence and conflict, is a political activity.[16] Bernard Crick and Tom Crick add that politics is about the study of these conflicts of interest and how they affect society.[17] Nicholson develops and restricts the theme, claiming that conflicts and force within individual groups in society do not constitute politics unless they are related to the 'political process'. A trade union negotiating conditions for its workforce, for example, is not engaging in a political act; however, when it subscribes to a political party it is contributing to the political process. Other groups, such as business and pressure groups, may claim similarities to 'politics'. They certainly attempted to influence the political direction of both NP and African National Party (ANC) policy in South Africa. Once again, though, they lacked the means of compulsion that exclusively belong to the State.[18]

As we examine the basis of Government and explore its significance, sources of strength and legitimacy, we find ourselves becoming immersed deeper into the art of political philosophy. However, if we restrict the study of concepts such as power and authority to the notion of Government it still enables an 'institutional' study to be carried out.

Politics as the art of debate

Aristotle began *Politics* with the observation that 'man is by nature a political animal'.[19] By this he meant that two or more men interacting with each other were engaged in a political relationship. Any society is a diverse unit, with interested parties contesting the scarce resources with which each community is bestowed. Politics, for its part, is a means by which individuals seek to influence others towards a particular stance or point of view. It is a means of resolving conflict through compromise and negotiation. Politics is thus an apparatus for arriving at decisions, and a political solution refers to one sought by negotiation and debate rather than by other methods. This idea places faith in the rationale of debate and assumes a belief in consensus above that of dispute. At its most desiring it claims that there are no irreconcilable conflicts.

The contribution of politics to the social sciences

The main advantages of the institutional approach are that it defines an area for study and allows for comparisons to be made. The question for the political scientist is whether this technique enhances our understanding of modern life. Should the study of politics be an exercise confined to narrow criteria or should it embrace the key issues and concerns of contemporary society? Radical theorists have suggested that politics should be analysed in its relation to the wider social and economic environment, for only then does it become relevant – both to the people affected by its actions and the effort to enrich an understanding of an increasingly complex world. What follows, then, is a brief outline of the criticisms of the institutional approach and an examination of alternative approaches to the problem.

Criticisms of the institutional approach

The emphasis on institutions has come under pressure in the latter half of the twentieth century. The limited state of nineteenth-century liberalism may have justified scrutiny on the institution of Government. The enormity and complexities of modern political life, however, ensure that any understanding of political and social behaviour requires an insight into territory far wider than the traditional process offers. Bilton *et al.* argue that the study of the machinery of Government merely represents one variable in the examination of politics.[20] Such a model, moreover, does little to assist an understanding of politics in the developing world. It fails, for example, to appreciate the politics of chieftainship or the role of village elders in agrarian societies.[21] If the role of the theorist is the pursuance of accuracy, can s/he accept a definition of politics based on the role and function of Government?

The State, it is argued, is a subsystem of a broader social system that is moulded by 'non-political' determinants such as culture, economics, geography and demography. Physical barriers to transportation and communication, for example, have made political unity difficult in some African and Central American countries, and the urban/rural distribution of the population is likely to affect the programme and outlook of a ruling regime. The relationships between all the dimensions that comprise human society should be reciprocal, which leads to a suggestion that 'politics is the integrating dimension of society – the subsystem through which the other dimensions of human activity are meshed.'[22]

Overall, by emphasising the role of Government institutions within a framework of the State, the institutional approach represents a defence of the social status quo. It is descriptive and restrictive, concerning itself with the trappings of power rather than exploring its sources and examining the merits of alternative political systems. Furthermore, 'There is … nothing *more political* than the constant attempts to exclude certain types of issues from politics.'[23]

Normative theory is criticised because it is subjective: its values are built on emotion and sentiment. If such standpoints are relative – in that no one position can be determined as better than another – then can normative theory have a future as a scientific discipline? Positivism argues that a specific meaning should be attributed to a particular phenomenon, and if it cannot be defined and subsequently tested then it is, in effect, devoid of analytic purpose.[24] Discourse theorists take the emphasis on definition further by examining the meaning given to political systems and how this shapes the individual's perception of their role in society and their conduct within it. They are concerned with how such meanings are produced and their potential for adaptation. Discourse theory, thus, affords a pivotal place in its understanding of social relations to the struggle over the structuring of social meaning. Lyotard argues that everything is a product of 'time and chance', and so not determined by some logic or principle.[25] For something to be tangible it has to be part of a wider framework of meaning. For example, concepts such as 'freedom', 'democracy', and 'justice' all assume competing definitions – and so does politics.

Politics and the study of society

Politics has to be about how we conduct our social affairs. It is principally a social activity and is continually changing throughout time:[26] the early Greek philosophers were concerned with defining an ideal type of organisation for man to prosper; medieval Christianity took an ethical stance, seeking how human society should be ordered and governed; following the Reformation, secular rather than religious order became the key interest. What is political, therefore, is determined by cultural trends. In the nineteenth century big business would not have been considered within a political context, yet its widespread influence in contemporary society ensures a place for it in any examination of politics.

What, then, do we mean by society? Society represents the complex of human relations. It features groups and institutions that express association, which vary in guise from the family and the caste to the Church and trade union; all of these influence social life. The State itself is probably the most important of these associations, but it is not totally independent of the others. Customs and ideologies can be prey to the desires and forces of the State; they are not, however, created by the central authority. The State differs from 'society' in that its main concern is with the institution of Government. Society is both reflected and expressed through the educational, religious and economic institutions of the State. It offers a greater insight into the normality and totality of human life, including – fundamentally – social and political behaviour.

Laver attempts to provide a definition that incorporates the larger groups or institutions: 'Politics is about groups of people. It is about the interplay of hopes and fears, aims and aspirations, that can be found in any human group.'[27] In other words, nothing should be excluded from politics if people decide that it is a political issue. To Leftwich, 'politics is at the heart of all collective social activity, formal and informal, public and private, in all human groups, institutions and societies.'[28] The trade union, the community group and the cricket board are engaged in dialogue over contested issues, and they also offer an insight into power structures and authority. The civic authorities that were established in the townships by the United Democratic Front following the uprisings in the 1980s were a classic case of a political authority that would have been ignored by theorists of the institutional school. As all these groups include the criteria used to outline the basis of the institutional approach, it follows that we should not always be concerned with the politics of the State. After all, 'There is politics in the board room, in the inter-departmental conference, in the school staff meeting, and in the annual conference of the dog lovers' association.'[29] It is just as legitimate, then, to be concerned with groups that are excluded from the mechanisms of central power.

Feminist writers have also attacked narrow conceptions of politics, arguing that what is personal is also political. Politics is about those decisions that affect peoples' lives, not merely those taken in the arena reserved for 'politics'. Thus, relations between individuals have to be examined as they reflect a situation of broader groups from whence the individuals came. At the root of the argument, once again, is the question of power. Family and personal life, for example, is political because one group of people is controlled by another. In the words of Bilton *et al.*, 'Politics is essentially "power behaviour", not by any means confined to particular governmental institutions or forms, but present in any social situation.'[30] The feminist perception is, largely, a holistic one, assessing the political, social, economic and cultural world of men and concluding that the dualism of gender is the root cause of oppression.[31] It has made an important contribution to the question of political enquiry, appreciating the necessity of cross-discipline analysis in an attempt to understand any society. Anthropologists, for example, first realised that 'sex-roles' varied from one society to another, and as such were determined by cultural constraints. This, of course, meant that they were not fixed – so could be changed.

Dearlove and Saunders argue for a political science that considered politics within the context of the social and economic environment, thereby relating it to other academic disciplines – notably sociology and economics.[32] Can political science continue to exist as a discipline autonomous to other areas of study? Is it not inevitable, indeed desirable, that there be some encroachment onto other terrain? Politics, at the institutional and normative level, does not exist outside the framework of law, history and philosophy. Yet, the division between politics and political economy or applied economics is almost non-existent, and an understanding of sociological theories and the use of research findings can only enhance the work of the political scientist. Other disciplines reveal themselves the deeper the student delves into the subject, and yet a tripartite division imposes a view of the separation of polity, economy and society that is not true.[33] Take the question of capitalism, for example. As an underlying feature of contemporary society, capitalism has largely been dismissed as a 'course ideological irrelevance'.[34] As a consequence, political scientists have overlooked the importance of economic power when assessing the nature of politics. Can we understand the politics of the NP without recourse to the economic environment in South Africa? It is my contention that we certainly cannot.

Politics arises, it is agreed by all approaches, out of conflict that stems from disputes. Leftwich claims that disputes have their origins in the production, distribution and use of resources in society, and attributes current problems such as unemployment and starvation to political decisions. Similarly, politics is defined by Dearlove and Saunders as 'the activities of co-operation and conflict ... whereby the human species [organises] ... production and distribution of ... resources.'[35] These resources are limited and, in general, insufficient to satisfy the requirements of the populace; competition exists for their control. Ownership of the major productive resources not only determines the structure of power and decision-making in society but also, in turn, dictates the customs and traditions of the people. Conflict arises when there is scarcity of requirements or when individuals or groups make demands that are incompatible. Laver argues that politics is about the blend of conflict and cooperation found in human interactions. He states that 'any mixture of conflict and co-operation is politics'.[36]

This is not to say that politics is not about governments: that would be absurd. Miller noted that Government is 'the prize of politics'.[37] Thus, political activity ultimately aims at putting a set of policies into practice, which can only be achieved through power. However, we have to account not only for the reasons behind policy but also for the effect that such actions have on the wider society. When people refused to pay Mrs Thatcher's poll tax, were they not – by their actions – engaging in a political dispute? Similarly, the township rebellions were part of a reaction to political initiatives to reform the apartheid system. In this situation, politics does not directly engage the institutions of Government but rather the effects that their actions have.

The contribution of Marxism to politics

A Marxist critique develops the claim that politics is about power. Real power in any society, though, stems from economics, not from politics. Lenin, in fact, described 'politics [as] the most concentrated expression of economics'.[38] We live in a condition of perpetual scarcity, from which a few people or a class are able, through the control of the means of production and distribution, to dictate or strongly influence the methods of allotment. Because society is organised according to the relationship to the means of production, economics is the predominant factor behind most of the world's 'political' disputes.

The Marxist model of society stresses the particular method of production – be it a slave, agricultural or capitalist society – known as the 'economic base'. From this foundation a superstructure emerges which encompasses the instruments of power. These include education, the judicial system, culture, knowledge, religion and politics, and their primary purpose is to reproduce the thought-process of the economic base. Marx argued, for example, that 'The ideas of the ruling class are ... the ruling ideas ... The class which has the means of material production at its disposal has control at the same time over the means of mental production.'[39]

So what purpose does politics serve? If it is merely to replicate the ideology of the economic base then wouldn't an authoritarian one-party rule be preferable? Politics, though, serves as illusion: it is a method to dampen the radical aspirations of the masses; it provides an excuse for why things can't be done; it allows for one powerful individual to declare war, yet it takes a whole parliamentary term to ban fox-hunting. Successive Labour governments have highlighted this illusion, having either reneged on 'progressive' aspects of their programme or have compromised under pressure from political and economic opposition.[40] Because conflict emanates from economic inequality, it is not inevitable that politics as we know it will exist in every society. As the class system is eroded and the State withers, there is little need for it. Politics would not feature in Communist society and so Marx called for its abolition and predicted that it would expire along with economic inequality.

The Italian Marxist Antonio Gramsci advanced the notion of 'hegemony' as being the all-important element in any study of politics. Hegemony is about ideology: the idea of an all-embracing dominant ideology whose scope extends throughout all social, cultural and economic spheres of a society.[41] It comprises an entire system of values, attitudes, beliefs and morality that serves as a support to the established order and the class interests that dominate it. Gramsci's ideas signify a break from the 'economistic' arguments of early Marxists in that they concentrate on the moral and philosophical leadership of a ruling class and its endorsement through the consent of the masses. Gramsci argued that the traditional Marxist stance allowed for too great an emphasis on the role of force and coercion in maintaining bourgeois rule. Whilst not ruling out methods of repression, Gramsci artic-ulated a dual process of domination – claiming that consent from hegemony was also necessary to maintain authority. As George Taylor notes, 'The political cannot therefore be understood as either force or consent: it is both force *and* consent.'[42] Thus, a class would only be deemed hegemonic once it had gained the approval of the masses.

The dominant class moulds a society in which subjective standpoints are accepted as fact and treated as 'common sense', thereby perpetuating its rule. In western Europe, for example, over the last 20 years successive governments have argued that liberal capitalism is now the norm. Economic measures such as low direct taxation, privatisation and emphasis on supply-side measures to reduce unemployment all seek to perpetuate the stance that 'private is best'. Is this fact or an ideological statement? It is hegemonic because it cuts across party lines. Evidently, though, it is still a point of view. Marxists see it as the task of socialists to challenge these world-views through an ideological crusade that advances a counter-hegemonic programme. This could only be attempted if the forces from education, the media, mass culture and politics were engaged in a 'total struggle'.

Gramsci did not reject the prominent role of economics in determining social and political nature. However, because he saw the superstructure as in a permanent state of fluctuation, he dismissed the notion that its components were subordinate at all times to the economic base. Clearly, economism was unable to account for the rise of fascism in Italy or to explain the grip that Catholicism held over the country. By challenging the orthodox stance, Gramsci claimed that spheres such as culture, politics and religion did enjoy a relative – though not ultimate – autonomy. In this case, they should at least be investigated, not assumed from a set of propositions. Socialist revolution, Gramsci argued, would not arise from the breakdown of the capitalist economy, but would be built through human action from a wide range of historical settings. Workers' struggles were largely confined to the workplace and so were based on motives of self-interest. Therefore, an external force was necessary to raise revolt to a counter-hegemonic struggle: politics was necessary to defeat bourgeois rule. This meant that Communists had to use the parliamentary system to advance their ideas and measure their support. A population had to be won over to the philosophy of socialism as a result of education and understanding, not by imposition by an elite. The political struggle, then, was part of the process of forging an alternative hegemony which would challenge the ruling group in ideological, cultural and moral fields. It is this struggle that should interest social scientists when they advance to a study of politics.

The adoption of such a broad-based theory of politics has alarmed liberal and conservative writers as the classical argument asserts that what is polit-ical is that which affects the State. By extending the territory under the scope of politics, the State is permitted the right to intervene further in society and hence encroach upon the private liberty of the individual. The main criticism of broadening the definition of politics, though, is that by including everything the term becomes meaningless. Society is a large and complex place. Can we treat all groups with equal importance, as Leftwich proposed? It is not possible to discuss all aspects of society in relation to politics. Critics counter the feminist argument by pointing to the reduction of enquiry to the 'woman-question' above all else and Marxism with its focus primarily on economics. In reality, is either analysis not dissimilar to the institutional theorists' attention to a narrow agenda?

Conclusion

An examination of the different approaches to 'politics' indicates two fundamental trends. The liberal method seeks to isolate the subject from other disciplines – a goal which is achieved by focusing the study on certain institutional areas, whereas a more radical perspective views the subject of politics in relation to the social sciences. Both have to coexist with another in the contemporary academic environment. Whilst both can claim a theoretical ascendancy, in reality proponents of each stance say more about themselves than the rigours of the discipline when determining what to consider when studying politics. Take for example, an analysis of the IRA. The British State has always condemned the IRA as terrorists. The IRA, on the other hand, views itself as a political organisation concerned with restructuring political forces in Ireland. It is for this reason that they demand political status whenever captured. There is, however, no such status in English law. So, the definition of politics ascribed to the dominant power prevails and a 'political actor' becomes a 'criminal'.

The subject of this thesis, an examination of South African society and sport, would be shunned by advocates of the institutional approach, who argue that politics and sport should not mix; it is, in other words, beyond the scope of politicians simply because political activity takes place within a defined area. If I accepted this stance there would be no justification for this work within the confines of political science. In reality, though, there was little in South Africa that was not tainted by the policies of apartheid. An independent examination of the institutions of Government would be both futile and meaningless without an understanding of the philosophy of racial segregation. Once embarked upon, the political scientist would find him/herself sucked into a whole range of social activities that were directly influenced by legislation and indirectly affected by the social environment created by apartheid. Thus, sport is one of many areas that is justifiably subject to research by students interested in politics.

Although my sympathies are firmly with the radical analysis of politics, I shall not shy away from demonstrating how the institutions of Government assisted in the creation of a systematic programme that embraced far-ranging features within South African society. A dominant hegemony was forged, of which sport was a component. Conversely, it became a formative player in the counter-hegemony of the liberation movement. This struggle provides a contribution to the increasing interest in politics and sport. This interest, though, has to be examined in the light of clear and concise definitions if we are to understand the nature of antagonisms about what should and should not constitute areas of study in political science.

2

The Ties that Bind:
The Relationship between
Sport and Politics

The emphasis on perspective was fundamental to an understanding of 'politics' and its relationship to the wider organism we call 'society'. 'Sport', surely, should not suffer from the same difficulties of definition and viewpoint that politics does. Sport is a part of leisure, a measurement of time free from the mundane routine of work and other obligations. It is an activity that usually, though not always, involves competition and the exercise of brain, muscle, or both. Sport has been a feature of human existence for as long as that history has been recorded. Is it not, therefore, a pursuit independent and remote from the rigours of political nature, an area which the liberal would consider inappropriate for analysis by the political scientist? If we accept sport in its innocence as an independent variable offering simple enjoyment to the world's population then, yes, scrutiny would be of little benefit to the student of politics. However, we know that this is a fallacy: sport is a reflection of the society in which it is practised. Could we examine sport in the Soviet Union or the United States, for example, without recourse to the social and economic environment? Attitudes to participation, competition and even which sports are played, are determined – in the main – by factors outside of sport itself. Contemporary sport, for example, has evolved in an age of urbanisation, industrialisation and technological advance, and it would be more than fair to outline the effect these social changes have had on sport.

The basis of this chapter is to examine what sport represents beyond its mere activity, the reasons that governments become involved in sport, the benefits that this association brings, how it has been shaped by social and economic phenomena, and the functions which it serves for that environment. Primarily, this chapter is an attempt to assess sport's relationship with politics.

Problems with defining sport

We have considered in the opening sentences that a conceptualisation of sport is not an easy one. Most definitions would agree that sport is a physical activity which involves the use of both exertion and skill. Even this basic definition, though, throws up a number of problems: what about chess and cards, for example? And what about motor racing, which involves a combination of both person and machine? These are amongst many sports that sit uncomfortably, or even outside, the basic consensus attributed above to sport. It becomes evident that perhaps not all physical activities can be considered as sport: two friends kicking a football in the park, for instance, has little in common with a professional contest in the Premier League.

In order to qualify, therefore, the activity would have to be engaged in a particular environment. Jay Coakley stresses a formal and organised format, involving 'the standardisation and enforcement of rules, an emphasis on organisation, and formalised skill development'. Sport thus becomes institutionalised.[1] Once you standardise sport you accept a willingness to conform to a set of rules. Rules and laws are major features of politics. In theory, then, the similarities are evident from the start.

From the formalised perspective, the two friends kicking a football are engaged in 'play' – an activity involving freedom from restraint and formality, and indulged in for its own sake by individuals voluntarily without financial reward at stake; a basic form of rivalry that has existed throughout time. Johan Huizinga is concerned that this 'play element' is lost as industrial society becomes bureaucratic.[2] Innovation is stifled by regulation, and the urge to win and gain monetary reward has replaced enjoyment as the key element in such activity.

From this very brief summary it becomes apparent that all is not what it seems. What constitutes a sport may well be determined by the preference of the individual. However, a formalised setting provides not only an acceptable grounding but also an audience. So why should sport be an area of concern for the political scientist? It becomes an issue because of its centrality to the lives of millions of people. If this importance was nurtured at the enjoyment stage, then we need progress no further. However, it is simply too big for this.

The importance of sport should not be underestimated.[3] It usually indicates how an individual occupies his or her leisure time, and is the antithesis of work. People devote more time to playing, watching and discussing sport than any other organised activity in public life. (In Britain, for example, 21.5 million adults and 7 million children participate in sport at least once a month.[4]) Furthermore, more money is devoted to sport in one way or another than for any other aspect of culture. A study in 1987 found that the British government received £2.4 billion in annual revenue from sport; this was five times its expenditure. Consumer spending on sport is equivalent to expenditure on electricity, gas and furniture in the personal sector.[5] As a result of this sense of importance to so many people, governments cannot allow sport to operate on a totally independent basis. They are, then, likely to seek to shape its development. The political scientist Art Johnson wrote that 'All governments regardless of … type, use sport to generate political support.' He continued that even in political systems that promote

belief in the separation of sport and government, it is likely that intervention ... will be needed to insure that sport serves the purposes of
government rather than its opponents. Sport, therefore, will become too
important to be left alone to excite the fans; it will be needed to service
the state.[6]

Issues surrounding sport and the State involve the institutions of power in
terms of funding, the availability of sports, and even attitudes towards
participation with other countries.[7]

Sport, though, is so much more than this. It has the capacity to give
meaning to life, to make sense of the world and to reinforce identity. As part
of leisure and culture it fits into Marx's superstructure, it represents a powerful means of enforcing hegemony and is representative of power struggles
and issues of opportunity which reflect the personal in politics. In short,
sport is not only framed by its social environment but is adapted and manipulated to reinforce the status quo. Such qualities are of particular importance
to the political scientist in the remit of understanding the role of politics in
society and its effects.

The autonomous perception

The notion that sport and politics should not mix stems from a world-view
of an order structured on autonomous phenomena. Hence, politics is
concerned merely with x, y and z, and usually associated with the institution
of Government. Sport is considered as an ideal, something distinct from the
discolouring qualities of greater society, mere amusement and pleasure, a
free voluntary action, and clearly outside the concerns of the State. The
competition and conflict that flow from sports are considered healthy
because they are distinct from social and economic issues. Outside interests
threaten the values which sport propagates by permitting decisions to be
made by people – such as judges, politicians or civil servants – whose main
concern lies outside of sport; when they become involved they invariably
'damage, corrupt, or pervert sport'.[8]

A counter-argument could be made that if sports' regulators were able to
adequately administer their respective interests then there may be little
motivation for intervention from the State. Unfortunately, they have not
been able to do this, if only because they lack the enforcing powers of the
sovereign authority. In the last decade or so the State has intervened in areas
such as the safety of spectators and the question of public order at events;
through the national lottery, moreover, it has actually sought to promote
sport through direct funding. Sports associations are ultimately subject to the
sovereignty of the legitimate power, that is, Parliament. Its regulations,
therefore, have to respect and be subordinate to the greater legislation of the

State. Crackdowns by the FA into violent behaviour and foul language on the pitch are a consequence of the fear of direct police intervention; a tougher stance by the Jockey Club against excessive use of the whip is taken under threat of the RSPCA suing individual jockeys.[9]

Policies and initiatives are not created in a vacuum: they are reflective of the social, political and economic environment. The move towards welfarism in western Europe after the Second World War encroached into areas not previously considered within the traditional domain of politics. The establishing of sports centres and swimming pools was viewed almost as an extension of the welfare state, a means whereby physical health could be enjoyed by the poor as well as by those who could afford to practise sports. Similarly, the policies of Thatcherism – such as compulsory competitive tendering, privatisation and the 'opting-out' of schools from local authority provision – have affected phenomena outside of the initial area of concern. In the period 1979–97, for example, more than 5,000 school and community sports fields were sold off to developers, 'who turned them into housing estates and supermarkets'.[10] Thus, what emerges is a structural relationship built between sport and political agencies such as local government, the State's bureaucracy and Parliament – a relationship so vast that in 1994 Grayson identified 15 different departments that were 'relevant to sport'.[11] As with Britain, sport in South Africa was determined by the wider forces that shape any society. Ignore the influence and impact that apartheid had on the country's sports and you can never accurately assess the history of cricket, rugby or football.

The machinery of government and its exploitation of sport

What does sport offer to our understanding of politics? In the opening chapter we analysed how both approaches to the nature of politics were concerned with the concept of power in society: one methodology to justify the sovereignty of Government as an approach to study; the other to assess the inequalities inherent when power belongs to a particular class or group. Taking the discourse a stage further, politics is about power because, in the end, it is the ultimate objective for actors, be they organised as parties or advocates of a particular ideology. Without power there can be no implementation of programmes or realisation of commitments.

Similarly, once in power the key objectives of any party or class is to legitimise and maintain its rule. This is achieved through a number of complex measures, of which sport fulfils a valuable role. It was, for example, undeniably a tool in internally legitimising the political system in the Stalinist bloc and exploited as a means of competition against the West. C. Offe, moreover, claims that the State is required to provide a range of services at an affordable cost or else access becomes so restricted that the 'legitimacy' of the regime becomes challenged.[12] This can certainly be applied to South Africa, where the State clearly failed to provide adequate facilities for the black population, and, in turn, sport became embroiled in the general antipathy towards the Government. How, though, can sport act as a means of legitimising the State?

Integration

All societies based and built upon a scarcity of resources will experience conflict. Similarly, all societies are integrated to a degree, otherwise they wouldn't exist. A number of factors have contributed to this 'gelling' process: sport is one of them. It assists national cohesion by providing a focus for people from different social, racial and religious backgrounds. Be it the community school or club, the city team or the national side, sport provides a 'something in common' for a diverse population. Eric Hobsbawm wrote as follows on such national integrative qualities:

> What has made sport so uniquely effective a medium for inculcating national feelings ... is the ease with which even the least political or public individuals can identify with the nation as symbolised by young persons excelling at what practically every man wants ... to be good at. The imagined community of millions seems more real as a team of eleven named people.[13]

How does a divergent population, keeping intact the distinct and core characteristics of its sum parts, become integrated? By assuming the norms and values implanted by the dominant group in society – be they racial, gender or economic. Augmenting this view, J. Galtung argues that sport is 'one of the most powerful transfer mechanisms for culture and structure ever known to humankind.'[14] It provides a method of socialising individuals in order that they adapt to mainstream society, and is thus an antidote to a variety of social problems such as alienation, juvenile crime, vandalism and hooliganism. Prime Minister Stanley Baldwin said in the year of the General Strike that the greater the facilities for recreation, the better would be the health and happiness of the people and 'the closer will be the spirit of unity between all classes'.[15]

By enforcing values that are promoted as beneficial in the 'real world', sport can be a useful aid for the development of 'good' citizens. In 1879 Harrow boys were informed that 'football brings out all the qualities that ought to be innate in a brave soldier'.[16] This association between sport and political socialisation dates back to the early Greek cities that provided funding for public gymnasia. These were used not only for sport but also to house political and religious discussion. Indeed, Plato's Academy takes its name from its location within the gymnasium of Akademos.[17] In modern society, sport emphasises the qualities of dedication, success and adherence to the rules: the individual learns how to be a 'gentleman'; the virtue of leadership is promoted; responsibility is encouraged; aggression is channelled. A government inquiry – the Clarendon Commission of 1861 – recognised the value of games for character-building, and argued that football and cricket provided durable qualities and manly virtues. Similarly, Nikolai Ponomaryov noted that 'when people engage in physical exercise their ideology and moral consciousness are shaped through acquiring information on sports ethics'.[18] As with society in general, the way to succeed is through competition, hard work and organisation. These values form the basis of Western cultures that incorporate the notion of the 'Protestant ethic'.[19] It follows that the notion of 'fair play' is dependent on the observation of the rules: the adjudicator has at all times to be respected. Leadership and authority – both political values – are enshrined in the ethos of all sports. Kenneth Brody writes that 'If any institution of this society serves as a model to such "Protestant ethic" values, it is most certainly the institution of sport.'[20]

We shall see that in South Africa in the 1970s the NP devised measures that incorporated many of these integrative tendencies in an attempt to hang onto power by winning over sections of the black community. As in South Africa, not all athletes will adhere to the core values of the larger society that are being displayed through sport. However, as Howard Nixon argues, if people accept aspects of the sports institution then it is expected that they will express faith in the order of established society because sport 'glorifies' that society.[21]

The promotion of integration through sport can, of course, have many positive sides. For example, African-Americans have been able to escape poverty through sport in the US, and the equal opportunities measures in the American education system came to fruition with the US women's soccer team winning the 1999 World Cup; in England, the influx of overseas footballers into the Premier League has undoubtedly aided the cause of multiracialism; and, following the success of José-Maria Olazábal in the US Masters in 1994, the *Independent* noted that 'even in the most xenophobic shire clubhouse, we are all European.'[22] In theory, anyone can come from humble beginnings and through hard toil can work their way to the top of the ladder: sport approximates to the notion of equality of opportunity more than any other sphere of social life.

On a grander scale, sport can assist international fraternity in that it can aid diplomacy, benefit international relations and offer a rare common interest between antagonists. Britain's imperial links were enhanced through a cultural assimilation largely built on literature, cricket, and – in the 'white' colonies – rugby. In the early 1970s a US foreign policy interest was identified 'in furthering mutual understanding and communication through sports.'[23] Perhaps the prime example, the Olympic Games is an event that draws the whole world community together. Baron Pierre de Coubertin, who relaunched the Games in 1896, envisaged that international sports competition would create 'international respect and goodwill and thus help to construct a better and more peaceful world.'[24] Such sentiments were exploited by the British government who persuaded the British Olympic Association to withdraw its bid for the 1940 Olympics in order to support Tokyo and thus enhance Anglo-Japanese relations. Christopher Lumer claims that it is the 'unserious' nature of sport that allows the possibility of such cooperation between states.[25] Sport also affords insights into the psyches of nations that a study of political institutions would not be able to. Adopting this perspective, Harry Pearson argues that there is more to be found about the politics of the Indian subcontinent in the cricket writings of Mike Marqusee than in the international pages of the press. Similarly, the north/south animosity in Italy had been apparent to fans of *Serie A* long before the exploits of the Northern League.[26]

The maintenance of social order

Governments become increasingly involved in sport through their mandate to maintain order within a society. Both sport and politics are embroiled in conflict over the division of scarce resources. The opportunity to enjoy sport, either as player or spectator, can only be pursued if the facilities are available and are for the usage of all. Governments become involved in sport to settle disputes that arise from such conflicts. Richard Thomas, for example, provides a peak figure of one-sixth of all criminal offences in England in the first half of the nineteenth century being prosecuted under the game laws.[27] Governments can, furthermore, become involved by policing the actual events: in the case of Test cricket between India and Pakistan, operations assume military proportions and involve the Ministry of Defence.

The promotion of sport, either through its integrative qualities discussed previously or as a means of diverting energies from undesirable activities, satisfies a requirement to dampen hostility to the prevailing social environment. The boys clubs and scouts founded in the Victorian age were amongst a number of socio-religious organisations established as a means of controlling the children of the growing industrial proletariat. The aim of the Boy's Brigade was 'The advancement of Christ's kingdom among boys and the habits of obedience, reverence, discipline, self-respect and all that tends towards Christian manliness.'[28] Both the Albemarle Report, *The Youth Service in England and Wales* (1960), and the Wolfenden Report, *Sport and the Community* (1960), highlighted the inadequacies of existing provision with the problem of idle juveniles:

> [We] … are not suggesting it [criminal behaviour] … would disappear if there were more tennis-courts and running tracks … and at the same time it is a reasonable assumption that if more young people had opportunities for playing games fewer of them would develop criminal habits.[29]

Many related reports were to follow: the 1973 House of Lords report *Leisure*, the 1975 government White Paper on *Sport and Recreation* and the 1977 *Policy for the Inner Cities* White Paper justified public expenditure on the grounds of alleviating social tensions and reducing delinquency; the Scarman Report on the 1981 civil disturbances reinforced this stance. The Sports Council, moreover, has sponsored sport programmes as an antidote to social problems among the young, the unemployed and ethnic minorities. In Belfast, for example, the population size warranted eight sports centres, but it was rewarded with fourteen – making it one of the most well-endowed [cities] in western Europe.[30]

Finally, the intervention into sport by the Thatcher government was dictated by ideological concerns. The Football Spectators Bill (1989), a response to the deaths of Juventus fans at the Hysel Stadium, came during a period dominated by the miners' strike and a government determined to enforce law and order. In this spirit, Mrs Thatcher appeared at the forefront of those demanding that English clubs be withdrawn from European competitions. So, then, far from stipulating the traditional stance regarding the separation of politics and sport, the issue becomes – in the words of an ex-head of the Sports Council – 'not whether or not politics should be involved in sport but rather "how" politics should be involved'.[31]

Maintaining and developing physical abilities and fitness

The reasons that governments promote fitness are threefold. The principal reason is defence of the State. Historical studies show that an army requires a pool of fit and healthy young recruits in order to meet its requirements. In Ancient Greece the hoplite race or race in armour over 400 yards was a reminder that athletics was, in origin, a preparation for war. The long jump was encouraged as it was useful in the assistance of travelling over the Greek countryside, cut as it was with small ravines and watercourses. However, it is the event of throwing the javelin, an important part of the infantryman's weaponry, which holds the closest link with training for war. Similarly, the tournaments of the feudal aristocracy in medieval Britain emerged from the demands of military training, and the War Office exploited football's popularity in 1914 when it linked with the game's governing body to promote a recruitment campaign for the war; by the end of the year half a million men had enlisted via football organisations – almost 50 per cent of the total number of volunteers.[32]

The other two determinants are economic. One, that prevention is better than cure: countries with a socialised health service will promote fitness in order to reduce the overall cost of running a health service. This was the reason given by the Canadian government in the mid 1970s as it was forced to cut health spending in the shadow of economic difficulty. Two, that a healthy and fit population is an aid to economic productivity. Ponomaryov, the Soviet commentator, noted that:

The main way to train people for work activity is to strengthen their health and improve their physical development ... Physical culture ... encourages a more rational use of work resources, since it extends the bounds of actual work capacity beyond (the normal retirement) age, i.e., it prolongs the active life of workers ... 'Athletic' employees are (also) less prone to sickness and therefore take less time off.[33]

The direct benefits of sport to governments

The previous segment touched on a number of reasons why governments become involved in sport. We now progress from this standpoint to an analysis of what sport can specifically do to enhance a ruling regime. All authorities seek legitimacy – it is a fundamental prerequisite in the claim for ultimate sovereignty, the key element that distinguishes government from other powerful groups in society. Sport can assist in this claim, especially on the world circuit. The footballer Davor Suker claimed that 'before the [1998] World Cup Croatia was recognised by 4 per cent of the rest of the world. Afterwards 45 per cent.'[34] So, sport assists simple recognition, a powerful concept in the claim for sovereignty. This is an issue that the International Olympic Committee struggled with for years over the question of two Chinas, two Koreas and two Germanys. Recognition of one over the other provided political approval to the sports body of the disputed territory, and hence the political regime. In this context, wasn't Nelson Mandela's determination to have South Africa included in the 1992 cricket World Cup a means of legitimising the country's ongoing peace process?

Governments will take advantage of prestigious sporting occasions to promote their country on the international stage. Why else would such events be so conducive to the display of such political symbolism as flags and anthems? Italian success abroad in the Olympics of 1932 and 1936 and the World Cup victory of 1934 exhibited the 'qualities' and 'prestige' of the fascist state. Janet Lever argues that 'long before economic and military strength back up political clout, sport offers a nation an opportunity for a high ranking in the world system'.[35] The South Korean government, for example, stated that their sponsorship of the 1988 Olympics was an announcement to the world of its emergence as a developing nation.

Familiarity with success in sport is also seen as being politically advantageous. In the quest for votes, wealthy and ambitious politicians paid for early Roman athletic festivals in an attempt to out-do their rivals. The emperor Trajan is reported to have celebrated his victory over the Dacians at the end of the first century AD with combat among 10,000 gladiators. This, though, was still behind Claudius in 52 AD, who claimed 19,000 combatants.[36] Another means of celebration was deployed by Emperor Augustus, who instituted the Games of Mars to commemorate Roman rule over Egypt. Like the Emperors of Rome, politicians began to see the benefits of associating themselves with popular sporting occasions.

Other, more recent examples, abound. In 1899 the FA Cup Final was attended by the Prime Minister, Lord Salisbury. Presenting the Cup to Bury in the following year, Lord Roseberry remarked: 'This is the second year running you have had a distinguished Cabinet Minister amongst you to preside over this sport. It is good for football, and it is not bad for the Cabinet Minister.'[37] Also capitalising on the popularity of sport were John Kennedy, who began the tradition of presidents ringing to congratulate winning Superbowl teams, and Harold Wilson (1966), General Videla of Argentina (1978) and President Pertini (1982) of Italy, who all associated themselves with their country's success in the football World Cup. Another use of sport was made by President Ronald Reagan, who exploited sporting metaphor to denounce his critics as backing 'the losing team'.[38]

Does the head of state view him/herself as leader or captain of his or her team, the nation state? It would seem that such association combined with winning and a general 'feel-good' factor can have positive political repercussions. Why else, the cynic may ask, would a government wish to decorate athletes in the New Years Honours list? Finally, the Wolfenden Report even suggested that success in sport might help toward offsetting Britain's declining influence in economic, political and military spheres.[39]

Hegemony: A critique of sport

The bases of any criticisms of organised sport have to be regarded in the social and economic setting in which the activity takes place. If sport can be used as a vehicle to channel particular ideals and norms, then it also holds that it acts as a mirror to the same society which it tries to influence. Cheating, drug abuse, excessive violence, racial and sexual discrimination and exploitation are all endemic in contemporary western civilisation. They also feature prominently in organised sport. Similarly, the conflicts between fox-hunters and those opposed to blood sports and over the provision of sports facilities are issues that concern politics.

Sport, moreover, is part of the social superstructure and so is influenced by the prevailing relations of production and the class relationships that stem from these relations. In traditional societies, for example, where the majority of the population worked the land, sport conformed to needs of the peasant and the landowner, and the timing of events was based on religious holidays and the needs and conditions of the land. The football games of the fourteenth and fifteenth centuries, for instance, were grand affairs usually played at Shrovetide or Easter. The contemporary fixation with financial reward represents a penetration into professional sports by the patterns and forms of capitalist society.[40] Disurbanisation and the demise of a predominately manufacturing economy have resulted in a more mobile population who practise their sport in the country, on the lakes or on snow.

If sport can justifiably be studied in a political and social context, it stands that a political examination of an individual country or a particular economic system can include scrutiny of sport as a means of relating the effects of political authority. My argument with regard to South Africa is that apartheid left no area of society untainted by its philosophy. Quite simply, a study of sport in South Africa holds no intellectual weight without a thorough appreciation of the extent of racial rule.

We have seen in the previous segments why governments become involved in sport and the benefits that they gain from it. Sport, as a means of transmitting the values of the ruling group, is a component of the dominant hegemony. Sport in Western societies is, therefore, a reflection of capitalist interests. The two worlds of work and leisure have to conform to the same truths and teach the same lessons.[41] Sport is controlled by big business and dominated by money, 'a tool for extracting incredible riches from the sports-hungry populace.'[42] Rules can be tampered with to suit the interests of promoters and sponsors. The days and times of competition have been selected to satisfy the demands of television and business interests: matches in the 1994 US World Cup were being played at the hottest time of the day to satisfy western European schedules, and the cigarette company Rothmans, which sponsored early one-day cricket, encouraged a more aggressive, attack-minded form of batting by paying bonuses for boundaries; despite the potential long-term difficulties this presented to techniques, emphasis was placed, not on the game, but on ensuring that boundary advertising reached its maximum audience.[43]

We have seen how certain values can be encouraged through the means of sport. In the second half of the eighteenth century it was the Church and public-spirited philanthropists who organised sports activities for the working-class communities. They sought to apply standards and principles into these activities, thus transforming undisciplined pastimes through the dominant themes of the industrial age. Bero Rigauer, in *Sport und Arbeit*, claims that at the highest level these values have actually taken on methods of industrial production: discipline, authority, competition, achievement and rationalisation.[44] It is not something 'in itself' divorced from the subtleties that comprise politics, and there is little interest in the concept of 'play' in organised sport as players become mere commodities – a means to an end. Bourdieu describes how, in France, traditional games between rival towns were transformed into a marketable entertainment form: 'In brief, sport, born of truly popular games, i.e. games produced by the people, returns to the people, like "folk-music" in the form of spectacles produced for the people.'[45] In this way, individual expression is sacrificed at the expense of time and output as rules and structure destroy spontaneity and freedom. Satisfaction is reached only if the contest is won or a record is set. An athlete that fails to perform to expectations risks being damned a failure. Those that are successful, though, become so at the cost of control of their bodies. They become 'gladiators' performing for the benefit of others, using their bodies 'in the mode of an efficient tool'.[46]

As sport is conceived as an element of hegemony, it is inevitable that it comes to reflect the economic antagonisms of any given society. Such economic forces dominate the direction of individual sports and participation in them. Taking an early example, slaves were the first athletes in Roman sports. They participated on behalf of their owners, who would either parade them as representatives of their state or territory or exploit them for themselves for political gain. In medieval society folk games such as football tended to be enjoyed by the peasantry, whilst the middle-class burghers and knights confined themselves to military sports. In general, access to the scarce resources of society, a fundamental prerequisite to politics, determined who played what. By the early twentieth century the middle classes were enjoying tennis, squash, skiing and badminton. Sports such as rugby (though not in Wales) and golf (not in Scotland) became associated with patrons of wealth. Many of these sports were middle and upper class in practice, not only because they held formal origins in the public schools but also because it was only the leisured class who had the time to devote to such pastimes. Football, in contrast, is the world's most popular sport because it is probably the easiest to play and the cheapest.

Whilst a preparation for the demands of industrial society, sport also assists its 'master' in becoming the modern-day opiate of the people by reducing 'the population to a position of complete passivity'.[47] Aggression from both athletes and spectators is channelled into formalised and acceptable activities which are strongly ordered, either through convention or regulation. It follows also that sport diverts the masses away from day-to-day problems and possible political solutions. Hoch, though, argued that sport actually perpetuates these problems by providing people with either: '1) a temporary high ... which takes their minds off problem[s] for a while but does nothing to deal with [them]; or 2) a distorted frame of reference or identification which encourages them to look for salvation through patently false channels.'[48]

The provision of 'bread and circuses' was one initially exploited by Imperial Rome. Ammianus Marcellinus noted in the fourth century: 'Now let me describe the mass of the people, unemployed and with too much time on their hands ... For them the Circus Maximus is temple, home, community, centre and the fulfilment of all their hopes.'[49] Such a strategy has also been known in British industry. For example, the Sheffield steel magnate Robert Hadfield said when opening the company's new playing fields in 1923, 'no-one had ever heard of a good sportsman rising among the Socialists or the Bolsheviks. Sport in itself was the best antidote to revolution and revolutionary ideas.'[50] Leon Trotsky wrote of the revolutionary fervour of the British working class being 'drawn off into artificial channels with the aid of boxing, football, racing and other forms of sport.'[51]

Furthermore, whilst sport is promoted as an agent for international cooperation and understanding, it can also prove to be a negative force by over-emphasising nationalism. This can be traced back as far as 1773, with Rousseau's pamphlet on *Considerations on the Government of Poland*, in which the political theorist states that games should be organised so that they 'make the hearts of children glow, and create a deep love for the fatherland and its laws.'[52] Spectators and participants measure a sporting occasion as the true power of the concerned parties: the national prestige is at stake. Stereotyping can heighten tensions: Russians are boring and don't smile; the Italians and Spanish temperamental; South Americans 'dirty'; and West Indians flamboyant but undisciplined. This only increases the potential for hostility. Tensions were such in 1969 that a football match between Honduras and El Salvador proved to be a catalyst for war. The internal, integrative qualities can also be overstated: the African-American athlete Tommie Smith expressed the frustrations of many black sportsmen, stating that 'when we're winning, we're Americans. Otherwise, we're just negroes.'[53]

The challenge to hegemony

Proponents of the hegemony argument – by criticising sport in a capitalist setting – were not condemning the activity in itself. Indeed, Lenin stated that 'wrestling, work, study, sport, making merry, singing, dreaming – these are things young people should make the most of'.[54] Furthermore, if sport is both a reflection and a component of the dominant hegemony, then it stands that it can also be considered within the forces that forge a counter-hegemony. Certainly in South Africa, sport became a feature of the political struggle since it allowed an arena for the contrasting philosophies to be played out. Marx pointed out that 'The changes in the economic foundation lead sooner or later to the transformation of the whole immense superstructure.'[55] It holds, then, that the nature of sport can be altered with changes to the socio-economic formation. Of course, not all societies emphasise competition. In the Soviet Union after the revolution, for example, health workers argued for a physical culture focused on health and fitness rather than competitive sports programmes. In England, too, such a link was made when the Greater London Council recognised the relationship between politics and sport and established the 'specific aim ... to increase participation among "underserved" groups.'[56]

Not all values promoted through sport are those of the ruling class. Therefore, the problem is not necessarily with sport but more the environment from which it evolves. In football, for example, emphasis is placed on teamwork. Discipline expresses the unity of the group and victory is in the interests of the collective rather than simply individual merit. This form of solidarity has often formed the basis of organised opposition to ruling groups. It lay behind the thinking of the black sporting organisations in South Africa, with their eventual emphasis on apartheid itself rather than sport as a discrete unit.

However, the 'genius' of the hegemonic order is its ability to absorb conflicting phenomena rather than stamp it out.[57] What it ultimately attempts to establish is the elimination of areas in which alternative ideas may be experienced. Therefore, only by absorbing competing values does the dominant culture remain one assessed as the 'common sense' ideal.

Conclusion: Towards an analysis of the connection between politics and sport

As with 'politics', a definition of 'sport' is determined by belief and ideology. However, what becomes increasingly apparent is that sport is not an isolated element developing independently of external influence. To begin with, it is linked to culture through leisure, and by this association to the decision-making process. Simply, sport is moulded by political and economic factors in order to recreate the value system of those in authority. What is meant, then, by keeping politics out of sport? The key concerns are that governments should leave domestic sports organisations to run their own activities. A judge declared in 1986 that 'sport would be better served if there was not running litigation at repeated intervals by people seeking to challenge the decisions of the ruling bodies'[58] and, secondly, that international sport should be protected from interstate politics. Sports, though, rely on the State for funding, promotion and policing. In fact, sport has relied on politics as a means of developing into an organised and popular international activity.

Can we be surprised then when the State exploits sport for its own purpose? Houlihan observed that 'It is one of the common clichés associated with sport that "sport and politics should not mix". Showing the naivety of such a distinction is fast becoming a sport in its own right.'[59] Garry Whannel has written that 'For "keep politics out of sport" read "keep the politics of sport the way they are".'[60] It is naive to expect non-governmental organisations to refrain from using sport in the same way that politicians do. Would the ramblers in Britain, for example, enjoy wider rights to roam without the trespasses of the 1930s? In the same way, was it not consistent with the analogies of Soviet athletes with robots to show that South African teams were all white (through policy) or to condemn English football's association with Nazi Germany? If a state does adopt the adage that politics should be isolated from sport, it does not follow that its neighbours will share the same belief: in the cold war both sides accused each other of combining the two to their advantage.

The theorist who views sport as an independent variable is likely to assess politics in its institutionalised form. If we accepted the minimalist definition of politics – and only concerned ourselves with political institutions – would we accept that what they discuss is politics? As well as individual governments, both the United Nations and the European

Community have become interested in questions and issues relating to sport. In 1975 the Brussels Conference of European Ministers for Sport, for instance, established the Committee of Experts on Sport. Its aims were:

(i) To place on record the important place of sport in civilisation.
(ii) To establish regular and effective machinery for co-operation within the Council of Europe.
(iii) To adopt a recommendation on the European Sport for All Charter.[61]

UNESCO meetings, to give a second example, have concerned themselves with the Olympic Games, apartheid, sporting connections with Israel, football violence and drug abuse. Political scientists consider both of these institutions legitimate subjects for examination. Furthermore, can political scientists ignore the increasing interest and concern in sport on an academic level? Politics can only be appreciated if understood within the boundaries of contemporary society; in the modern world sport is a central characteristic, maybe even akin to the role of religion in the past.

Finally, an examination of sporting relationships can be of invaluable assistance to the student of modern politics. If we are to understand a society and determine how it functions we need to know more about it than simply how Parliament works or the characteristics that make a good president. If we want to take the politics out of sport, we need to re-evaluate attitudes to 'play'. We are moving away from a world dominated by the State and towards globalisation, in which alliances between nations become the predominant form of rule.[62] Sport provides a 'something in common', not just for diverse communities within a single geographical unit but within regions and the world itself. Are not the football World Cup and the Olympic Games unique in involving just about all the countries of the world? Housing, law and order and environmental issues are amongst subjects that are being studied by political scientists. My proposal is that sport, too, is a legitimate area of study.

3

On a Sticky Wicket:
The Ethos of Cricket

Because sport is viewed, through leisure, as a component of the superstructure and a key actor in the formation of hegemony, it holds that it is also a purveyor of values that serve the interests of political elites who, in turn, represent the concerns of the dominant economic forces. The previous chapter attempted to provide a definition for sport and place it within the context of the political environment. The task of this one is to further scrutinise sport – through cricket – and to highlight just what virtues the game upheld and how they could be manipulated to serve the ideals of the status quo. The purpose of this is not only to advance an understanding of the relationship between politics and sport but also to examine what qualities are distinct to cricket. The bulk of this thesis focuses on cricket in South Africa; in order to avoid a simple dismissal of events and attributes as unique to only that country, I am keen to isolate and assess the characteristics that belong to cricket in order, then, to determine what effects particular social and economic factors had on the game in South Africa. To do this, I have examined cricket in a number of countries – focusing on the early stages of the game's history – in order to identify trends.

Attention to the game's social values forms the first of four segments within this chapter. Once the game's ethos becomes established within the dominant political culture it is inevitable that it will be extended to wherever that culture expands. Cricket became a popular pastime in England during a period of overseas territorial acquisition – and a component of the forces that shaped the social and political environment of these regions. The Empire provides the social scientist with the basis of who plays cricket. An examination of the social and economic structures within the cricket-playing nations suggests why particular groups take to the game. Within this analysis I am interested in determining the specific role that politics plays in the formation of cricket. The final segment considers the growth of the game within an institutional setting, highlighting the role of the legislature. The conclusion ties in the politics of cricket with the conceptualisation of politics and sport in order to forge a structure from which to scrutinise cricket in South Africa.

Ethos

Numerous writers have concerned themselves with the subject of cricket. This is because, according to P.F. Warner, 'Cricket is something more than a mere game.'[1] Neville Cardus, for one, deduced that 'cricket somehow holds up the mirror to the English nature',[2] and E.W. Hornung, in *Keynon's Innings*, wrote: 'My dear fellow, it was only a game – yet it was life.'[3] In *Tom Brown's Schooldays* a master of Rugby School describes it as a noble game:

> 'It is more than a game, it is an institution,' said Tom.
> 'Yes,' said Arthur, 'the birthright of British boys, old and young, as Habeas Corpus and trial by jury are of British men.'[4]

The Victorians considered cricket to represent a system of ethics and morals which embodied all that was favourable in the Anglo-Saxon character. These values were quickly adopted and promoted by politicians, philosophers and poets, so that by the end of the nineteenth century Lord Harris could claim that 'Cricket is not only a game, but a school of the greatest social importance.'[5]

Such values stemmed from the institutions of private education and organised religion. They represented the belief system of the landed gentry, and, as such, were hegemonic. Although the land-owning class were no longer the dominant economic power in late nineteenth-century Britain, their influence – especially political – remained significant. Through sport – via the public schools and the church – they were able to install certain 'common sense' ideals on the populace, espousing the virtues of the 'gentleman' to which all should aspire. Moreover, through the military and missionaries these values were exported to the colonies.

The notion of 'fair play' is a trait that runs through the game even in the modern commercial age: the spirit as well as the letter of the law should be upheld at all times; the player should conduct himself with dignity; a batsman should 'walk' if he knows he is out; it is the contest rather than the result which is paramount; spectators should applaud good play, not simply that of their own side – it is even common for the fielding side to applaud an opponent's century or other landmark; most importantly, the umpire should be respected and obeyed at all times, for they are the protectors and defenders of 'fair play' and should never be abused. In 1867, for example, *Lillywhite* advised young cricketers: 'Do not ask the umpire unless you think the batsman is out; it is not cricket to keep asking the umpire questions.'[6]

Cricket soon became embroiled in the vocabulary of decency: 'It's not cricket' referred to unreasonable, immoral and ungentlemanly conduct; 'keep your end up' became a call for a worthy cause; 'hit straight from the shoulder' denoted approval; 'keeping one's end up' related to doing one's share for the greater cause; and 'playing the game of life with a straight bat' depicted conduct of a correct and courageous type. Indeed, the author Hornung told an audience that 'Being "a sport", as we use it among ourselves, has come to signify every virtue which is dearest to our hearts: courage, honesty, unselfishness, chivalry, you cannot have a sportsman without all of these; and if you have all these, you must be a good man.'[7]

Through cricket's moral code youths learned the rules of society, such as discipline and respect for authority. They also learned to be respectful and to practise self-control, enabling the Cricket Association of the United States to have as its motto: 'No selfish, conceited, lazy or irritable man can be a first-class cricketer.'[8] On his eightieth birthday Lord Harris wrote: 'You do well to love it (cricket), for it is more free from anything sordid, anything dishon-ourable, than any game in the world. To play it keenly, honourably, generously, self-sacrificingly is a moral lesson in itself ... '[9]

Cricket championed masculinity. One of the very first literary exertions on the sport was James Love's ode *Cricket, an Heroic Poem*, in which he 'Hail[ed] cricket, glorious, manly, British game'.[10] This belief in cricket's manly virtues was soon echoed in the colonies. The first advertisement for a contest in South Australia in November 1838 requested support for this 'old English and manly game'.[11] Bill Bundey, prominent in the move to found the South Australian Cricket Association in 1871, claimed that 'manly' sports assisted the formation of character and that cricket was the prince of all games in this scheme.[12] 'There is no more agreeable sight to me', commented the Mayor of Bombay in 1886, 'than of the whole maidan overspread by a lot of enthusiastic Parsi and Hindu cricketers, keenly and eagerly engaged in this manly game.'[13]

The ethics and values of the game were part of a greater ideology that was forged in Britain during a period of unprecedented social and economic change. Throughout the eighteenth century the emerging force of capital was overriding old customary rights. The rules of cricket, although framed in a previous age, came to reflect a new society founded on the principle of law.[14] Dean Farrar, headmaster of Marlborough School 1871–76, commented: 'no one can be a good cricketer ... who does not attend to the rules.'[15] Through 'fair play', encompassing competition, free trade, hierarchy and tradition, Britain became the primary industrial nation. Its philosophy was founded on the principles of justice and the belief that such 'enlightening' beliefs should be passed onto others. Cricket came to represent these beliefs and so aided in the establishment of an overseas Empire. In order to maintain control of such a vast area it was essential that certain values were instilled onto the native populace.

'Playing the game', submission to the rules and ultimate respect for the umpire were characteristics, then, of something greater than a sporting code. Accepting defeat meant acceptance of the system in which the contest takes place. Such values were representative of the dominant hegemony, embraced the attitudes of the establishment and were ultimately promoted through society's superstructure – of which education, religion and politics were paramount.

The purveyors of ethos

Educators encouraged participation in cricket out of the conviction that it produced better men as well as scholars. Thomas Arnold, the headmaster at Rugby School (1827–42), even placed gentlemanly conduct above the acquisition of knowledge or possession of ability, and Dr George Riding once said: 'Give me a boy who is a cricketer and I can make something of him.'[16]

It was the public schools which furnished the requirements of Victorian amateur cricket. Between 1827 and 1854, for instance, Eton alone produced 63 university 'blues', Winchester 43, Harrow 34 and Rugby 23.[17] By the 1860s the annual contest between Eton and Harrow had become an important social occasion, to which the Prince of Wales and 1,200 carriages 'conveying the élite of English society' accompanied the King of Greece in 1876.[18] The public schools provided the majority of amateur players for the County Championship and, along with the universities, they founded numerous clubs in the second half of the nineteenth century.

These centres also reproduced the backbone of political leadership. By 1864 the Clarendon Commission commended the public schools for 'their love of healthy sports and exercise' which had helped to teach Englishmen 'to govern others and to control themselves.'[19] Theodore Cook, writing in 1927, showed that this attitude was still a hardened one: ' ... the most deep-seated instincts of the English race – the instincts of sportsmanship and fair play ... [are] to be found in the public schools and universities'. The purpose of this education 'is the formation of an elite, not for its own sake, not for its own glory, but for the advancement and benefit of society at large'. This leadership would come from 'men whose character and hearts have flourished in the sunshine of the fair play they are always ready to extend to others', for it is a 'fundamental fact of nature that some people are born to govern and others to work.'[20]

Thus was cricket analogous in its formative years with elitist institutions and, merely by association, with politics. Justification for this lofty stance was sought in organised religion. The church has enjoyed a lengthy rapport with cricket: according to Lisle Bowles, Bishop Ken encouraged the game at Winchester School about the year 1650;[21] in the 1760s, the Revd Charles Powlett was a founding member of the Hambledon club; the Revd James Pycroft in 1851 published the first serious work on the early history of cricket, *The Cricket Field*, which contained the earliest printed reference to behaviour being 'not cricket'; a number of religious leaders took up the game at the highest level; and one in three Oxbridge cricket blues between 1860 and 1900 (209 amateur players) took holy orders, of which 59 played county cricket.[22]

There are, moreover, remarkable similarities between the terminology of cricket and that of religion in the Victorian age. L.C.B. Seaman wrote that

'Cricket was associated with religion: just as freemasons referred to God as the Great Architect of the Universe, young cricketers were taught to think of Him as the One Great Scorer and almost to regard a Straight Bat as a second in religious symbolism only to the Cross of Jesus.'[23] By the turn of the twentieth century, Revd Thomas Waugh wrote in *The Cricket Field of a Christian Life* that cricket, morality and religion had been intertwined in the Victorian ethos. He saw the Christian side batting against Satan's bowlers, who disregarded the laws of the game – so the godly batsman had to cope with both the quality of the bowling and the attitude of the bowler.[24]

Being the first country to industrialise, Britain enjoyed a unique status – one that suggested that the embracement of capitalism bestowed on it an air of superiority. The Christian religion – a 'civilised' hierarchical social-structure and an economic system based on the maximisation of profit, in which each of the participants was assigned a specific role – gave Britain an advantage over its neighbours. As we have seen, Theodore Cook argued that Britain owed this position to the notion of 'fair play',[25] a concept that was enshrined in the game of cricket. It was the sport's ethos that encouraged Philadelphians to steer their sons toward cricket with the intent of furnishing them with a strong moral fibre, and allowed a writer in *Temple Bar* to claim in 1862 that 'It is a healthy and manly sport; it trains and disciplines the noblest faculties of the body, and tends to make Englishmen what they are – the masters of the world.'[26] Enjoying such a status, it was, of course, the duty of the Englishman to spread the effects of 'civilisation' among the 'heathen nations'. So, armed with the Bible, the classics and the cricket bat, the missionary laid the foundations for the imperialist, and the modern British Empire came of age, enabling Benny Green to define cricket as a 'compromise between a religious manifestation and an instrument of policy' which came to represent 'the white man's burden'.[27]

Empire

By 1899 the total global area under British control was the equivalent size of four Europes and had a population of around 400 million.[28] The acquisition of overseas territories provided for an expansion of production and trade by opening up new markets and capturing raw materials. Colonies, for their part, could add international prestige to the nation and assist it in the defence of its economic and military interests. Though the British Empire was acquired for economic concerns, it was maintained using political and cultural manipulation – applying the 'superior' moral 'civilised' qualities discussed before. Thus, the British did more than merely exploit:

> For every buccaneer like Henry Morgan, for every slave-owning plantocrat, who were both the builders and the beneficiaries of the empire, there was an earnest missionary or an idealist pedagogue who

revelled in the role of apostle of British values such as Christianity, law or parliamentary democracy; or British culture in the form of Shakespeare, the romantic poets, and cricket.[29]

The apparatus of Government and Civil Service in the colonies was replenished with the graduates from British public schools, who were presented with an opportunity and the means to put into practice all that had been taught them in these elite institutions. A dominant group cannot rule by force alone. It relies on persuasion and by implanting particular attributes that, combined, form a 'common-sense' understanding of society. It became evident that the moral code which cricket celebrated could prove beneficial to this emerging ruling class if imposed on the native population: impartial umpires (the British judiciary) ensured that the rules were adhered to, their decisions never being questioned; cricketers always played fair and accepted defeat with grace – they knew 'their lot'; and for 'fair play' read free trade (to be encouraged by the advanced economy, not so rewarding for the under-developed). Thus, cricket became a component of the strategy of imperialism – and, according to the historian Cecil Headlam, the subtlest component: 'First the hunter, the missionary, and the merchant, next the soldier and the politician, and then the cricketer – that is the history of British consideration. And of these civilising influences the last may, perhaps, be said to do least harm.'[30]

The conveyors

Engaged in securing the pretext for the foundations of hegemony were three principal actors on the imperial stage: the military, the schools and the organised church.[31] Benny Green outlines the thinking behind this as follows:

> They knew that if insurrection were to rear its ugly head at two or three outposts simultaneously, then their resources, already stretched to the limit, might snap altogether … The answer, they felt, lay in a combination of psychological warfare, discipline and decorum, good manners and plenty of churches, propaganda by polite pretext.[32]

Can we argue, then, that the most significant political development associated with cricket thus far was its introduction into the Empire? Indeed, a military presence and cricket appeared to be introduced simultaneously to the colonies in the eyes of some observers. 'The Englishman carries his cricket bat with him as naturally as his gun-case and his India-rubber bath', remarked *Blackwood's Magazine* in 1892.[33] Moreover, each country's early origins of the game begin with matches involving the armed forces of Britain, for 'the men who win boat-races and cricket matches are the men who win battles and change the fortunes of nations',[34] and Pycroft recorded that 'Every regiment and every man-o'-war has its club; and our soldiers and sailors astonish the natives of every clime, both inland and Maritime, with a specimen of a British game.'[35]

An estimated 45,000 migrants of upper- and middle-class origin settled in the Dominions between 1875 and 1900.[36] Many brought with them the idea that through sports and scholarship they could have a civilising effect on the native population. C.L.R. James wrote:

> our masters, our curriculum, our code of morals, *everything*, began on the basis that Britain was the source of all light and leading, and our business was to admire, wonder, imitate, learn: our criterion of success was to have succeeded in approaching that distant ideal – to attain it was, of course, impossible.[37]

Elite colonial schools were established, based on the lines of Eton, Harrow and Winchester. These establishments provided many of the earliest crick-eters. The three main elite schools in Barbados – Harrison, the Lodge and Combermere – helped to lay the foundations of organised cricket before the emergence of the regular club format; when club cricket eventually became established, the leading teams contained many players from these institu-tions. Clubs in the major Australian centres soon depended on local schools for their membership rather than rely on new settlers. The King's School in Parramatta was indeed strong enough to play first-grade opposition in the second half of the nineteenth century, and Hutchins School and Launceston Church Grammar School, both founded in 1846, developed a number of players who went on to represent Tasmania.

The missionaries, many of whom saw cricket in God and God in cricket, assisted in establishing the game overseas. *Carr's Dictionary of Extraordinary English Cricketers* includes the Revd Elisha Fawcett 'who devoted his life to teaching the natives of the Admiralty Islands the Commandments of God and the Laws of Cricket'.[38] Even where they failed to win converts to Anglicanism, missionaries were often successful in winning them to cricket – prompting Keith Sandiford to note that if they 'could not always make Anglicans of natives, they frequently succeeded in otherwise anglicising them'.[39] For example, in 1938 Edward B. Knapp left Harrison College in Barbados after 25 years of service with a farewell address which held that cricket was one of the most effective instruments for developing good Christians and that character was perhaps even more important than education in this regard.[40]

Once established in the colonies, cricket proved a valuable asset in the conducting of relations with the 'mother country'. Lord Hawke was 'certain that a properly-arranged tour does a good deal for the spread of Imperial Federation. Wherever Englishmen go they take cricket with them.' The visit of an Australian touring team in 1880 prompted Lord Harris to claim 'the game of cricket has done more to draw the Mother Country and the Colonies together than years of beneficial legislation could have done'.[41] British rulers, for their part, considered the enjoyment of 'our' games for 'our' people to be an expression of the naturalness of Empire.[42]

Democracy?

We have noted already that the social environment determines not only the nature of sports but which ones are played and by whom. Cricket, like most folk games, was originally enjoyed by peasants and workers, but rarely by 'gentlemen'. Indeed, John Stowe, in his *Survey of London* in the seventeenth century, placed cricket among the amusements of the lower classes.[43] Early forms of competition, mainly between villages and parishes, took place in the Weald – the area between the North and South Downs that encompasses the counties of Sussex, Kent and Surrey. This area was the heart of the iron industry in England, and research by Peter Wynne-Thomas claims that it was these ironworkers who were the first to play cricket.[44] On holidays, the whole community – both men and women – would participate. As late as the turn of the eighteenth century the game was still ranked with vulgar amusements and any nobleman would be denounced by his peers if he partook in a contest. The earliest surviving laws of cricket stem from a match played, not on a village green, but in London in 1727. At the end of the eighteenth century, artisans in Sheffield, Nottingham and Leicester – who on piece-rates determined their own hours of work – took up cricket.

It was later that the gentry became interested in cricket, seeing in it a means to assert their authority over the local community and enabling them to mix-in whilst maintaining social distinctions. John Nyren was at pains to stress 'the style in which we were always accustomed to impress our aristo-cratical playmates with our acknowledgement of their rank and station'.[45] The widespread gambling which accompanied the game was also a crucial inducement to take up the sport. Early newspapers reported cricket not for interest in the actual game but to record the social dignitaries who attended. As the social elite became engrossed, cricket became more than a game.

As in the past with tennis, the upper classes sought to turn their favourite pastime into an exclusive affair. A number of great amateur clubs were formed in the eighteenth century: I Zingari, Quidnuncs and Harlequins, to name a few. Many others were formed later based on counties or particular public schools. Membership of these clubs was restricted and highly elitist. The Hambledon club charged three guineas a year membership (the same price that Hampshire County Cricket Club were charging in 1970!),[46] and membership of I Zingari was by invitation alone. Moreover, as late as 1914, 50 per cent of the Marylebone Cricket Club (MCC) committee still had aristocratic origins and, on purchasing the land that is now Lord's, the club erected a fence around the ground so that ordinary men and women would be prevented from spectating for free: ' ... the London masses do not care much for cricket, probably because they have little chance of exercising any taste they may have for the noble game; but if they did, the half-crown gate-money [at Lord's] would effectively keep them out.'[47] As the dust jacket of Tony Lewis's history of the club proclaims, 'The story of the MCC is the history of cricket.'[48]

Thus, from the outset of the modern game, cricket is associated with elitism and segregation. Within the organised formal structure of the second half of the nineteenth century the distinctions between amateur and professional became so embedded that they determined where a cricketer got changed, his entrance onto the field of play, accommodation and even menu. The social status of a batsman could also determine his style of play, with amateurs preferring the offside for their shots.[49] If democracy is the opportunity of all – regardless of race, sex and economic status – to partake in the activities that compose social life, then cricket was certainly not democratic. Its ethos espoused dignity – rather than competitiveness – in contest, enforcing social status rather than actual ability as the key determinant to participation. The nobility has dominated the game's hierarchy in England. Of 111 presidents of the MCC between 1825 and 1939, only 16 were neither knights nor peers.[50] The post-war years have seen one prime minister (Alec Douglas-Home), two supreme commanders (Earl Alexander and Viscount Portal), a head of the Foreign Office (Lord Caccia) and the earl marshal and chief butler of England (the Duke of Norfolk) as president of this elite institution: the monarch's husband has even held the post twice.

However, the working classes continued to support and play the game, plying their trade either as 'servants' of the clubs or in the value-free arenas that became league cricket. Contests here were more reflective of the contemporary one-day competition and were naturally frowned upon by the elite clubs. So, what emerged in industrial Britain was one code but two traditions. Moreover, the dominant tradition, established by a hierarchy and club system rooted in the middle and upper classes and maintained by the emphasis on amateurism, brought with the game a set of values that were representative of the political system that they personified.

This informal segregation was transmitted to the colonies. In India organised cricket was based upon exclusive clubs that were open to Europeans only. Games were organised between a civilian team and a regiment or gymkhana, and fraternisation was strictly between one European and another. When the first English teams visited the continent in the 1890s it was to partake in competition against these European sides. During the 1840s a group of Parsis witnessed military officers playing the game and attempted to duplicate their actions. At least 30 Parsi cricket clubs were formed in the 1850s and 1860s.[51] Despite this enthusiasm, the Parsis were not given a match against a British team until 1877 and were forced to play on inadequate pitches which did little to develop their techniques. The mixing of races was clearly not encouraged.

Once it was considered politically expedient to encourage contests with

Indian sides, it was on the premise of religious segregation that such competition took place. The annual Presidency matches between the Parsis and the Europeans became India's first cricket tournament. In 1907 the Hindu team made it a triangular contest, the Muslims joined the Tournament in 1912 and, in 1937 a team composed of Indian Christians and Jews made it a five-way competition. Governors encouraged communal cricket because it satisfied their concept of Indian society. Lord Harris, a one-time governor of Bombay and leading MCC administrator, did not look upon India as a nation but a collection of races and castes without any common bonds. The cricket field would provide a meeting place where social intercourse was achieved – but in separate team identities.

Although club cricket in the Caribbean allowed a wider share of the population to become involved in the sport, this participation was on strictly economic – and thus racial – terms. Through cricket the benefits of the hierarchical structure of society were displayed. Each island had a team that represented the white elite, other teams represented the coloured and black middle class, and the working-class mass of the population formed their own sides – from which a number of players could hope to be called on to play for the elite clubs for financial reward. By 1906 players of African descent were representing the national team. However, early West Indian sides were led by white captains (Archer Warner in 1900 and H.G.B. Austin in 1906 and 1923) and the leading batsmen were of European descent.

Membership of the early prestigious Philadelphian clubs was by subscription, thus reinforcing the social status of the club. Eighty per cent of the members in the major clubs held white-collar positions, while blue-collar workers tended to play for the minor clubs – which included an equal share of white-collar members.[52] Clubs, moreover, came to represent more than simply sides that played cricket: they increasingly organised social gatherings (where like-minded people would congregate) for a membership in which inactive cricketers at some clubs outnumbered actual players by ten-to-one.[53]

Only the Australians rejected the prejudice of elitism when it came to cricket. Emphasis on winning – especially against England – was the side's *raison d'être*, and they cared little for the social apartheid that so absorbed English cricket: 'The Australians, whether amateurs or professional, will never consent to be spat upon by dirty little cads whose soap-boiling or nigger-murdering grandfathers left enough money to get the cads' fathers "ennobled" and to enable the cad himself to live without working.'[54] The 1884 touring side, for example, refused to be labelled and asked for its players to be regarded not as 'amateur' or 'professional' but as 'cricketer'. This was evidently divorced from the attitude in England. Consider the synopsis from S. Canynge Caple in 1960:

> If the purpose of a cricket tour abroad is merely to foster good relations
> with that particular country and at the same time encourage the devel-

opment of the game there, then by all means send a side which contains a goodly proportion of amateurs who can sustain the social side of the trip and a reasonable number of first-class professionals who ... could 'sell' cricket with an eye to the future. If, on the other, the tour is one in which the honour of English cricket depends ... then it is obviously the bounden duty of the selectors to choose the strongest possible combination *even if this means weakening the after-dinner speech capacity of the side*. Singleness of purpose wins not only battles but also Test Matches, and it was because they were imbued with this inevitable attribute that for so many years the Australians lost so few Test rubbers.[55]

Despite this, there have been accusations of racism cast at Australian cricket. No Aborigine has represented the land of his birth, even though players such as Jack Marsh, Alex Henry and Eddie Gilbert were certainly good enough.[56] Racism was evident in every country that took up the game.

Leadership

Nowhere was the hierarchical nature of the game enforced so efficiently and purposely as in the question of leadership on the field of play. Whilst professionals and native cricketers were grudgingly accepted, the captaincy of the team – especially when that side was the national team – had to go to the 'right sort of fellow', even at the detriment of the side, for the game was not simply about winning. A journalist wrote that 'County sides are best led by a man socially superior to the professionals.'[57] Cricketing ability, then, was not the first priority. When Lord Hawke retired from the Yorkshire captaincy in 1910, the county were led first by Everard Radcliffe, who had a poor batting average and took two wickets at 67 each, and then by Archibald White, who batted at number ten and did not bowl. For the period 1907–10 Sir Arthur Hazelrigg captained Leicestershire, even though he had never participated in a first-class match in his life and was not even in his school XI.

Test captaincy, moreover, was the monopoly of the amateur. Of 47 amateurs who represented England between the wars, 16 did so as captain. The 45-year-old Gubby Allen led the MCC in the West Indies in 1947–48 even though he had only represented Middlesex twice in the previous season. It was not until 1952 that Len Hutton became the first professional to captain his country.

Palwanker Baloo, the greatest Hindu cricketer of his day and a Harijan, never captained the Hindu XI. The costs of the cricket trials for the 1932 tour to England were funded by the Indian prince Patiala, who also underwrote the total costs of touring. Perhaps unsurprisingly, selection for the side was not based on merit but on association with Patiala. The Maharaja of Porbandar succeeded Patiala – who was too busy with domestic politics – as captain. He faced widespread criticism as he was a non-player and resigned after having batted only three times on tour, scoring 0, 0 and 2 – making him the only cricketer to have owned more Rolls-Royces than he scored runs on a tour to England! Such princely patronage only declined amid the social and political currents that swept across India, resulting in independence, and the selection of Armanath as captain in 1947 signalled the beginning of a selection process based on ability.

A similar history of selection is apparent in the West Indies. In 1930 the West Indian captaincy was offered to Jack Grant. Grant, a white 23-year-old Trinidadian, had only recently completed his studies at Cambridge, and had never captained a first-class team and never played in a first-class match in the region of his birth: 'It could not be disputed that my white colour was a major factor in my being given this post.'[58] Gerry Alexander, of mixed-race, was made captain for the 1957–58 home series against Pakistan. A veterinary surgeon from an upper middle-class family in urban Jamaica, Alexander was also Cambridge-educated, and 'although not white by race', was seen by many as being 'white by class and colour and ... regarded as "Jamaican white."'[59] In 1959 Frank Worrell was appointed captain for the coming tour of Australia, and was thus the first black man to be appointed captain of the West Indies in his own right. Blacks had been in charge for occasional matches when the official captain had been unable to take part, but Worrell was the first to be appointed for a series. Under his leadership the West Indies played 15 Tests in the period 1960–63, winning 9 and losing 3. Nonetheless, Worrell was still considered to be a 'safe' choice as he had attended a leading school in Barbados and graduated from a university in England. Furthermore, he was sympathetic to the established perception of racial society in the Caribbean: 'Nobody cares two hoots about a man's colour, and there is no obvious colour bar to advancement in any trade or profession ... It is not easy for a West Indian to write about "the colour problem" because there is ostensibly no such thing on our islands.'[60]

Within four years he had handed over the leadership to Gary Sobers. Coming from the 'lower' orders, Sobers did not enjoy the same comfortable upbringing as Worrell. He was the first working-class player to captain the West Indies. The revolution was complete.

Once again, it was the Australians who proved the exception to the rule. Both early state sides and the national eleven were known to elect their captain democratically. Indeed, the players selected the captains of seven of the first eight Australian teams to England.

Australia aside, where did this lack of democratic sentiment fit in with the values of cricket? Learie Constantine argues that cricket is the 'most obvious, and some would say the most glaring, example of the black man being kept "in his place"'.[61] This had adversarial effects on the West Indian team as they struggled to unite as a single unit. The sport was supposed to be a stage where the act of 'civilisation' could be paraded and dispersed to the far corners of the globe. The message, then, was all-important, and authority through leadership overrode any sentiments towards equality and was central to the objective. However, emphasis on the qualities of the man as a social being rather than a cricketer did not make for successful sides. It certainly wasn't cricket.

Politics

To say that the modern game owes its existence to politics would be an oversimplification. What is beyond doubt, however, is the role of politicians in both the 'take-off' stage of cricket and their influence in shaping the sport's development. Indeed, if we were to adhere to the proponents of the 'keep politics out of sport' argument, there would be no history – as we know it – to record.

The emergence of cricket as a popular pastime came about through political legislation. The Tudors, as a move to preserve and encourage archery, banned sports. A way round this prohibition was for people to invent new games that were not covered by the statute, but this led to a blanket ban on all activities. However, this did not cover children's recreations and as cricket was, in the main, an activity enjoyed by the young it is to be assumed that adults took the opportunity to partake in a game that invoked no legal penalty.

The early patrons of cricket had two things in common: they owned large country estates in the south-east and were Members of Parliament or Crown appointees. The Duke of Dorset (Ambassador to the Court of France), Horatio Mann (MP for Sandwich, 1774–1807), and the Earl of Tankerville (a Privy Councillor) were all responsible for many of the early 'great' matches. Indeed, Dorset and Tankerville, along with a number of other prominent politicians, were members of the Star and Garter Committee who issued the laws of cricket at Hambledon. Furthermore, Thomas Lord sold the cricket ground that bears his name to William Ward, a director of the Bank of England and an MP for the City of London, and William Pitt made a reference to the game when introducing a Defence Bill during the Napoleonic Wars. Dorset, though, fell victim to politics when the first ever overseas tour – to France in 1789 – was cancelled because of the Revolution.

The Victorians were equally keen to dabble between the pastimes of politics and sport. Lord Harris was chancellor of the Primrose League, a Conservative-front organisation that argued for the unity of classes and the imperial ascendancy of Britain; many MPs were members of the MCC; and prominent administrators such as Hawke, Harris, F.S. Jackson and P.F. Warner were well known for their adherence to the cause of conservatism. In fact, interests were such that in 1888 a section of the Great Railway Bill, which threatened the Lord's ground, was defeated. This personal link between politics and sport continued throughout the twentieth century. Stanley Baldwin often sported an I Zingari tie; Clement Atlee installed a tickertape outside the Cabinet Room in order to obtain the county scores; Alec Douglas-Home played ten first class matches; and John Major portrayed his ideal of Britain as one of warm beer and village cricket matches.

In India, cricket was only promoted among the population once it was considered politically advantageous to British rule. We have seen that the Parsis took up the game in the 1840s, but it was not until the 1880s that the imperialist authorities acknowledged them. This turnabout was caused by the formation of the Indian Congress in 1885. The British were faced, for the first time, with organised criticism of their rule. The imperial authorities sought allies or at least a buffer between themselves and the populace at large. The Parsis fitted this role nicely. In 1886 they were invited to play at Royal Windsor. Regular fixtures were then established against the Bombay Presidency XI, during which players mixed with Sahibs and Memsahibs – which allowed seeds to be sown in the prosperous Hindu and Muslim circles. This procession of events led to an acceleration of the game's popularity, which in turn led to the 'take-off' of Indian cricket.

Moreover, politicians saw in cricket a vehicle that could be manipulated to secure popularity. For example, leading Australian colonial figures often frequented the first intercolonial games: in New South Wales the governor was a regular visitor; in Tasmania the governor was the patron; and in 1871, when the South Australian Cricket Association was formed, J.A. Ferguson, ADC to the governor, became the Association's first president. Robert Menzies, the Australian Prime Minister 1939–41 and 1949–66, also made use of cricket. Although Menzies was not known for his affections toward sport before he entered politics, on obtaining the highest civil rank he became one of the nation's most enthusiastic cricket observers; it was also interesting to witness that his missions to London always seemed to coincide with the Lord's Test match. A similar nexus was evident in other outposts of the Empire. In India, the Governor of Bombay declared the first day of the first ever Test match in India in 1933 a national holiday. In Barbados, the swearing-in ceremony in 1954 of the new administration had to be rescheduled in order to avoid a clash with an important fixture, and in 1966 independence itself was celebrated with a cricket match.

Many colonial rulers also sought promotion of cricket as a means to enforce ties with the 'mother country'. This would certainly explain the patronage of the sport by the early princes in India. It suited neither them nor the British authorities to see the rise of the Indian Congress Party. Additionally, a prince with cricket connections carried political clout in the Chamber of Princes:[62] Ranjitsinhji was Chancellor of the Chamber before his death, as was Patiala (1926–30 and 1934–35).

Finally, politicians became involved in cricket as it was an important means of promoting the nation state. For example, cabinet ministers have headed the Indian Board of Control (founded in 1928), which has as one of its functions 'to improve or develop cricket through organisational and scientific means so that the cricketers enhance the nation's prestige by their victories and give a sense of achievement and well-being to 800 million Indians'.[63]

Conclusion

The social scientist is constantly engaged in conceptualising matter in order to enhance an understanding of the world in which we reside. Whilst definition is a valuable aid, though, it has to be conceded that the discipline of political science does not always conclude studies with an actual fact or a right or wrong answer, and that differing approaches yield conflicting responses. This is, indeed, the issue with the three criteria discussed in the opening section of this book. In order to comprehend the relationship between politics and sport it is necessary to be aware of not only one's personal viewpoint but also of the understanding applied to the issues in question by others.

As discussed in the first chapter, the conceptualisation of 'politics' will undoubtedly determine the individual's approach to its relationship with sport. A study of politics in institutional terms divides matter into acceptable and unacceptable areas of analysis. Sport is not an issue, it is argued, for a political scientist for it represents activity in a setting beyond the jurisdiction of the State. To allow government's access to such areas is to permit encroachment of the individual's natural rights. In which case, what is within the legitimate confines of analysis for the student of the simplified model? Politics is about the functions and institutions of Government. It is normative and deals in the concepts of power, sovereignty and justice.

So, politics is about power and, by definition, disputes and conflicts over its application and distribution. Power, though, exists in associations and relationships other than those concerned primarily with the legislative process. Are these political? They are if they are directly influenced by the same factors that determine political institutions. By introducing a philosophical influence we are immediately drawn into a more spacious terrain for investigation. By thorough scrutiny it is clear that sport is beyond mere 'play' and activity. It is subject to wider concerns and is also influenced by the same concepts of power, sovereignty and justice. By being so, sport and politics now have something in common. This is all at a theoretical level, but when we apply a more in-depth analysis of a particular sport in any given society then it becomes evident that it is subject to far wider influences. Cricket's ethos was constructed by the purveyors of hegemony in order to maintain and strengthen their political and economic power, both at home and throughout the Empire. Such forces embraced not only sport, leisure and culture, but politics as well. As social scientists, therefore, if we are seeking to define 'politics', 'sport' and 'cricket', we can only do so with certainty if we assess them in relation to the environment in which they have evolved.

The brief study of cricket in this chapter highlights how the same forces that shaped political direction also moulded the game. Cricket promoted the values of 'fair play', acceptance of the rules, masculinity, common decency and respect for the rules and rulers. This ethos was not simply adopted by athletes because it sounded like a good idea; it was carved out of a social, economic and political philosophy in the elite establishments of church and private education for the purpose of promoting contemporary values. Cricket was also subject to the accompanying tendencies of social segregation – on grounds of class and race – in all of the countries where it has been played at first-class level. So, what comes first: political ideology or the social value system? In all probability the latter of these options is more likely and therefore politics has to be about more than institutions, as do leisure, sport and cricket – simply because they are all prone to the wider persuasions of a more powerful source.

Having established the connections between politics and sport and examined the rationale for the relationship and the benefits from which politics derive, the book advances to the core of the study: a history of South African cricket. The justification for a theoretical analysis of politics, sport and cricket is to show that each criterion is subject to greater convictions. Segregation, according to racial classification, has dominated the economic and political structure of South Africa. It is, therefore, impossible to compile a study of South African cricket without considering the effects of such a 'tradition'. By emphasising cricket as a means of imparting political values, this chapter has attempted to show that the sport – in all countries – is subject to and conditioned by its social environment. This is not something unique to South Africa, nor is the segregation of players. What follows is a thorough scrutiny of how politics dictated the terms of reference for South African cricket. At each stage, the government – as a key component of the economic superstructure – mapped the game's development. This was acknowledged by opponents of apartheid and reversed so that sport became a means to inflict political damage on the ruling administration. Still, there were those who chose not to see the intimacy of the relationship between sport and politics, and viewed the former as autonomous. The following analysis, then, is as much an examination of conservatism as it is about South Africa.

4

Programme and Practice:
Apartheid and Sport

Chapter 2 examined the rationale for the relationship between politics and sport. Assessing this connection in the context of *what* governments do, it was determined that sport provides a valuable means of integration, of maintaining social order and ensuring a fit and healthy populace that can be called on in times of conflict. It was further suggested that sport offered benefits to professional political actors, if only because it was a means by which to promote the nation state. Finally, sport and politics were examined in the broader context of the social and economic environment to outline the manner that they serve, recreate and reinforce the dominant hegemony.

All of these themes are examined further in this section, which explores the ideological trends that have formed and dominated the history of South African cricket. If the previous section provided the theoretical foundation for the analysis of the relationship between politics and sport, the following puts in place the structure or 'pillars' of the book. Each of the four chapters is interrelated and is positioned in an ascendancy of importance.

Before 1948 the game evolved in relation to the patterns of the wider society. Initially, it was introduced into South Africa by the British military and later by settlers and seen as a means of cementing imperial ties and pacifying hostile elements. Following the election of the National Party in 1948, 'informal' segregation was tightened up and the philosophy of apartheid (separateness) applied to virtually all areas of public and private life. One such area subject to scrutiny by the state was sport. This chapter formulates an analysis of apartheid and then examines the role of the state in determining the fortunes of South African sport. It is concerned not only with legislation, but with the reasons that reforms were enacted. As such, it is an attempt to view both politics and sport within the medium of the traditional institutional approach to political science whilst maintaining that the mere examination of policy is insufficient in understanding political behaviour.

Theoretical principles in the early history of South African cricket

Cricket's elitist ethos, discussed in the previous section, ensured the involvement of men concerned with issues of status and stature. Similar 'qualities' probably enticed the same individuals into politics. A feature of the early days of Natal cricket was the interest taken in it by many 'leading men' in the colony.[1] The first inter-town match, for example, featured Harry Escombe and Henry Binns, both future prime ministers of the colony; in 1887 C. Henwood, a future mayor of Durban and member of the Union parliament, captained the side; and in the Western Province early cricket matches were fashionable occasions and would be graced by the governor and other distinguished guests. Cricket, then, immediately forged a relationship with those sectors of South African society that would become the political and economic ruling class.

The whole rationale of the South Africa colony, in the eyes of the British authorities, was to maintain and strengthen the Empire by ensuring safe passage around the Cape. Sports, as part of an imperial ethos, proved crucial to the overall 'masterplan'. Lord Harris, for example, described Lord Hawke's 1895–96 tourists as 'a strand in the elastic which unites the colonies and the Mother Country.'[2] South Africa soon joined Australia among the most important Test playing sides when, with England in 1901, they formed the Imperial Cricket Conference (ICC). In 1909 the MCC suggested that the nations should engage in a triangular contest. So important was this to the English authorities that when the Australians argued against it on account of South Africa not being strong enough the MCC threatened to cancel the proposed 'Aussie' tour to England. The two sides compromised and the tournament was arranged for 1912. The wider significance of the competition was not lost on its instigator, the South African diamond magnate Abe Bailey:

> … the cricket result should be a secondary consideration to all lovers of Empire. That a spirit of true national comradeship will be produced must be the desire of every cricketer throughout the king's Dominions. Other colonies will be as deeply interested in the matches as those immediately concerned, and if the strengthening of the bonds of Union within the Empire is one of the many outcomes of the great [triangular] Tournament …[3]

In 1907 both Australia and New Zealand were granted dominion status within the British Empire; they were joined by South Africa in 1910. Sport became an important means of maintaining relations between these semi-independent countries and the imperial centre. Cricket became one component of the ideological forces that assisted in the maintenance of Empire and, later, Commonwealth. Internally, it aided the same political and economic interests by providing the classic 'opiate'. Consider the remarks made in the newspaper the *Natal Witness* concerning the first recorded match to be played in 1852 by the townsmen of Maritzburg: 'The goodwill and cheerfulness visible in every face, the happy picnic and the active cricket match would lead strangers to suppose that the cry about hard times and financial difficulties had only its origin in distorted imaginations.'[4] This was a time before the discovery of gold and diamonds, an age in which Natal – as with other provinces – suffered severe economic difficulties. Cricket even acted as a dampener on the spirits enraged by the Jameson Raid:[5]

> Coinciding as they did with the Jameson Raid, our men had some curious experiences. They were hurriedly summoned to Johannesburg to distract local attention from political issues, were held up on their way by an armed posse of Boers, from whom, however, by presenting two bats, they parted excellent friends, and on arrival at the Rand saw Cronje march through with his victorious commandos, and dined with the English 'prisoners'.[6]

Such were the healing qualities of cricket that the correspondent S. Canynge Caple believed that international tension would be less great 'if only Russia and China could be persuaded to take up cricket'.[7] In other – somewhat more minor situations – cricket was actually used in such a placatory way. Floris van der Merwe relates how sports were encouraged in the Afrikaner prisoner-of-war camps during the Boer War in order to placate thousands of bored captives.[8] Indeed, prisoners were shipped throughout the Empire and given provisions to establish cricket clubs, and Afrikaner prisoners of war engaged in contests against British soldiers and the indigenous populations of countries such as Ceylon, India and the island of St Helena.

Sport in general served a similar purpose in other situations, too. The compound and the slum were consequences of a mining industry built on the principle of low labour costs, and such conditions inevitably led to tension and industrial disputes. The promotion of sports offered a means of channelling energies away from political and economic concerns, as *Abantu-Batho*, the ANC-linked newspaper, remarked in 1931:

> The biggest weapon to keep a native quiet is to give him sports and our present administration and employers know this and they want to use it to the fullest extent. When our intelligent young men are given sports they forget everything which is dear to them and their country. It is harmless to give him sports it keeps him contented they say, while they exploit the poor native to the fullest extent.[9]

The rise of the Communist Party and the increasing black membership of trade unions alarmed liberals, who then sought to devise a means whereby a greater understanding of African attitudes would defuse any potential hostility. Departments of Bantu Studies and Social Anthropology were opened in the major universities, and black newspapers such as *Umteleli Wa Bantu* were launched in order to provide white liberal representation in the black communities. Additionally, in the early 1920s a number of prominent individuals established the Joint Councils Movement in order to advance cultural and leisure activities among blacks. These bodies were composed of an equal number of Africans, coloureds and Indians on one side and Europeans on the other. The composition of the 18 European members who founded the Johannesburg Joint Council included 'academics, lawyers, priests and missionaries ... directors of a mining company and of an insurance company, the former chairman of the Stock Exchange, chairman of the Chamber of Commerce, the manager of the Native Recruiting Corporation and the President of the Typographical Union'.[10] They invited the black 'elite' to represent the voice of the African population. This is not surprising considering that the political leadership – people such as Abdurahman (the president of the first nationally based black political movement, the African Political (later People's) Organisation, founded in 1902) – had argued for segregation, claiming that this would shelter Africans from white vices.[11]

The aim of such bodies was to 'enlighten' African cultural life by introducing black workers to the ideas and beliefs of European 'civilisation'. Improvement was seen as moral rather than economic or political. The Revd Dexter Taylor outlined the benefits of leisure for Africans in a speech to the National European–Bantu Conference (Joint Councils) in 1929:

> Proper and adequate provision for Native recreation would mean better workers, keener mentally and physically, better citizens less likely to be criminals, better neighbours, less likely to be anti-white, more likely to possess a true sense of community values ...[12]

Dorothy Maud of the Anglican Church's Community of the Resurrection believed it a 'blessed truth' that 'games break down colour prejudice quicker than anything else'.[13] By the end of the 1930s the Social Welfare branch of Johannesburg's Native Affairs Department supervised and organised a number of African teams, including 230 football and 60 cricket sides.[14] 'With a little encouragement', wrote Ray Phillips in 1936, 'the cordial relationships which have developed in the field of sport will, undoubtedly, continue, and will act as a positive factor in shaping the attitude of the hundreds of Africans who are finding an outlet for their energies on the Witwatersrand playing fields'.[15] Sport had become a class issue, a mechanism to cement the relationship of the white peoples, reward the black elites and pacify black labour. The Communist Party, though, attacked the ANC and other intellectual leaders for cooperating with such schemes, arguing that 'Liberalism and the lure of fat jobs corrupted the leaders. "All the black reformists and charlatans, all the discarded race-betrayers and unprincipled time-servers suddenly became protagonists of sports, education and inter-racial co-operation." The young were made sports minded and dance crazy; and Congress fell back into inactivity.'[16]

Whilst not as formally structured as apartheid, the segregated society was built on a number of laws that were designed to satisfy the requirements of capitalism for cheap units of labour. Africans were stripped of their land, were tied to employment and informed where they might reside and what occupations they might pursue. White South Africans, it appeared, wanted the service of the native population, but not their presence. Where they encouraged sport it was to occupy time in order to prevent a hostile reaction to very poor conditions.

To hard-line Afrikaner Nationalists, though, this was not enough. They advocated a more formal and strict system of 'separateness'. In 1942 B.J. Vorster, assistant chief-commandant of the pro-Nazi Germany *Ossewa-Brandwag* and future prime minister (1966–78), outlined his political philosophy as follows: 'We stand for Christian Nationalism which is an ally of National Socialism. You can call this anti-democratic principle dictatorship if you wish. In Italy it is called fascism, in Germany German National Socialism and in South Africa Christian Nationalism.'[17] After the Christian Nationalist victory in the 1948 general election, South African society anticipated the future prospect of this Afrikaner nationalist rule.

Apartheid

The 1948 general election was the first to be contested following the Second World War, a conflict that had divided the political elites into two opposing camps.[18] The defeat of fascism ushered in a period of expectation for colonised peoples throughout the imperial globe. Indeed, there had been a change of attitude amongst the creators of Empire: cooperation and influence would now replace domination. The age of imperialism, as it was known, was coming to a close. In South Africa, 134,000 African workers had been recruited into industry during the war to absorb labour pressures as a result of the expanding economy and white recruitment to the armed forces.[19] Africans were increasingly becoming urbanised and unionised and were prepared to adopt extra-parliamentary tactics in an attempt to improve their quality of life.[20] Liberals reacted to this by proclaiming universal educational and employment rights as a means to integrate the nation's parts into the capitalist organism. Conservatives rejected this stance and advocated stricter segregation as a means to blunt militancy and preserve racial exclusiveness. These two contrasting energies, offering distinct versions of segregation, engaged in one of political history's most memorable contests – with the National Party unexpectedly defeating the United Party on seats, though with a smaller share of the vote.[21]

Afrikaner nationalism, as a political philosophy, has been constructed out of the experiences of the Dutch settlers in South Africa. Based upon fear of the unknown, it considered itself susceptible to the economic dominance of the English, the uncouth manner of the native African and the foreign doctrine of communism. Each would undermine the Western civilised standards that the Afrikaner had taken upon himself to uphold. Emphasis was stressed on *volksgebondenheid* – the belief that the ties of blood and *volk* come first. Individuals could realise their full potential only through the *volk*.[22] Nationalists feared that in the absence of formal segregation the European race would eventually disappear, as did the British in Egypt and the Dutch in Indonesia. They also held that the Afrikaners were a repressed minority in South Africa. This gave rise to a 'national anxiety', which could only be overcome through a thorough re-evaluation of the social and political apparatus of the state.[23] Thus the Afrikaner nationalist philosophy led to the strategy of apartheid, which aimed at the maintenance and protection of the white population 'as a pure white race' and the maintenance and protection of the indigenous race groups 'as separate national communities' residing in allocated 'homelands'.[24] They fought the 1948 election with no English candidates and a constitution, in Transvaal, which explicitly excluded Jews.

Apartheid represented the value systems of racial superiority. It held that all whites were above all blacks.[25] Dr Strijdom (prime minister 1954–58) stated that the policy of apartheid was to be carried out 'to perpetuate the rule of whites in their areas'.[26] The idea of a nation of all races was never entertained; the indigenous population were considered an inferior people: 'The Bantu were a race who never through all the centuries developed more than a primitive civilisation.'[27] Surrounded by such a population, the hold of 'advanced civilisation appeared all too tenuous, as Dr J.E. Holloway – high commissioner for South Africa – warned the South Africa Club in London: 'to undermine the all too limited number of pillars of civilisation which existed there was to invite the return of barbarism'.[28]

Nationalism claimed to be above politics, and sought inspiration and justification in religion. The Dutch Reformed Church was the co-author of apartheid, 'some would say its initiator'.[29] Political leadership was ultimately responsible to God, in whose name they acted. The philosophical basis for this stand was to be found in Paul's admonition in Romans 13:

> Everyone must submit himself to the governing authorities, for there is no authority except that which God has established. The authorities that exist have been established by God. Consequently, he who rebels against the authority is rebelling against what God has instituted, and those who do so will bring judgement on themselves.[30]

A Calvinist doctrine of predestination provided the white Protestants with their theological justification for racial superiority. 'God's hand was always clearly "visible" in the history of the nation, which had a task, or mission, or calling ...'[31] Moreover, Article 2 (ii) of the National Party's constitution stated: 'The Republic is grounded on a Christian-National foundation and therefore acknowledges, as the standard of the government of the state, in the first place the principles of the Holy Scriptures.'[32] For the Nationalist, then, this was not politics, but destiny. In the words of Dr Malan, a former minister of the Dutch Reformed Church and prime minister (1948–54), 'We are not a party political organisation in the ordinary sense of the term. We are far more than that.'[33]

The argument followed that there are two kinds of people: those who are predestined by God to be saved and those who will be damned. The Afrikaner, as is his calling, would have the 'best interests' of the African at heart: 'If to do this effectively and avoid being submerged or absorbed entailed the domination of other groups, so it had to be.'[34] The task was to construct a society in which each of the separate identities would be preserved, enabling them to function for the well-being of South Africa.[35] This became the so-called 'native problem'. P.W. Botha, secretary of the Cape National Party, suggested the lengths to which the Nationalist regime would go to in order to realise their ambitions:

> to gain a clear view regarding fair treatment and the rights of non-Europeans, we should first answer another question and that is: do we stand for the domination and supremacy of the European or not? ... For if you stand for the domination and supremacy of the European, then everything you do must in the first place be calculated to ensure that domination.[36]

As a key element in the philosophy, each group of races was to be segregated in both the workplace and habitat. Therefore, black South Africans were to be allowed to enter white areas for the purpose of employment only, provided that they carried permission to do so. Self-government was offered to the reserves in exchange for the relinquishing of all political aspirations in the 'white territories'. National differences replaced racial superiority in the justification for segregation, and became an honourable pursuit of traditional social practices.

The effects of apartheid on sport

When the National Party succeeded to power following the 1948 election it did not have to impose apartheid on sport since it was already segregated. This does not mean, however, that affairs simply continued as before or that measures undertaken by the new regime were not to have an effect on all walks of life, including sport. Harold Wolpe has maintained that a failing of many historians on South Africa is that of the 'continuity of history' in that an assumption is made that apartheid was simply a formal continuation of the segregation policies of the previous epoch.[37] Apartheid, whilst building on segregationist foundations, was unique. Its structure, distinct from segregation, was based on a number of acts, the totality of which affected the whole social environment and had the effect of outlawing multiracial sports:

- Legislation governing migrant and temporary labour was strengthened. Before black workers were permitted to work in the cities, the requirements of farmers had first to be satisfied.
- Africans were obliged to carry Pass Books, which informed the authorities of which urban area s/he had permission to be in, whether s/he has permission to work in this area and for whom s/he was employed.
- Racial zoning of residential areas was accelerated.
- The Group Areas Act (1950) determined where the African could live, and with whom.
- The Bantu Laws Amendment Act (1970) prohibited non-Africans from entering into an African residency without permission.
- The Job Reservation Act outlined the type of work each racial group was allowed to perform.

In effect, blacks were treated as interchangeable labour units rather than as human beings. Apartheid was introduced for park benches, buses, railway waiting rooms and even the beaches. A Race Classification Board determined the individual's colour. In addition to these general regulations which would ultimately affect leisure activities came the measures that directly related to sport:

- The Urban Areas Act (1955) reserved sporting facilities for the use of one racial group.
- The Reservation of Separate Amenities Act (1953) imposed racial segregation in stadia and other public places. It granted municipal authorities the power to prohibit black spectators.
- The Native Laws Amendment Act (1957) allowed for the withholding of permission to Africans to attend gatherings outside of their own residential area. It was later amended to extend segregation into churches, places of entertainment, buses and sport.
- The Liquor Amendment Act forbade the social interaction of Africans with other races to consume alcohol, preventing athletes from mixing after matches for a social drink.
- The Group Areas Act (1950) prohibited the mixing of races in cinemas, restaurants and sports clubs without a permit.

The minister of community development explained how the Group Areas Act would affect sports venues:

> A sports facility in a white area ... should generally be used only by whites. However, if separate entrance, seating and toilet facilities were provided, blacks could attend provincial and international events if it did not disturb the whites. Africans could never attend events below the provincial level, while Indians and Coloureds could – provided it did not disturb the whites.[38]

This was the initial extent of political involvement by the state in sport. It marked a direct encroachment into areas considered out of bounds by liberal sentiment.

South Africa, then, was assuming features that were compatible with a totalitarian state. There were very few areas of life that remained unaffected by the command of 'Christian Nationalism'. The Customs Act and the Publications and Entertainments Act of 1963 informed the African of the books s/he could – or rather could not – read, what films s/he could enjoy in segregated cinemas and the art that s/he would be allowed to contemplate. This was a country that banned *Black Beauty* as subversive literature, condemned swimming on Sundays as a moral outrage and claimed that the 1966 drought was God's punishment for white women wearing the miniskirt.[39] Sexual relations with whites were regulated, and the Courts were bestowed with powers to prosecute if satisfied that there was even intention to practise intercourse. Known opponents of the regime were subjected to intimidation, banning and physical violence. An editorial in the *Times* argued that '... the more the policy of apartheid is developed in practice the more it becomes apparent that it involves outrage upon liberty in every aspect – freedom of body, of mind, and of spirit'.[40]

Sport enjoyed a status in South Africa that was similar to its status in Australia. Not only was it a means to unify the white race, it proved an impressive instrument on the international stage to display the strengths and qualities of South African nationalism and political standing. It was Dr Malan, the newly elected National Party prime minister, who cabled F. Allen, the captain of the All-Blacks Rugby football team, and thanked him for 'stimulating to an unprecedented pitch the interest of all sections of South African people in Rugby football',[41] and similarly to the captain of the Springboks following the tour to Britain in the 1951/52 season for the way in which the team had achieved world fame for South Africa.[42]

This is a clear-cut example of how politics involves itself with sports without actually formally doing so. It cannot be disputed, though, that the programmes in place prevented great sections of the population from engaging in 'normal' sporting relations. Blacks, of course, could not hope to represent South Africa since mixing was prohibited. It was seen as essential by the National Party to enforce that principle because of the relevance sports had to South Africans and for reasons expressed in an editorial in *Die Transvaler*: 'In South Africa the races do not mix on the sports field. If they mix first on the sports field, then the road to other forms of social mixing is wide open ... With an eye to upholding the white race and its civilisation not one single compromise can be entered into.'[43] In other words, if the races played together they would soon want to worship and study together. Not one leak could be permitted in apartheid's dam, less the whole thing be washed away. It was inevitable, then, that sport became a part of apartheid's 'grand scheme'.

Official policy

Scrutiny of individual pieces of legislation offers the political scientist a possible answer to the problem *why* governments initiate policy. Segregation in sports was such that further regulations did not need to be drawn up and, until 1956, there was no specific programme relating to sport. In June 1956 Dr Dönges, the minister of the interior, announced South Africa's first official policy on sports. This was forced on the regime by a number of developments which indicated the distaste toward racial sport: in 1956 the International Table Tennis Federation withdrew recognition of the white South African body and recognised its black counterpart; FIFA became embroiled in the soccer structure of the nation; a number of black organisations (including the South African Cricket Board of Control) pressed for international recognition; and Dennis Brutus formed the Coordinating Committee for International Relations in Sports – the first South African sports protest group.

The government reacted to this breach of its philosophy with a statement that enshrined a collection of wider policies and 'traditions' into an official sports policy. It outlined that:

- whites and blacks should organise their sports separately;
- no mixed sport would be allowed within South Africa;
- no mixed teams could compete abroad;
- international teams competing in South Africa would have to be all-white;
- black sportsmen from overseas would be allowed to compete against blacks in South Africa;
- black sporting organisations wishing to apply for international recognition would have to do so through the established white associations;
- the government would refuse visas to anyone who sought to criticise South Africa's policies abroad.[44]

In 1963 Jan de Klerk, the then minister of the interior, claimed that the sporting policy merely reflected the 'custom' by which all policy was conducted in South Africa: whites would compete against whites and blacks against blacks;[45] this was how it had always been. In practice, the official sports policy afforded the government the right to determine not only which teams could play abroad but also the racial composition of these sides. The government even laid down which sporting bodies should be affiliated to international associations. Successive ministers defended this stance in parliament to the extent of discouraging foreign countries from inviting South African sides to tour outside of South Africa.[46]

Olive van Ryneveld of the Progressive Party warned the government that its attitude would lead to South Africa's expulsion from overseas sports.[47]

This warning, though, was ignored by de Klerk, who endorsed the sports policy on 26 June 1964 in an official statement:

> The participation in international or world sports tournaments or competitions by mixed teams representing South Africa as a whole can in no circumstances be approved ... The South African custom, which is traditional, finds expression in the policy that there should be no competition in sport between the races, within our borders, and that the mixing of races in teams taking part in sports meetings within the Republic of South Africa and abroad should be avoided.[48]

The multinational policy

The multinational idea allocated each race its own territory. Once assigned an area, Africans could only enter white territory for a temporary period for an established purpose. To enforce this, strict influx controls were introduced and greater use of migrant labour exploited and justified as being in 'the interests of the Bantu'.[49] Africans were divided along ethnic lines into eight (later expanded to ten) 'homelands', which totalled something in the region of 14 per cent of South African territory and comprised 81 large and 200 smaller blocks of land. Not only were these of the poorest agricultural terrain but none had a chance of viability without an investment, both in their own infrastructure and in their links with the rest of the country – far in excess of what any white South African electorate could be persuaded to finance.[50] To seek employment in the prosperous white sector the African had to assume the status of temporary worker. The idea was that – as independent sovereign states – the homelands would export labour to South Africa in a similar way as Turkey does to Germany, with no questions about political rights in the host country. In effect, the African population would no longer be considered as South African. Verwoerd described this as his 'good neighbour' policy.[51] It was a 'divine task ... which dare not be denied or destroyed by anyone'.[52]

Relaxation of official policy

In the 1950s the ANC issued the government with an ultimatum that demanded an end to a number of unjust laws and threatened them with passive resistance if their demands were not met. A defiance campaign, similar to the civil rights movement in America, was soon initiated. In March 1960, 69 protesters were shot dead by police in Sharpeville; others were killed in Cape Town's Langa and Nyanga townships. This outrage became a watershed in the history of South Africa. The African political movement – increasingly radicalised by the experiences of apartheid – organised shutdowns, strikes and boycotts. The ANC adopted a position of non-cooperation with the regime, went underground and planned an armed wing. Sharpeville had transformed a civil-rights campaign into a civil war of sorts, which replaced any possibility of a political solution to the racial problem with the certainty of confrontation.[53]

South Africa found itself on the front pages of the world's media. Panic gripped the economy, with millions of Rand fleeing the country. In just two weeks South Africa's reserves of gold and foreign exchange had fallen by about £9.5m;[54] they plummeted by a total of over R100 million, falling below the R200 million safety limit.[55] The regime, then, had managed to alienate both its black population and international opinion. This posed a threat to export markets, to supplies of foreign capital and political stability. Multinational companies with interests inside the country and mining houses with concerns outside became alarmed. Liberals were joined for the first time by Afrikaner businessmen and *Die Burger* in the demand for a relaxation of policy. Senior Cape ministers such as Dönges and Sauer called for concessions to the coloureds and evidence of the positive aspects of separate development.[56]

Nonetheless, Dr Verwoerd, the Dutch-born prime minister (1958–66), stood his ground. He stated that not the slightest deviation, not a single concession, could be permitted without destroying the fabric of apartheid, which for him had become synonymous with preservation of the white race generally and of the Afrikaner in particular.[57] The authorities reacted with a series of repressive measures intended to restore stability and order so as to indicate to its international backers that it had the situation under control. It invoked the General Laws Amendment Act – commonly known as the Sabotage Act – which increased the powers of government over the activities of citizens and stiffened penalties for offences considered to be political. The ANC and Pan African Congress (PAC) were both banned and the African trade unions intimidated out of existence. Police circled townships that practised stay-at-homes and community leaders were beaten and arrested. State spending on the military increased by 63.6 per cent between the budget years 1960/61 and 1961/62, and by a further 80 per cent in the following year.[58] Within this remit the homes of officials of the South African Sports Association (SASA) were raided and documentation seized. This tactic appeared to be successful as foreign exchange reserves were slowly restored, white immigration increased and manufacturing output expanded from R1 billion in 1960 to R1.76 billion in 1965 – a rise of 76 per cent.[59] However, it signalled the demise of any possibility of a political settlement to the 'race question' and put South Africa on a path towards further confrontation.

In an attempt to forestall future conflict, though, the regime sought to complement its aggressive tendencies with an approach that suggested a softening of attitude toward the rigidities of racial life. One such area for consideration was sport. South Africa had been excluded from the 1964 Tokyo Olympic Games as its apartheid policies did not conform to the Olympic Charter. In an attempt to regain admission to the 1968 Games, the government offered black athletes – in exchange for cooperation with apartheid sports – the carrot of international competition. B.J. Vorster, determined that the Republic be an important player in world affairs, announced a 'liberalisation' of sports policy to parliament on 11 April 1967. He declared that athletes selected for the Olympic Games would take part as one team under the South African flag:

> The Olympic Games is a unique event in which all countries of the world take part, and our attitude in respect of that event was that if there were any of our Coloured or Bantu who were good enough to compete there, or whose standard of proficiency was such that they could take part in it, we would make it possible for them to take part.[60]

The various racial sporting bodies would choose their own representatives, but all would go as one team representing South Africa abroad. However, there would be no racially mixed trials for the Olympics. Furthermore, Vorster would not object to South Africa hosting the Canada Cup and Davis Cup and playing against coloured countries if necessary: '… because here one has to do with an inter-state relationship … We must draw a very clear distinction between personal relations on the one hand and inter-state relations on the other.'[61]

The political elite had always to be conscious of international opinion as well as that of its own MPs and supporters. This theme, more than any other, dictated the political strategy towards sport by South African rulers. Vorster was not claiming to have abandoned his principles by accepting, in theory, that blacks could represent South Africa in international sports. Indeed, he was reworking the role of sport into the multinational framework of apartheid philosophy. A new policy for foreign visitors, for example, was always compatible with the theory of separate development. During the speech that ushered in moves towards improvement, the prime minister set out sport's place within the framework of apartheid. Foremost, it is an area that 'should not be dragged into politics' as it was part of the wider policy of separate development, 'which has never been based on hate or prejudice of fear.' Vorster reiterated that 'no mixed sport between whites and non-whites will be practised locally.' Overseas countries would have to appreciate and respect South Africa's approach, just as it would adhere to their policies. Vorster would not be held to blackmail by those who did not like South Africa's segregation laws. He chillingly concluded that 'in respect of this principle we are not prepared to compromise, we are not prepared to negotiate and we are not prepared to make any concessions'.[62] He later reminded his audience that 'If there are people who in any way believe or think that it can be inferred from my speech that all barriers will now be removed, then they are making a very big mistake.'[63] In a rebuff to cricket followers, while ties with 'traditional' friends should be strengthened, Vorster saw no reason why relations with the West Indies, India or Pakistan should be entered into.[64] When a tobacco company offered to sponsor a series of international matches between the West Indies and South Africa (to be staged in Britain), Frank Waring, the South African minister of sport, intervened: 'If whites and non-whites start competing against each other, there will be such viciousness as has never been seen before.'[65] The prime minister, in turn, accused the company of interfering in the activities of the National Party.

Despite Vorster's commitment to racial segregation in domestic sports, his statement was received positively by the international sporting community – especially as it seemed to imply that the selection of both Maoris and the Cape coloured Basil D'Oliveira would be left to the 'good judgement of the sporting bodies concerned'.[66] Indeed, Lord Exeter, a vice-president of the IOC, said: 'The suggestion of mixed sports teams of any kind visiting South Africa is a big step forward. I am sure it will help their case at Tehran next month when the committee consider whether South Africa can be brought back into the Olympics.'[67] Alan Paton, the leader of the Liberal Party, though, reminded any appeasers that 'in many centres here Africans are not allowed into the stadiums in which Test matches are played – not even as spectators …', and added that, 'Mr. Vorster has made it clear that South African non-whites will never be allowed to play against whites on the sports fields of this country.'[68] This was no multiracial policy.

The setting of sport within the economic and political environment

What is the basis of a political action? This is a question that has intrigued political philosophers throughout history. Can we be satisfied that political actors react out of virtue or in self-interest, or are they motivated by a whole range of social and economic phenomena at work in wider society?

In South Africa, the sports policies were not invoked simply because the white population held that sports were very important: they became absorbed in a strategy to placate economic concerns and prolong the longevity of apartheid. South African capitalism, as well as framing the ideological forces that entrenched society, was – to an extent – affected by these same influences. The problems inherent within every capitalist economic system came to be compounded by those deriving particularly from the politics of apartheid. Rates of economic growth, particularly during the 1960s, suggested that the racial programme advocated by the National Party was working. A survey completed by the Council for Scientific and Industrial Research, for example, showed that in 1965 the Republic enjoyed the lowest overall cost of living in the world and the highest actual annual increase in GNP.[69] Impressive accounts, however, cannot sustain a long-term trend. The 1960s signalled the 'take-off' phase of South Africa's industrialisation, involving a shift in emphasis from the primary sectors of mining and agriculture – built on large quantities of cheap unskilled labour – to a manufacturing base dependent on skilled labour. At the turn of the decade the South African economy experienced a slowing down: the real rate of growth, for example, declined from 7.1 per cent in 1969 to 3.3 per cent in 1971.[70]

South Africa's impending economic problems were structural in that they were a consequence of the policies that stemmed from racial segregation. Verwoerd had set out his economic policy as not anti-capitalist but manipulating capitalism to make it compatible with apartheid. A labour force built on the doctrine of low unit costs proved fundamental to the establishment and the high profitability rates of labour-intensive industries such as mining. The accelerating effects of this industry were such that it dominated the whole economy, but in the long-term, of course, this would prove to be a distortion – especially with the price volatility of gold and diamonds. Until the 1960s, the primary sectors had accounted for a larger share of GDP than manufacturing and had provided a significant base for government revenue to finance economic growth. Mining, though, was now gradually surpassed by manufacturing as the dominant industry in the economy. Manufacturing was dependent on a domestic market and skilled workforce: it inherited neither from mining. The small size of the South African market made it essential that manufacturing break into the export sector. However, the high costs of manufactured products made South Africa internationally uncompetitive. The increasing international hostility to apartheid threatened not only export markets but supplies of foreign capital and technology as well. Faced with restrictions on potential output, voices within manufacturing advocated an improvement in the status of black labour as a means of expanding the production-possibility frontier: 'Not only would there be enormous gains from the development of skills and increases in motivations [as a result of such measures] but the resulting growth in Black incomes would so expand our domestic markets as to magnify the scope for applying greater economies of scale in our manufacturing industry.'[71]

Moreover, South Africa's consumer goods production was highly labour intensive (wages in mines, for example, consumed 50 per cent of working costs). Improvements in wages were only possible if they were matched by an expansion in productivity. In turn, productivity could only be increased by improvements in the status of labour, not simply in monetary terms but in terms of longevity and education as well. Blacks were not trained for the skilled tasks that made use of the technology, and not only in manufacturing. The du Plessis/Marais Commission (1971) found that only 10,000 of 180,000 tractor operators had received formal training, and, as Merle Lipton puts it in *Capitalism and Apartheid*, 'At a certain stage in the development of capitalism, cheap untrained workers become a burden to employers, not a boon.'[72] The only way to break this increasingly downward spiral was to rely on Western capital and technology, but the imposition of economic sanctions threatened this traditional source of funding. Finding it increasingly difficult to generate infusions of international capital, the government was forced to show to the world that not merely was it misunderstood but that it also had the ability to adapt.

At the Transvaal National Party Conference in September 1969 sport was identified as one of four areas which offered the potential for reform. Recognising the threat to the fabric of apartheid, which any relaxation of laws regarding segregation supposed, the government called on the Broederbond[73] to draw up guidelines for a new policy. The Nationalist consensus was now under severe strain. At the conference Dr Albert Hertzog, who had been dropped from the cabinet in the previous year, clashed with Vorster, describing his sport policy as the 'thin edge of the wedge' and an approach that would open the way to social mixing between the races in South Africa:[74] 'They [Maoris] will sit at the table with our young men and girls, and dance with our girls.'[75] Hertzog, though, was cast out of the National Party and formed the Herstigte Nasionale Party (HNP – Restored National Party). In the ensuing panic, Vorster brought the general election forward by a year in order to prevent his right-wing opponents gaining momentum from an issue – sport – which threatened to divide South African political life. Vorster aligned the National Party with a *verligte* (enlightened) outlook consisting of maintaining apartheid at home with an outward-looking attitude to the world – including black Africa – which encouraged white immigration, conciliation over 'petty-apartheid' and a welcome to black diplomats and selected sportsmen.

Theoretical apartheid and the 'multinational' sports policy

The South African government unveiled the 'multinational' sports policy to parliament on 22 April 1971. The prime minister, Mr Vorster, informed his audience that the internal sports policy of the country would remain unchanged and that it had to be viewed against the policy of separate development. However, this separation was no longer based on notions of biological or genetic differences but on cultural distinction, and the right of each racial group to preserve their identity. The multinational policy, in effect, was simply formalising the more relaxed stance adopted towards the end of the 1960s. South Africa clearly needed something to change in its situation in the international sports arena as it was running out of opponents to engage in competition. It had been expelled from the IOC and had had cricket tours against England and Australia cancelled. The new programme, if nothing else, was a reminder to the international community of South Africa's capacity to adapt. It reaffirmed three key principles:

• Sport had to acknowledge its position in South African society. It could not be considered above the country's national and international interests. South Africa was a multinational country, with each of the various nations on the path to autonomous development. Organised sport had to reflect this.

- Mixed sport between whites and blacks remained prohibited at club, provincial and national level. However, black sportsmen would be permitted to affiliate to white sports bodies and by doing so would be allowed to partake in competition against white sides. The international implications were greater: in events such as the Davis Cup, the Olympics and golf, where the individual rather than the team performed, competition would be open.[76] Mixed South African teams would not wear the Springbok emblem. Blacks still could not represent South Africa at cricket or rugby, though, because contests were not decided on a world championship level. However, mixed 'invitation' sides selected for friendlies rather than as official Springboks would be approved, if only to appease international opinion.
- Mixed teams from countries with traditional links with South Africa would be allowed to tour South Africa and perform *separately* against white and black sides. New relations with other countries would not be considered. The government promised not to interfere in the composition of the touring side, provided that there were no ulterior political motives.

Specifically on the subject of cricket, Vorster confirmed what had previously been claimed – that blacks had never been allowed to belong to the white South African Cricket Association (SACA). Under the new policy they would be able to arrange tours and similarly receive visitors as long as they functioned as a black unit or 'nation'. Apartheid would continue to be rigidly enforced as before in sport at club, provincial and national levels, and mixed trials would not be allowed. Multiracial cricket, therefore, remained prohibited at all levels. Technically, though, mixed sport could take place provided it did so using private facilities, players did not share amenities, no spectators attended and that there was no socialising after the game. A racially mixed team in any sport except for the Olympic Games would not represent South Africa abroad. Waring, the minister of sport, warned supporters of mixed contests that 'should cricket bodies in South Africa wish to contradict and confront government policy, they must bear the full responsibility ...'[77]

The multinational policy was intended to strengthen, not to dilute, apartheid, and as such became part of the dominant ideology. The Broederbond executive, who had drawn up the Bill's initial drafts, defined the aim of official sports policy as 'the maintenance of the white population in South Africa through and within the policy of separate development'.[78] Dr Koornhof, Waring's successor as the minister of sport, informed the white electorate in 1973 that: 'Announcements in respect of certain points of departure relating to sport should ... be seen as adjustments, development and progress without sacrifice of principles.'[79] Therefore, Koornhof added, it was wrong to speak of 'a new sports policy' or 'concessions' and more appropriate to speak of 'a developing policy' which was being applied to new situations. Sport could not be placed before South Africa's other interests.[80] 'All these petty apartheid measures', Dr Connie Mulder – the South African minister of the interior, told British journalists

> are not there simply to belittle people. They are based on the pure principle of diversity and the fact that we put a high premium on the maintenance of our identity as a separate nation. Even if the whole world would try to force South Africa to do something that would endanger the identity of the nation, we would resist. We can't give way. We can't, even if it is unpopular. Whatever the world may say, this is one of the fundamentals on which we can't give an inch.[81]

In reality, reforms were permitted because 'international sporting ties, especially in rugby and cricket, have serious implications at this critical stage for our country, regarding international trade, national trade, military relationships and armaments, and strategic industrial development'.[82] The selection of a single black team was an interim measure designed to influence international attitudes and was to be replaced once the Bantustans became independent. Concessions were permitted in order to uphold the system of law and order in South Africa – and to assert the dominant political will:

> By means of sport, a new dimension is being given to our policy of multi-nationalism and to the South African set up, which, since 1652, has been in embryo what it has become today. We should not lose sight of the fact that we are dealing with an historic situation. Sport is being used to create a spirit and attitude which have a positive value, a spirit and attitude which are giving new dimensions to our multi-national set up.[83]

Segregation in the sports grounds, then, would continue to be pursued and free social mixing would remain prohibited. The *Sunday Times* (England) described this multinational policy as 'a contribution to institutionalising apartheid.'[84] Cricket would not be subject to merit selection because to do so would involve integration at all levels, a position the authorities were not prepared to consider. 'If I should advocate multi-racialism', Vorster told a seminar at Potchefstroom University, 'I should know that what could happen in America on the hottest summer day would be child's play in South Africa on the coldest winters day.' Everything South Africa had built and hoped for would be destroyed, Vorster asserted, if multi-racialism were to prevail.[85] At the same time, Koornhof argued abroad that the multinational policy 'normalised' sport in South Africa. By 1977, he could boast that 99.9956 per cent of sport was still played according to the segregated sports policy and that there were only 56 cases of people joining clubs of other racial groups. Still, he warned, the government might be forced to take action if the policy was contravened too often.[86]

The autonomous strategy

Apartheid in crisis

South Africa's economy continued to spiral downwards. Between 1946 and 1970 the average annual growth rate for South African manufacturing was 7 per cent; from 1969 it declined to 2.6 per cent; by 1977 it was negative. Total investment declined 13 per cent between 1975 and 1977 as the state was forced to cut spending. The budget deficit rose from the equivalent of $220 million (£122.5 million) in 1973 to $865 million in 1974 and $2,323 million in 1975.[87] (The reality behind these figures was an increase in black unemployment to 2.3 million African workers) and double-figure inflation.[88]) To make matters worse, there was a decline in the gold price by up to 40 per cent in 1976 over the previous 12 months; for every $5 fall in the price of gold, the reduction in revenue was R90 million a year.[89] Following the Soweto uprising in 1976, foreign capital dried up.[90] As a result, South Africa had to seek out bank loans at high rates of interest. Mining companies such as Barlow Rand, Gencor and AAC had worldwide interests and required access to Western technology and capital; they naturally became concerned at the growing international hostility towards South Africa. As manufacturing became more capital-intensive, it required larger markets in order to sustain and expand rates of profit. Businessmen argued that 'the basic reasons for the concern felt by foreign investors about South Africa are not financial or economic but political and they can only be removed by action in the political field'.[91]

To the structural causes of economic decline, discussed earlier, can be added the growth in the militancy of the liberation movement. The 1970s witnessed an unprecedented increase in black membership of trade unions and in the level of unofficial and illegal strikes. From two unions with 16,000 members in 1969, membership increased to 25 unions with 70,000 members in 1977, and, after the Wiehahn inquiry into labour, there were 35 unions (1984) with over 1,400,000 members.[92] In the period 1973–75 the mining industry faced a wave of strikes which 'rocked the economy'[93] and was forced to concede increased wages; there was further disruption in the period 1979–81. Soweto became another landmark from which analysts could divide events into before and after. Unlike Sharpeville, it was viewed as a rebellion rather than a massacre, and the liberation movement now directly challenged the legitimacy of the apartheid state. The ANC's Francis Meli noted that the confrontation between the masses and the apartheid regime 'would, to all intents and purposes, be continuous and uninterrupted'.[94]

Moreover, there were many, especially in business, who feared revolution. Whereas they supported reform previously for economic concerns, they now added political reasons. It was significant that the few companies that owned over 75 per cent of shares listed on the Johannesburg stock exchange were among the leading proponents of reform.[95] They argued that the government should offer greater concessions – better even to concede political power than for them to lose their economic stranglehold, though the concession of political rights to blacks was still very much a minority viewpoint.

Afrikaner unity was becoming fragile. As increasing numbers moved into industry they began to embrace similar economic ideas to English manufacturers. Many Afrikaner sons and daughters received a university education, including a growing number who studied abroad. They could no longer be relied upon to perpetuate the mythology of racism. Politically, the National Party faced the potential threat of the HNP. Even a previous bulwark of apartheid such as the church raised doubts and sought alternative answers to the race question. The regime was becoming one of self-defence alone: 'The fortress of the *volk* is to be defended, but there is no faith within its walls.'[96]

The collapse of the Portuguese empire and the resulting independence of Mozambique and Angola in 1976 signalled another defining moment in South African history. Not only did it inspire the resistance movement, providing it with foreign bases and with the confidence that revolutionary change was possible, it transformed Pretoria's strategic thinking as it was looking to Africa to develop its expanding market.

The increased military threat and domestic unrest meant an even larger role for the forces of order. The Riotous Assemblies Act gave the police power to ban or close any meeting by anybody, anywhere, at any time. Towards the end of 1977 the government closed down newspapers and banned hostile political organisations. Steve Biko became the 40th black person to die in police custody under detention-without-charge laws. The defence budget grew from $60 million in 1960 to $3 billion in 1982. The army tripled in size during the same period, from 11,500 permanent members, 56,000 part-timers and 10,000 national servicemen, to 28,300, 157,000 and 53,000 respectively.[97] By 1975 defence expenditures were 17 per cent of the total budget.[98] Additionally, the state's share of gross fixed investment rose from 35 per cent in 1950 to 53 per cent in 1979.[99] Spending on defence, coupled with the fall in the price of gold, led to serious balance of payments difficulties. This concentration of resources meant that it became increasingly more difficult to fund new investments from internal sources. Business was now forced to compete with the state for what scarce capital was available. Private sector borrowings in the second quarter of 1976, for example, fell to R158 million from R614 million in the last quarter of 1975, while government borrowing rose from R36 million to R340 million in the same period.[100]

'Total war' and 'total strategy'

South Africa was in the classical situation described by Gramsci as the 'organic crisis', whereby:

A crisis occurs, sometimes lasting for decades. This exceptional duration means that incurable structural contradictions have revealed themselves (reached maturity) and that despite this, the political forces that are struggling to conserve and defend the existing structure itself are making every effort to cure them, within certain limits, and to overcome them.[101]

Overcoming the structural problems involved the economic, political and ideological task known as 'total strategy'. Its fundamental aim, according to the South African Defence Force (SADF) organ, *Paratus*, was 'a guarantee for the system of free enterprise.'[102] The 'total strategy' was originally developed by the military in response to the 'total war' or 'total onslaught' allegedly facing South Africa, which was portrayed as an offensive from Moscow designed to groom South Africa for the world communist cause. The sanctions campaign, the armed struggle by the ANC and internal disorder were all seen as examples of the offensive.

The 'total strategy', though, came to take on a significance far greater than simply military. It held that 'the resolution of conflict ... demands interdependent and co-ordinated action in all fields – military, psychological, economic, political, sociological, technological, diplomatic, ideological, cultural, etc ...'[103] Magnus Malan, the minister of defence in 1977, said that 'The [total] war is not only an area for the soldier. Everyone is involved and has a role to play.'[104] Politically, the 'total strategy' envisaged an increasing centralisation of power and a prominent role for the armed forces. Increasingly, security replaced ideology as the dominant political theme.

Financially, the government's primary concern was attracting back frightened foreign capital. This involved the dual process of taking on proponents of sanctions and introducing further reform. On his accession to power, P.W. Botha announced that apartheid must 'adapt otherwise we shall die'.[105] Leading capitalists were in favour of granting additional concessions to the African workforce in order to stave off further difficulties. *Volkshandel*, the organ of the Afrikaner Chamber of Commerce and Industry, called for rights for urban blacks to buy their own houses and to receive better education and job opportunities.[106] The *Financial Mail* declared that

> If South Africa is to enter an era of (relative) stability and prosperity, government must ensure that as many people as possible share in that prosperity and find their interests best-served by an alliance with capitalism ... Defusing the social time-bomb ... can only be achieved through negotiation – not with men with kalashnikovs but with the authentic leaders of the black people.[107]

Self-interest fed this recent concern for black conditions. Estate agents and builders pressured the government to support black home-ownership.

Producers of electrical goods hoped that the electrification of Soweto would lift them out of the mid-1970s recession. The big chain-stores, such as Pick-and-Pay and Checkers, condemned apartheid legislation that excluded them from the African townships, South Africa's fastest growing market. Manufacturing could only thrive through a prosperous domestic market where more people had the resources to purchase its goods.

Domestically, the total strategy sought to divide the African masses in order to strengthen the status quo. The *Financial Mail* described it as involving moves which 'strike out, albeit extremely cautiously, in the direction of moderate adjustment and building up a black labour elite and middle class which will have a stake in stability and provide a counter to the process of radicalism'.[108] The authorities convinced themselves that the radicalisation of the black working class was not the result of genuine economic concerns but the actions of troublemakers. A number of commissions were established which reported that the state should relax certain key policies in order to subdue the revolutionary potential, aid industry and provide the regime with greater – if less obvious – forms of control:

- the Wiehahn Report (1979) recommended trade union rights for African workers;
- the Riekert Commission (1979) dismantled white job reservation;
- the de Lange Report (1986) called for universal compulsory primary education and black technical training at secondary and tertiary level (a single education authority for all was rejected by the government except for private institutions);
- the Lombard Report (1980) argued that stable government could only be provided by 'the emergence of new, legitimate political institutions that allow the effective participation of the governed.'[109]

A package of reforms included limited self-government in the Bantustans (Transkei (1976), Bophuthustwana (1977), Venda (1979) and Ciskei (1981) actually became 'independent') and, through the 1977 Community Councils Act, administrative powers in black urban areas. These measures were designed to create a black elite that would owe its position to the prevailing economic order.[110] Botha's economic advisor, Simon Brand, explained that it would be 'naïve' to expect that African political demands could be defused by economic concessions alone but that 'by satisfying the economic aspirations of Africans, we could play a major role in changing the climate in which political demands are made'. If this change could be made to take place, African demands may then be made 'in a more constructive and peaceful way.'[111]

Therefore, the 'total strategy' sought a restructuring of society away from a hierarchical racial order to one based on class in order to lay 'the foundation for resisting communism.'[112] It was envisaged that the African masses would then focus aspirations and discontent locally against their own 'rulers' rather than against capitalism and racism in general. The *Financial Mail* observed that

> by and large this strategy has been successful as far as Bantustans are concerned. Most homeland 'governments' have gone along with administering key aspects of the labour system ... One effect of setting up governments and parliaments and civil services all over the show is to put the educated elite on to official payrolls, which is a good deal healthier than having them fomenting unrest.[113]

In the urban areas an attempt was made to create a black aristocracy of labour, an 'insider class' of workers who would benefit from this latest package of reforms. This consisted of skilled and professional employees, who were offered greater job security, increased wages, trade union rights and – provided that they were not hostile to the regime – access to permanent accommodation for themselves and their families. Thus, in 1983 about 500,000 state-owned houses were put up for sale, mainly to Africans, at cheap prices. It was, moreover, increasingly advantageous to urban businessmen to invest in their workers and give them a stake in society. For workers to be able to reside with their families and to be provided with the social niceties that whites took for granted would hopefully reduce employee turnover, make for a less explosive social situation and – through higher consumption – provide a larger domestic market for goods. It also represented the abandonment of a key principle of separate development – that the black urban population was temporary.

Other changes were made. Blacks became entitled to join public libraries, serve behind the counters of shops and take on other employment previously reserved for whites. Petty-apartheid, such as segregation in restaurants and on trains and buses and park benches, was abolished in many districts. Blacks could attend some performances in previously segregated theatres. The gates of the private schools opened to the small number of black families who could afford to send their children there. The Immorality Act and the Mixed Marriages Prohibition Act were both abolished, and the scheme of job reservation removed. An article in the *Durban Times* suggested that sport would now be open to all races and would also be allowed to determine its own future.[114]

The third South African sports policy

Following the Soweto uprising in 1976 and the 1977 Gleneagles Agreement which committed Commonwealth governments to a policy of discouraging sporting links with South Africa, Pretoria made further gestures towards relaxing apartheid in sports. A circular issued on 27 October 1979 stated that in future 'all sports activities will be disassociated from the Group Areas Act, that is to say no permit, as required by the Act, is in any manner

applicable to sport'.[115] Dr Koornhof, minister, claimed that sport reflected a
new way of thinking in that people should have the right to play with
whomsoever they choose. They had not done so in the past because of
social and cultural differences – not because they were prohibited from so
doing. The regime even claimed that 'as late as a decade ago there was little
interest in multiracial play ...'[116] In a Department of Information publication, Koornhof stated that there was now no law that prohibited mixed
teams in any sport. It was the 'inherent' right of any sports club in the
country to control and decide its membership, to become, in other words,
autonomous. Multiracial teams would also be allowed to socialise after
matches and share facilities.[117] A statement from the Federal Information
Council of the National Party suggested that multinational participation at
the international level would also be possible:

> That if so invited or agreed upon, teams consisting of players from all
> population groups may represent South Africa if such a sport is an
> Olympic sport or not, and such players or participants may be awarded
> colours and an emblem, if so desired, which can be the South African
> flag or the colours thereof.[118]

Thus, the national squad became – in theory – open to all races, and the
minister for sport could claim that South Africa was now 'at a complete
par as far as merit selection is concerned with any other country in the
world.'[119]

   This granting of autonomy to sporting organisations was a constituent
part of the strategy of defusing aspects of contentious matter. The state
was now of the opinion that, far from causing racial conflict, sport could
play a valuable healing role. The Broederbond said that it had considered
'the recent drastic changes in the internal security situation' which made
'the promotion of internal peace and good relations between whites and
non-whites essential'.[120] It was also part of a process that, once initiated,
was proving difficult to slow down. The South African government, and
those who wished to re-engage in competition with the Springboks, had
long argued that politics should not be a factor when considering sporting relations. Furthermore, the Human Sciences Research Council's
report on sport in 1980 argued that sport should be taken out of the
mainstream of everyday life. It argued that discriminatory laws applied
to sport were an 'unwarranted extension of the state's authority in a non-
state terrain.'[121] Koornhof wanted to 'see dirty, bloody politics out of
sport and let the sportsmen get on with it.'[122] Acting on such criticisms,
the government therefore disbanded the Department of Sport and
Recreation in 1980 and handed the administration of sport over to the
Department of Education.

   The regime now claimed that its only involvement in sport was to
maintain law and order: 'autonomy' was the fruition of this stance. In reality,

it was embroiled in the wider strategy that envisaged racial assemblies for what came to be known as areas of 'own affairs' and 'general affairs'. The government would determine which areas of policy should be subject to regulation by local authorities and which would be subject to central control. It was a means of redefining what politics is in order to pursue a particular approach. Local authorities, as owners of most sport facilities, had the power of sanction over mixed events. Many simply refused to allow them. In January 1981, for example, the Oudtshoorn Town Council rejected an application from its cricket club to allow a coloured person to play cricket on a municipal pitch. More importantly, the new initiative only applied to organised sport. Recreation and leisure facilities, as well as training, remained segregated. The overwhelming majority of athletes, then, continued to train and play in segregated schools and clubs.[123]

Each reform of the sporting process was not only an admission of the involvement of politics but also an attempt to prolong Nationalist rule. Despite this, change once again proved too much for *verkrampte* (cramped) influences within the National Party. In 1978 leading conservative Andries Treurnicht argued that 'if petty apartheid is completely eliminated, grand apartheid becomes stupid, superfluous and unnecessary'.[124] In 1982 Treurnicht led 16 MPs out of the movement and formed the Conservative Party. This caused a serious threat to the Nationalist cause for within months of their existence opinion polls showed that support for the National Party had fallen below 50 per cent.

Conclusion

The sporting polity under apartheid can be divided into three key stages: the first formal statement on sport, the 'multinational' policy and the 'autonomous' policy. Each one of these programmes was part of a wider strategy devised to shape the development of apartheid. No matter what the aims or the potential benefits that reform in sport offered, they were ultimately enacted because it was felt that they would help prolong racial rule.

The National Party genuinely believed that apartheid was a philosophical quest that may have included political and economic measures but ultimately was greater or higher than both of these: it sought its justification from God. Racial separation was not only considered as natural but was advocated on the basis that it benefited all sections of society. So, when the regime came to view issues such as sport it did so within the confines of what it believed to be a natural order. Therefore, how could sport be political?

It is not enough simply to observe the policies of a government. To understand political behaviour it is necessary to relate how legislation affects its target, and from where such measures derive. When the effect of a sports policy allows the state a say in the selection of sides, the relationship with international sporting bodies and even a sanction on whom teams may play against, sport enters the arena of politics. It does not matter that those academics who maintain an institutional approach to politics may wince at this, for what is important is how political actors perceive such measures. This brief study of the relationship between economic difficulties and political measures shows both how policy was determined by economics and, in turn, how economic problems were exacerbated by ideology: the two cannot be divorced. It is the same with sport. Once the government directly intervened, or once sport became overtly affected by ideology – even if disguised as some form of 'higher authority' or 'natural order', then sport became explicitly political in character.

5

Banishing Tradition, or Prejudice?
Politics and the Winding Road
to Multiracial Cricket

It is traditionally held that cricket was championed by South Africans of English descent. Rugby, for its own distinct social and political reasons,[1] was adopted by the Afrikaners, whilst the Africans took to the world's simplest and cheapest sport – football.[2] Whilst this pattern could be termed as accurate for the purpose of rough generalisation, it is not established in stone, nor for that matter can such claims be made without recourse to *why* such trends exist. This chapter is concerned solely with the development of cricket in South Africa, a sport played by all the races. It examines the *why* of segregated sport, and then places it into the context of the political struggle – initially by black organisations for recognition of their existence and then of the attempts by the white authorities to forge a single body and promote 'normal cricket' within the context of the dominant hegemony in order, simply, that the game would survive. As such, it builds on the previous chapter that showed how politics became formally integrated into the fabric of South African sport. Emphasis, then, is to show the effects that the various sporting programmes had on cricket.

The path towards integrated cricket was shaped by political events, as sport increasingly proved a means by which the government chose to display to the international community that it was prepared to adapt and reform. In essence, progress was defined and measured using three key phrases:

- 'Racial sport', by which each of the races belonged to distinct organisations.
- 'Multiracial sport', which involved the selection of a team from all the racial groups. In reality, as was shown with cricket, it meant signing up to the white sporting body – which then claimed to be representative of all races.
- 'Non-racial sport', defined as that practised by those who would have no truck with the apartheid regime.

Whilst most cricketers – both black and white – wanted an end to segregated cricket, the issue that divided them soon came to be politics: on what terms would this unity exist? Mixed cricket in a deeply segregated society would have been a farce; allowing oneself to be used as a means to prolong apartheid was viewed as even worse. It was within this atmosphere that the struggle, which culminated with the formation of the United Cricket Board of South Africa, was fought. Once again, it shows that the relationship between politics and sport was fundamental – and that sport could be exploited by all sides for political gain.

The origins of South African cricket

South Africa became a feature of European interest in 1652 when 100 men landed at Cape Town in order to establish a strategic posting for the Dutch East India Company. The English War of 1665 and the French War of 1672 then highlighted the geographical importance of the Cape Province. In order to consolidate their position, the Company encouraged immigration – and it is by this decision that those who would become known as Afrikaners can trace their origins.

The British became involved in the Cape in 1794 when the Dutch East India Company went bankrupt. They inherited a colony which was 'economically more undeveloped, politically more inexperienced, and culturally more backward than any of the greater colonies of settlement'.[3] From this point South Africa accommodated two distinct groups of white settlers, who had to make their home among the numerous native tribal inhabitants – each of which had its own set of customs, grievances and social and political agendas. The British introduced cricket during periods of intense conflict over land and political control. A brief examination of the key players involved in the introduction of the sport shows how cricket became a key ideological component in formatting white hegemony.

The military

As in other countries that played cricket, the game was introduced into South Africa by the armed forces. Research has not been precise on this question but it would appear that cricket was first played in Southern Africa during the occupation of the Cape by British troops between 1795 and 1802. The first written reference appeared in *The Cape Town Gazette & African Advertiser*: 'A grand match at cricket will be played for 1,000 dollars a side on Tuesday, January 5, 1808 between the officers of the artillery mess, having Colonel Austen of the 60th Regiment, and the officers of the Colony, with General Clavering. The wickets are to be pitched at 10 o'clock.'[4] Cricket was introduced into Natal by the 45th Foot, stationed at Fort Napier, Maritzburg, in 1848, just three years after the formation of the Surrey County Cricket Club. The 86th regiment and HMS *Rattlesnake* both entered teams into the Western Province domestic competition.[5]

The Champion Bat tournament, the precursor of the Currie Cup, was inaugurated in Border in 1876. It was South Africa's first national domestic competition; Capetown, Port Elizabeth, Grahamstown and King were the initial competitors. These teams each had a number of soldiers in their sides, enough that at the end of the tournament a separate game was held between the civilians and the troops. The link between the armed forces and cricket continued in the form of individual military figures representing their country. Major R. Stewart represented South Africa in their first ever Test side. 'Dave' Nourse, one of the greatest players to represent South Africa, came to the country as a bugler with the West Riding Regiment; he would appear in 45 consecutive Test matches and still be playing first-class cricket at the age of 58.[6] So, the earliest known games were between teams of men who were stationed to establish economic and political control in foreign climes. If we want to know the origins of the association between politics and sport we need look no further.

Education

Colonial education policy was double-edged: English schools prepared the officials and rulers of the next generation, whilst the education of the indigenous population comprised of being taught the values and norms of this ruling class. Both, nonetheless, encouraged cricket. Indeed, they were to become the nurseries that supplied the region with its cricketers.

There were differences, moreover, in the education offered to the indigenous population. The black 'elite' were enticed with concessions by the ruling authorities in exchange for support and cooperation. Sons of chiefs and political leaders attended the better-resourced black schools and colleges, and were encouraged to discover the qualities of 'Englishness'. Furthermore, African clergymen and teachers were trained at Lovedale, Healdtown and St Matthew's colleges. These establishments provided an education based on the 'best' traditions of the English public schools, including, of course, cricket. On the Queen's birthday in 1877, for example, all the pupils celebrated the occasion by engaging in sports.[7] Zonnebloem College was founded by the Cape governor, Sir George Grey, with the aim of 'civilising' the sons of chiefs. The records of the college describe the enthusiasm for cricket, and in 1910 the mayor of Cape Town 'remembered a time when the College had the best cricket team in the whole Peninsula'.[8]

Gold and diamonds

Studies of the early history of cricket reveal that its imperial roots dictate its pattern of development. Cricket was introduced by the military and promoted through the education system in every one of the leading participant countries. In each, however, distinct environmental factors have influenced the progression of the sport: in India, the role of the Princes, in the West Indies, sugar, and in Australia, the forces of nationalism.

The 'independent' variable in South Africa was the mining industry.

Diamonds were discovered in South Africa in 1867 and gold in the 1880s. The mining industry transformed a largely agrarian society into an urban, industrial one. The adoption of the gold standard as the basis of the major currencies ensured and cemented stability in the industry.[9] The nature of extraction required significant inputs of both labour and capital, and – in order to receive a worthwhile rate of return and ensure the longevity of the industry – production had to be inexpensive. This required the 'conscription' of a black workforce and the full involvement of the state.

The mining industry's role in the history of cricket was significant in three key areas: firstly, it encouraged sports in order to negate potential hostility to the working and living environment. Employers organised the compound system in order to control their workforce. These camps were little more than prisons with up to 2,000 miners packed into a single building. This type of environment could prove somewhat volatile, so in order to provide entertainment and channel energies sports were introduced and strongly encouraged. Reflecting on this unstable environment, the Revd Ray Phillips – an American Board missionary – stated that 'We must capture the physical and mental life of these young men during the six days of the week besides preaching the gospel to them on the seventh.'[10]

Secondly, the proliferation of mines provided the means to stimulate growth in the game at a higher level. Following the discovery of diamonds, Kimberley became one of the most important sporting centres in the country. They were the recipients of the first Currie Cup, presented to them by Major Warton as the side who proved the best against his tourists. Finally, it encouraged racial sport. The mining industry displayed its support for racial cricket when, in 1897, the De Beers Consolidated Mines company presented the Barnato Memorial Trophy to the Griqualand West Coloured Cricket Board. This body represented the only black union that served the requirements of Africans, coloureds and Malays. African cricket was first organised on the Witwatersrand by the Native Recruitment Corporation Cricket League, which was sponsored by the Chamber of Mines. Black cricketers continued to play for the Native Recruitment Corporation Cup until 1976.

'Englishness'

The roots of South African cricket, then – the military, education system and mining industry – all shared one thing in common: 'Englishness'. As pointed out in Chapter 3, cricket was viewed as a means of securing the legitimacy and ethos of the British Empire. This represented something more than simply games: it was a way of life, one considered so important to the advancement of 'civilisation' that all should be encouraged to further the cause. Therefore, when English cricketers visited the colonies they did so for more than just entertainment. The first tour in the 1888/89 season saw Major Warton's English side defeat a South African XI 2–0 (by 8 wickets and an innings and 202 runs) on matting wickets. To the South Africans, such visits were vital to the game's development: 'Taking a survey of the game from 1860 until today, it is clear that the visit of Major Warton's team in 1888 marks the turning point in its history in many ways. This visit undoubtedly was very largely responsible for the tremendous and splendid subsequent progress in the standard of play …'[11]

In the 1895/96 season, South Africa was afforded three Tests against Lord Hawke's tourists. Although England won all three matches comfortably, the association between the two nations was becoming firmly cemented. In 1906, in its 12th Test, South Africa defeated England by one wicket after Dave Nourse hit an unbeaten 93; they went on to win the series 4–1.

As industrialisation led to an increasingly segregated society, cricket – a game enjoyed by all the races – became a symbol of status. This status was both racial and economic. The 'elitist' attitudes that impregnated the game, though, soon gave way to a more sinister form of exclusiveness – one determined by the social environment in which the sport evolved.

Racial cricket

Although introduced and dominated by the English, cricket was not an exclusive pursuit of one group of South African inhabitants. Each racial group – English, Afrikaner, African, coloured, Indian[12] and Malay[13] – can trace their history of the sport. Furthermore, despite the obstacles presented by a political and economic system reliant on inequality, cricket within the various racial groups proved to be of remarkable quality.

White cricket

The British imperialists heaped scorn on the Afrikaners, regarding them as uncouth and irresponsible. 'Newspaper cartoons portrayed them with very dark skins', implying that they were only marginally above the blacks. Letters to editors complained that they were unable to follow simple instructions.[14] Such opinions were displayed most prominently in their approach to sport: 'It is worth while considering the Boer in sport, for it is there he is at his worst. Without tradition of fair play, soured and harassed by want and disaster, his sport became a matter of commerce, and he held no device unworthy… [The Boers] are not a sporting race.'[15]

Despite such feelings, though, the support of Afrikaners was vital in ordering a stable and unified state. Sport, as we have seen in other countries, provided an opportune vehicle to cement political objectives. Therefore, it is not surprising that Afrikaners were among the early cricketers in South Africa. Krugersdorp, a Dutch stronghold, was a leading cricket centre; the game was also played at Potchefstroom, Pretoria, Barberton and

Johannesburg.[16] Moreover, W.H. Mars lists the pioneers of South African cricket as those in the Cape in the 1860s: C. Neuman Thomas, C. van Renen, A. van der Byl, T.J. Anderson, Canon Ogilvie, Percy Vigors, Collard, Dan Cloete, F. Puzey, S. van Renen, J. van Renen, Maitland Twentyman, Shearman, H. de Smidt, E. Judge, C. Jones, Overbeek, Home, Powell and Atmore.[17] Although he does not state the origins of these players, it is clear by name that not all were English. A.W. Wells confirmed that Johannesburg's first cricket team in 1886 was captained by and featured an equal number of Dutch speakers.[18] The Afrikaners Arthur Ochse and Nicolaas Hendrik Theumissen played in the first Test of 1888, as did Jacobus Francois du Toit and Charles Gustav Fichardt in the 1891/92 series – and Fichardt again in 1895/96. The fast bowler Johannes Jacobus Kotze toured England with South Africa in 1901 during the Boer War.[19] Pelham Warner, who took the 1906/7 MCC side to South Africa in part as a goodwill mission following the Boer War, was informed by the *Cape Times* that 'the world of cricket was a united South Africa', suggesting that any ill feeling between the two white populations had not yet penetrated into cricket.[20]

However, despite early Afrikaner interest, cricket became a game dominated by the English population. For this we owe the intrusion of politics. In 1901 the ICC was formed. South Africa took its seat at the inaugural meeting of the world's governing body at a time when the two white groups were engaged in combat. In the concentration camps of the Boer War the British attempted to stamp out the burgeoning Afrikaner culture. Afrikaans was banned in the schools, and prisoners of war were encouraged to take up 'English' sports such as cricket.[21] By definition, membership of the ICC was subject to those countries that accepted the British monarch as head of state. Apart from stifling development of the game in Northern Europe and Philadelphia, this move caused offence to a group of people that had considered themselves humiliated by British imperialism. In 1914 J.B.M. Hertzog formed the National Party as an organisation designed to assert the sovereignty of the Afrikaners. Test cricket between England and South Africa was now considered to be an Anglophile 'family' affair. Indeed, no Afrikaner played for South Africa until Jacobus Petrus Duminy in 1927/28,[22] and no significant writing on cricket would appear in Afrikaans for 50 years.[23] This lack of unity proved detrimental to the performance of South Africa in the international arena.[24]

Whilst mainly English, cricket also remained predominantly white. The South African Cricket Association (SACA) was founded in 1890 to 'foster and develop cricket throughout South Africa.'[25] Its initial intercolonial tournament provided competition with Portuguese East Africa, British Bechuanaland (now Botswana) and Rhodesia. There was no invitation, though, extended to the black communities who played the game in South Africa itself. John Nauright suggested that 'racial solidarity was more crucial in this context than national-based solidarities.'[26] Within this, though, M.W. Luckin, the first chronicler of South African cricket, suggested in

1927 that the English looked to 'our Dutch friends' to provide fast bowlers,[27] somewhat reminiscent of the early approach to cricket in the West Indies.[28]

However, the victory of the National Party in 1948 resulted in a transformation of the Afrikaners from a largely agrarian and insular people to one ready to exploit the immense economic potential of the state apparatus. They entered industry and the bureaucracy, and, more importantly, they became urbanised. The new political leadership sought means to impose their 'Afrikaner first' hegemony on the new South Africa – and sport is one method that an aspiring nation manipulates to gain recognition and prestige.

Cricket became increasingly popular once South Africa had left the Commonwealth in 1961. There are a number of possible explanations for this. It could be that once the game became divorced from its English hierarchical structure it could be examined minus its baggage and viewed solely on its merits. Of course, there was always the prospect of defeating the English at their own game. Thirdly, once South Africa was expelled from the ICC there must have been the urge to 'rally round' and defend the cause – and what better way than to ensure the maintenance and upkeep of the game.

By the 1960s South Africa was becoming a good side, and sport, moreover, benefited from a period of unprecedented economic growth (an average of 7 per cent per annum between 1960 and 1970) – which allowed for increased leisure time for whites.[29] The Sports Federation, which represented all sports in South Africa, saw its membership rise from 14 to 90 affiliates between 1951 and 1977,[30] and between 1955 and 1970 the number of white cricketers doubled. Even in the press box at Kingsmead for the third Test against Australia in 1967 there were nine Afrikaans writers where previously there had been only two.[31] Afrikaans newspapers, which had once paid little attention to cricket, were now on occasion leading both their front and back pages with it.[32] Furthermore, Afrikaner schools were encouraged by the authorities to take up cricket. Roland Bowen, for one, noticed that 'The game is no longer an English and therefore an alien institution: it is a South African game, and now that the political connection with England has been severed, the Afrikaner can play cricket with a quiet conscience.'[33] The prime minister even graced the first two days of the Cape Town Test against Australia in 1970 with his presence.[34] It cannot be ignored that this was also a period when the National Party sought the support of the English-speaking South Africans in its attempt to consolidate its rule. As part of this, Vorster sought policies that would embrace the white population in South Africa rather than simply the Afrikaner.

Black cricket

White South Africans believed that the country belonged to them, and tended to treat the native population as 'aliens' in their own land. To them belonged the toil of hard manual labour. Blacks were 'cursed, and ... none [shall] ... be freed from being bondmen, and hewers of wood and drawers of water'.[35] The 1961 Republic of South Africa Constitution Act stated that 'God is credited with having given South Africa, "this their own" land, to a specific people.'[36] Indeed, the idea that white civilisation had to erect a border to protect themselves from the 'black barbarians' is central to the white South African psyche.[37]

From this perspective, the history of cricket was incorrectly viewed as exclusive to the white and occasionally coloured sections of the population. In fact, just about all of South Africa's communities can point to a long and rich lineage, even if it has been unappreciated or even ignored. *Wisden* provides an early reference to a match between 'Hottentot and Africander [sic] Boers' at the Cape Province in 1854 which the Hottentots won;[38] John Sheddon Dobie, who came to Natal in 1862 to farm, noted in his journals a game of cricket involving a farmer and some blacks;[39] *Wisden* writes of the Queenstown Cricket Club, formed in 1865, and notes that 'Bantu (Kafirs)' had partaken in the sport in the preceding three years;[40] the *South African Cricket Almanak* records that black cricket began in Kimberley in 1876;[41] *Wisden* writes of a 1890/91 natives cricket tournament in Port Elizabeth involving four teams – and a match at Kroonstad between 'Natives (Bantu?) of Potchefstroon and the native CC of Kroonstad' is also mentioned.[42] Even in the Afrikaner republics, where blacks were not allowed to walk the same pavements as whites, they played cricket. In fact, it appears that only in Natal did the game not penetrate the culture of the indigenous population – soccer being more popular from the start.

The *Mfengu* (the name given to the first groups of Africans who converted to Christianity) were among the first African communities to become interested in sport. They became familiar with 'Englishness' via their over-representation within the growing black bureaucracy. Moreover, by the 1880s, sport was becoming more widespread and organised, being enjoyed by the African petty bourgeoisie and the coloured community. The African newspaper *Imvo Zabantsundu* reported on cricket matches, and a number of clubs were formed who competed with teams from the Indian, Malay and coloured communities in the Griqualand West Coloured Cricketers Union (1892–95) and, later, the Griqualand West Colonial Union. Fixtures between 'Duke' and 'Eccentrics', two of the prominent teams, came high up on the social calendar of Kimberley's African petty bourgeoisie. It was the major entertainment, for example, of Christmas Day 1895.[43]

The enthusiasm for cricket among the African middle class and the coloured community had definite political undercurrents. Despite the annexations of land and the 'Christianisation' of native institutions, the absorption of the Cape blacks into wider society was considered to be dependent on the maintenance of imperial rule. 'Direct Imperial control', as *Imvo* put it in 1897, 'is the talisman engraved on the heart of every Native in the land.'[44] By adopting the most gentlemanly of English pastimes, the black middle classes were displaying attributes in order to be considered worthy of citizenship. This thought-process highlights how different sections or groups within a society, not only the ruling authorities, can manipulate sport to satisfy a political agenda.

So, amidst this enthusiasm for sports by the black populations, how can we explain segregation? The orthodox response has been one of 'tradition': blacks either do not play cricket or are not good enough.[45] We have seen that the argument that they do not play the game fails to withstand close scrutiny, and even if they had not would it not have been beneficial to teach the black communities the merits of cricket? Analysis suggests that the argument over ability is also based on little foundation. A combined Malay XI was considered strong enough to take on the second English team to visit South Africa in 1891–92. The match was arranged as an additional fixture on the tourists programme and was the last between a black side and a white touring team until an African XI played the Derrick Robins' side of 1973. For the Malays, despite a loss by ten wickets, 'Krom' Hendricks took four wickets for 50 runs in 25 overs and L. Samoodien hit 55 – one of only two South Africans to score 50 against the tourists all summer. Hendricks, described by English Test players George Rowe and Bonnor Middleton as one of the fastest bowlers they had witnessed, was included in the 1894 South African team to tour England. However, he was later omitted, a result of 'the greatest pressure by those in high authority in the Cape Colony.'[46] One leading English cricket magazine rued the fact that those responsible for the South African team were so particular about the colour of their players.[47] Pelham Warner recorded in his *Lords 1787–1945* how 'They wanted me to send a black fellow called Hendricks to England. I said I had heard that he was a good bowler, and he replied, "Yes", but I would not have it. They would have expected him to throw boomerangs during the luncheon interval.'[48]

There was also depth to this ability. The King William's Town cricketers won the first black inter-town tournament, challenging and beating the victors of the corresponding white competition. At the same time (1885), the *Imvo* recorded a victory by the Port Elizabeth African team over the white Craddock side.[49] These were not exceptions to the rule. However, regular competition between white and black sides did not take place.

There were, moreover, a number of outstanding individual players: Armien Hendricks, a wicket-keeper, and C.J. Nicholls were two impressive black cricketers at the turn of the century. Nicholls, who was asked to play for Kent, was a most feared left-arm pace bowler. He once earned ten gold half-sovereigns for bowling in three afternoons at Pelham Warner's 1905/6 MCC side. In his book of the tour, Warner described how, at practice, Nicholls, 'a young Malay with a fast left-hand action hit my middle stump nearly every other ball'.[50] Frank Roro – 'the WG Grace of African cricket'[51] – compiled over a hundred centuries in senior league cricket at an average of well over 100. Taliep Salie, the Malay googly bowler, once took all ten wickets in a 'friendly' match against an all-white XI that included the Test players 'Dave' Nourse, X. Balaskas and A.W. Palm. Clarrie Grimmett, the

Australian googly bowler, commented that Salie would win a place in any international side.[52]

Indeed, there have been claims that a 'coloured' actually represented South Africa. Brian Crowley writes of C.B. 'Buck' Llewellyn, a very good all-rounder and son of white and coloured parents,[53] and, in *Overthrows, a Book of Cricket*, J.M. Kilburn noted that Llewellyn (one of *Wisden's* 'Cricketers of the Year' in 1911) 'was dark-eyed and dark-skinned and South Africans called him coloured'.[54] Herby Taylor, the Springbok, has stated that his father employed Llewellyn as a coloured clerk and paid him accordingly.[55] Roland Bowen claims that he was subjected to racial abuse from his team-mates during the 1910/11 tour of Australia.[56] Despite this wealth of evidence, though, Llewellyn's daughter refutes the claim that her father was of mixed race and claims that both grandparents were of pure British descent.

To solve the problem of segregated cricket, one has to look beyond the logistics of the game. The reasons that black cricket failed to keep pace with the white game have their foundations in the state's economic programme. Thousands of natives were left without land after the wars of dispossession. Many were forced to enter 'white South Africa' in search of any work they could get for whatever reward. These migrants were further forced to seek employment in order to meet the increasing demands for taxation and rent on the reserves. Cecil Rhodes, leading mine owner and premier of the Cape Colony, sponsored the 1894 Glen Grey Act. Its land tenure and tax provisions would, he argued, act as a 'gentle stimulant' to blacks to work and 'remove them from that life of sloth and laziness ... teach them the dignity of labour ... and make them give some return for our wise and good government.'[57] Because of his relationship to the land through the extended family networks, the migrant would not only return home in periods of harvest or when required but would also have to provide the means to account for the inevitable shortcomings from agriculture.

The extended family on the reserves also provided the important function of social insurance – and the industrialist took advantage of this. He paid the male worker way below the cost of reproduction, taking into account perceptions of agricultural production when determining remuneration. Thus, the 'migrant' worker was offered a wage sufficient for his maintenance in the urban area alone, ignoring the provision of subsistence to his family.[58] The state, unsurprisingly, obliged the industrialist. A Master and Servants Act, which was passed in 1856, made it illegal for blacks to leave their jobs. Blacks were therefore forced to work but were unable to sell their labour to the highest bidder or to acquire the skills needed for better paid work. The 1922 Stallard Commission established the principle that an African should only be in the towns to 'minister to the needs of the white man and should depart therefrom when he ceases to minister.'[59] Practically all African mineworkers were recruited from the reserves and returned home after a period of economic activity. Apart from their periods of work at the compound, black urban workers had virtually no access to sport. In conditions such as this – the foundations for apartheid – it is nigh on impossible to establish the organisation required to develop coaching of talent or to provide any form of regular competition.

Furthermore, segregation proved popular with traditional African leaders who wanted to reassert their authority and with coloureds who wished to preserve their status over Africans. Nor did it conflict with the initial political ideology of the liberation movement. The ANC was founded under the ideological influences of Gandhi's doctrine of non-violence and Booker T. Washington's notion of advancement within the framework of segregation. There was, then, no strategy for entering government. The early leadership was composed of the African elite (teachers, priests, lawyers and doctors), and tended to look to English liberalism as a source of political guidance. All of this enforced segregation as a natural order. Indeed, in 1943 the African leader Anton Lembede described the goal of black unity as 'a fantastic dream which has no foundation in reality'.[60]

Racism merely added the finishing touches to this already segregated situation. The King William's Town Council banned Africans from the pavilion at the town's sports ground in 1885;[61] the Wanderers Cricket Club refused to set aside a number of seats for coloureds in 1913;[62] and the 1923 Urban Areas Act confined Africans to segregated townships or locations.

Along with such obstructive instances, there was also little or no encouragement of black cricket. Even if the cruel environment produced players of a standard to enjoy the first-class game, Gerald Howat believed that 'he would not find selection for South Africa or any provincial side.'[63] Social Darwinism and eugenics prevented blacks playing with whites – the risk of defeat by 'inferiors' was too great. Cricket encapsulated the values of the ruling regime and formed part of the boundary behind which white civilisation protected itself from the 'black barbarians'.

Black sporting organisations

The multinational policy, examined in the previous chapter, envisaged different groups of people residing in distinct territories, who would cross these for the sole purpose of employment. The justification for this was that not only were there racial differences but separate world-views and cultures as well. The intellectual rationale for racial separation, then, was moving away from biology and genetics to culture and ethnicity. To show this, games and activities of a 'tribal' flavour were sponsored by the state. Black dance groups were sent abroad to represent 'African culture' and provide publicity for the regime. The illusion was propounded of a mythical 'homeland' where the blacks could 'develop along their own lines'. This, of course, was a reinforcement of the concept of separation. 'The goal', declared Connie Mulder, cabinet minister in charge of black affairs in 1976, 'is that eventually there will be no black South Africans.'[64]

However, despite all obstacles and difficulties, cricket continued to flourish amongst the black population. Father Botto's survey in 1954 showed that
one-quarter of the Africans in Cape Town belonged to a sports club or
association, of which nine played cricket.[65] Basil D'Oliveira considered
them to include a number of promising players: 'Make no mistake: there is
a lot of ability among the non-whites of South Africa. Their love of the game
thrives though the playing facilities are poor. In good conditions and against
better players, their cricketing status would improve overnight.'[66] Still, some
players and teams did manage to transcend these unfavourable playing
conditions. Milnrow, the Central Lancashire League club, signed C.
Abrahams, a 25-year-old coloured, as a professional for 1961. The last
recorded cricket match before isolation involving players of more than one
race in South Africa took place at Johannesburg on 1–2 April 1961: a white
team, led by John Waite and containing 8 other Springboks (including Ali
Bacher), played against an XI made up of coloured players – and lost the
game by 20 runs. S. 'Dik' Abed, a coloured all-rounder in English League
cricket, had a substantially better average in the same league conditions in
both bowling and batting than Pat Trimborn, who was picked to tour
England in 1970.

In order for any sport to flourish it has to be organised for the sake of
competition. In South Africa, any attempt to extend the game beyond its
narrow clientele moved it into areas that were overtly political. Black organisation firstly questioned the nature of racial sport and then directly
challenged the principles of apartheid by demanding equality for all sportsmen. Such demands were often accompanied with support for the
Springboks' opponents, further enraging the authorities. By these acts alone,
sporting organisations entered the political arena.

The South African Cricket Board of Control

In the early 1950s the ANC demanded that six laws be repealed, threatening
disruption if they were not. This marked a new phase in the history of the
organisation and of the liberation movement in general. A new wave of
young members was assuming control within the Congress. The ANC's
Francis Meli noted that this new campaign recognised 'the fact that the liberation of the oppressed people in South Africa could only come about as a
result of extra-parliamentary struggle. Our duty as an oppressed people was
to fight by all means possible.'[67] A Programme of Action proposed a
National Academy of the Arts and Sciences to coordinate cultural activities.
The 1955 *Freedom Charter* stated that 'The colour bar in cultural life, in
sport and in education shall be abolished.'[68] The ANC proved successful in
arousing the consciousness of thousands of people and shaping the political
culture in the townships. Alliances were made with the South African Indian
Congress, the Coloured People's Congress and the South African Council of
Trade Unions (SACTU). South Africa became engaged in an ideological

civil war. Just as the policies of the National Party affected all walks of life, so did the resistance.

After competing in racial leagues, black cricketing organisations came together as the South African Cricket Board of Control (SACBOC) in 1948. Inter-race tournaments were arranged, taking a similar format to the communal cricket of India.[69] An increase in political consciousness, though, led many to question this form of competition, and a tour by Kenyan Asian cricketers in 1956 led to the selection of a South African side based on provincial lines. Then, in 1958, SACBOC shed its racial constitution and Africans, coloureds, Malays and Indians now represented their provinces; the South Africans won all three of the 'Tests' against Kenya. (This shows the importance of overseas visits in the development of the game – and was one of the reasons that white South Africans were so enthusiastic about tours by England, and later Australia, at the end of the nineteenth century.) The South Africans reciprocated the Kenyan visit with a tour to East Africa in 1958, losing only one of 16 matches. In the following year, they tried to organise a tour by a West Indian XI. This was obviously more prestigious than the Kenyan tour and aroused the interest of the government, who insisted that any games be played against only black sides and that segregation be enforced at all times.

SACBOC, who, according to Roland Bowen, represented the majority of South African cricketers,[70] first sought the support of the ICC in 1955. Their application for membership was rejected, in part because it did not have the funds and facilities to accommodate overseas visitors, and also because South Africa was already represented on the ICC by the South African Cricket Association (SACA). In 1960 SACBOC reported SACA to the ICC for practising discrimination in its selection policy. The white body, for its part, offered no help to their fellow countrymen and turned down a request for a match against the 1956/57 MCC tourists as the itinerary was full. When the ICC sought the opinion of SACA on the question of racial cricket, the white body approached the government for an official response. The commitment to multinational sport was henceforth accepted as the policy of SACA.[71]

SACBOC's own policy was one of multi-racialism, with teams selected on ability rather than the colour of skin. Participation in its leagues was open to all races, though no white players participated. Hassan Howa, the secretary of the board, outlined his organisation's stance to the Johannesburg *Sunday Times* on 29 January 1967:

> We would like to see South Africa playing all the cricket countries of the world, including the West Indies, India and Pakistan, but with a truly South African side picked on merit only, regardless of race or colour. Sport should be left to find its own salvation and politics, race and colour should be left out of it altogether.[72]

To pursue this objective it refused all cooperation with white cricket, and campaigned for the isolation of racial sport.

The South African Sports Association

SACBOC was affiliated to the South African Sports Association (SASA), an organisation of 70,000 founded in 1958, whose initial objective was 'To co-ordinate non-white sport, to advance the cause of sport and the standard of sport among non-white sportsmen, to see that they and their organisations secure proper recognition [in South Africa] and abroad, and to do this on a non-racial basis.'[73] Furthermore, SASA sought to undermine racist sport structures on three fronts:

- it appealed to white organisations to reject discrimination and to select sides on merit, in effect requesting that they break the law;
- it appealed to international sports organisations to insist that South African sides were representative;
- it appealed to the population of countries involved in competition with South Africa to campaign against racial sport.

The demand for full integration in sports, however, was a number of years away.

SASA successfully campaigned in 1959 for the cancellation of a West Indian tour to South Africa to compete against black cricketers. Its critics argued that SASA was using the means of protest and politics in areas where they did not belong.[74] SASA countered these criticisms by pointing out that the black population had no recognised legitimate means in which to pursue political protest, that sport had become politicised by the measures of the Nationalist regime and, finally, that sport was viewed as central to the South African psyche and as such was a 'legitimate target'.

Despite these counter-arguments, SASA's main weakness lay in the fact that it challenged racial sport in a manner that offered only minimal resistance to the state overall. Initially, it campaigned for 'international participation for black sportsmen within the framework of segregation in national sport',[75] but the appeals made to white sporting organisations were largely ignored. Dennis Brutus, for instance, complained that his letters to the MCC often elicited no reply.[76] Following the Sharpeville massacre in 1960, the government's repressive arm used emergency powers against any individual or organisation considered a threat to public order. Additionally, the Unlawful Organisations Act (1960) discouraged any form of black organisation. As a result, SASA was practically intimidated out of existence. The lesson to be learned from this episode was that a separation of sport and politics failed to achieve relatively tame demands. In the future, the policy of non-racial sport had to be linked to the wider political forces trying to break down racism in South Africa.

The South African Council on Sport

In SASA's place emerged the South African Council on Sport (SACOS), formed out of a conference of non-racial sports associations in 1970. SACOS was more aware of its relationship towards politics than its predecessor. It cleverly invoked the principles of the Olympic Charter[77] as its founding philosophy and sought relations with non-sporting organisations in constructing an anti-apartheid alliance. By 1980, 26 different sporting bodies had affiliated to it.[78] SACOS's programme included a number of points that directly challenged the concepts of the government's policy of multi-nationalism:

- It recommended that affiliates should refuse to apply for permits to play sport; to collaborate 'in their own humiliation'.[79]
- It sought to determine what was acceptable sport and what was not. It defined 'non-racial' sport as that partaken outside the confines of officially recognised racial sport. To belong to SACOS, a sporting body had to pledge itself against such sport. This approach was part of the wider political stance of the liberation movement in the 1970s, which was increasingly advocating black autonomy and a policy of non-cooperation with apartheid.
- It sought facilities that were deserving of all athletes, irrespective of colour.
- It demanded a moratorium on international sporting relations until apartheid had been demolished, arguing that under such restrictions it was impossible to partake in non-racial sport. Reform was no longer an option.
- It demanded equity of sponsorship for both non-racial and multinational sport. A memorandum published in September 1972 by the Ad Hoc Committee for Non-Racial Sport showed that the Department of Sport and other bodies had contributed R2,708,900 to white sport and only R102,150 to black sport.[80] When companies gave to black sports it tended to be to those who had affiliated to white bodies. The memorandum noted that sponsorship from foreign companies was similarly skewed.[81]

On this final point Sam Ramsamy suggested that sponsors played a significant role in luring black South African sportsmen and women into multinational leagues,[82] and Hassan Howa noted: 'People who are compromising in sport all of a sudden take a huge leap in their everyday lives, financially and otherwise. I know of several administrators who were bankrupt at one stage and who are very rich men today.'[83] By focusing on the sponsors of sport, SACOS was drawing into the equation the role of big business. This enabled it to fix its sights on the perpetuators of the problem whilst challenging the classical liberal assumption that capitalism would bring an end to apartheid.

SACOS, then, sided with the liberation movement and, as such, assumed their platform. They were unashamedly political, and their role in isolating South Africa was paramount. Whilst international sports organisations had sought to integrate South African sport, SACOS devised a strategy that invoked a boycott against apartheid itself.

The stance of white cricket

On the whole, white sport was ignorant of the rich history of black cricket. An ex-Springbok captain declared in 1981: 'Don't forget that the blacks have really known Western sports [only] for the last ten years';[84] the Department of Sport and Recreation informed the British Sports Council inquiry in 1980–81 that 'sport in South Africa has evolved methodically in a sustained manner over the past twenty years – when non-white population groups also became interested and started to participate in the wide variety of sports';[85] and Kim Hughes stated after the first Australian rebel tour in 1985 that 'Cricket isn't the beat of the blacks.'[86] This ignorance was part of a social outlook that argued that blacks were unaccustomed to the traditions of the West, such as their sports, and, more importantly, their concepts of democracy and political power:

> Power cannot simply be handed to the blacks overnight … for the obvious reason that they are, as a race, not yet capable of exercising that power democratically. Of course, they possess many educated men with qualities of leadership, but in general they still need to be further educated and to be seen to be capable of putting that education to good use.[87]

Dr J.E. Holloway, high commissioner for South Africa in 1955, argued that the very mental processes of the primitive Africans reacted differently from those of the European to the normal stimuli of civilised life.[88] How could they, therefore, be expected to take to cricket or to democracy?

Heribert Adam reminded his audience that prejudice is not endemic in an individual because he is depraved: it is a product of situations.[89] There were no actual laws prohibiting the various races from playing cricket together, but white cricketers were, as such, victims of the Christian Nationalist hegemony in that their world-view was distorted by 'common-sense' perceptions of racial superiority. In part, this stemmed from the white cricketing authorities themselves. Consider that SACA's annual report of 1955 noted the death of the wife of Englishman, Pelham Warner, yet it took five years before the South African Cricket Annual acknowledged the death of C.B. Llewellyn (the first 'coloured' to play for South Africa) – and then without an obituary.[90] Racial mixing, in the country overall – via the multi-national initiative – was not realistically considered until the 1970s. Even if SACA had wanted multiracial cricket, there is little they could have done without the approval of the government. Despite this, white sporting bodies were guilty of only accepting their black equivalents once they became subject to international scrutiny and the threat of boycotts. When in 1956 a Kenya–Asian team toured South Africa, for example, they had to play their Cape Town Test match at Hartlevale soccer ground – where a matting wicket had to be specially laid. The South African all-rounder Mike Proctor conceded that 'Hassan Howa always said that white cricketers in South Africa didn't give a damn about the interests of black players before isolation and he's probably right.'[91] The 'Stop the Seventy Tour' organisation criticised the South African cricketers in 1970 for not declaring themselves against apartheid and – by their silence – condoning it as such. *Wisden* noted that 'An unequivocal statement against sports segregation by either the captain, Ali Bacher, or the tour manager, Jack Plimsoll, would have been welcomed in the absence of one from the South African Cricket Association itself. But presumably they regarded apartheid as the national policy and not the responsibility of sportsmen.'[92]

Ali Bacher said, shortly after his appointment as captain for the English tour, that he would welcome multiracial cricket in South Africa 'as soon as the government finds it practical.'[93] He was not prepared, at this stage, to make a stand against racial sport. The South African Cricket Association, however, displayed no sign of supporting multiracial cricket. Anthony Steel, joint secretary of the Campaign Against Race Discrimination in Sport, said that they had been trying to get SACA to discuss at least the possibility of including non-European players in the trials for the 1960 tour to England, but 'The SACA rejected every approach and in fact did not reply to most of the letters. The only acknowledgement ever received was that correspondence had been noted.'[94] Additionally, in 1971 it cancelled a tour by a mixed-race England XI, which included Basil D'Oliveira; the profits from the tour were to go to the development of black cricket. A couple of years later they also rejected Mike Proctor's plans to bring a mixed-race International XI to South Africa 'worried that South Africa would be beaten out of sight inside a couple of days because the opposition would be strong and our players would be out of season and not geared up for such a big match. The morale of South African cricket would be badly damaged as a result.'[95]

By the end of 1970 South Africa had found itself excluded from practically all international sporting bodies. Whether inspired by a prick of conscience or self-preservation, white cricketers accepted that reform was necessary if they were to once again engage in Test-match competition. Dennis Gamsay, a Springbok player, was one of the first to articulate this new line of thinking:

> In my own mind, there is no question but that we should have mixed sport here. What has happened now is only the thin end of the wedge. If we turn back into the laager because of it, our position can only worsen, not only in sport but also economically.

We are only four million whites in a continent of several hundred millions of blacks. If we go on the way we are, we could find ourselves being sacrificed to rid the world of one of its niggling problems.[96]

Others followed. Peter Pollock, who had once condemned demonstrators as Communists, now urged all sportsmen who wanted multiracial sport to step forward and be heard. He was supported by Ali Bacher, the South African captain. SACA even conceded that it would select blacks for the forthcoming tour of Australia if they were good enough.[97] The government, though, immediately intervened and overturned this announcement.

However, the cancellation of this tour in 1971 by the Australians proved to be the final straw for many leading cricketers. Barry Richards recounted how 'Five or six senior players, including myself, decided that now was the time for the players to speak out.'[98] Along with Mike Proctor, he led colleagues from the field in April 1971 during a contest to commemorate the tenth anniversary of the Republic, and presented the Association officials with the following written statement: 'We cricketers feel that the time has come for an expression of our views. We fully support the South African Cricket Association's application to invite non-whites to tour Australia, if they are good enough, and further subscribe to merit being the only criterion on the cricket field.'[99] Their stance was supported by their fellow players when an opinion poll in 1971 demonstrated the thaw in racial attitudes: out of 292 leading white cricketers, 276 were prepared to play with or against blacks. Before 1969, the number answering in the affirmative could probably have been counted on one hand.[100] Ali Bacher joined this swell of opinion and now argued for blacks to be allowed to represent South Africa.

This conversion has to be viewed in the light that South Africa was now isolated from international cricket. Players such as Barry Richards, Peter Pollock and Mike Proctor feared that their international careers were now over. Owen Wynne, the former Springbok, commented: 'Only now that they [white sportsmen] are being ousted from world sport do they, in the hope of again being accepted, turn to the non-whites and say: "All right, we'll give you a chance."'[101] The South African *Sunday Express* berated those

who allowed, encouraged, supported, tolerated or simply ignored apartheid in sport as in everything else in your lives. Half-heartedly, belatedly, some of you tried to change ... You saw that you were being thrown out of international sport because of your country's racial ways. And you started to panic, to seek ways of keeping yourselves in ... Unfortunately, your initial efforts were clearly motivated by self-interest rather than moral conviction. You were prepared to compromise not because you accepted the injustice of racial discrimination, but because you feared the isolation that would result ...[102]

David Frith later stated that 'historians would be hard put to name any of the 235 Springbok Test representatives who were blatant racists',[103] only to add to the same issue of *Wisden Cricket Monthly* a conversation between retired internationals, Neil Adcock and Peter Heine:

> 'Peter, what would you have done if a black traffic warden had booked you 20 years ago?'
> 'I would have murdered him.'
> 'And what about today, Pete. What would your reaction be today?'
> 'Today, Addie, it would be ok.'[104]

The resistance of black sporting organisations resulted in the isolation of South Africa and an acceptance that if it wanted to enjoy international cricket again it had to do so with the support of the black community in a multiracial setting.

Multiracial cricket

Following the cancellation of the tour to England in 1970, SACA set about placing its house in order so that it could gain swift entry back into the international fold. The English authorities had warned the South Africans that it would only play them once they selected their sides on a multiracial basis. When talks began in April 1971, the white authorities offered money to SACBOC and its affiliates to amalgamate with SACA. The South African African Cricket Board took the bait and signed up for multinational cricket in April 1972 on the basis that SACBOC was not serving the interests of African cricketers and that they could not wait for society to be changed before they could play at a higher level.[105]

SACA proposed that the now three organisations continue to organise separately and that touring sides be able to play against them individually. In addition, the three bodies would compete against each other in a national tournament. This would act, if permitted by the government, as a selection procedure for Springbok sides. This, in effect, was a reflection of the multinational policy and was rejected by SACBOC's Hassan Howa, who argued that there was no reason why mixed cricket could not be played now at all levels. This was supported by legal advice which suggested that there was no law to prevent mixed cricket provided that it took place on a private ground, without spectators, where players did not share facilities or drinks afterwards.[106] Nonetheless, Barry Richards commented that his country would have to do a lot more towards integration in sport before they would again play Test cricket; Mike Proctor believed his chance had gone.[107]

Two events marked a further softening in the SACA attitude. Ali Bacher and Joe Pamensky headed a group of businessmen who assumed the levers of control. They were considered to be more liberal than their predecessors and so more likely to be sympathetic to the cause of multiracialism. They watched over the inauguration of an international World Cup limited overs tournament in 1975 (ironically, introduced into the gap which a cancelled tour to England by South Africa had left), an event that was to signal the popularity of the one-day game and radically transform cricket. This prestigious competition, then, did not include or need South Africa. It was to prove an enormous blow.

Progress towards multiracial cricket remained slow, but on 18 January 1976 it was announced that the three groups had merged and pledged themselves to the promotion of 'normal cricket'. Rashid Varachia of SACBOC explained that 'normal cricket shall mean at this stage participation of and competition between all cricketers regardless of race, creed or colour in cricket at club level under one provincial governing body.'[108] Boon Wallace, president of SACA, said: 'Cricket is not only a game in which a man's colour is neither significant nor important, but cricket is indeed a great catalyst of goodwill in the field of race relations.' He also said that the government's apartheid policy was not that of SACA's and that mixed cricket was inevitable.[109] This was a departure from the traditional position that such matters were beyond the sporting domain. The decision was greeted with disdain by Albert Hertzog of the HNP, who called it an attempt to 'undermine the white man's self-respect'.[110] The MCC and the Australian Cricket Board, on the other hand, were delighted, with the 'Aussies' offering to tour later in the year, and Peter Hain, a leading voice in the Stop the Seventies Tour (STST) organisation, promised that he would not organise protests against the united body.[111]

The merger, moreover, offered opportunities to black cricketers. The Datsun Double Wicket International Competition in 1973 was actually the first event in the history of South African first-class cricket to allow all races to compete at an 'international' level. It also introduced black cricketers to a large white audience for the first time. Edward Habane and Edmund Ntikinca, the first African participants, defeated the New Zealanders Bruce Taylor and Bev Congdon – both Test players. In 1975 an African XI toured Rhodesia, were given games against Derrick Robins' XIs[112] and even competed in the domestic Gillette Cup. An International Wanderers XI, captained by the Australian Greg Chappell, were the first overseas side to compete against 'multiracial' teams when they toured South Africa in March 1976. In one contest Babu Ebrahim bowled the South Africans to victory with 6 for 66 from his slow, left-arm spin. When Ali Bacher was asked about the chances of South Africa fielding a multiracial Test team and of the emergence of black players like Basil D'Oliveira, he announced: 'to be honest, a Test team picked on merit now would be all white, but in two or three years it may be a different story. We don't have anyone in Dolly's class at present, but there are many promising Indian and coloured players and a few outstanding blacks.'[113]

The Cricket Club of South Africa, founded by former Springbok Dennis Gamsy, and the Aurora Club of the Maritzburg Cricket Union were among the first multiracial teams. Marshall Lee and Colin Henderson sacrificed the comforts of racial cricket to play for SACBOC's formerly all-black College Old Boys Club in 1975. Progress at club and provincial level, though, was slow and when Billy Woodin, the president of SACA, revealed that Dr Koornhof, the minister of sport, had never agreed to multiracial club cricket – '[He] has spelt out the new policy to me and other cricket administrators on several occasions and we and the Minister agreed to cricket matches between clubs of different races. We never agreed to multiracial clubs'[114] – the brief experiment was over.

Elements within the National Party, under the tutelage of Dr A.P. Treurnicht, had made it clear that they would not support multiracial cricket. In fact, little was done to prevent the staging of matches involving mixed teams. The regime, in shock at events in Mozambique and Angola and the June 1976 Soweto uprising, was trying to evolve a social system that, at least, would not entail the blacks becoming a fifth column in South Africa. Still, Koornhof refused to be pinned down without the backing of his party, reflecting the dual nature of policy – placation of both international opinion and the NP right wing.

The South African Cricket Union

Despite this setback, a second attempt was made at reconciliation and, on 18 September 1977, the South African Cricket Union (SACU) came into existence. Its president, Dennis Dyer, outlined the new organisation's aims and objectives for normal cricket:

- membership of clubs to be open and not governed by race, creed or colour;
- merit selection from club level upwards;
- sharing of all common facilities.

Dyer concluded that the cricketing authorities had now met the conditions set by the ICC for South Africa's readmission to international cricket. Two of the three SACBOC provinces, however, refused to join the new organisation. They claimed that SACU remained multinational in its approach as virtually no white clubs had accepted black membership and, therefore, very few teams were mixed. They reformed themselves as the South African Cricket Board (SACB) and advocated a series of measures to be implemented before they would re-join the SACU experiment.

1. All racial, tribal, religious or other labels should be abolished from club to national level.
2. There should be equal facilities for all and immediate steps must be taken to ensure that everybody enjoys the same facilities.

3. All cricketers and potential cricketers should be given the same opportunities to develop their skills and to participate in the game. This means that training facilities, coaches and other teaching methods should be made available to all on an equal basis.
4. All cricketers and potential cricketers must be placed in a position which will enable them to play and enjoy a game of cricket.[115]

Such initiatives, then, not only required the participation of the state but also challenged the very nature of apartheid. Equal facilities, equal opportunities and the removal of racial, tribal and religious labels so that all men and women were equal in the eyes of God was anathema to the ideology of Christian Nationalism.

More practically, though, the South African Cricket Union could not deliver them. Whilst the Transvaal province became the first to open its leagues to multiracial cricket, the Natal Cricket Association initially refused mixed leagues – preferring white teams and black teams to organise their own competitions, with the two winners meeting in a final. This avoided the possibility of the strongest black sides defeating the weakest white sides and so threatening centuries-old ideological notions of racial superiority. As Heribert Adam later commented,

> It is indicative of South African racialism that even in the somewhat unreal world of sport a white cannot allow himself to be defeated by a non-white … South African whites prefer to suffer the humiliation of exclusion from the world's sports scene rather than accommodate an even symbolic abandonment of their colour privileges and master role.[116]

SACB's withdrawal, however, did not spell the death of mixed cricket. In the Transvaal leagues more than 30 black teams joined the existing 60 white clubs;[117] Yacoob Omar became the first black cricketer to play for Natal in the Currie Cup; and in the first season of 'normal' cricket eight blacks played first-class cricket for various provinces. By the end of the first season, though, most of the ex-SACBOC players had returned to the non-racial SACB.

Despite the still unresolved upheavals, the ICC, at their meeting in 1978, accepted that there was now in place a single South African body that represented cricketers of all races and that it actively promoted 'normal' cricket. However, neither Australia nor England were prepared to propose South Africa's readmission (as founder-members they were the only countries eligible to do so) for fear of upsetting relations with India, Pakistan and the West Indies, who still had their doubts about the extent of multiracial cricket.

The events in 1976, namely the massacre at Soweto, showed once again that sport is affected by the wider currents affecting any society. The 'goalposts' were now moving and South Africa was to enter into the bitter-est chapter of its turbulent history. It was felt that the relaxation of measures that enabled mixed cricket to be played were a gesture on the part of the government in order to appease sectors of the black opposition. SACU was accused of using the promotion of black cricket simply as a means to re-engage itself in international cricket. The liberation movement committed itself to a campaign of non-compliance and civil disobedience. Alfred Nzo, the ANC's secretary-general, had already stated that his organ-isation 'totally reject the notion that ... the struggle of our people is aiming at reform within the apartheid system ... our objective is the seizure of power, which our people will use to bring about the radical political, economic, social and cultural transformation of South Africa'.[118] SACOS argued that: 'If at this juncture we accept commissions grudgingly given, the reluctant suggestions of amalgamation from our new-found fair-weather friends, and lose sight of our non-racial objectives, we may as well temporarily halt the march towards truly non-racial sports in a truly democratic society ...'[119] SACB aligned itself to this position and distanced itself from the unified body.[120]

SACU's self-interest did nothing to undermine apartheid – the extent of multiracialism, especially after stumps were drawn, was negligible – but, on the contrary, acted as a promoter of the government's supposed willingness to reform. In return, SACU made regular appeals to Pretoria to assist in breaking South Africa's isolation. This enabled its opponents to accuse SACU of being in the government's pocket. Such an accusation appeared justified when the government offered to assist in the financing of rebel tours to South Africa, both directly and through tax concessions to sponsors. Previously, Koornhof had praised Varachia in parliament for 'touring abroad to put in a good word for South Africa.'[121] The relationship was strongly denied by the cricketing authority, but, on the two occasions that SACU threatened to sue over the allegations, charges against the claimants were dropped.

Hassan Howa, the SACB's head, declared that 'normal' cricket could not operate in an environment soiled by the policies of apartheid, and he coined the phrase 'no normal sport in an abnormal society' to outline its new approach. Howa challenged SACU to accept that South African society was 'abnormal': 'If they say that and ask us for help and ask us to play sport on the understanding that it is abnormal and they are working to normalise it, they would find us co-operative.'[122] It meant that, as the National Party was beginning to embrace the idea of 'normal-ity' in sport, the opposition advanced onto the question of apartheid per se.

However, SACU condemned the position taken by SACB and accused them of subjecting cricket to political concerns. SACB was further criticised as an organisation run for the benefit of the middle-class coloured and Indian communities. Joe Pamensky of SACU claimed that most Africans were affiliated to his organisation.[123] He further pointed out the knock-on potential that multiracial cricket offered to the wider society: 'it is no coincidence that the government has moved to scrap several apartheid laws affecting sport since the SACU demonstrated that it was indeed possible to play non-racial sport in South Africa without major problems or friction'.[124] Still, South African cricket remained divided and Michael Owen-Smith could write in his notes as editor of the *1980 Protea Cricket Annual of South Africa* that 'there is no sign of any solution being found to the differences which exist between the SACU and the SACB'.[125] This was because the disagreement was rooted in political rather than sporting terms.

The development programme

A key component of the 'total strategy' was the emphasis on 'Winning Hearts and Minds' (WHAM). Its aim was to eliminate 'the underlying social and economic factors which have caused unhappiness in the population.'[126] Roads were built in the townships and a massive housing programme was started. Political power, though, remained firmly entrenched in white hands. Accompanying coercive measures included mass detentions, assassinations and the creation of a special township police – who were aided by black vigilantes. Attempts at an illusion of democracy through municipal government were rejected, often violently. The insurrection of 1984 was to last for three years, led to 3,000 deaths and caused untold damage to the national economy. The United Democratic Front (UDF), which was formed in 1983 to galvanise opposition to the new constitution,[127] grew out of this turbulence. They encouraged a wave of political activism in the black communities. Street committees, welfare groups and mutual aid societies were formed to organise the townships, placing them outside the remit of the state. Police and troops were sent into these areas to 'restore order'. This triggered a huge campaign of civil disturbance. In 1985 a partial State of Emergency led to the arrest of over 8,000 people, which escalated until, by June 1988, tens of thousands had been detained.[128]

Against this backdrop, Ali Bacher took mini-cricket into the townships. This was an abridged version of the real thing, though it was a courageous move for it challenged the implied assumption that blacks were not interested in cricket, a belief that had been used to justify their exclusion from the top levels of the game. These so-called development programmes forged part of a philosophy that promoted sport as a racial and social equaliser. Mervyn King, the chairman of the South African Executive Cricket Club, stated that 'By taking cricket to the children in the townships we can do a great deal towards making South Africa a better place in which to live.'[129]

Bacher's motives have obviously been questioned. One township coach, Nicholas Selana, resigned, accusing SACU of using mini-cricket 'to get into the townships' and using the townships 'as a ticket to the international test arena.'[130] The development programme, moreover, was instigated at the same time as the government's new initiative to defeat the liberation movement: the 'total counter-revolutionary strategy', which was an extension of the 'total strategy'. It argued that in order to defeat the revolutionary movement the state had to counter the tactics being adopted in all spheres – political, social, labour and sport. The government had to initiate schemes to build roads, schools and playing fields in order to offer an alternative to the revolutionary movement. Nearly two thousand urban renewal projects were launched in 200 townships.[131] Radio and television appeals urged youngsters to take up cricket in Soweto. The development programme attracted the support, through sponsorship, of a number of South Africa's largest companies (First National Bank, South African Breweries, Slazenger, Form-Scaff, De Beers – to name a few). These companies, attracting considerable tax concessions, have claimed that their actions were both assisting the campaign against apartheid and the healing process in the new South Africa. The same companies, though, supported the Labour Relations Amendment Act (1988) and resisted the Confederation of South African Trade Unions' (COSATU) campaign for a living wage![132]

Bacher, for his part, claimed that the development programme was more than simply sport as 'bread and circus' in an attempt to divert people away from the political issues (better to bowl cricket balls than throw rocks). He claimed that he took the game to the country's poorest sector because of a belief that cricket could achieve things beyond the reach of politics.[133] The programme also forced racial integration onto a previously reluctant education system.[134] Another consequence was that, for the first time in any cricket-playing nation, female teachers played a prominent role in the coaching of children.[135] In 1989 Joe Pamensky boasted how the development programmes had introduced 60,000 black South Africans to cricket; he estimated that this figure would soon reach 100,000. 'The one certainty of tomorrow's cricket in South Africa is that black people will be re-writing the record books.'[136]

In essence, the development programme was a further component of the political process, a continuation, in more subtle form, of the multinational and the autonomous sports policies. It was, in other words, a showpiece to disguise the realities of a racist society. Only this time it was conceived in an environment of social turmoil. Ali Bacher conceded that fear was a main reason for its launch: 'Back in 1986 I was really scared, and I honestly thought my country was on the verge of a bloodbath.'[137] Douglas Booth argues that the programme was devised in order to preserve these threatened existing structures: 'Their objective is to create the illusion of harmony while co-opting a carefully selected small group of elite black players and administrators who pose no threat to long term white control of sport.'[138] As with the wider 'reform process' in South Africa, its long-term objective was the maintenance of existing power imbalances – albeit in a slightly modified form.

The politics of compromise

By the early 1980s SACOS was confident that world opinion recognised them as the legitimate authority on sport in South Africa. When the townships exploded in 1984 the slogan 'no normal sport in an abnormal society' appeared particularly apt. Mixed sport may well have made advances in the large cities like Johannesburg and Cape Town, but in the small towns and rural areas there was little or none. In a survey of sports facilities in the Natal town of Pietermaritzburg, for example, 11,567 white school pupils shared 32 cricket fields and 65 cricket nets, while 13,608 coloured and Indian pupils enjoyed one field and five nets; there were no sports facilities for African children.[139]

Amid the turbulence on the ground, the liberation movement sought to reassess its tactics and strategy. The two warring sides appeared to be engaged in a lengthy process of stalemate. The state was sufficiently strong to keep revolutionary forces at bay but not so strong that it could banish the spectre of revolution permanently. The liberation movement could not seize control from below; the state could not impose its authority from above. The ANC shifted its stance so that it would only negotiate with a defeated white regime – to one that called on whites to embrace the tenets of democracy and multiracialism. This 'Call to Whites' campaign was endorsed by the UDF in 1986. It was being suggested that the white hegemony should be challenged through cooperation with individuals and organisations who were prepared to embrace such qualities. The ANC sought to broaden its appeal and to develop contacts with a wide range of actors, including elite sectors of white opinion – academics, clerks, opposition figures, student groups and, most notably, big business. Significant steps had already been taken by the cricketing authorities to move towards multiracial competition on the field of play, and some members of SACOS now began to question the longevity of the policy of non-cooperation.

> We started the debate within SACOS in 1984. It was a hot debate. No normal sport in an abnormal society was all right but it was not a solution. It was a cul-de-sac. Just to repeat the slogan was a weakness. We could blame apartheid for everything – but that wouldn't get rid of apartheid. We had to do something to normalise sports.[140]

In February 1988 the government placed restrictions on 17 extra-parliamentary organisations, which effectively banned the UDF and prevented the trade unions engaging in political work. Leaders of the UDF and COSATU reformed themselves as the Mass Democratic Movement (MDM) and called for a campaign of widespread civil disobedience to challenge segregated facilities and institutions. Emphasis focused on individual bodies and gave the impression that the black opposition was prepared to negotiate change on a one-to-one basis in order that this might undermine the grand scheme of apartheid.

The National Sports Congress

Muleleki George began to organise a dissident faction within SACOS. He was a member of the ANC, whereas many in SACOS drew their inspiration from Steve Biko's black consciousness movement. The UDF/MDM was so broad as to embrace a number of lines of thought, all of which were united by the common determination to rid South Africa of apartheid. This meant that, in stark contrast to the philosophy of the black consciousness movement, it was prepared to countenance deals with the traditional foe in order to advance its cause. Trade unions, for instance, had recently become accustomed to bargaining and winning concessions and benefits for their members and, at the same time, power and influence for themselves. The tactic of collaboration, therefore, could be beneficial.

SACOS now began to be challenged on the basis that it was not representative of all black sportsmen, and, further, that it was hampering the development of a mass non-racial sports movement. SACOS was largely Indian and coloured, and strong in areas such as Port Elizabeth and the Western Cape, and although its membership included a number of educated Africans, it never made progress within the townships. As George stated: 'Soweto was not part of SACOS, nor was Umlazi or Lamontville [black townships in Natal] ... SACOS ... represented only one section of the non-white people.'[141] Its hardened principle of refusing to budge until apartheid had been eradicated was seen as a long-term objective, but one which offered no sense of power to the victims of racial rule. In fact, George reinterpreted the slogan of not playing normal sport in an abnormal country by arguing that there was not one South African sporting sector but two. Apartheid sport had to be boycotted, but multiracial sport should be encouraged: 'The normalising of society and the playing of normal sport needn't be locked into the same timetable.'[142] This was a major concession on the principle that apartheid had to be abolished before sports links could be resumed with South Africa. As a strategy it was condemned by P.W. Botha as part of the ANC's terrain of 'subtle subversion'.[143] However, it showed that the liberation movement was prepared to be flexible and to accommodate the needs of the white population. In Hain's words, 'From then onwards, sport – instead of being a means of confronting whites with the realisation that they had no alternative but to change – became a means of offering them a glimpse of a new post-apartheid South Africa in which their beloved sports tours could resume.'[144]

In 1988 George and his dissident group formed the Interim National Olympic and Sports Congress and, in April 1990, the National Sports Congress (NSC), which was aligned to the MDM but effectively the sports arm of the ANC. This, in itself, was quite remarkable considering that the ANC, at the time, had not even debated a sports policy. The truth was that the ANC was effectively becoming the legitimate voice for black South Africa and had, therefore, to explain itself on issues not usually recognised as its forte. SACOS refused to join the NSC, but a number of its affiliates – including SACB – defected.

South Africa's internal resistance movement now had two black sporting bodies and two strategies. The inexperienced NSC remained on the periphery of the political struggle until afforded the opportunity to assert its muscle and exploit its relationship with the ANC and MDM by the rebel tour of Mike Gatting's 'England' team in 1989. Following a mass and successful campaign against Gatting's side, the NSC was able to establish itself as the pre-eminent sporting organisation in South Africa. When Nelson Mandela was released, the NSC – in accordance with the ANC – abandoned the policy of non-collaboration and acted as a force to unify sporting organisations on non-racial principles: 'Every deracialised democratic institution is a victory for non-racialism and every victory, no matter how small, contributes to the cumulative building of post-apartheid society.'[145] This formed an element of the ANC's compromising of a number of its core beliefs: it suspended its armed struggle in August 1990, and 'democracy' and 'growth with redistribution' replaced 'socialism' and 'nationalisation' as the principal priorities. This was part of a general process of placating white apprehension about possible majority rule.

The United Cricket Board of South Africa

The merging of the cricketing bodies into the United Cricket Board of South Africa (UCBSA) was as much a process of politics as anything to do directly with sport. Negotiations between SACB and SACU took eight months before a 'Declaration of Intent' was agreed and the UCBSA finally came to fruition in June 1991. All sides committed themselves to redressing the injustices generated by apartheid. Priority was to go to grass-roots development rather than international competition. Despite this, the formation of the UCBSA ensured that South African cricket rejoined the world stage even before more traditional multiracial sports as soccer and athletics.[146] A tour was quickly arranged against India and the regulations guiding the 1992 World Cup were altered to accommodate cricket's latest readmission. Nelson Mandela dismissed critics of the pace of merger as 'extremists … sport is sport and quite different from politics'.[147]

Ali Bacher, for one, was enthusiastic about the prospects for multiracial cricket in South Africa: 'If we had a South African Under-15 or Under-17 team, there is no question it would be composed of players from all the population groups.' The potential among young players was such that he was convinced South Africa would dominate world cricket by the end of the decade: 'We were a force when the teams were all white. Can you imagine what the potential will be when we utilise all our people, all our resources?'[148] He also finally acknowledged the role of the SACB cricketers 'who deserve even more credit than we for keeping the game alive with very poor facilities'.[149]

Conclusion

All the races in South Africa have a history of playing cricket. If the social and economic environment – which culminated in informal segregation – resulted in racial cricket becoming the 'tradition', it has to be accepted that politics enforced a division based on colour. Black cricket became embroiled in politics because, by demanding firstly recognition and secondly equality, it directly challenged the philosophy of the apartheid state. The white establishment, of which cricket was a paid-up member, responded to the call for multiracial cricket only when it feared for its very existence. It is significant that whites only joined the 'integrated' leagues after the 1976 split into SACU and SACB.

Multiracial cricket appealed initially to SACA as a means of re-engaging in international contests, to the government as a demonstration of the willingness to reform and, finally, to the liberation movement – and especially the ANC – as a token to white South Africans that all would be well under majority rule. Amongst these expedients, the platform of the old SACOS and the long-term policy of SACB for non-racial cricket was conveniently overlooked. However, it will not go away and will ensure that cricket in South Africa remains a political issue. It is interesting, with the luxury of hindsight, that Bacher's predictions for black cricket have not come to fruition. The premise underpinning non-racial cricket is that equality of opportunity can only exist once the inequalities that resulted from apartheid had been attacked and eradicated. The 'no normal sport in an abnormal society' slogan, therefore, had much more to do with politics and economics than it did with sport. Only by examining the thinking behind this phrase in greater depth can we hope to understand why the simple enjoyment of games was such a contentious issue.

6

'No Normal Sport in an Abnormal Society'

What does a society have to do in order for it to be perceived as out of the ordinary? In any number of states, opposition forces could claim their existence to be the consequence of gross inequalities. Are not revolt and revolution both end-results of a political rule that is deemed unreasonable? In South Africa, the political scientist could focus on any number of variables – from measures to control the flow of information, to the deliberate undermining of its sovereign neighbours, to the belief in a 'science' of racial superiority to determine policy – to demonstrate the abnormalities of the state. Whilst a similar approach could be used when studying other nations, South Africa was a unique case in the later 20th century, especially amongst cricket-playing countries.

The concern of this book is the relationship between politics and sport. It began with an assessment of the problems of defining 'politics'. It is argued that the political scientist had to venture beyond the institutional study in order to have an understanding as to *why* politics exists. The previous chapter asserted that the refusal of the black South African Cricket Board to join the South African Cricket Association merger was for political rather than purely sporting reasons. The goal of 'non-racial' cricket could only be obtained following political and economic change. Hassan Howa withdrew his support for 'multiracial' cricket, arguing that it could not exist within an abnormal society. His organisation was criticised by both the 'multi-racial' body and the government for dragging politics into sport; the SACB, in turn, attacked the regime for the social and economic conditions that necessitated this stance. Both sides, though, gave credence to a definition of 'politics' that lay well beyond the scope of a purely institutional analysis.

The task of this chapter is to examine how racial legislation affected cricket within the black community – to scrutinise, in other words, Howa's claim. Opportunities to play competitive sport are not only determined by the availability of facilities, they are rooted in the education system, in the living conditions and in the economic well-being of the population. These provide the technical grounding, the facilities to play and the personal resources with which to purchase basic equipment. When one section of the population enjoys a privileged access to sport denied to another, and when that privilege is certified by racial origin, then there is some legitimacy to the claim that that society is abnormal. This does not have to be quantified by political scientists but rather perceived by the disadvantaged and formed into the ideology of political opposition. This is what happened in South Africa.

Education

'It has become an accepted fact that where Englishmen are banded together, either by reason of duty, self-advancement or force of circumstances, there cricket will be played.'[1] Throughout the British Empire educational institutions were established as a means of recreating English lifestyles, and through these the ethos of sports was propagated. Indeed, as early as 1740 Lord Chesterfield acknowledged the merits of both a 'sound' education and the game of cricket: 'If you have a right ambition, you will desire to excel all boys of your age at cricket as well as in learning.'[2]

Cricket of a remarkably high standard was being played in the English schools in South Africa by the mid nineteenth century. In 1870, for example, the Diocessan College in the Cape Province tied with Western Province and beat the Garrison by eight wickets – both amongst the strongest sides around. In the 1898/99 season, eight members of the Diocesan team played for the Combined Colleges XVIII vs. Lord Hawke's side in the only match of the tour that the English lost. The resources ploughed into it showed the interest given to games: 'At the present time [1915] the College is probably better equipped in the matter of cricket grounds than any other scholastic institution in the world, for it has no less than three separate specially laid-out playing fields of full size.'[3] St Andrews became the nursery of Orange Free State cricket. A number of prominent players – such as T.L. Graham, future judge-president of the E.D. Court, H.W. Court, colonel of Prince Alfred's Guard, Port Elizabeth, and E.W. Douglas, attorney general for Natal – represented the school.[4] The dominance of Transvaal in the early domestic game owed itself to 'those great nurseries of Transvaal cricket, King Edward VII High School, Jeppe High School and St John's College.'[5] Many of these traditional English institutions had the funds to employ an English professional coach.

These elite public schools were not the only educational establishments to partake in cricket. Dale College has proved invaluable for Border as a provider of cricket players. In the 1912/13 season Selbourne College was admitted into the East London Senior League and managed to maintain their place. Two Selbourne boys, L. Miles and R. Osthuizen, represented Border vs. MCC at East London in February 1913.[6] There were also various school and college sides in the Eastern Province Cricket Union leagues.[7] Dudley Nourse, a sporting legend in South Africa, described the importance of a cricketing education as follows:

We attribute much of the success of Natal to the watch kept over the younger players. It is not only the more fortunate boys who attend schools where they can obtain regular coaching advice from men who are both enthusiastic and possess a good knowledge of the game; but the less fortunate boys get their equal share of attention. There has been a steady scheme of expansion which will serve the province and the country well.[8]

How prophetic it was when he stated that 'Today I realise more fully the necessity of a correct start.'[9]

On the other hand, the lack of cricketers from the South West districts of the Cape Province has been attributed to the neglect of sports in the schools:

Hardly a schoolmaster in the districts has played a game of cricket in his life, and it is not encouraged in the boys. Unfortunately, also, the population is principally Dutch, who, though they have taken up Rugby football with great success, do not care for cricket, consequently it is only amongst the English section that the game is played.[10]

Such a start in life, clearly essential to assimilate the basic technical requirements to play cricket, was not afforded to African children. At the turn of the nineteenth century, though, the London Missionary Society opened a number of schools in order to provide elementary education in reading, writing and arithmetic. Its philosophy was integrationist, focusing on providing skills to African labour in order to satisfy the demands of the market and imparting cultural values to the black elite who schooled there. The Bible, Shakespeare and easy Greek offered a path from barbarism to civilisation. Sports, especially cricket, represented the values and ethics of this 'civilisation'. In 1865, 2,827 African pupils had been enrolled into these schools; by 1885 the number had grown to 15,568 in 700 schools.[11] In 1915 Fort Hare was founded to provide further education to the most gifted students from mission colleges. One of the first acts of the students was to lay out a football and cricket pitch, 'Proof indeed of the extraordinary influence exercised by the public school ethos, which produced "gentlemen" on an almost industrial scale throughout the British Empire'.[12]

By the end of the century, the education system had become multi-tiered, and featured elite white public schools, state-sponsored white education, mission colleges for the black 'elite' and the standard mission school for the African masses. In the Afrikaner republics, though, Africans were rarely offered even the basic education as it was not considered necessary. Jack and Ray Simons argue that segregation in education gave white children a 30-year head-start over their black counterparts: 'It is quite impossible to assess the damage suffered by the coloured people through their children being confined to the inferior mission schools.'[13]

Despite the benefits that physical education presented to the state, it was not made compulsory in government schools until 1939. This, of course, did not affect the black population as so few of them attended schools. In 1932 an estimated 80 per cent of African children still lacked an education.[14] The fear that they would acquire the skills of white settlers and so demand equal pay dominated policy in the era of segregation. Inferior teaching methods and resources were merely one of numerous means to ensure that the racial make-up of the state satisfied the requirements of concerned interests.[15]

The Nationalist government of 1948 attached enormous prestige to education, valuing its promotion of the 'Afrikaner first' hegemony:

> Afrikaans schools, Afrikaans teachers' colleges, Afrikaans universities and other educational institutions were essential to lead the Afrikaans child through his mother tongue into the cultural life of his own people, an introduction through which the Afrikaans national spirit was formed to achieve its highest prestige potential. In these educational institutions the flame of Afrikaans nationalism, as the bearer also of Afrikaans republican independence, constantly burned high and brightly.[16]

White schooling, a diet of 'Christian Nationalism' based on the Holy Scripture, was both free and compulsory. It promoted the national cause, this being a 'love for everything that is our own, with special reference to our country, our language, our history and our culture.'[17] Within this cause, sport was given a high profile. Tony Greig, the South African-born England captain (1975–77), recalled that the academic side of the school day would be over by lunchtime and the remainder of the day devoted to games:

> Looking back on those years, I cannot fail to be impressed by the complete involvement of all the masters in every aspect of the school and the pupils. The extra-mural activities like sport and music were all efficiently and enthusiastically supervised despite the fact that they were officially practised outside school hours.
>
> Masters generally adopted a particular sport as a matter of course. It was expected of them and any who refused to co-operate would have been looking for another job before long ...
>
> Just like their boys, the staff would finish lessons, eat their lunch, and within a very short while be out on the sports field. I am sure the majority enjoyed the involvement as they organised net practices with regimental efficiency and built everyone up towards the challenge of the following Saturday's match.[18]

There were, of course, far less fondly remembered aspects of the 'Afrikaner first' initiative, which involved the removal of thousands of blacks from employment and their replacement by higher paid white workers. In the expanding state bureaucracy, preference was given to whites.

Education and training had to reflect these proceedings. It was spelt out by Dr Verwoerd, the minister of native affairs, in a speech on the Bantu Education Act in 1953:

> There is no place for [the Bantu] in the European Community above the level of certain forms of labour ... it is of no avail for him to receive a training which drew him away from his own community and misled him by showing him the green pastures of the Europeans but still did not allow him to graze there ... the much-discussed frustration of educated natives who can find no employment which is acceptable to them ... must be replaced by planned Bantu education ... [with] its roots entirely in the Native areas and in the Native environment and community.[19]

Therefore, African students were to receive a separate education, one commensurate with the programme for development of the African people as a whole. The government set out to destroy the influence of the mission schools, who continued to provide a basic primary education to a number of Africans. Grants were cut back and then abolished. The number of mission schools fell from 5,000 in 1953 to 438 in 1971 and 132 in 1977 – a decline of over 95 per cent.[20] It was these institutions that played cricket. Those allowed to remain were forced to teach the national curriculum. Conversely, in the period 1953 to 1960 the number of government and government-aided schools increased from 992 to 6,750.[21] Expenditure on education was tied into revenues from black taxation. Equipment in these schools was therefore negligible and reliant on the poorest sections of the community for donations towards furniture and repairs, with pupils even having to provide their own writing equipment. In competition with housing, health and education, sport assumed a low priority.

There were no such handicaps for white children. In 1977, for example, the ratio of white to black spending on education was 14:1. Indeed, the increase in defence expenditure in 1975/76 was greater than the whole total allocated to African education.[22] In 1986–87 R2,299 was allocated by the state to educate each white child; the figure for each black child was R368. In white schools a single teacher taught on average 16 pupils; in black schools the figure was 41.[23] Whilst 30 per cent of white children could expect to go to University,[24] nearly two-thirds of Africans left school after primary education;[25] an estimated 50–60 per cent of African and coloured children remained illiterate.[26]

Before 1976 the state's policies had ensured that there would be no racial mixing on school playing fields. Following Soweto, this policy was 'relaxed' and the multinational sports policy was extended to schools. White sides could compete against 'non-racial' teams provided that permission was obtained from both the Department of Education and the minister of sport and recreation, and that attendance permits – which had to be made 30 days in advance of the contest – had been issued.[27] These measures, though, placed such a burden on interracial competition that they were very rare. There was barely any mixed-schools cricket because whilst the Transvaal Cricket Union, for example, could afford to hire Bob Woolmer (Kent and England cricketer, and later South African coach) to coach at four Afrikaans primary schools in 1970, as late as the 80s there were still very few black schools with equipment. In 1983 Ken Andrew, a Progressive Federal Party MP, complained that the government spent '2,400 times as much furthering the participation in sport for each white child compared with each black child.'[28]

The 'autonomous' sports policy was part of an overall strategy from which emerged the Republic of South Africa Constitution Act (1983). This separated government business into either 'general' or 'own affairs'. Matters affecting only one racial group were classified as 'own affairs', those pertaining to more than one racial group were 'general'. Sport fell into both categories: school sport was an 'own' issue, whilst sport outside of school fell under the scope of 'general' affairs. The policy, whilst appearing to the outside world as a recognition of the rights of sporting bodies and educational institutions to conduct their own affairs, further condemned the poorest sections of society. Sports such as cricket rely on a number of basic skills that are assimilated at a young age, as Hassan Howa pointed out:

> The best time to start teaching a youngster about cricket is at six or seven and at 13 he should have learnt the basics, then you develop what he has. Not so with this [black] chap. He doesn't get any coaching because his teachers know nothing and there are no facilities. As a result his technique is hopeless and he probably does not even know how to grip a bat properly.[29]

It was not enough for blacks to be selected for sides on the basis of their ability as the struggle became one of opportunity. Merit selection is meaningless if players do not have an equal chance to learn and practise their skills. The school that you attended was a greater determinant of destiny than raw ability. Prior to 1981, for instance, the KwaZulu Department of Education and Culture did not employ any fully trained physical education teachers.[30] With the matriculation rates in the African schools being low, additional time would usually be spent on extra lessons rather than sports. Yet, the cause was and is not a forlorn one: Joe Pamensky wrote how SACU 'found that people whom we thought had no aptitude for cricket in fact have the ability providing they are given the right kind of support and encouragement.'[31]

Urbanisation

Between 1891 and 1911 South Africa's urban population grew by more than 200 per cent. The primary cause of this was the discovery of gold and diamonds and the subsidiary industries to which they gave rise. The fact that over 10,000 people lost their land during the Boer War added to the population of the towns, as did the Native Land Act of 1913 – which attempted to squeeze the African population into reserves. Africans were prohibited from buying or leasing land outside of these designated areas. Amounting to only 12 per cent of the country, the reserves proved too small to sustain the large numbers of people dependent upon them. Furthermore, none of the country's known natural resources happened to be found in these areas. Inevitably, people left to seek better prospects in the town.

Initial thinking held that towns were not the right place for blacks as this was where a 'good kaffir' could be 'spoiled'.[32] However, the municipal and state authorities came to the opinion that if blacks had to reside in the towns then they at least should be controlled and segregated from the white residential areas. White South Africans wanted the black man's services but not his presence. They feared for the purity of both race and national identity. By formalising urban segregation in the Native (Urban Areas) Act of 1923, the authorities accommodated such prejudice.

With apartheid, Africans were not permitted to leave their 'homelands' unless they were contracted to work. In the cities they were accommodated in townships, which were designed on the periphery of white areas to allow the state to maintain what it considered to be a migrant population. Here, people lived in appalling conditions: an average of 14 occupied each dwelling in Soweto.[33] Less than 20 per cent of township dwellings had electricity, and water and toilets were outside.[34] Conditions were purposely sub-standard to deter further migration. Each town had a separate black quarter, where the curfew bell reminded people of where they should be. There were distinct sections for blacks at the post office, the bank and the doctor's surgery. Amid such deprivation, how do you rank sport? A 1981 survey of the problems in the eastern Cape placed the lack of recreational facilities as 14th out of 21 – behind more pressing concerns such as housing, employment, transport, electricity and street lighting.[35]

Recreational facilities in the black areas were, of course, virtually non-existent. While whites enjoyed sports grounds with stands and dressing rooms, blacks had to improvise – taking over spaces outside of the centres and adapting them for recreation. Omar Henry, the coloured cricketer, recalled that outdoor sports would be played 'on whatever areas of rough ground that were available, or in the street'.[36] The facilities available in 1944 to the 112,000 Africans living in Johannesburg, for example, covered the requirements of only 7,000 people.[37] Alan Cobley noted that 'throughout the first half of the twentieth century the primary areas for African sport and recreation in the city … were the streets and slum yards, or adjoining strips of waste grounds'.[38] Father Botto recorded that in the Cape: 'not more than 30 acres were available for fields in 1954 for 44,300 Africans, whereas by the standards of the United States and Germany 220 acres would be required'.[39] The situation was, of course, entirely different for the white population. What data existed, and even parliament could not produce complete records for all groups, highlighted the discrepancies.

TABLE 1
TOTAL PUBLIC EXPENDITURES ON SPORT (IN RANDS)

Years	Whites	Africans	Coloureds	Indians
1965–72	2,708,900	?	102,105	?
1974–75	1,217,612	464,317	333,792	?
1975–76	1,417,609	415,439	449,112	20,300
1977–78	1,585,724	495,394	187,420	?

Sources: Archer and Bouillon, *The South African Game*, p. 168; Brickhill, *Race Against Race*, p. 71. Official figures released by ministers in parliament.

TABLE 2
GOVERNMENT FINANCIAL EXPENDITURE ON SPORT DURING 1979 (%)

Department of Sport & Recreation (white)	86.6
Department of Plural Relations & Development (non-white)	4.19
Department of Coloured Relations (non-white)	0.003
Department of Defence (non-white)	9.21

Source: Judy Seidman, *Facelift Apartheid: South Africa After Soweto* (London: International Defence & Aid Fund, 1980), p. 31.

On a per capita basis the period 1965–72 represented a ratio of 120:1 in favour of white sports. For the period 1974–75, expenditure per head of the population was as follows: whites 29.3 cents, coloureds 14.5 cents, and Africans 2.6 cents (see Table 1).[40] Public funds distributed in the ratios given in Table 2 provided for as low as 7 per cent of the African sports budget. In contrast, it paid for just about the whole of the white sports budget.[41] 'This means that, to the extent that the labour of blacks contributes to the wealth of the country as a whole, and therefore to government revenues, blacks actually subsidise white sport.'[42] The 'autonomous' sports policy provided further reason to cut back on the limited grants to black sport. In 1988 the director of sport in 'coloured' areas estimated that it would cost R239 million to upgrade facilities: the government voted just R20 million.[43]

This poverty of resources was manifested in the sub-standard quality of pitches that black cricketers had to use. Basil D'Oliveira described how they were both overused and under-maintained:

So many teams played on this space that you would often get thumped in the back by a ball from another game; the batsmen regularly hit sixes because the ball was deemed 'lost' in the thick grass ... And the ball would do crazy things as it careered from boulder to rock from a batsman's stroke. Even if we understood such weighty matters like how to use the seam and to swing the ball, it wouldn't have mattered because the ball was soon kicked out of shape by those rocks. We would play with a ball until its cover came off – then we'd use the cork. Only when the string unravelled was it time to buy another ball. And whenever you won a cricket award you always said, 'forget the trophy, please can I have a bat?'[44]

Matting wickets, moreover, allowed bowlers to hurl down the ball with such unpredictable results as to render a decent batting technique improbable.[45] Such wickets, which were the norm in the early history of South African cricket, were blamed for the poor showing of the national side in its infancy.[46] Yet, this would be the norm for the black cricketer – 'a grassless, matting wicket, corrugated iron sort of place that a 6th Division white cricketer would have hesitated to play on.'[47] So, whilst in Pietermaritzburg at the time of the England rebel tour of 1981, SACB had a league of 17 teams playing on four wickets: 'One is turf with the expected accompanying facilities, the other three are matting with no facilities whatsoever. The rival "official league" with 13 teams enjoy municipal funding for four turf wickets.'[48]

Amid such conditions, there was no shortage of funds for overseas cricketers who were prepared to break the international boycott against South Africa. More than 600 people filled a banqueting room to meet the rebel Australians in 1985. The scene resembled something from a royal pageant. The room was lit by 3,220 chandeliers and served by 130 waitresses, with a further 200 staff behind the scenes.[49] A SACB spokesman commented that 'they will be getting practically a black man's lifetime earnings in two years', and added that 'there is so much malnutrition that these earnings alone could feed thousands who are in need.'[50]

Poverty

A number of surveys showed that South Africa, a country in which white living standards matched those of any in the West, suffered from both widespread relative and absolute poverty. In 1939, for instance, a study claimed that 52 per cent of coloured, 48 per cent of African and 6 per cent of white families lived in a state of poverty. Poverty was defined as living on the bare means of subsistence, 'the minimum income, barring sickness or any other exigencies, on which physical efficiency can be maintained, assuming the wisest expenditure of available income.' It provided for food, clothing and basic lighting and fuel. It did not, though, include funds for medicine, education or amusements such as sport.[51] O.P. Horwood, professor of Economics at Natal University, informed the South African Institute of Race Relations in 1958 that the minimum cost of living for an African family of five was £20 a month. Only 9 per cent of individual workers earned more than £15.[52]

The causes of this poverty and the fact that it was almost entirely centred on the black population were the reasons opponents of the government charged it with the responsibility for maintaining an abnormal society. Such abuse did not, of course, originate with the establishment of apartheid. In 1896, mining companies colluded to reduce black wages in their industry. A ceiling was placed on remuneration rates and fines imposed for those who broke them. At a shareholders meeting in 1899 it was declared that: 'It is preposterous to pay a Kaffir the present wages. He would be quite as well satisfied – in fact he would work longer – if you gave him half the amount. His wages are altogether disproportionate to his requirements.'[53] This attitude shaped capitalist approaches to wages for black employees and, unsurprisingly, low incomes became the major cause of poverty in urban areas.

South Africa was not the only country from which historians can draw examples of the extreme exploitation of labour. However, it must rank as one of the few to legally impose substantial differentials based on the criteria of race onto employers. In manufacturing, the white-to-black wage ratio throughout the first 90 years of the twentieth century was roughly 5:1. In mining the figure averaged 14:1, with a peak of 20:1 in the early 1970s.[54] The state sector, in accordance with the 'civilised labour' policy, paid whites more than blacks for the same job. The government argued that, since black doctors, for example, pay fewer taxes and have less expensive training, it is logical that they should receive lower salaries.[55] Incomes in the 'homelands' were about 40 per cent less than the African average wage, thus forcing African workers into the migrant labour system in order to maintain a very basic subsistence.

These low incomes, exacerbated by high unemployment, had significant multiplier effects on the welfare of the recipients. Whilst the white population enjoyed an infant mortality rate that was below that of the United Kingdom, a report in the *Sunday Tribune* noted that in 1976 three African children were dying of malnutrition every hour in South Africa. As Archer and Bouillon noted, 'Between 15,000 and 30,000 die every year of malnutrition, without counting the diseases like tuberculosis which it encourages.'[56] In 1973, African children were getting much the same amount of food as those in other parts of Africa and considerably less than children in orphanages in Vietnam.[57] Even as late as 1989, Wilson and Ramphele stated in *Uprooting Poverty*, 'two million children are growing up stunted for lack of sufficient calories in one of the few countries in the world that exports food'.[58] South Africa was two countries – one prosperous, healthy and white, the other in poverty, low paid or unemployed, and black.

Against this backdrop, cricket seemed rather insignificant. It well suited the perpetuators of these inequalities to argue that politics should be kept out of sport and that one should 'play up and play the game' rather than seek political solutions to worsening problems. Hassan Howa, though, considered that it would be irresponsible of him not to consider the wider picture, that multiracial cricket could not take place in a racially segregated society: '... the child doesn't get the right food, he doesn't get the right education. If he does, his father has to starve to pay for his fees. He can hardly afford a pair of shoes to go to school, never mind cricket shoes.' [59] When you reflect that the major causes for African mortality were diseases related to low socio-economic and poor environmental factors – and that the principal causes of disease among whites related to lifestyle – 'it is not a question of what sport black children play, rather it is a wonder that they play sport at all.'[60]

Conclusion

The data given above indicates the disadvantageous social and economic position of black to white South Africans. It would be difficult to maintain that the development of cricket in the black communities would not be handicapped by such inequalities. Indeed, the whole style and standard of black cricket was dictated by circumstance. Most matches could only last a day because that was all that was available free from work. Batting, there-fore, was inevitably adventurous, especially when coupled with the dangers of 'playing safe' on such poor pitches. Those still in doubt should consider how the lack of cricket in schools and poor pitches have been held to blame for England's recent demise.[61] Ronnie Pillay and Khaya Majola, top black cricketers with the non-racial SACB, told Peter Hain how cricket was dying through causes other than sporting: 'They explained that they could not afford the plane fares to travel hundreds of miles to away matches in towns like Johannesburg, with the result that a three-day match turned into a five-day excursion by road – and their players could not get the time off work as white cricketers did.'[62] Furthermore, it was not possible for the non-racial game to make similar progress to its white counterpart because of 'the hopelessly inadequate facilities for black cricketers.'[63] Slowly, even officials in SACU recognised this:

> We drew up a new constitution in 1976 and told the world our cricket was non-racial but, in reality, that was all nonsense. There was still no effective structure in which a black boy from, say, Rocklands (Bloemfontein), could develop his cricket. Without coaching, facilities or encouragement, how could he? A piece of paper didn't help him very much.[64]

In the modern age, economics still determines sporting opportunity. Blacks have not broken into the national or provincial teams as expected. Ali Bacher, the 'godfather' of the contemporary game, admitted in 1992 that South Africa 'cannot pretend to have merit selection until there are equal opportunities to progress in the game ... [Township children] still feel like orphans because they cannot reciprocate on a home-and-away basis, which is something that lies at the very heart of cricket.'[65]

A policy statement by SACOS pointed out that 'there is an inter-dependence between a society and its sporting system. Sport is a by-product of society. It reflects the spiritual wealth of a society. Or it reflects its political decay.'[66] Thus, any changes by the apartheid regime made to accommodate sporting participation at international level cannot be viewed in isolation from the conditions that drew criticism of South Africa. Can the regime credibly claim that its sporting structures were 'multiracial' when the life chances of its inhabitants were determined by the colour of their skin?

Opponents to racial rule were subject to state intimidation. Penalties such as banning, fines and beatings were handed out to those who protested peacefully. They were placed under surveillance and risked losing their jobs and being forcibly removed to the 'homelands'. This aggressive terror was accompanied by an ideological campaign that used propaganda and censorship to ensure that the government's views were the predominant ones. Institutionalised separation further made it difficult for black and white to establish political and social relationships.

In such societies, one also has to assess the order of relevance of sports. Whilst we have examined the qualities and potential for the exploitation of sports, when a community has no school books and poor or little sanitary conditions, housing and health care, when it lives in fear of 'visits in the night', sports take a low priority. The curfews installed by the State of Emergency Acts ensured that practice and competition was difficult in the evenings. The apartheid philosophy was built upon a hierarchical racial structure where all whites were above all blacks. No black could become the equal of a white. Because of this, sport was a victim of a political system:

> It is the greater morality that transcends the sports struggle that dictates that, for as long as the stifled sobs and tear-stained cheeks of our children haunt the darkness of dejected corners in dignified pride, for so long must those who express a commitment to the cause of non-racialism, in sports and society, refuse to succumb to cosmetic changes. The sum total of South African society clearly underlines the truth that South Africa's sports structure has not changed. Only the nuances have. Can any acceptance of it be compatible with the cause we espouse?[67]

This was no normal society. Sport has a reputation for being egalitarian, apolitical and able to transcend the social order. In South Africa, the political system frustrated this and so led to the politicisation of sport.

Hassan Howa argued that 'For true merit selection everyone has to be given the same opportunities to develop his latent talent. This cannot happen in South African society ...'[68] It fell to international pressure, to those who detested such abnormalities, to assist in its demise.

7

Isolating the Disease: International Politics and the Arguments for Sanctions against South Africa

In philosophy, an extrinsic force is supposed to motivate moral agents to adhere to the social norm and perform their conscientious duties. Sanctions are usually invoked against those who stray from the lines of acceptability. They are a means of ensuring some basis of order. In the social sciences, sanctions assume a similar function, only on a larger scale – usually being a measure taken by any number of states to enforce international law or to demonstrate opposition to particular regimes and their practices. Sanctions are defined as the denial of customary interactions (strategic, economic or social). They are intended, as a punishment for wrong actions, to promote reform in the target state. The imposition of sanctions may well suggest further measures, and would almost certainly involve their lifting if the target satisfies certain requirements.

The previous chapters have highlighted how a political ideology steeped in notions of racial superiority affected areas of life normally considered beyond the realm of the political scientist. In an era that was coming to terms with the destructiveness of world war and the demise of colonialism, it appeared inconceivable that South Africa should be attached to a political theory that had been not only rejected but also disproved. South Africa, then, stood outside the bounds of acceptability. The question was what would the international community do about it?

One of the most psychologically important sanctions the international community placed on South Africa was the sporting boycott. Through ostracising the Republic, the international community was serving notice that if South Africa hoped to engage in an act as inconsequential as a game, it had to mend its ways. This chapter explores the debate around the sporting boycott. It considers its role within the wider campaign for economic sanctions, assesses the merits and rationales of those arguing for and against measures and offers a further insight into the nature of power in a society.

The international campaign against racial cricket

South Africa was valued as an important trading partner with the white Commonwealth. The UK was by far its most important overseas investor, and South Africa offered British investors and manufacturers 'the prospect of good profits, low taxation, a long record of industrial peace and political and economic stability and, above all, security from expropriation'.[1] Although never integrated formally into Western defence structures, South Africa was considered a vital member of the cold war alliance against the influence of the Soviet Union. So, when in 1957, the United Nations, by 55 votes to 5, urged Pretoria to 'reconsider its position [on apartheid] and revise its policies in the light of its obligations and responsibilities under the [UN] Charter', the United Kingdom and Australia were amongst those who voted against (New Zealand abstained).[2] Similarly, in 1963, when the Security Council called upon all states to 'cease forthwith the sale and shipment of arms, ammunition of all types, and military vehicles to South Africa' there were only two abstentions – Britain and France.[3] A failure to achieve results through formal diplomatic channels forced the opposition to white rule to seek alternative methods of applying pressures against the regime.

A bus boycott in South Africa in 1957 provided evidence of the tactical strength that could be mustered and the economic harm that could be inflicted by resistance. In the following year the British urban council of Longbenton placed a ban on all South African goods and the apartheid sports policy was openly condemned by prominent sportsmen including Danny Blanchflower, Johnny Haynes, Jimmy Hill, Stanley Matthews, Don Revie, David Sheppard and M.J.K. Smith. An editorial in the *Times* accused South Africa of turning 'its back on the twentieth century'.[4] The Indian government further established the precedent for intervening in another state's sporting matters when it called on the Frank Worrell-led West Indian team to cancel a visit to the Union. Such unorthodox intervention appeared to be firmly established on the political agenda. Following the Sharpeville massacre, leading Maoris called on the New Zealand rugby board to reconsider its relationship with South Africa.[5]

Protesters first gathered in England to greet the 1960 tourists who arrived in the wake of Sharpeville. The Springboks were met with protests at a number of the grounds where they appeared. The 'Campaign Against Discrimination in Sports' charged the South African government with introducing politics into sport. The Revd David Sheppard announced that he would not play against the South Africans and the Revd Nicholas Stacey refused to preach the 'Sportsmen's Service' before the Edgbaston Test. Both the Welsh Council of Labour and the Welsh National Union of Mineworkers called on Glamorgan to cancel their match against the Springboks.[6] The MCC countered that it was 'wholly unjustifiable to identify members of the South African cricket team with political issues.'[7] John Arlott noted that most cricketers and a substantial body of non-cricketers agreed with this viewpoint. He also recorded the fact that this was the first tour to make a financial loss since 1912.[8] In 1963–64 the South African tourists to Australia met protests due to the exclusion of Basil D'Oliveira from the side.[9] The Springbok captain actually met with Prime Minister Verwoerd to discuss how he would handle questions whilst in Australia. On the New Zealand leg of the tour the wicket at Wellington was damaged by anti-apartheid protesters before the first Test match. In both countries attendances were down. Protests were once again mounted against the visiting South Africans to England in 1965. Demonstrations on this tour were both larger and better organised than anything previous. Individual players were also singled out for retribution by governments of countries that South Africa refused to play against. In 1962 T.L. Goddard, R.A.A. McLean and N.A.T. Adcock were refused permission to compete as part of a Commonwealth side in Pakistan.[10]

Whilst these campaigns succeeded in keeping the South Africa issue in the headlines, they were confined to small numbers and had little actual impact in either preventing play or in changing attitudes among the white cricket authorities. However, the refusal of the South African government in 1968 to allow Basil D'Oliveira to represent England in their country transformed the whole debate. The arguments, presented in the previous three chapters, of the relationship between politics and sport were overridden by the blatant abuse of a head of state determining the composition of a visiting sports team. This one aspect enabled South Africa's opponents not only to condemn the racism of their foe but it also allowed them the opportunity to press for a thorough scrutiny of racial sport. The tour was cancelled, and, with one exception (the Springbok visit to Australia in 1969–70), the international cricketing fraternity turned its back on one of its founding members, refusing to play them until cricket was played and teams selected on a multiracial basis.

A combination of domestic extra-parliamentary activity, international government condemnation and black cricketing pressure ensured that there would be no route back for apartheid cricket. Such actors, and the methods that they pursued, alarmed not only the white cricketing establishment but conservative and liberal ideologues as well – who had maintained that politics should remain distanced from sport. Their allegiance to this cause ensured that the debate over the State's domain would be fought on ideological grounds.

The philosophy of boycott

Sport in South Africa has been exploited for political ends since its inception by the armed forces of Her Majesty's government in the early nineteenth century. It can be of little surprise, then, given the evidence presented in the previous chapters, that it became embroiled in the unfolding political drama of apartheid South Africa. Discontent with racial sport was initially expressed during international contests by supporting the opposition.[11] When Neil Harvey scored 151 not out at Durban in 1950 every shot was cheered by the black spectators, one of whom was Nelson Mandela.[12] Annoying as this may be, it was unlikely to threaten the structure of racial sport.

Once the opposition to racial sport became organised, though, a more direct assault on the very vestiges of apartheid sport could be made. Initially the black sporting organisations were concerned with being treated as equals with their white counterparts in multiracial sides. Once their requests for membership of international federations were rejected, the black bodies demanded that white sports be isolated. As a tactic it was roundly condemned by both white and international sporting organisations. On reflection, it is difficult to imagine what else the opposition could have done. If anything, they were pushed and intimidated into a cul-de-sac – from which they had to clutch at the faintest hope of 'justice'. Sport, so central to the psyche of white South Africa, became the hope that a better future not only could be achieved but that it was worth fighting for.

The black cricketing organisation, SACBOC, charged the white SACA with contravening a basic tenet of sporting philosophy, namely the non-racial principle that imbues the Olympic Charter, and applied directly for membership to the ICC. There were, however, a number of difficulties with this tactic. South Africa had been a founding member of the ICC, an organ-isation whose constitution forbade the recognition of more than one organisation from each country. SACA did not purport to be white-only, despite the fact it had no black affiliates and none of its constituent unions admitted black clubs. Furthermore, as apartheid prevented the playing of mixed sport in South Africa, the black organisations could not claim to be multiracial. The white federations denied that they supported apartheid, but that they had to respect the laws of their country; the government countered that the sports bodies were loyal to the tradition of separate development and that they would defend this right. Less convincingly, it was also argued that players were chosen on merit and that there were no blacks sufficiently well qualified to represent South Africa.

By challenging racial sport, bodies such as SACBOC became immersed in the whole campaign against apartheid. Their case, being directly related to the issues of distribution of resources and notions of sovereignty and power, became political. Furthermore, they were in a position to wound the all-abrasive and encroaching apartheid state. The tactic of ostracism against racial sport became somewhat inevitable given the limited number of channels through which black South Africans could express their discontent. The United Party, the official opposition, accepted the doctrine of 'white leadership' – only differing over details of how to secure this.[13] Its leader, de Villiers Graaff, stated that: 'When we get into power again there will also be discrimination.'[14] It was the same leader of the opposition who persuaded Verwoerd not to resign following Sharpeville, offering him his party's full support for firm measures to restore order.[15] The 1953 Criminal Laws Amendment Act and the 1953 Public Safety Act outlawed publications that were even slightly hostile to the regime. Constitutional trade unionism was prohibited by the 1953 Native Labour (Settlement of Disputes) Act, which prohibited strikes by African workers. Peter Brown, the chairman of the

South African Liberal Party, argued that boycotts were a legitimate weapon because the government's behaviour criminalised all other peaceful tactics.[16] Thus, the only option lay in extra-parliamentary activity. Similarly, in sport, it was the international campaigns against South Africa that raised the profiles of black sports organisations. Only an appreciation of this reality can allow an appraisal of the use of sport for political ends.

The sports boycott was a component of a wider strategy to isolate South Africa economically and culturally. The other forces for change included labour organisations and mobilisation in the communities and via the liberation movements. Mark Orkin argues that none of these separately had the power to displace the regime, but in unity they could exert pressure on an ailing economy.[17] It was anticipated that this would contribute to securing peaceful change in the Republic. The role of the boycott was to undermine white morale and keep the question of racial rule on the international agenda. Sport created shared values and identities. By reflecting racist structures, sport, in its own way, legitimised them, rewarding them with a 'common-sense' status. The ambition of the boycott was to address issues in a way that delegitimised particular policies. The Johannesburg *Sunday Times* recognised that 'the main target of attack is the racial policy of South Africa or, to put it more precisely, the racial policy of the Nationalist Party.'[18] This may explain why resources were concentrated on team, rather than individual, sports. A South African writer argued that the sport boycott 'deeply offends South Africans. Success at sport has been seen throughout history and throughout the world as a matter of national honour, indicating as it does a degree of physical superiority, excellence in training and tactics, and a measure of diligence and courage.'[19]

By disrupting everyday activity the boycott challenged the normative basis of apartheid. Sanctions work by ensuring that such arguments are heard and their psychological effects ran deep. Donald Woods believed that Dr Koornhof 'felt that while South Africa remained excluded from international sport this constituted a political pressure-point against the whole Afrikaner nationalist regime and the main body of political apartheid.'[20] Tony Greig wrote that 'The South African people live for sport and with sport to a degree that I have not seen equalled in any other country in the world. They will tolerate a good many shortages and inconveniences in other spheres, but, if their sport is affected, they will want to know why.'[21] To many Afrikaners, the boycott confirmed their sense of persecution, and placed a further hurdle in their path to righteousness.[22]

Such high-profile campaigns provided visibility for the anti-apartheid movement, increasing global awareness of racial segregation and raising the issue of further measures. If South Africa violated norms in the 'trivial' world of sport, then surely it deserved punishment in political and economic areas too. It is claimed that British business, for example, for so long the leading source of trade and investment in South Africa, found itself forced to reconsider its attitude to investment in the Republic following the publicity surrounding the abandoned 1970 tour to England. In August the construction firm Wates Ltd declined a contract in South Africa on moral grounds. The director of Bovis Holdings, another construction company, argued: 'Speaking personally, I've always taken the view that the City putting an embargo on South Africa is the only way, putting aside bombs, of changing the system.'[23]

Finally, a boycott of sport was relatively easier, compared with alternative options, to enforce. Schalk Pienaar pointed out in *Rapport* in 1971 that 'the sports boycott is the only one that is succeeding … Sports is a cheap way of boycotting. It is "expendable".'[24] Sport, in other words, was less likely to arouse the resistance of powerful interests. Tertius Myburgh argued in the *Sunday Times* (Johannesburg): 'for many leaders of overseas governments sports boycotts are really quite handy lightning conductors; a politically useful, but inexpensive way to demonstrate their disapproval of apartheid without actually giving up something truly valuable like trade'.[25] It also proved to be a morale booster to a people who rarely tasted political victory. Success was more likely to derive from challenging racial sports structures than by taking on the might of the military or international capital.

Criticisms

The anti-apartheid campaigners were challenged on the philosophical preferences for focusing on both South Africa and cricket. Why single out South Africa and not confront oppressive regimes such as Greece and Spain? There were more dictatorial countries in the world. Politically, it had traditionally been the United Kingdom's position not to interfere in the affairs of another sovereign state.[26] Christopher Martin-Jenkins noted prejudice in India, Pakistan and Guyana and also noted that 'cricketers from these countries have cheerfully played with and against South Africans in England.'[27] The Soviet Union was routinely proposed for comparison: 'For every Biko, there was a Sakharov and a Solzhenitsyn in Russia. We didn't want to penalise Russian sportsmen for the policies of their government, so why should our sports be subject to isolation for a political policy we didn't support?'[28]

However, by arguing that all teams should be selected on merit, the anti-apartheid campaigners were not making a commitment to boycotting all countries whose 'policies' one may disapprove of. If that were so, there would be little international sport. Avery Brundage, president of the International Olympic Committee, once remarked 'if participation in sport is to be stopped every time the laws of humanity are violated, there will never be any international contests.'[29] Inequalities do indeed exist in all societies. What distinguished South Africa, though, was that its inequalities were not merely economic, but racial. Allister Sparks argues that a world post-war consensus found any public declaration of racism objectionable.[30] The Soviet Union did not have in statute a series of laws that promoted racial segregation:

In any other oppressive country, and under any other oppressive system, sportsmen have a choice, albeit a limited one: they can decide whether or not they are going to oppose the particular regime; they can change their politics. In South Africa, the black man cannot change the colour of his skin: he has no choice.[31]

Race, moreover, was becoming a serious international political issue in the 1970s. 'Powellism', for example, was influential within the Conservative Party, and far-right political organisations such as the National Front were gaining popularity as Britain headed toward economic difficulty.

It was felt that by using the Soviet Union as a counter-example to South Africa those who defended the apartheid state were merely engaging in the cold war rhetoric of the day. This was, in itself, a legitimate political statement, but then to condemn those who campaigned for isolation because politics was mixed with sport left the apologists open to the charge of double-standards. As for Martin-Jenkins' other points, despite its widespread influence and effect, the caste system was actually outlawed in India. More importantly, those Pakistani, Indian and Guyanese cricketers who competed with South Africans in the English County Championship could not engage in Test matches against the Springboks because the South African government refused to allow it – until isolation.

Christopher Martin-Jenkins complained of the injustice of singling out sport – and especially cricket – for attention by isolationists. He pointed out that the economic relationship between the West and South Africa did far more to sustain apartheid than sporting links ever could.[32] Sporting authorities were being called on to commit themselves to an approach that was ignored by political and economic elites throughout the world. Businessmen and traders were able to conduct their affairs and move freely within South Africa without having to contribute to racial integration. Cricketers who coached and played in the English winters at least became involved in the communities, where perhaps they could exchange liberal values and ideas towards race.

It was further argued that focusing on cricket was also aiming at the wrong party. It was pointed out that it was the national pastime of the English speakers. The Afrikaners played rugby, they formed the bedrock of Nationalist support – therefore, to cause the maximum impact, rugby should be singled out. Opponents viewed the issue differently.[33]

Is it a coincidence that this, the most serious and sustained argument there has ever been about sport, certainly in Britain and probably in the world, concerned cricket? What was at stake, as it so often has been in arguments about cricket, was what cricket symbolised to those involved – more than a game, more a way of life. And is it a coincidence that the school of thought that exalts cricket as a symbol of true and lasting values has so often aligned itself with things that are manifestly 'not cricket'? Apartheid is one. It seems a feeble defence, when opponents of this savage and selfish injustice point it out, for supporters or 'neutrals' to argue that cricket is, after all, only a game and that politics has no place in sport.

Cricket-lovers from *Tom Brown's Schooldays* on have invested the game with profound political and social significance. It has been an emblem of the British way of life.[34]

An Athlone schoolboy told Bob Woolmer that 'If you have a cause to fight, then you must give up some luxuries, and cricket is a luxury.'[35]

Could anyone be absolved from the sin that was apartheid? The English-speaking South Africans found it far easier to accept the status quo – the policy of 'baasskap' – than to advocate a policy of change that would have meant, in reality, moves towards equality.[36] By the 1980s English-speakers were increasingly supporting the Nationalists; even before then, the English-speaking United Party's racial philosophy was little different.

The pro-business lobby argued that economic relations could not be subject to the same restrictions as cultural dealings. The West relied on South Africa for a number of industrial and strategic minerals, for which the only alternative was the Soviet Union. South Africa is also strategically important to the West because it commands the sea route between the Atlantic and Indian oceans, which is important for the supply of oil.

In view of this, the question has to be asked as to whether the focus on sporting sanctions was a smokescreen to protect the continuing trade relations between South Africa and countries that were prepared to isolate her on the sporting field? Was it not 'satisfying theatre', enabling punishment of an offender's behaviour without upsetting the general equilibrium?[37]

It allowed world leaders to appear pious in their condemnation of racial discrimination whilst at the same time providing the very lifeline that maintained an economic system created and sustained by the very policies of segregation that they claimed to detest. Sportsmen, moreover, have higher profiles than businessmen and so concentrating on them may have had immediate short-term benefits.

Indeed, apartheid would surely have been jettisoned earlier had it not been for the economic support it received from global capitalism. Foreign capital was crucial to South Africa's economic development because of the skills and technology that accompanied it. In computers, electronics, chemicals and even nuclear energy this technological 'bridge-building' linked South Africa with the latest Western trends.[38] Economic investment also aided political rule in that it highlighted to the resistance groups that powerful economic interests would not permit the stability of minority rule to be destabilised. This, in essence, is the nature of the beast. Politics is dictated by economics. Western economic sanctions were only applied once it became apparent that this would be in capitalism's best interests. Apartheid had to be attacked through whatever means rather than on an all or nothing basis and sporting isolation proved effective – as even its critics came to acknowledge.

Countering the boycott

Prime Minister Vorster painted a picture of a South Africa threatened by communism on three fronts: the international sports boycott, the permissive society and the threat to the strategic Cape sea route.[39] To the ruling elite in South Africa the idea of business as usual was fundamental to the morale of the Republic. International sport, being a central component of the nation's psyche, provided an indicator by which the government could measure its success on the world stage. The Springbok Peter Kirsten summed up its relevance: 'There is always that ardent wish – merely to take part in the contest of country versus country to show where one's identity lies.'[40] 'Identity', of course, was a fundamental political issue in South Africa. Enormous prestige was showered on those prepared to defy the boycott. At Johannesburg, for instance, the 1970 All Blacks were greeted by more than 3,000 supporters. They were received, in the words of one newspaper editorial, 'not only as sportsmen but as envoys from a part of the world that has not altogether deserted us.'[41] Another example is the ICC's invitation to South Africa in 1980 to submit a written report on progress towards racial integration of cricket, which made front-page news.[42]

Furthermore, third parties were encouraged to advance Pretoria's cause. The South Africa Foundation was established by industrialists 'to promote international understanding of South Africa, her achievements, her problems and her potential, and by doing so to advance the welfare of all her peoples.'[43] The remit of the Committee for Fairness in Sport was to perform a similar role for sport. Among its membership was businessman Louis Luyt (a friend of Dr Koornhof), the golfer Gary Player, Wilf Isaacs and the president of the South African Breweries, Dick Goss. Activities included placing advertisements in newspapers all over the world and organising extraordinary tours. The Muldergate scandal in 1978 exposed that $73 million was made available from the South African Department of Information to persuade the Western media and businessmen to support South Africa. Gary Player alone was provided with $30,000 to invite directors of major companies (Chrysler, Ford, Boeing and the Bank of America) to play golf with him in an attempt to weaken the American campaign against investments in South Africa. In Britain, Freedom in Sport (FIS) was founded to promote links with South Africa 'in the midst of all this massive political interference in sport throughout the world ...'[44]

Denied official international competition, the cricket authorities attempted to provide contests with a cast of known cricketers – in any possible format. The Datsun Double-Wicket Competition allowed the South African public to see blacks and whites competing together. The Indian, Pakistan and West Indies Boards of Control had all refused permission for any of their players to participate, but – by defying their authorities – Younis Ahmed, Saeed Ahmed, Bill Ibadullah, John Shepherd, Mohammad Ilyas and Geoff Greenidge became the first cricketing 'rebels'. In 1974, cricketers from this competition formed the International Wanderers and played against Transvaal before touring Rhodesia. Such tours provided the cricketing authorities with acclaim from prestigious players such as Greg Chappell and the tennis star Arthur Ashe, who urged the sporting world to resume links with South Africa.[45] Derrick Robins, the one-time Warwickshire amateur, organised tours of cricketing professionals to South Africa and Rhodesia. These exhibitions were blessed by the South African regime, who guaranteed permission for them to play against black teams, and by the English authorities, who recognised the games as first class. Younis Ahmed and John Shepherd became the first black cricketers to be included in a touring side to the Republic when they were recruited for the Derrick Robins side. Their game against a South African team in October 1973 was the first match between a black side and 'white' tourists since 1892.

Bridge-building

Arguments for maintaining cricketing relations with South Africa ranged from the economic to expressions of concern for the welfare of the black population. If they had anything in common it was an intense dislike of political methods to disrupt the international sporting calendar.

Foremost, though, it was argued that sports apartheid could not be blamed on the sporting bodies as it was a direct consequence of government regulation. Furthermore, the argument continued, only through direct contact such as that through sport will South Africa be forced to change its policies. In this way, engaging in competition with racial sport actually undermined apartheid. This really was the crux of the 'bridge-building' argument. S.C. Griffith, secretary of the Cricket Council, stated in 1970 'that more good is achieved by maintaining sporting links with South Africa than by cutting them off altogether'.[46] John Woodcock, in his 'Notes by the Editor' in the 1982 *Wisden*, commented that 'When it comes to overturning racial prejudice cricketers believe that the best contribution they can make is to compete together, whether in the same team or on opposite sides.'[47] Thus, they believed that by participating with South Africa they were showing the regime the merits of a liberal society. Kim Hughes, the captain of the 1985 and 1986 Australian rebel tourists, maintained that: 'Through sport, barriers are broken. Barriers are built through politics and religion. Sport is one vehicle through which people of all races can come together.' Far greater progress had been made through sport, he continued, than any other aspect of the South African society since the early 1970s.[48] South African cricket should be rewarded for such steps. The continuance of links, therefore, will only hasten the moment that South Africa advances back into 'civilised' society.

Critics of this argument point out that the situation is far more complex. Black sports, as shown in the previous chapter, were not being engaged on a level playing field. White newspapers did not promote or record details of black cricket. Compare Hughes' thoughts with the official stance of the South African government:

> Sport is a wonderful catalyst which brings peoples of various international convictions together and makes them forget their differences in the challenge of the sport. We must not relegate sport to an insignificant component of our international counter-offensive, but South Africa should rather use the platform that sport offers in order to build bridges between nations.[49]

Gordon Ross asked whether President Nixon would change his policies in Vietnam if America engaged in sporting contest with them? 'Of course not.'[50] Politics does not work like that.

The main contention, however, is that the white bodies themselves did little to advance multiracial sport. The *Post* (Natal) berated the silent compliance of white sportsmen and their organisations:

> South Africa's chances ... are not helped by the deafening silence of white sportsmen. White sportsmen should say clearly that, while they have to keep the laws of the land, they are against these laws.
> South Africa is condemned by its own mouth – a tight-lipped mouth that, it seems, only opens to condemn other nations for bringing politics into sports and never raises a voice against the cause of the trouble – apartheid.[51]

Given the fact that white teams had enjoyed regular competition with South Africa before 1968, it is difficult to argue that sporting contact helped to break down apartheid. Since liberalisation was largely a phenomenon of the 1970s and 1980s, it is evident that the boycott was a more effective weapon. The denial of international sport, then, was a means of generating the discontent of white South Africans against their government.

A more sophisticated argument attacked the whole philosophical basis of sanctions. Liberals such as Merle Lipton claimed that the reforms of the 1970s were the product not of internal or external pressures but of the dynamics of economic growth. Sanctions and boycotts are therefore counter-productive because they threaten growth rates, which, in turn, hinder the reform process. There was not one white political party, it should be noted, that supported South Africa's isolation from sport. Michael Ellis of the Progressive Federal Party argued in 1989 that the period of isolation had been extended far too long. He argued that sports' capabilities to break down barriers within the Republic would be extended if international competition was permitted. Continued isolation not only added to the despair of the white community but left it of the opinion that whatever they did would not be enough, and therefore why bother? Worse, it was argued by Bill Hicks of the UK Sports Council among others, that the boycott actually strengthened the hand of those opposed to reform.[52] R.A. Pape argued that sanctions were rarely successful because their costs can be passed on to weaker sections in society whilst bolstering nationalism.[53] This is evident, for example, in Iraq, Cuba and Libya, where support for the regimes has appeared strong. Ellis concluded that the rise of Conservative Party support in South Africa was in part due to these very attitudes.[54]

The bridge-building argument, thus, was nothing less than a political counter to the isolationists. As an ideology, though, it was incoherent compared to the advocacy of sanctions, being a patchwork of vested interests. For example, Bruce Francis, the Australian rebel-tour organiser, paid $9,000 to place a full-page advertisement in *The Australian* (22 July 1985) countering the 'misinformation ... dishonesty and ... half-truths' which appeared in the Eminent Persons Group's report into conditions in South Africa.[55] His concerns lay beyond mere sport, thereby contradicting earlier arguments about distancing one from the other. Similarly, in 1976, Greg Chappell, in a call to open up relations with the Republic, stated that 'The South African government is relaxing its restrictions in many ways ... They are making concessions.'[56] Was this not an explicitly political justification? Chapter 4 concluded that the reforms of the 1970s and 1980s were indeed induced by economic pressures (including sanctions), but they were designed to modernise and strengthen racial rule.

The sudden interest in the well-being of black South Africans also invoked cries of cynicism. Chris de Broglio pointed out that:

> After eighty years of sports relations with white South Africa it is hard to believe that the people who support these relations are at all concerned with the fate of black South African sportsmen. The non-whites have been systematically boycotted for all that time so cannot be any worse off.[57]

It was difficult to envisage who exactly in the black population would suffer because of sanctions. Besides, the ANC, PAC and the UDF, unequivocal representatives of the black populace, all supported comprehensive and mandatory economic and cultural sanctions. The Black Renaissance Convention, representing black church, educational, cultural, trade union and professional organisations, resolved in 1976 'that legalised racism in South Africa is a threat to world peace'. It called on 'all the countries of the world to withdraw cultural, educational, economic, sporting, manpower and military support to the existing racist government and all its racist institutions.'[58] ANC leader Oliver Tambo considered sanctions to be 'the most important' weapon in the struggle: 'That is the trump card with which we can mobilise international opinion and pull governments over to our side.'[59] A CASE survey of black attitudes in 1987 found that only 14 per cent of respondents were opposed to sanctions, 52 per cent favoured conditional sanctions (until the government meets certain conditions) and 29 per cent supported unconditional sanctions to force the government to surrender power.[60]

The sporting boycott was condemned by the bridge-builders because it amounted to interference in South Africa's domestic affairs by foreign powers and so contravened the liberal 'realist' tradition of international relations. A government was being condemned and sanctions imposed upon it for its domestic policies. It should be for the people of South Africa to work out their own destiny, free from outside interference. Sir Garfield Barwick, the Australian attorney general and acting minister for external affairs stated in 1960 that 'the time when you need a comrade is not when you are dead right it is when you may be wrong.'[61]

Criticism of this stance is to be found in an examination of the virtues of liberal political philosophy. The question of political sovereignty in the western liberal tradition stems from the writings of the English philosopher John Locke. Locke argued that men and women are moral beings, able to choose the correct law in accordance with reason. In this 'natural state' each has the right to punish disobedience to this 'moral law'. This system of rule proves inefficient and so people decide to make a compact with each other, out of which emerges a central government given the authority to keep peace and enforce the law. Black South Africans were not recognised as citizens of the state and as such were not signatories to the social contract from which derives the existence of government. They had the right, therefore, under the moral law to appeal to external assistance.

For Robert Wolff all the arguments for maintaining or not maintaining links – political, economic or cultural – with South Africa were somewhat inappropriate. His starting position was where does the individual stand in the anti-apartheid struggle?[62] Perhaps this refrain touches on the nub of the argument. Were the bridge-builders concerned solely with sport or was this part of a wider agenda, a world-view (that is, conservatism) for which they were prepared to use cricket as a propagator? Conversely, opponents of South Africa felt justified in acting outside of the constraints of liberal philosophy. Socialists, for example, argue from an internationalist perspective, claiming that an injury to one is an injury to all. Emphasis on solidarity ensures an obligation to intervene wherever there is injustice.

What appeared to concern cricket commentators more than any other issue was the threat of banning players who had or intended to ply their trade in South Africa. Ian Chappell, the then captain of Australia, had said that South Africa would be back in Test cricket if the decision were left to the players.[63] They were, then, to be the actual labourers of bridge-building. To threaten their livelihood struck at the conscience of liberal philosophy: '... No-one should seriously suggest they [English cricketers] should be deprived of their right to go there [South Africa] if they wished to do so. Indeed, this would be a direct contravention of English law, [and] the liberty of the individual.[64] Mike Brearley, an outspoken critic of apartheid, could not countenance such actions:

> In my view our Board were right to warn English cricketers that flirting with South Africa may put international cricket at risk. But I doubt whether, even if they wished to, they could go further, and I also doubt whether they should. It is a bulwark of an open society that people should be allowed, where possible, to do as they wish. They can be dissuaded, even disapproved of, but not prevented.[65]

Christopher Martin-Jenkins pointed out the inconsistencies of the Indian and Caribbean governments banning English players who had been to South Africa from touring in their territories whilst allowing their own cricketers to come to England to partake in the County Championship against South Africans.[66]

This question of individual liberty, more than any other, focused the energies of those who decried the involvement of politics with sport. It struck at the heart of the issue as to what governments could and should concern themselves with. Sport was certainly considered a 'no-go area'. This was not just the opinion of certain cricket correspondents but of the white Commonwealth regimes. Jack Marshall, the Conservative opposition leader, condemned the New Zealand government for instructing the Rugby Union to withdraw its invitation to an all-white Springbok team to tour in 1973, calling it a denial of democracy.[67] Neil Macfarlane, British minister for sport 1981–85, outlined that 'The British government does not stand in the way of individuals going to play sport anywhere and it would be a sorry day that saw us impounding passports and using immigration controls – individuals with British passports have the right to come and go as they please.'[68] Indeed, according to Margaret Thatcher, the prime minister, if the government were to ban sportsmen and women visiting any country, then 'we would no longer be a free country'.[69]

Critics of the bridge-building argument point out that the cricket correspondents missed the point. What they wanted to avoid was giving any credence to the regime in Pretoria. Sport was exploited in order to promote the apartheid state and present to the international community an image of normality and respectability. James Roxburgh, the Australian rugby union player, recalled how during the 1969 tour of South Africa that 'the local mayor would remark how South Africa and Australia were two great countries with so much in common, and how alike our ideas and policies were.'[70] The organisation of rebel tours – with teams representing England,

Australia or the West Indies – was a source of invaluable propaganda for Pretoria. Individual cricketers who competed against players from South Africa in the English County Championship were hardly likely to be serving the same master. Furthermore, the whole thrust of the isolation concept was to cause maximum disruption and harm to the South African authorities. How could banning Barry Richards, Clive Rice and Jimmy Cook achieve this? The snubbing of the mighty Springboks, though, did damage the morale of a nation obsessed with sport.

The bridge-builders also failed to acknowledge just how reprehensible the apartheid regime was to the black cricketing nations: 'For a region so keen to establish an independent identity and international respect as the West Indies, that South African attitude was anathema, especially when the background of Caribbean slavery was so easily equated with what was happening in South Africa.'[71] A letter to *Wisden Cricket Monthly* seemed to put the whole debate into context:

> It is not true that playing cricket is all-important, even in the United Kingdom, much less in any other part of the world. Finding a job, feeding a family, getting an education, avoiding floods, famines and genocide, are all 'all-important'. Attaining political freedom and justice is 'all-important' to blacks, coloureds and Indians, not playing cricket.[72]

There was vociferous support for the idea of sending an MCC XI to South Africa. The proposal originated from the right-wing organisation Freedom in Sport and was fronted by the ex-England cricketers Denis Compton and Bill Edrich. It is clear that the English cricketing 'establishment'[73] was largely sympathetic to South Africa's claim for readmission. It was felt that 'the MCC can make some contribution to a return to justice and fair play'.[74] The proposed tour was intended to 'encourage all races in South Africa to work towards full integration, by receiving ambassadors from this country' and to 'halt the slide of international sport towards total political influence'.[75] The sending of an MCC team was only reiterating the recommendation of the ICC delegation to South Africa in 1979, so why did cricket's governing body not seize the initiative? The answer lies at the essence of all political phenomena: power. It would have jeopardised MCC's influence within cricket, and Lord's as the headquarters of the game:

> Recognising that although now a private club with no direct responsibility for running the first-class game in England, MCC does still have a public role, the committee rejected the idea of a tour because of the 'absolute necessity in an increasingly political climate of keeping Test cricket as played by the member countries of the ICC alive.
> ... it would undoubtedly lead to the disruption of the World Cup, probably to the resignation of the MCC committee and probably also to the threatening of MCC's traditional role as guardian of the ICC.[76]

The Test and County Cricket Board (TCCB), though, continued to be a good friend to South Africa, and it afforded SACU a full hearing at the meeting called to determine England's response to the ICC agreement on relations with South Africa.

Finally, the cricketing authorities were also subject to the wider international approach to South Africa. Western governments eventually embraced the idea of sporting sanctions as a means of applying pressure on the South African administration to reform. They considered sanctions as a tactic which would force the regime to change but make it safe for capitalism. It also enabled foreign governments to gain credibility and seek to influence the liberation movement. The sports boycott was thus a convenient manoeuvre which directly affected few people whilst providing publicity which diverted attention from the economic relationships with the republic. When P.W. Botha came to power promising reform, governments and Cricket Boards congratulated themselves on the role which each had played.

International politics and the boycott

National governments had the ultimate authority to prevent a tour to or from South Africa. The New Zealand government in the 1970s, for example, refused admission to sides selected on the basis of race. The Australians, similarly, denied entry to Boon Wallace of SACA to put the case for 'multiracial' cricket. Conservative thinkers were alarmed that such powers should be enacted. By distinguishing between the subjects of apartheid and sport, they could both condemn racism and satisfy the requirements of a sports-mad electorate. For example, Keith Holyoake, prime minister of New Zealand (1957 and 1960–1972), stated that he was 'not in the business of sport' shortly before hosting an official farewell to the 1970 All Blacks team to South Africa.[77]

Was not the attitude of conservatives political in itself? By seeking to determine which areas of public life the state was entitled to concern itself with, the debate centred on what could legitimately be defined as politics. Sport, it was argued, was clearly an area in which government should not involve itself. What was at stake was tradition and as such the hegemony of political and sporting codes. That the two should be intertwined, as they had always been, was lost on those whose focus was both singular and narrow.

The traditional standpoint of the West has been that there was little governments could or should do to influence South Africa's evolution. Events that followed the Sharpeville massacre in 1960 drew the same regimes to concede South Africa as a special case and apartheid as contrary to the spirit of the United Nations. Many became vociferous in their condemnation of that doctrine and some were prepared to evoke sanctions to force change. A distinction had to be drawn, however, between economic and other sanctions. Economic sanctions, it was initially argued, would be counterproductive, forcing the government into the laager rather than onto the path of reform. Therefore, even Conservative governments, such as Robert Muldoon's (prime minister 1975–84) in New Zealand, could actually see advantages in a sporting boycott.

It should also be noted that the question of the sporting boycott was configured during the 1970s, a decade in which social democratic parties in Australia, New Zealand and Britain all enjoyed periods in office. Conservative administrations had, in the main, been sympathetic to South Africa's cause. In New Zealand, the newly elected Labour government informed the South African regime that teams selected on a racial basis would not be allowed into the country. It officially withdrew an invitation to the rugby team to tour New Zealand and announced that it did not approve of tours to the Republic and would actively discourage them. Indeed, no further racial sides from South Africa would be allowed to visit New Zealand.[78]

The Australian government had historically followed a 'white Australia' policy in which it was criticised for its treatment of Aborigines, barred black immigration and refused independence to Papua New Guinea. This attitude was abandoned with the election of Gough Whitlam's Labor Party in 1972. Whitlam was determined to rid Australia of its racist image abroad, and this was demonstrated by the denial of visas for racially selected sporting teams. The Liberals were returned in 1975 but were resolved to maintain pressure on the South Africans. Prime Minister Malcolm Fraser's view was that the future of Western influence in the region was dependent on the eradication of apartheid: 'Far from being a bulwark against communism – as it frequently asserts – South Africa is inviting the spread of communism in the region. Its current policies are inimical to Western interests.'[79] This position was later supported by the Commonwealth's Eminent Persons Group, of which Fraser was a member, which recommended sanctions as the only means to prevent a possible communist victory.[80]

In Britain, the 'Basil D'Oliveira affair' and the proposed South Africa tour of 1970 polarised political opinion, in the main along party lines. In 1974, the Labour foreign minister Joan Lestor instructed the British Embassy to withdraw courtesy facilities for the visiting British Lions to South Africa. In contrast, Ted Heath, the leader of the Conservative opposition, greeted the team home at Heathrow airport.[81]

The question of sporting sanctions was not restricted to Commonwealth countries, or, for that matter, to sporting bodies. During the 1970s, the United Nations passed three resolutions which firmly called for political solutions to apartheid sports. Resolution 2775D (1971) pointed out that the Charter of the United Nations promoted and encouraged 'respect for human rights and for fundamental freedoms for all without distinction as to race, sex, language or religion'.[82] It requested sporting organisations to suspend contests with South African teams whilst they were selected on a racial basis. The United Nations also called on individual sportsmen to refuse to participate in South Africa and called on 'national and international sports organisations and the public to deny any form of recognition to any sports activity from which persons are debarred or in which they are subjected to any discrimination on the basis of race, religion or political affiliation'.[83] It further called on national governments to 'act in accordance with the present resolution'.[84] Another resolution, 3411E (1975), attacked the multinational policy by 'rejecting the attempts of the racist regime to gain acceptance for participation in international sports by superficial and insignificant modifi-cations of apartheid ...'[85] A third resolution, 31/6 (1976), recognised the importance of sport in the international campaign against apartheid. It further urged states not simply to 'persuade' sportsmen of the folly of going to South Africa but to 'deny facilities to sports bodies or teams or sportsmen for visits to South Africa'.[86]

In June 1977, following the lead set by the United Nations, the Commonwealth heads of government issued a communiqué which aimed to discourage sporting contact with South Africa. The Gleneagles Accord justi-fied itself on the grounds that apartheid ran counter to the founding principles of the Commonwealth. In all truth, it was forced upon the Commonwealth in order to prevent any further disruption to sporting relationships, especially the 1978 Commonwealth Games. While 'conscious that sport is an important means of developing and fostering understanding between people ... of all countries', the heads of government recognised that 'sporting contacts between their nationals and the nationals practising apartheid in sport tend to encourage the belief that they are prepared to condone this abhorrent policy ...' The communiqué committed members of the Commonwealth to take 'every practical step to discourage contact or competition by their nationals with sporting organisations, teams or sports-men from South Africa ...' Thus, the heads of government jointly announced that it was unlikely, in the near future, that members of the Commonwealth would engage in competition with South Africa.[87]

Both the United Nations and the Commonwealth, then, considered it acceptable and legitimate for national governments to take action to prevent individual sportsmen and women from competing in and with South Africa. Indeed, Leslie Harriman, the chairman of the UN apartheid committee, directly requested that the mayor of Hastings prevent a proposed visit by two South African cricket teams in 1977. The United Nations advanced the process still further when, in 1980, it produced a 'blacklist' of sportsmen and women who had connections with South Africa. The Supreme Council for Sport in Africa urged members of the United Nations to use their influence to ostracise players who appeared on the list. Donald Carr, the chairman of the TCCB, reacted angrily to this 'blackmail', stating that cricket authorities would do nothing to dissuade English professionals from playing and coach-ing in South Africa during the English off-season. 'This is a free country in which we don't presume to dictate what our players should or should not do', he said.[88]

Apartheid and the developing world

There are often spillover effects from sanctions which involve more than the principal actors. The role of developing African nations against South Africa is one such case, and provides the political scientist with a valuable insight into the capabilities of cooperation among traditionally weak countries. Nations who struggled to compete on economic and political terms with the large powers in the West found in sport a playing field where they could be considered, if not on equal terms, then with respect, especially when aligned as a greater unit. The developing world benefited from greater democracy in world-governing bodies: forums such as the General Assembly of International Federations and the Permanent General Assembly of National Olympic Committees provided platforms to challenge the traditional domination of sport by white, Western interests. In 1963, African states formed the Organisation of African Unity (OAU), of which the charter held that 'liberty, equality, justice and dignity are the essential objectives for the realisation of the legitimate aspirations of the African peoples'.[89] Unlike their Western counterparts, African nations – often supported by other developing countries as well as the Soviet bloc – realised the potential benefits of a sports boycott. The OAU established the Supreme Council for Sport in Africa in 1966 to persist in this cause. Their threatened withdrawal from the 1968 Olympic Games led to South Africa's exclusion.

The black cricketing countries in the Caribbean as well as India and Pakistan also played a leading role in the isolation of South Africa, not just from sport but from other areas of 'civilised' life. In 1946 India became the first country to impose a trade embargo against South Africa. In 1953 the government of Pakistan first submitted a memorandum to the UN requesting that it study the racial situation in South Africa.[90] It condemned the policy of racial discrimination pursued by the South African government as a violation of the basic principles of human rights and the fundamental freedoms enshrined in the UN Charter. As early as 1969, Pakistan, India and the West Indies advocated banning cricketers who had played or coached in the Republic.

Association with apartheid sport was not merely condemned: nations that did so risked being ostracised themselves. In 1976, for instance, African countries boycotted the Montreal Olympics because of New Zealand's presence (the All Blacks had recently toured South Africa. They were also the only country to send a full team to the 1969 South African Games). In 1983 the governments of Jamaica and the Bahamas scuppered a tour by an amateur England Women's XI because five of their party had been on an unofficial tour to South Africa in 1979. In 1986 Bangladesh and Zimbabwe cancelled tours by the England B team because some of the party refused to sign undertakings not to play in South Africa. The Australian government similarly banned the 'rebel' West Indians from playing cricket in Australia.

This political oligopoly (sport's OPEC) was condemned by some Western governments as unfair, just 'not cricket'. Abraham Ordia, the chairman of the Supreme Council for Sport in Africa, explained:

> Those who choose to remain insensitive to the feelings of millions of their fellow men, those who arrogantly and flagrantly defy world opinion and the IOC, have no moral right to expect to play with those they defy … The best means to break down apartheid is to isolate the country concerned. Those who are not with us in this fight are against us.[91]

It should also be remembered that during the early years of the cold war nearly all Western states prevented sportsmen and women from travelling to the Soviet Union.[92]

Conclusion

In terms of effectiveness, the sports boycott was the most successful of all sanctions against South Africa. It contributed to the process of change in a number of significant ways: as a form of punishment for apartheid; as a delegitimising influence on the hegemony of the white state, sapping the morale of a once-invincible ethos; and as an inducement to change. It is difficult to claim that the weapon of sanctions was not a most capable one. Many prominent white South Africans sportsmen – direct 'victims' of sanctions – confirmed their effectiveness. Mike Proctor, a member of the 1970 'world champions', wrote that 'sanctions were justified in the early 1970s, because they helped break down the sporting segregation which had existed'.[93] Tony Greig argued that the advances towards multiracialism 'would probably not have been considered but for the interference of Hain's group which robbed South Africans of so much international competition at a time when their stock as a sporting nation was reaching a peak'.[94] Dr Danie Craven, president of the South African Rugby Board, admitted that the changes now being made in South African rugby stemmed from the isolation imposed by the outside world; they would have been much longer in coming had the bridge-builders been allowed to maintain the contact they desired.[95] Finally, Ali Bacher put the argument beyond dispute: 'There is no doubt the cancellation forced us to change. We wouldn't have done so otherwise. It was the turning point. There was no way back for us. You were right – we were wrong.'[96]

To the political scientist, the role of sporting sanctions offers an intriguing and modern insight into the usage of power. Through sport, a coalition of South African exiles, Western activists and governments of developing nations were able to pressurise South Africa. In this context, sporting sanctions have been viewed as a catalyst for stronger international pressures.[97] This shows the potential of political actors who have traditionally been viewed as weak in relation to the formal political process. It could well prove that this unorthodox approach to the 'art' of politics was what really upset those who claimed that politics and sport had no relationship. It defied convention and acceptability. Politics was to be conducted through institutions that had evolved over time, not 'on the street'. Viewed as an act of empowerment by those normally marginalised in the decision-making process, the procedures enacted by this coalition actually threatened the traditional political process – and threatened to turn it upside down.

These four thematic examinations provide the backbone of the book by exploring the interaction between politics and sport. We have seen how political hegemony directly influences policy, and, through this, determined the very structure of sport and cricket in South Africa. The role of politics in sport, then, becomes very clear. Whether this is desirable is subject to discussion; the fact that it exists is not. If a 'trivial' activity such as sport is subordinate to the State's all-embracing ideology, then it stands that social and economic criteria will also be. Apartheid ideology in South Africa was so comprehensive as to determine the life-chances of the population according to racial classification. When assessing the relationship between politics and sport, the political scientist has to account for wider variables – most importantly opportunity. The case of South Africa highlights how important this is in the study of politics.

Finally, no political study can be complete without an analysis of the prospects or the reasons for change. There have – and will continue to be – many examples of sanctions being applied against a 'rogue' nation, usually by powerful Western interests, such as those against Cuba, Iraq and Libya. The study of South Africa shows that pressure for international action came from a variety of sources and was built from the bottom up. This not only threatened the traditional decision-making process of international affairs but also opened up the meaning of politics to a wider audience.

Thus far, this study has largely been theoretical, assessing the different stances of protagonists. These theoretical positions are given a more practical application in the next section through an examination of four case studies: South Africa's withdrawal from the Commonwealth; the 'Basil D'Oliveira affair'; the cancelled 1970 tour to England; and the rebel tours. Each of these episodes raises issues about the relationship between politics and sport. Each, though, has a unique role in the unfolding history of not only South African cricket but its political history as well.

8

Isolation (of Sorts): South Africa's Withdrawal from the Commonwealth

By the end of the 1950s the formal segregation of South African society was at an advanced stage. The movement and employment of African labour had been brought under state control, parliamentary representation for the Cape coloureds had disappeared and Christian-National education was being introduced into the schools. In 1961 South Africa became a Republic. This was a further part of the process of 'Afrikanerisation', and set the country at an increasing distance, politically, from the United Kingdom. In the same year, the new Republic walked out of the Commonwealth.

Certain events in history encourage a re-evaluation of attitudes: this was one such occasion. The Commonwealth had traditionally been a loose body of ex-British colonies which met in order to further interests, mainly economic and cultural. The question of South Africa – especially after the events at Sharpeville – now aroused particular concern, and the Commonwealth became engaged, as the United Nations would over the next decade, in the affairs of another sovereign state.

South Africa's withdrawal from the Commonwealth was not only an issue for political organisations. Cricket's relationship to the Empire was such that its international governing body, the Imperial Cricket Council (ICC), determined that all members should bear allegiance to the British monarch. Its constitution forbade membership to countries outside of the Commonwealth. South Africa, one of the three founding members of the ICC, suddenly found itself isolated. This presented the three black members – the West Indies, Pakistan and India – with a political leverage that they could not enjoy on other platforms.

This chapter marks the beginning of the history of modern South African cricket. The fabric of the discussions that were to dominate the international game for the next 30 years was laid out well before the Basil D'Oliveira affair brought the issue to a head in 1968. The attitudes of both the cricket boards and governments were first influenced by the question of whether South Africa should be excluded from the Commonwealth and, then, from international cricket. Not only could attitudes be quantified by race, but those of international cricket boards also showed a remarkable similarity to those of their respective national governments. This can only reinforce the suspicion that political and sporting hierarchies were both subject to the existing social and economic structure, and were, in effect, intertwined.

The National Party's worldview pitted the Afrikaner 'small man' against the 'imperialist-oriented' monopolies that dominated the economy. In this context, the NP was anti-imperialist in its outlook, at least in the sense that it was anti-English establishment. It attacked symbols such as the flag, anthem, currency and the monarchy as alien to the Afrikaner cause. Similarly, it held little respect for the Commonwealth. When it came to power, the NP set about replacing the English hegemony with its own. The education system would promote the cultural life of the Afrikaner people. Based on Christianity and nationalism – with reference to country, language, history and culture – the NP set out to build a new society. The crown was removed from military regalia; white schools were segregated as pupils were to be taught in their mother tongue; and the Nationalists withdrew support from the immigration programme, professing that they would prefer Dutch and even Germans to English. The state existed now to serve the interests of the *volk* and the NP: Afrikaners replaced English-speaking civil servants, as loyalty to the cause became the prerequisite of advancement; the senior ranks of the armed forces and the police were similarly purged;[1] Afrikaner businessmen were appointed to key positions in state industries; and government accounts were switched to Afrikaner finance companies and contracts awarded to Afrikaner firms.

Having narrowly won a referendum to establish a Republic in October 1960 and facing the threat of expulsion, South Africa resigned from the Commonwealth in March 1961. *Hoofleier*[2] Verwoerd declared that South Africa had been freed 'from the pressure of the Afro-Asian nations who were busy invading the Commonwealth. We are not prepared to allow these countries to dictate what our future should be ... Therefore, we go now forward alone. We are standing on our own feet.'[3] The Nationalists had finally shaken off the yoke of the British and formally severed the imperial connection: 'The last shot had finally been fired in the Boer War: the enemy of 1899 had been pushed aside and vanquished ...'[4]

Rule 5 of the ICC regulations provides that membership of the organisation shall cease should a country concerned no longer be part of the British Commonwealth. Therefore, by its political actions, South Africa immediately forfeited its ICC membership, assuming the role of observer. Under the constitution of the ICC there could be no official Test matches against a non-member. Cricket was not the only sport that had existed to strengthen the ties of imperialism. Within a month of it leaving the Commonwealth, South Africa's invitation to the 1962 Empire Games at Perth, Western Australia, was withdrawn as only Commonwealth teams were invited to compete. To many English-speaking South Africans, it was all becoming too much as they witnessed their institutions, values and way of life being eroded by the Afrikaner onslaught. Such rebukes, though largely a response to Sharpeville, contributed to the exodus of British capital in the early 1960s.

SACA requested a change in the ICC rules to accommodate non-

Commonwealth teams, and was met with a decision of delay for a year following a vote which pitted England, Australia and New Zealand against Pakistan, India and the West Indies – the first time an international sports body had split along racial lines. In the meantime all Tests against South Africa would be 'unofficial', starting with the forthcoming visit of New Zealand. So, whilst – in effect – cricket against South Africa would not be sanctioned as official, it was not actually outlawed by the ICC. The suspension of a decision (in fact it was 30 years before the Springboks rejoined the ICC) presented opponents of apartheid with an opportunity to air their grievances. Black cricketers had written to the ICC as early as 1955 requesting that it apply pressure to SACA to remove racial barriers; SASA suggested that the white Association be expelled if it failed to comply. Their arguments were now met favourably by the boards of Indian, West Indian and Pakistani cricket.

However, C.O. Medworth, the South African cricket commentator, condemned the black cricket boards for

> allowing politics to encroach on the noble game of cricket. By depriving South Africa of her status on the ICC it is the players who are suffering, not those who frame the laws of the country … there is precious little chance for some time to come of South Africa changing her views on the playing of mixed sport. That is government decree and there it must remain. There is absolutely nothing that cricketers or cricket legislators can do about it, try as they would. Springbok teams would only too gladly visit the West Indies, India and Pakistan – if they would have us. But the trouble is that we could not reciprocate without causing our guests some embarrassment on the social side and in the matter of accommodation.[5]

This is an argument that reoccurs: that the conditions in which cricket was played were not the fault or responsibility of players or the cricketing authorities. The same fears were expressed when the issue of South Africa's membership of the Commonwealth was being discussed. The Commonwealth, it was argued, is not merely an association of governments, but of peoples: 'South Africans in these grim days of their destiny, need to have – and to know they have – the support and sympathy of the outside world. South Africa is greater than the clique of men with closed minds who now tyrannise over her – and she will outlast them.'[6] The message was, punish the regime in Pretoria and you do more than harm a stubborn government. The West, then, should maintain relations with the Republic, if only for the sake of the black population who would surely suffer if it did not. Thus, the political and the sporting arguments for maintaining relations with South Africa were as one.

The positions of black and white cricket boards over the Republic's relationship to the ICC bore a strong similarity to that of their national governments to the question of South Africa and the Commonwealth. There had been pressure within the Commonwealth for South Africa to be expelled because of its apartheid policies. This had, in the main, been rejected by the white power brokers. When Pretoria forced the issue by becoming a Republic, there was despair on the part of the white Conservative members. Robert Menzies, the prime minister of Australia (1939–41 and 1949–66), expressed that 'this is a very unhappy day for those who attach value to the Commonwealth as an association of independent nations, each managing its own affairs in its own way, but all co-operating for common purposes.' Keith Holyoake, New Zealand's prime minister, stated that 'the decision of South Africa to withdraw from membership of the Commonwealth is indeed a matter of deep regret.' Harold Macmillan informed the British parliament of his deep regret at contemplating the severance of the Commonwealth's 50-year-old ties with South Africa.[7] What lay at the root of this anxiety was the key question of the rights of nations to determine their own policy, a right enshrined in the Balfour Declaration of 1926.[8] It was not the government of Verwoerd that had been forced to withdraw, it was the Union of South Africa – a nation that fought along other white colonies during two world wars. This stance was the key to the conservative position over South Africa for the next 30 years.

In contrast, Jawaharlal Nehru, the first prime minister (1947–64) of independent India, viewed South Africa's departure with regret, but said the policy of apartheid was incompatible with membership of the Commonwealth as he understood it. Furthermore, the Commonwealth would be strengthened by the virtue of underwriting a moral principle.[9]

On the cricket field, the Pakistani position was that South Africa could not return to the international fold unless it agreed to play all constituent members of the ICC, irrespective of colour. Sardar Majithia, the Indian deputy defence minister and president of the Delhi Cricket Association, said that as South Africa was no longer a member of the Commonwealth it should not be readmitted to the ICC as long as it pursued a policy of apartheid. It was 'not cricket' to segregate anyone on the basis of the colour of their skin.[10]

On the other hand, S.C. Griffith, assistant secretary of the MCC, implied that South Africa would be welcomed into some newly constituted world-wide cricketing body and emphasised that it was the MCC's intention to continue to meet them – both home and away – whether matches be official or not. English caps were awarded for the 1965 tour and cricket statisticians refused to consider the South African games as anything other than official.[11] The New Zealand Cricket Board, for its part, refused to meet a SASA deputation that was demanding the Kiwi's boycott the South African tour of 1961–62 unless the Springboks included blacks. In contrast, the visiting South Africans were welcomed as guests to New Zealand in 1964 by no less a figure than the prime minister. They received hospitality at the Parliamentary Buildings – dining and mixing with New Zealand's political elite. The Australian Board of Control was also supportive of South African cricket, stating that the visit of the team to Australia in 1963–64 would be regarded as a full-scale Test tour.

This was, to all intents and purposes, a straight political issue between – on the one hand – England, Australia and New Zealand and – on the other – the West Indies, India and Pakistan. On the South African question both cricket and politics divided along racial lines. In 1965 the governing body did become 'International'. The United States, Fiji and Ceylon were the first to join. There was, though, no proposal to readmit South Africa, nor was one likely until there was a change in the policies of the South African government.

The reaction from South Africa was typical of the arguments that have been discussed in the previous section. Former Springbok captain J.E. Cheetham accused South Africa's critics of introducing politics into sport, claiming that South African cricketers would be prepared to play anyone provided that it does not conflict with policies over which they have no say. There was also a fear that the public might not support unofficial tours, and that this could have a detrimental effect on SACA's finances.[12] The tour of England in 1960 resulted in a loss, and support for the Currie Cup – South Africa's domestic competition – was declining. The game clearly needed overseas support.

Dr Verwoerd had stated that he wished to maintain relations with those Commonwealth countries that he already cooperated with. This seemed to be acceptable to South African cricket commentators: 'as long as South Africa can continue to enjoy the friendship and good will of England, Australia and New Zealand they will be quite content.'[13] By implication, this suggested that neither politician nor cricket authority had any interest in furthering acquaintances with other – that is, black – nations. Verwoerd said that the United Party was worried about what South Africa might lose by leaving the Commonwealth. Yet, he suggested, even if it lost everything, it was better than losing its soul:[14] what could be more important? On the other hand, as the cricket journalist C.O. Medworth summed up: 'a voice in the affairs of cricket is denied us by countries who cannot see eye to eye with our national way of life'.[15] We had reached the classic South African political scenario: the stalemate.

So, cricket becomes embroiled in the political history of South Africa because of political actions. Chapter 4 highlighted that it was politics that immediately influenced sport, not the reverse. South Africa's withdrawal from the Commonwealth came shortly after the Sharpeville massacre. Both events served to shape the outlook of member nations to South Africa. Furthermore, by applying pressure on the Republic whilst within and, then, outside the Commonwealth, it enabled this rather loose organisation to construct a set of principles by which it should be guided. This was no longer the laissez-faire approach of an association whose primary task was economic, and it was a further reason to alarm conservatives.

The ICC, because of its constitution and the fact that it was forced to take issue with South Africa, also became directly involved in the political environment. Countries, moreover, were suddenly forced to examine their attitude towards the Republic. This afforded opportunities to opponents to influence the decision-making process. Protests were held outside of cricket grounds, and the black sporting bodies in South Africa were taken seriously for the first time. This groundswell of discussion – which largely resulted in criticism of apartheid, if not of South Africa – had a profound influence on Verwoerd's government. The 'multinational' policy examined in Chapter 4 was a result of not merely economic but political pressure also. Such actions were effective because white South Africans could begin to envisage the effects of isolation.

The ICC split on the question of whether South Africa should be afforded 'official' status. This division was racial *and* political. The white bodies sought vindication for their approach with the announcement on 11 April 1967 that the South African government was considering relaxing its stand on sporting apartheid. This raised the possibility that blacks could tour South Africa provided that they were members of teams with which South Africa had a traditional relationship. They would not be admitted, however, if they were to be used for political reasons, nor, as it turned out, if they were South African-born.

9

A Defining Moment:
The Basil D'Oliveira Affair

The evolution of South African cricket had been directly influenced by the prevailing political hegemony. So-called 'tradition' had shaped the early game, and, when this required tightening up, regulation ensured that a mere activity such as sport would not contradict and undermine government philosophy. This meant that the Springboks would not enjoy relations with three of the other six leading cricket-playing nations, simply because they were black. Whilst this may have caused discomfort among white federations, South Africa was placated – even when it left the ICC – on the basis that cricket is cricket and politics is something else. When Pretoria directly intervened in the selection of another side, however, the white boards were forced to re-examine their approach.

The refusal of the South African government to grant permission for Basil D'Oliveira to tour with the MCC in 1968 sparked the furnace that was to become the 'South African problem'. No single event did more to focus the eyes of sports administrators on the question of apartheid in sport. D'Oliveira was initially left out of the original touring party. This chapter seeks to locate the reasons for this. It enquires as to *how* decisions are reached. What influences are at play? Is it possible that the composition of an English cricket side can be determined by factors other than ability? If we accept that it is, then there are no grounds to cry foul when sport becomes part of the political agenda.

Basil D'Oliveira, the Cape coloured, was a cricketer of unquestionable ability. A genuine all-rounder, he was considered to be the best black cricketer of his time and captained the first combined black South African side to tour overseas (Rhodesia and East Africa in 1957–58) as well as leading them to victory on home soil against Kenya. By 1958 he had scored over 80 centuries in the black leagues. Still, he was not afforded any credit because of the colour of his skin. 'To quote D'Oliveira's phenomenal bowling performance of nine wickets for two runs evoked only "and what kind of wicket did he do that on?" … his innings of 225 in seventy minutes elicited: "But what was the opposition?"'[1] White cricketers did not believe that their black counterparts could be good enough for top quality sport: 'You'd be surprised how many top cricketers said Dolly wouldn't make the Transvaal B side.'[2] A lack of first-class opportunities led D'Oliveira to seek his fortune in English league cricket.

Whilst Tony Greig's school boasted of three cricket squares and eight turf nets,[3] D'Oliveira's performances in league cricket were his first on grass wickets. He became such a talent that he was signed by Worcestershire and, in 1966, made the England side to face the West Indies, playing in all but the first Test. He finished third in the batting averages, with 42.66, and only two other bowlers surpassed his 8 wickets. In the following year, after only two years in the first class game, he was included as one of *Wisden's* five 'Cricketers of the Year'. Speculation became rife that on current form he could be selected for the MCC tour to South Africa in 1968–69.

England were touring New Zealand in 1966 when the New Zealand Rugby Board cancelled a scheduled tour to South Africa because they were refused permission to include Maoris in their side. S.C. Griffith, the MCC secretary, went on record as agreeing with the cancellation, and stated that the MCC would do the same in similar circumstances.[4]

In January 1967 a report appeared in the Johannesburg *Sunday Express* claiming that Peter le Roux, minister of the interior, had implied that D'Oliveira – if chosen to tour with England – would not be accepted in South Africa: 'Our policy is clear. We will not allow mixed teams to play against our white teams here. If this player were chosen, he would not be allowed to come here. That is our policy. It is well known here and overseas.'[5] Le Roux later confirmed to parliament that D'Oliveira would not be allowed to visit the Republic as a member of an MCC team. This caused unease amongst the black ICC members and, in Barbados, invitations to the Pollock brothers and Colin Bland to play on the island were cancelled. In a statement, the sponsors, Banks Breweries, said: 'While regretting the embarrassment this decision may cause to three fine players, and the disappointment it will create for those looking forward to seeing them in action, we feel that the situation has been drastically changed by the recent statement of Mr. Le Roux, the South African Minister of the Interior.'[6] The decision was clearly political. Dennis Howell, the Labour minister with special responsibility for sport, told the House of Commons that he was confident that any tour to South Africa would be abandoned if any member of an English team was rejected. 'MCC would find such a condition wholly unacceptable', he added.[7] This smacked of political interference to Jack Bailey, a member of the MCC staff, and later its secretary (1974–87):

> In those early days the Labour government of Harold Wilson was in power. For the first time we had a Minister for Sport. His powers were strictly limited under the law of the land but, as is often the case with socialist regimes, this did nothing to prevent interference of a direct kind in the affairs of various sporting bodies, in so far as they would allow it. Denis Howell had been quick to take an interest in cricket, both as to the way it was being governed and by whom, and the position vis-à-vis England playing against South Africa; or, as his government would prefer, not playing.[8]

Despite views such as these, the MCC confirmed their position to the British government – that its side would be selected on merit, and if that upset South Africa then the tour would have to be cancelled.[9]

The MCC contacted SACA in early 1968 for an assurance that there would be no preconditions on its choice of players. Alec Douglas-Home, a former Conservative prime minister and then president of the MCC, visited the Republic in his capacity as the foreign affairs spokesman for the opposition. He sought council with Prime Minister Vorster and left with the opinion that the South African government would not intervene on the subject of personnel. As part of the 'multinational' sports policy, the government had said that they would not interfere with the selection of sides provided that they were not politically inspired. This suggested, though it was never actually stated, that D'Oliveira would be allowed to play for England in the country of his birth. Lord Cobham, a former president of the MCC, had also met with Vorster, and informed his MCC colleagues that the political authorities in South Africa would not allow D'Oliveira into the country.[10] Ian Wooldridge noted in the *Daily Mail* that the MCC had a choice: 'They must choose either to sacrifice D'Oliveira to the doctrine of apartheid or to cancel the test tour scheduled for the winter of 1968–69.'[11] SACA didn't reply to the MCC's request for clarification. The cricketing authorities placed their trust in Home; Cobham was either ignored or swept under the carpet.

One might wonder what agenda was being drawn up here. For Jack Bailey, the 'villain of the piece' was Denis Howell for having the audacity to suggest that the MCC seek assurances from SACA regarding the selection of players: 'No government would answer a hypothetical question of the kind posed by our letter.'[12] To have pressed for an immediate answer, commented *Wisden*, would have appeared to have been politically inspired.[13] Yet, what was the purpose of the Home and Cobhan visits to the head of the South African government if not to anticipate potential difficulties? Furthermore, the MCC showed that they would be prepared to act on the basis of a political position when they ruled out the Rhodesian leg of the South African tour, 'in the light of present circumstances'.[14] The South African government was gambling on a waiting game, for it wanted to avoid an international situation. Sport offered the regime a means of useful publicity. The South Africans had just beaten Australia by three Tests to one, and it was between them and the West Indians as to who was the world's best side. Cricket was also increasing in popularity and being taken up by Afrikaners. If the MCC were to cancel, the Springboks could look forward to precious little Test cricket on their own grounds during the forthcoming decade. The New Zealand team was not due before 1972 and the Australians until 1975 at the earliest. The government was adamant that they would not play India, Pakistan or the West Indies. All hope lay with the non-selection of D'Oliveira.

D'Oliveira was picked for the first Test against Australia in 1968. England were beaten by 159 runs, of which he scored 87 not out in the second innings, the highest English score in the contest. Despite this, *Wisden* argued that 'the value of his belated effort was difficult to appraise. England needed him as an all-rounder and he had failed as a first-change bowler.'[15] In his defence, figures of 25-11-38-1 and 5-3-7-1 'if not penetrative were Scrooge-like in their economy.'[16] Furthermore, D'Oliveira was not a recognised first-change bowler, his forte as a medium pacer was that of breaking up partnerships. Indeed, prior to the Test he had taken only four first-class wickets all season.

D'Oliveira was left out of the England side for the next three Test matches and must have considered that his dream of competing in an international contest in South Africa was over. His luck appeared to change when Tienie Osthuizen of Rothmans cigarettes offered him R40,000, a car and house to coach cricket for the South African Sports Foundation.[17] This 'offer' was far in excess of what a player could expect for coaching. Part of the deal was that he would have to declare himself unavailable for the forthcoming tour. Whilst considering this, D'Oliveira was called up for the final Test match at the Oval (22-27 August) and made the most of his selection by scoring 158 and taking the wicket of Barry Jarman in the second innings, which gave England the breakthrough they needed to win the match. The significance of his knock was described as

> an innings which perhaps more than any other deed on the field of play has helped shape the destiny of South African cricket. The D'Oliveira affair might have been avoided until that innings. Although Dolly had already played in fifteen test matches his chances of making the side until then were, on his own admission, fairly slim.[18]

Colin Cowdrey, the England Captain, told Jack Bailey: 'It's good to have beaten the Aussies. It looks as though we shall have problems with South Africa, though. They can't leave Basil out of the team. Not now.'[19] Knowing the Captain's influential position, Bailey prepared for the fallout. Later that week, Doug Insole asked D'Oliveira about his availability for selection. Cowdrey seemed to confirm selection by quizzing D'Oliveira toward his feelings about playing at Newlands, Cape Town, which would have been his home ground.[20]

On Wednesday 28 August 1968 the MCC selectors announced their side to tour South Africa. D'Oliveira, who had just scored 128 for Worcester, headed the batting averages against Australia and done more than any other player to win the final Test, was missing. D.J. Insole, the chairman of selectors, explained that: 'from an overseas tour point of view [D'Oliveira was considered] as a batsman rather than an all-rounder. We put him beside the seven batsmen that we had ...'[21] It was felt that Tom Cartwright, a medium-pace bowler, would be more likely to succeed on South African wickets than a man who had grown up in the Cape. There were places for Keith Fletcher and Roger Prideaux, neither of whom had been selected for the squad at the

Oval. As for Cartwright, he had not represented England all summer and had missed nine of Warwickshire's last ten championship matches with trouble from both a shoulder and knee.

Sport provides an area of discourse fraught with disagreement about the merits of this or that player. Whatever the activity it is unlikely that any two enthusiasts could agree on the same world XI. However, cricket is a statistical game and it enables an examination of factual data, even if we accept that conclusions are subjective. The facts presented here led to accusations that the selectors had omitted D'Oliveira for political reasons so as not to prejudice the South African tour. Michael Parkinson wrote in the *Sunday Times*:

> Last Wednesday a group of Englishmen picked a cricket team and ended up doing this country a disservice of such magnitude that one could only feel a burning anger at their madness and a cold shame for their folly. The dropping of Basil D'Oliveira from the MCC team to tour South Africa had stirred such undercurrents throughout the world that no one but the impossibly naive can any longer think that politics and sport do not mix, never mind believe it.[22]

According, though, to S.C. Griffith, the MCC secretary: 'No preconditions as to the selection of the touring party have ever been laid down by the South African Cricket Association (SACA). The team has been picked solely on the basis of providing the best players in a cricketing sense to beat the South Africans.'[23] Graeme Wright, the editor of *Wisden* 1986–92, believed that 'The only sound louder than the cries of conspiracy was the sigh of relief blowing out of South Africa.'[24] Indeed, an NP rally in Potchefstroom broke into cheering and applause on hearing the news.[25] Joe Lister, secretary of the Worcestershire team stated, 'I find it hard to believe that form alone has kept D'Oliveira out of the side.'[26] A player who was the winner of the Gancia Award for his batting during August, who was considered good enough for the final XI in the last Test, who had had a good game, was not considered one of the best 15 players after it. *Wisden* concluded:

> When so many voices in England were discussing the political side of the affair, it was hard for anyone at a distance who did not know them to believe that D.J. Insole, A.V. Bedser, P.B.H. May and D. Kenyon, augmented by G.O. Allen and A.E.R. Gilligan and the captain, M.C. Cowdrey, were impervious to political influences and were picking a side purely on cricketing qualifications.[27]

Nineteen members of the MCC resigned in protest at his omission and Labour MP Ivor Richard called on the Race Relations Board to investigate it. Amid the outcries, investigations and controversies the *News of the World* offered D'Oliveira a contract to report on the tour. This could potentially inflict greater embarrassment on the regime. Under the Group Areas Act, for example, D'Oliveira would not have been able to eat or drink with the players for the purpose of interview and would have had to sit in the 'non-white' stands whilst watching the cricket. As a player, under the policy of accepting 'non-whites' in touring sports teams from countries with which South Africa has ties, he could have been granted a blanket exemption from the Group Areas Act. It all proved too much for Prime Minister Vorster, who stated that 'Guests who have ulterior motives or who are sponsored by people with ulterior motives usually find they are not welcome. When you visit a foreign country you are a guest and you are expected to behave like one. Guests observe rules – they don't make them.'[28] Furthermore, the inclusion of D'Oliveira in any format would have undermined South Africa's way of life. Despite this, Vorster reiterated that his government valued 'those relations, not only in the field of commerce but also in the field of sport. These relations will not be and have not been put in jeopardy by us.'[29]

A couple of days after this statement the MCC announced that Tom Cartwright would not be fit to tour and that D'Oliveira would replace him. Cartwright was principally a bowler who could bat a little, and D'Oliveira's substitution for him was not consistent with the selectors' initial arguments. Cartwright's obvious replacement was Barry Knight, but it became known later that he had been ruled out by the MCC for allowing articles to appear under his name without permission.[30] A batsman was replacing a bowler, and whilst the omission of D'Oliveira in the first place appeared suspect, his inclusion in place of Cartwright suggested factors at play other than merit on the cricket field.[31] Jack Bailey, assistant secretary of MCC, made the following statement: 'The selection committee have decided to replace him [Cartwright]. They consider that there was no direct replacement for a bowler of Cartwright's specialist abilities and felt that the balance of the touring party had inevitably to be altered.'[32]

It is unlikely that we will know the extent of pressure applied on the MCC from public opinion. Were they swayed under pressure of government policy on South Africa, by the international climate or by the need to maintain a semblance of unity within the international cricketing fraternity? This whole sorry history is one of events being forced by protest. This undoubtedly was one protest too far for the apartheid regime. Vorster told his NP Conference that D'Oliveira's selection was unacceptable:

> We are not prepared to accept a team thrust upon us by people whose interests are not the game, but to gain certain political objectives which they do not even attempt to hide.
>
> The team as constituted now is not the team of the MCC but the team of the Anti-Apartheid Movement, the team of SAN-ROC, and the team of Bishop Reeves … The matter passed from the realm of sport to the realm of politics … Leftist and liberal politicians had entered the field of sport and wanted to use it to suit their own purposes and pink ideals.[33]

At every opportunity, the South African regime accused the MCC and the government of bringing politics into sport, thereby absolving Pretoria of any possible wrongdoing. It was further evidence that the world was conspiring against the Afrikaner people.

Nonetheless, the English authorities reiterated their position: 'if the chosen team is not acceptable to South Africa, the MCC will call the tour off'.[34] When SACA officially informed them that D'Oliveira's selection would not be sanctioned, the MCC duly cancelled the tour.

The MCC had considered itself a natural ally of the white South African cricketing authorities. Griffith held to the opinion that there was no colour bar in the SACA constitution, and that racial segregation was not the responsibility of the sporting bodies.[35] The two countries had been traditionally tied in the cold war alliance by the twines of trade, political interest, culture, blood and a sense of sacrifice through war. It was considered with contempt that politics within the arena of the cricket field could potentially damage this relationship. When David Sheppard summoned a meeting of the MCC membership to criticise the committee's handling of the D'Oliveira affair, the committee, led by Aidan Crawley and Dennis Silk, implied that South Africa's domestic policies were not of concern to the MCC.[36] They further re-emphasised the need to encourage cricket in all circumstances. This was a firm endorsement of the doctrine that politics should not mix with sport in any situation.

This was by definition, however, a political position taken by a group of people with known right-wing sympathies. Crawley had been an MP for both the Labour and Conservative parties; Dennis Silk 'rejoiced in the third name of Whitehall.'[37] Every one of the ten selectors had played cricket in South Africa. The Chairman, Alec Bedser, later became a founding member of the right-wing Freedom Association, which received funds from the South African government. The MCC president Arthur Gilligan had been for many years a member of the British Union of Fascists. For John Arlott, the MCC represented an antiquated establishment that still considered itself relevant: 'Most of the many MCC members of my acquaintance are such purely bred conservatives that they regard themselves as non-political.'[38] The *Guardian* quoted Lord Monckton as once having said 'I have been a member of the committee of the MCC and of the Conservative Cabinet and, by comparison with the cricketers, the Tories seemed like a bunch of Commies.'[39]

The doctrine of laissez-faire appeared obscure in the context of cricket's imperial ethos. Certainly, the fostering of the game overseas was seen as unworthy as a major criterion for touring South Africa. Cricket in West Africa had made important advances, especially in the Gambia, Sierra Leone, Ghana and Nigeria. However, there was little encouragement from the white cricketing nations and the game fell into decline.[40] What formal encouragement was offered to the black cricket organisations in South Africa? SACB complained of having their requests for support ignored, and *Wisden* didn't even provide a contact address. No representative South African black teams had been invited to England. On the other hand, a 'flood' of schoolboy and club sides had gone to experience the hospitality of the South Africans, assisting the propaganda campaign of the increasingly isolated apartheid administration.

One of the key questions in this study concerns the intervention of politics. By determining when politics became involved in sport, we are able to enquire as to its interpretation. The South African government believed the mere suggestion of D'Oliveira being selected for the MCC was political. His eventual selection, because he was not in the original squad, was deemed political. Vorster told a meeting in South Africa: 'From then on D'Oliveira was no longer a sportsman but a political cricket ball. From then on it was political body-line bowling all the way. From then on the matter passed from the realm of sport to the realm of politics.'[41] It was politics that had forced the selectors' arm, not ability. The South African 'multinational' sports policy allowed for blacks to represent international teams against South Africa provided that their selection was not on political grounds. For many, the omission of D'Oliveira in the first place not only smacked of political interference but opened up the matter to the merits of sending a team at all to South Africa.[42] Despite all of Vorster's cries of 'foul-play', he had no intention of allowing D'Oliveira into South Africa as part of a side to compete against the national team. He had told Douglas-Home as much in the previous year, and not hidden his intentions from his party.[43] Harold Wilson, the British prime minister, was able to rise above these arguments and in response to Vorster state that 'Once the South Africans had said that they were not taking a player we wanted to send, I would have rather thought that put them beyond the pale of civilised cricket.'[44]

It would be naive to suggest that the approach of the British government and the cricketing authorities to the D'Oliveira affair was not influenced by the wider political and sporting climate. An Olympic delegation report on South Africa suggested that the government's 'multinational' sports policy cleared the Republic for readmission to the Olympic fold. The vote in favour of this report threatened to split world sport – not just on racial but on ideological grounds. There had always been alternatives to the Olympic Games: the workers Olympics in the 1930s, for example, and the South African Games in the 1960s. Neither, though, threatened the prestigious position of the world games. There emerged in the Far East a movement on Olympic lines as the Games of the New Emerging Forces (GANEFO). If a significant number of African countries were to boycott the Olympics and opt for this alternative, the authority of the whole Olympic movement would be undermined. John Hennessy in the *Times* even suggested that this break could 'lead to new international realignments'.[45] The West had to act.

The assassination of Martin Luther-King not only shocked, but frightened. This was an era of increasing violent protest, as governments were not tackling issues such as the Vietnam War and racism. Politicians such as the Conservative MP Enoch Powell were stoking the furnaces of racial hatred. Opposition to these positions came in the form of extra-parliamentary activity. The IOC feared that the Mexico Olympics would become a platform for protest against South Africa and racism in general, which could escalate into far wider disruption against the Vietnam War – and against capitalism. Sport would provide the arena, because sport was part of the problem.

The actors involved in cancelling the tour to South Africa were not merely representative of insular interests. Ultimately, the Olympic movement was forced – by the threat of becoming impotent through boycott – to expel South Africa. In May 1968 a United Nations Human Rights Conference called for a total ban on South Africa's participation in international sport until it mended its ways. The West was forced into re-examining South Africa within the context of wider political currents. Inevitably, the ultimate ambition of power is its retention and reproduction. Any possible split along racial or ideological grounds not only threatened the dominant position of the white sporting elite but could also have repercussions in the field of international politics. No decision on cricket relations with a country – whose founding philosophy was strict racial segregation – could be made on sporting grounds alone.

It would now be difficult to argue that there was no place for politics in sport. Instead, the discussion progressed onto the precise nature of that role. David Sheppard, noting the impact of politics on sport on this occasion, said following his defeat at the MCC extraordinary meeting: 'What is more important than votes … is that ideas have been ventilated. Nothing will be quite the same in English cricket after the debate.'[46]

10

Cricket and the Actual Institution of Politics: The 1970 South African Tour to England

The arguments for maintaining or severing links with South African sport were discussed in Chapter 7. A case study of the proposed and subsequently cancelled tour to England in 1970 provides the political scientist with a cast with which to demonstrate certain key points. It draws apart two separate and distinct groups that are sharply divided on ideological grounds. Sport became embroiled in a struggle of ideas, not only because it represented – and represents – qualities that are ripe for exploitation but also because it was an additional ingredient in a turbulent period. Britain was coming to terms with the fact that it was now a multiracial country. Questions relating to race-relations and law and order would dominate the political agenda of the 1970 general election.[1] Furthermore, the question of whether arms should be supplied to the Republic forced the political parties to evaluate their position towards apartheid and how best to influence change.

This chapter explores the notion that politics is ultimately about ideas. The dominant ideological force in any society is essentially fundamental to the piecing together of a hegemonic order in which elements that do not subscribe to notions of 'fair play' – that is, the determined legal framework – are considered by the standards of 'common sense' to be standing beyond the boundaries of acceptability. Political challenges should come through agreed and approved channels and should not exploit areas such as sport and culture that were primarily non-political. Both of these key beliefs were challenged by the crisis that became the 1970 cricket tour, and, more importantly, so was the concept of ultimate authority – the basis of liberal government.

Protests against the visiting Springboks had been taking place since the 1960 tour. The putrid taste left in the wake of the D'Oliveira affair ensured that the campaign against the 1970 trip would be unprecedented. This, remember, was the era of the 1968 Paris insurrection, the anti-Vietnam War movement, college occupations and a general flourishing of radical sentiment – not simply emanating from Europe, but from Indo-China, Latin America and the black civil rights movement in the United States. Ideas are not contained within defined or restricted areas. They develop through scrutiny and spread, influencing social thinkers and political strategists. Such trends represented a breakdown in the traditional method of political activity since the belief that politics was concerned mainly with issues relating to the constitution or to political institutions rang hollow with advocates of direct action.

A number of groups were formed with the purpose of preventing sporting contact with South Africa. Some were prepared to take direct action. This represented a change in the strategy of the anti-apartheid movement, whose previous protests had been essentially symbolic and concentrated on raising awareness. John Arlott described the 1960 protestors as 'woolly and gentle; they seemed to be there from habit rather than from conviction ...'[2] Peter Hain reflected that 'the tactics of polite and reasonable persuasion simply had not worked. And it was clear, particularly with cricket and rugby, that they would never work. New tactics had to be employed.'[3] The Stop the Seventies Tour (STST) was formed to annul, or at least disrupt, the forthcoming Springbok visit, as Richard Thomson explained: 'The aim was to create an "atmosphere of siege" making life for any visiting Springboks "so unpleasant, so hostile and so unbearable" that they would not come again. This, it was hoped, would force sports to invite non-racist teams only.'[4]

Early seeds of this new approach were evident when the Wilf Isaacs South African Invitation XI team – which toured England in 1969 – faced demonstrations at a number of grounds. At the Parks, home of Oxford University Cricket Club, over 70 protestors invaded the pitch and stopped the match for over 40 minutes, causing play to be abandoned for the day. In the months preceding the proposed 1970 tour, STST daubed 14 of the 17 county cricket grounds with slogans. A patch of the Glamorgan outfield at Cardiff was also dug up and weedkiller was sprayed on the Edgbaston pitch. The actual game of cricket was becoming synonymous with barbed wire; it would take an operation of military proportions to ensure the smooth running of a major tour.

A cricket field provided an ideal setting to advance one's cause: it is difficult to police and demonstrators could exploit international contests to seize newspaper headlines and global television coverage. Moreover, Peter Hain, a leader of the STST, projected that about 200,000 demonstrators could be called on. This kind of organisation gave an expression to protest politics and to a radicalism that was not represented by the major political forces. For the first time white radicals worked alongside immigrant and race relations organisations. The West Indian Campaign Against Apartheid Cricket devised plans to mobilise the African-Caribbean community in Britain against the tour. Tasadduq Ahmed, chairman of the League of Overseas Pakistanis, promised moral support 'for any social action through non-violent means.'[5] These groups, through their actions, were campaigning not only against racism in sport but also against the stance taken by right-wing politicians such as Enoch Powell on the subject of race.[6]

Furthermore, STST claimed that 23 trade unions had signed up to its demands. Black workers on London Transport threatened to stage a strike to coincide with the Lord's Test. The television technicians union called on members not to cover any matches involving the South Africans – indeed, Granada television had withdrawn from broadcasting the contests because 'it would be wrong to present these matches as entertainment.'[7] A motion was proposed at the *Observer* chapel of the National Union of Journalists which called for the implementation of a newspaper, radio and television ban on reporting the sports aspects of the tour, and journalists on the *Middlesbrough Evening Gazette* voted to 'boycott' all scores and match reports. No facilities on premises controlled by the Inner London Education Authority (ILEA) would be made available during matches at Lord's and the Oval. The British Council of Churches had instructed its 6-million membership to boycott the tour. The protestors, then, were not simply a rump of left-wing ideologues.

At a parliamentary level, more than 100 Liberal and Labour MPs signed a letter to the MCC saying that they had every intention of joining the protestors if the South Africans came to England.[8] The London Labour Party announced that it would be organising mass, peaceful demonstrations at the Oval and Lord's. Harold Wilson (prime minister 1964–70 and 1974–76) considered that the MCC had made 'a big mistake' in inviting the South African team – 'a very ill-judged decision'.[9] He later hoped that people 'would demonstrate against the South African cricket tour. Everyone should be free to demonstrate against apartheid.'[10]

Beyond the interests of sport and the strains that it would place on the Commonwealth, the government was concerned by the tour's threat to both race relations and law and order. At the end of January the chairman of the Police Federation came out against the tour because of the risk of disruption. The *Observer* reported on 5 May 1970 that 'Nine out of ten head teachers questioned in the London Boroughs of Lambeth and Southwark, which have large immigrant populations, said that they thought it would be foolhardy to allow the South Africans to play at the Oval.'[11] Despite this, the government was 'reluctant to interfere with the traditional rights of people to carry on a lawful pursuit, even though it is an unpopular pursuit'.[12] They could, though, refuse financial support for groups or individual athletes to compete in or against South Africa. Furthermore, the government did not want to be seen as defenders of the South African tour. More importantly, however, it did not want to be identified with the protestors so close to the general election. Its tactic was to pressurise the Cricket Council into taking the decision to call off the tour for them. 'I believe that that is correct and that it is not unfair to throw the responsibility upon the Cricket Council. It invited the South Africans, it can uninvite them if it chooses to do so.'[13]

The first South African cricket association was established on 8 April 1890 by British interests in the colony. The benefits of planting these roots have been discussed in Chapter 3. Needless to say, officials in Britain were keen that all relations with South African cricket be through official

channels, deeming them as traditional and 'the norm'. When this arrange-
ment was challenged the cricketing and political establishment winced at the
perceived threat to their world-view. Jack Bailey of the MCC proclaimed
that 'We are fighting for the world of cricket as we knew it; for the right to
play cricket under the law of the land.'[14] H. Doughty of the *Daily Sketch* said
that 'If the tour is cancelled it will be another victory for the vicious, phari-
saical leftist meddlers who are dedicated to the destruction of the British
way of life.'[15] The cricketing authorities alone should determine the choice
of the South African side. It was not the role of the MCC or, even worse, the
government to dictate conditions. The cricketer Peter Pollock was convinced
that sinister agents were at work: 'I see these demonstrations and riots as
part of a Communist-inspired idea to smash the vital links which have for
years forced the Western nations firmly together ... A principle is involved
and any measure of success for this kind of defiance would see the idea
spreading far beyond the realms of sport.'[16]

Did any group, despite the righteousness of its stance, have the right of
veto over lawful events that the majority desires to take place? Edward
Heath, the Conservative leader, didn't think so. He declared that the tour
should go ahead,[17] and later confirmed that he was glad the South Africans
were coming.[18] Heath had told an election gathering that the difference
between himself and Powell was a matter of 'tone' and not of substance.[19]
The Shadow Chancellor Ian Macleod attacked Harold Wilson's belief in
the right to demonstrate: 'The silent majority will go unrepresented unless
peoples of all parties speak now for them ... But there can be no respect
for a Prime Minister who deliberately encourages a minority whose
declared object is to stop the majority from enjoying their lawful
pleasures.[20]

Just as anti-apartheid demonstrators had taken the issue beyond the level
of argument, so a number of pro-South Africa groups were established to
counter the effect of the STST and its allies. A 'Save the Seventy Tour
Committee' was set up by the right-wing Monday Club. Several MCC
members who were 'financial moguls' in the City established the 'Save the
Seventy Tour Fund'. The '1970 Cricket Fund' was established with the aim
to finance precautions against anti-South African protests. It was launched
at Lord's under the chairmanship of Lt. Col. Charles Newman, and included
amongst its patrons the Duke of Norfolk, the Duke of Beaufort, Viscount
Portal, Lord Wakefield, Judge Sir Carl Aarvold, Sir Peter Studd, M.J.C.
Allom, Alec Bedser, Brian Close and Colin Cowdrey. A glimpse of the
composition of these groups did more than suggest an interest beyond
cricket. Peter Tombs, leader of the Anti-Demonstration Association, for
example, criticised West Indians who protested against the tour: 'We are
becoming so overwhelmed by the colour question in this country that we are
allowing these people to dictate to us.'[21] One county secretary told the
Observer: 'This was their opportunity to apply all their dislike and loathing
of permissiveness, demonstrators and long hair. Staging matches [with

South Africa] is their chance to make a stand against these things.'[22]

Those who supported links with South Africa tended to base their arguments on law and order rather than the issue of racism in sport. Peter Hain's prosecutor, for example, argued that, if found not guilty, Hain's actions would lead to politically inspired law breaking on a massive scale, the possibility of which threatened the very fabric of England's civilisation.[23] The pillars of law and order were under threat by a minority force which was prepared to engage in extra-parliamentary measures to force their opinion onto others. This displayed scant respect for both sport and the belief in what constitutes the legal process, that is, 'politics'. As Reginald Maudling, the Conservative MP for Barnet, put it: 'Any man was entitled to do what was lawful in this country and to expect the state to protect him from unlawful interference. This must be the first duty of government.'[24]

Those who opposed the relationship with racial sport took the argument back a stage and showed that the threat to law and order came from the potential and long-term damage that would be inflicted on race relations because of the visit of the South Africans. Without the initial problem, there could be no protest. This, in effect, encapsulates the notion that politics is about a struggle between rival ideas. It is certainly what has interested philosophers throughout time. What are the legitimate powers of the state? Does the individual have the right to ply his or her trade unhindered in all circumstances? Who and what determines policy? This really was what was at the heart of the whole issue. A *Times* editorial complained that if the tour was cancelled it would show that 'physical disruption had proved more effective than argument.'[25] This was all about power and its legitimacy. The demonstrators had not lost the argument; they simply did not have the means, beyond exerting their numerical strength, to influence policy. Does that mean they should simply submit?

And what of cricket? Both the Indian Cricket Control Board and the Pakistan Board of Control for Cricket came out against the tour and instructed their players on English county sides not to take part in contests against the South Africans. At the same time as announcing that it would join the Commonwealth Games boycott, Pakistan called off its under-25 cricket tour to Britain – which would have coincided with the visit of the Springboks. A planned tour of Kenya, Uganda and Zambia by the MCC in early 1970 was cancelled. Mansinde Muliro, Kenya's minister responsible for sport, stated that 'as long as the MCC has been playing in matches with South Africa I do not want to see the MCC playing in Kenya.'[26] The West Indies Board of Control set out its opposition to the tour. It informed the English authorities that a visit by the West Indies Young Cricketers due for the summer of 1970 would have to be cancelled if the South Africa tour went ahead. The commentator and journalist John Arlott announced that he would not cover the tour: 'Commentary on the game demands, in my professional belief, the ingredient of pleasure; it can only be satisfactorily broadcast in terms of shared enjoyment. This series cannot, to my mind, be enjoyable.'[27]

In contrast, the MCC Cricket Council, which had recently taken over the governing of the game from the MCC, offered assistance to its sister organisation in South Africa. At its very first meeting in January 1969 it recommended that the South Africans be invited to tour in 1970. Such support was on the basis of the long-term well-being of cricketers,[28] the belief that SACA would select its side on merit and 'their resolve to uphold the rights of individuals in this country to take part in lawful pursuits, particularly where these pursuits have the support of the majority.'[29] It later added the sop that it would engage in no further Tests until cricket in the Union was multiracial. By continuing with the current tour they were suspending sentence in the hope that future reforms would rule ostracism out: 'It was agreed that in the long term this policy was in the best interests of cricket, and cricketers of all races in South Africa.'[30] An editorial in *Playfair Cricket Monthly* dressed these sentiments in the game's ethos: 'There is no game anywhere in the world where creed and colour has no part whatsoever in the game, where friendships of a lifetime have been made between men of all races; all that matters is that they are cricketers.'[31] Nowhere, except possibly Australia, India, the West Indies, England (see Chapter 3), and certainly South Africa!

There were definite political undercurrents in the Cricket Council's position. The recognition that change had to come through 'legitimised' channels (SACA) and the undisguised attack on the protestors represented further discourse on the question of law and order. Of course, the authorities didn't see their role as being political, and stated: 'It should be stressed that the Council have taken into account other matters of a public and political nature, but they consider those matters to be the responsibility of the government who are best equipped to judge and act upon them.'[32] However, 'they were aware of the dangers of a minority group being allowed to take the law into their own hands by direct action.'[33] Their approach to relations with South Africa neatly fitted into the liberal capitalist model that argued that relations with South Africa should be maintained for, in the long run, exposure to economic growth and more enlightening cultures would lead to the demise of harsh racial rule. Revolt and isolation, in other words, were not the answers.

In May 1970 it was discovered that the Cricket Council had paid a £50,000 premium on an insurance policy that would pay out £250,000 if SACA or either of the governments cancelled the tour. This introduced financial incentive into an argument that the Cricket Council were clearly losing. Their cause was further impeded when the establishment 'heavyweights', prestigious journalist E.W. Swanton and former England captain Ted Dexter, withdrew their support.[34] Still, on 18 May, the day that the government called a general election – which would have coincided with the first day of the Lord's Test, the Cricket Council met in secret session and voted to continue with the tour.

The acceptance that there were political connotations to the tour and that these best be resolved by the state provided the government with an opportunity to openly intervene. The Sports Council, of whom the minister for sport was chairman, stated that the responsibilities of governing bodies were first to their own sport, and secondly to sport in general, and that, thirdly, a governing body should take into account the influence which their actions might have on the community as a whole. The Cricket Council could not view the issue as being simply about cricket, for that was 'not cricket'. James Callaghan, the home secretary, informed the cricket authorities of his concern for the impact on relations with other Commonwealth countries, race relations in Britain, the threat to law and order, and the consequences for the Commonwealth Games. What possible benefit could be achieved from staging these matches, especially as the MCC had admitted that no future tours could take place until there was reform in South Africa? 'The government have come to the conclusion, after reviewing all these considerations, that on grounds of broad public policy they must request the Cricket Council to withdraw their invitation to the South African Cricket Association.'[35] The day following the home secretary's request the Cricket Council cancelled the tour, being of 'the opinion that they had no alternative but to accede to the request',[36] and deploring 'the activities of those who by the intimidation of individual cricketers and threats of violent disruption have inflamed the whole issue.'[37] It is from this point onward, argues Christopher Martin-Jenkins, that sportsmen lost control of the whole situation:[38] South Africa's fate now lay in the hands of politicians.

Conservative reaction was hostile to the cancellation. It was painted as a failure by the government to uphold the principle of law and order in the face of an unruly mob of political agitators. 'It is not cricket or sport that loses, but the forces of law and order', proclaimed *Hoofleier* Vorster.[39] The Conservative home affairs spokesman, Quintin Hogg, called it 'a classical illustration of the inability of this government to preserve freedom in this country or to maintain law and order'.[40] Enoch Powell compared it to the loss of the 'Prince of Wales' and the 'Repulse ... beneath the waters of the Gulf of Siam'.[41] Jack Bailey of the MCC believed that 'the rule of threatened mob violence had won the day'.[42] This threatened the very fabric of the social equilibrium that the representatives of conservative hegemony had sought for so long to maintain. Tradition, not only in sport but also in how politics is understood and practised, was being undermined. C.R. Yeomans, chairman of the Council of Cricket Societies, said: 'Many cricketers will probably rejoice that if the Labour Party meets defeat it will come on the same day that a Test match against South Africa was due to start.'[43]

Moreover, Bailey saw the decision as a 'bitter disappointment ... because it led to the isolation of South Africa's cricketers as representatives of their country'.[44] But that was the point. The Springboks were more than simply athletes engaging in a politically valueless pursuit. Vorster outlined this perfectly from a South African standpoint:

... This particular cricket relationship between South Africa and Great Britain was a relationship of the MCC with white South Africans.

Even in previous years, when there was nothing against it whatsoever, Britain did not include coloured players when sending a team to South Africa, because they recognised the particular sporting relationship which existed between the countries.[45]

The effect upon South African sport was instant. Three days after the abandonment, Dennis Gamsy, a white cricketer, wrote an editorial in the Rand *Daily Mail* calling for a national sports conference, a view supported by Alf Chambers of the white tennis body.[46] Peter Pollock called on his fellow sportsmen to demand multiracial sport and requested the government to assist. Eddie Barlow, the South African all-rounder, said that his country's cricket authorities would have to overcome the racial problem and choose their Test cricketers on individual merit or face international isolation.[47]

Shortly after the English cancellation, the Australians withdrew their invitation to the Springboks, who were due to visit in 1971–72. South Africa had now entered the cricketing wilderness. It no longer had anyone to engage in contests with. That this ostracism was rooted in political phenomena and was sanctioned by institutional political means highlights the close relationship between politics and sport. This intimacy was no longer denied; rather, it was the format of this relationship that would determine debate in the next two decades. Politics remained a battle of ideas, but these ideas would now be open to a far wider audience for scrutiny than simply MPs and civil servants. The manner in which such forces influenced cricket was highlighted in the 1980s when South Africa attempted to break its isolation by inviting a number of rebel teams to play cricket in the Republic.

11

Treachery and Despair:
The Rebel Tours

Sport offered a means to display to the international community the South African commitment to relax the harsher elements of apartheid. The advances towards integration by cricket in the 1970s presented a model to other organisations. To utilise such progression, though, it was necessary that sporting teams be afforded regular competition. When the ICC continued to fudge SACU's pleas for readmittance, the white-led organisation bypassed the world's governing body and organised rebel tours of cricketers – providing South African cricket with a much-required fillip and the sports-starved population with international competition.

Such were the perceived changes that the authorities invited teams from nearly all the Test-playing countries (the exception being New Zealand. The attempt to lure cricketers from India and Pakistan was unsuccessful). For the first time in the history of the sport black international teams could compete against the Springboks. Not only that, but they were openly supported and encouraged to do so by the regime in Pretoria.

South Africa had now surely done more than meet the requirements of the ICC. However, these tours were clandestine. They proved disruptive to domestic cricket in the respective countries and threatened a further split among the Test-playing countries.

This chapter seeks to assess the justification for such tours and analyses the response of both cricketing and political forces in a further assessment of their relationship. It examines the role of the South African government in the promotion of rebel tours and views how they intensified political protest in a decade that proved to be the most turbulent in South Africa's history. By doing so, it provides the political scientist with an insight into the importance attached to 'power' by so-called non-political organisations. It also displays how compromise can emerge from seemingly polarised positions, and offers an example of the disobedience to a law on the basis of principle and the sanctions that that would attract.

Throughout the 1970s South Africa's white cricketing authorities concerned themselves with preparation for a return to the international fold (see Chapter 5). In 1979 an ICC delegation visited the Republic, appeared impressed with the changes afoot and recommended that a side of players from all countries tour South Africa.[1] The ICC did not act on the delegation's recommendations and no member was prepared to propose South Africa's readmission to a body from which it had forfeited membership in 1961. It was Sri Lanka ('a very minor cricketing body'[2]) rather than South Africa who were elected as the next full-time member country of the ICC. The island's inclusion brought the number of Test playing nations up to seven, with white countries now being outnumbered for the first time.

England were probably South Africa's best hope for support on the ICC. This, according to the Transvaal chairman Don Mackey-Coghill, could not be relied on as it was considered to be dependent on the British domestic political situation: 'The Thatcher government can't remain in power long, and once they go, we go.'[3] Any attempt by England to push for South Africa's readmission, though, raised the spectre of international cricket splitting into two racial camps. This ultimately concerned the MCC who feared isolation: Australia was unlikely to back the South Africans as the Commonwealth Games were being held there in 1982. Any signals of support towards welcoming the Springboks back into the international community would be countered by the fear of widespread absenteeism from the Games. Without Australia, England would not act. South Africa's situation appeared desperate.

South African players and officials began to conclude that their country's plight no longer lay with parties concerned primarily with cricket, and that political pressures would ensure isolation for the foreseeable future. Jimmy Cook, the man who opened the batting for the Springboks throughout most of the 1980s, argued that SACU had a duty to both supporters and players to bring cricket of the highest level to the country.[4] This could only be done by bypassing the ICC and organising private tours of international-strength teams. Clive Rice, future captain, demanded that administrators seize the initiative.[5]

On 28 February 1981 it was announced that a team of English cricketers would tour South Africa: the Republic's isolation from international cricket was at an end. Following the English tour, a side from Sri Lanka became the first black team to tour South Africa who could 'stay in the same hotels, eat in the same restaurants and walk on the same side of the street'[6] as their white counterparts, even if this required a mass of permits authorising permission. In January 1983, the greatest coup of all – 'a major accomplishment by the South Africans both political and cricketing'[7] – involved a team from the West Indies. The West Indians made two visits, as did a team from Australia in 1985 and 1986. Finally, an England side became the last to make an 'illegal' visit to South Africa when Jack Bannister, secretary of the Cricket Association, disclosed in the summer of 1989 that eight of their current senior players would prefer to go to the Republic next winter rather than the Caribbean – if the money was right.

With the exception of the West Indies, though, the tours could hardly be described as a success in cricketing terms. All the teams were composed of players who were at the end of their international careers and were unlikely to play Test cricket again, or who were disgruntled with their own boards. Alvin Kallicharan, for instance, had come to South Africa to play for Transvaal the year before, claiming dissatisfaction with the West Indian selectors that he wasn't being selected because of his Asian descent.[8] Mike Gatting had been sacked as England captain in 1988 because of a sexual liaison in a Rothley guest house, whereas Gooch – who had deserted the England cause by leading the first ever rebel tour, and has stated since that he had no regrets over his actions – was now being made captain. The standard of competition was not particularly high and this was reflected in the low attendances for the 'Tests'. The visit of Sri Lanka, for example, was witnessed by less than 10,000 spectators for the two four-day Tests,[9] and resulted in a R600,000 loss.[10] The four Tests for the second Australian tour drew an aggregate attendance of 104,247, a daily average of 5,487. Gross takings of R2.185 million accounted for less than a quarter of the costs of staging the tour. Chris Harte believes that these disappointing crowds probably reflected the standard of cricket: 'The serious South African commentators, [regarded] the series as the dullest since England's visit in 1964-5 …'[11] The first Gatting Test, which was over in three days, was watched by a total of only 16,000 people – leaving SACU well short of the 200,000 crowd figure for which it had budgeted.[12] The exception to this trend was the visit of the West Indies. Once again, this appeared to be political. The prospects of seeing white South Africa defeated not only raised the gate but stimulated the game in the black communities, highlighting black support for cricket. Mike Proctor felt at times that the South Africans were playing an away fixture, such was the vociferous support for the West Indians from the black communities.[13]

The politics of rebel tours

Justification

In *The Rebel*, a work about political ideology, the French philosopher Albert Camus argued that the true rebel is not the man who conforms to orthodoxy, but one who could say 'no' to injustice.[14] Many commentators felt that South Africa had been treated unjustly by the ICC. SACU, the case went, had taken moves to integrate the sport and it should, therefore, be applauded and encouraged for such actions. Moreover, the South African government no longer interfered in the selection of teams. Thus, the conditions that the South Africans had to achieve in order to be accepted back into the ICC had at last been met. Finally, it was the duty of all international bodies to facilitate the global development of the game. The players, by going to South Africa, then, were assisting in the reform process. This is certainly how many of them saw their participation in the rebel tours. Graham Gooch, the England captain in 1982, proclaimed that 'we want to encourage multi racial sport in South Africa'.[15] Kim Hughes described his Australian team as 'ambassadors for sport and humanity'.[16] Furthermore, according to Bruce Francis, the organiser of the Australian visits, they were obliged to do so because the ICC had abdicated its responsibility.[17]

Criticisms of the moral standpoint stem largely from an examination of cricket in the context of South African political developments. Peter Hain outlined the case that:

> changes were made, not with the honest objective of establishing truly non-racial sport, but on the basis of seeing what the government or white sports leaders felt was the minimum they could get away with ... Ultimately, fundamental political changes were necessary to eradicate apartheid before South Africa could win a ticket back into international sport.[18]

Many club and all school sport remained segregated. Political authority still held sovereignty over the rules of engagement of cricket. Individuals may have been considered as equals on the field of play, but remove 'the whites' and the grim reality was a society built on – and totally riddled with – a culture of racial segregation:

> ... outside the cricket ground we have, obediently, to fit into our allotted place in apartheid society. I am 'white'; my provincial umpiring colleague is 'black'. We cannot live next door to one another or vote together for those institutions which control our lives; our children cannot attend the same school; we cannot share a railway compartment or even a beer in a public bar after a match. Yet some will argue that 'normal' cricket can be played and that South Africa should be welcomed back into international sport.[19]

The West Indian Collis King and Springbok Vince van der Bijl could not go to the same movie. King's team-mate, David Murray, whose wife is white, could not tour with his family for fear of breaking the Mixed Marriages Act. The couple, moreover, could not travel on a train together and in most cities would have to go on separate buses. Reflecting on this situation, Sam Ramsamy, the chairman of the South African Non-Racial Olympic Committee, claimed that the West Indian tour could be considered as 'normal cricket – but only for a day'.[20]

The West Indians, classified as 'honorary whites', witnessed the harsh reality of racial authority. The fast bowler Colin Croft was thrown out of a railway compartment that was reserved for whites only, and Alvin Kallicharan was refused service for food because of the colour of his skin. When the coloured cricketer Omar Henry was selected for the third Test of the second Australian tour, the player he replaced, Alan Kourie, launched a verbal attack on him – questioning his ability as a cricketer and making a number of racial slurs.[21]

The touring cricketers, it is clear, were not primarily concerned with racial justice. Geoff Humpage, the Warwickshire batsman/wicketkeeper, described how 'It was strange going into the off-licence and seeing one entrance marked for whites, and another for non-whites. But it did not bother me.'[22] Asked by his old school headmistress if he would have played cricket with Nazi Germany, Humpage replied, 'Germany doesn't play cricket.'[23] Geoff Boycott, when asked about the ethical reasons for the visit, replied that 'There was no talk of bridging ideologies or nurturing international understanding. It was a job and it would make money for us – that was the unglamorised and unpretentious truth of the matter.'[24] The first England tourists were to receive around £30,000 each for one month's work. Geoff Cook, who turned down a place on the first England tour, said that he was offered the opportunity to earn in one month what would take six years as a Northants player.[25] Albert Padmore, the West Indian player-manager, confirmed that 'We have realised that our respective economic positions and our outstanding liabilities render it impracticable for any of us … to refuse the renewed offer to us to participate … for a brief cricket tour in South Africa'.[26] The Australians received A$200,000 each.[27] The rules on overseas players in domestic cricket were also changed to accommodate many of the 'mercenaries' in future years. Jack Bannister claimed that most of the players agreed to the Gatting tour because they were disillusioned with English cricket.[28] However, these were the highest paid cricketers in the world, who could look forward to regular international competition. Disillusionment came from losing – it had little to do with any belief that South Africa deserved to return to world cricket. It was, then, a financial rather than a moral crusade.

For SACU the tours were about sustaining cricket in South Africa. Starved of international competition, the sport was declining in popularity:

> In 1970, when South Africa had beaten Australia seven times in three years, all 12 primary schools in Bloemfontein, which is as much the heart of Afrikanerdom as Newmarket is of racing, played cricket. Now, after 12 years of isolation, none of them do. As a result of the recent series being televised, one or two may start again.[29]

Players such as Allan Lamb and Robin Smith were turning their backs on their country of birth in order to qualify for England and so play international cricket. What option did Bacher's Board have?

> The International Cricket Conference meeting of 1981 unanimously passed a resolution supporting the view that 'every encouragement should be given to the continued development of multi-racial cricket in South Africa'.
>
> I asked a leading official what had been done to follow through that resolution. He replied, honestly, 'nothing'. I received the same answer when I asked what was likely to be done.

> ... We are tired of being fobbed off with soothing words. We would dearly love justice to prevail.[30]

Without international competition – the argument developed – the domestic game would not only suffer but be fighting extinction. This, in turn, would undermine attempts to introduce the black population to cricket and remove an important means of integration. It was the duty of cricket supporters to prevent this from happening, not just for the benefit of the sport but for the wider effects that it had in South Africa. The SACU leadership were convinced that cricket could assist in breaking down the more extreme vestiges of apartheid. Ali Bacher used the *Wisden* dinner in 1989 to describe how, through the township programme, his cricket union was trying to attack the foundations of apartheid, such as the Group Areas Act, the Separate Amenities Act and the ignorance and fear that apartheid both fed on and generated. International tours provided an impetus to the coaching schemes that accelerated the integration programme. Township cricket, he claimed, had made white cricket sensitive to black feeling, now it was necessary to build for the post-apartheid society he was sure would emerge.[31]

In reality, this argument was a variation of the 'trickle-down' theory that was in vogue amongst political elites in the 1980s and early 1990s: if you reward the people at the top, the benefits of such recompense will work their way down to the lower sectors of society. Rebel tours, therefore, were to be commended because of the potential accelerator effects they presented for increasing benefits to the lower sectors. A percentage of the gate receipts from 'international' tours, for example, were used for the township initiatives. Further frustration could only harm the development programme, for the loss of international cricket would give SACU no incentive to continue attempts to integrate.

No incentive, certainly, but was this a threat? Was this an admission that SACU were only interested in developing multiracial cricket to benefit themselves? The multiracial question was exploited because it presented the liberation movement with a real dilemma. Very few questioned the merits of the development programmes, only the motives. At the *Wisden* dinner, Bacher's address implied that a key role of international guests was to promote cricket in the townships. Now it appeared that, without international competition, the whole thing could come to a grinding halt. Well, so be it. Reforms in sport were only introduced because of pressure; this was no time to let up.

Moreover, it is difficult to believe – considering the evidence – that the tours did nothing to bolster the confidence of the Nationalist regime. Sport contributes to national identity. Commenting on the West Indian tour, the education minister, Gerrit Viljoen, stated that: 'The government profoundly appreciated the exceptional initiative displayed by the cricket chiefs in achieving this breakthrough. The tour struck an important blow not only in the sporting field but also in general against the concentrated efforts to isolate South Africa.'[32]

Would the players be worth the thousands they were paid if it were not to the political advantages of the South Africans?[33] Joe Pamensky had justified the Gatting tour on the basis that it benefited domestic cricket because it provided an opportunity to represent an individual's country, to encourage hero worship and provide a sense of national pride.[34] Sport, in this case, gave meaning to political concepts such as national identity and nationhood. In 1989 the South African state could certainly have done with an injection of national pride. Irrevocable damage had been caused by the township rebellions, the increasing wave of strikes and international sanctions. The white power structure was 'defending its Berlin'; cricket was coming to its aid.

The rebel tours serviced the requirements of the developing political agenda. It would be incomplete to examine them outside of the context of the 'total strategy', an initiative which drew on the collective strengths of all components – political, military and cultural – in the struggle against 'communism' (see Chapter 4). The cricket also helped to divert attention from South Africa's domestic situation. The 1980s proved to be the decade that white hegemony was successfully challenged and was forced to compromise its all-embracing features. The Australians, for example, played at a time when the townships were in insurrection, the turning point for the apartheid state.[35] Ali Bacher stated that the visiting cricketers had given South African people their

> only bright ray of hope this year … South Africa has had a terrible year, financially and politically … Speak to people and they will tell you that since the 1930s and 1940s there has never been a bad year like this. There is a lot of gloom and despair around the country. The attitude is very pessimistic. The Australians' tour here has given the people the only thing they can look forward to. This cricket tour is a big thing in this country. It would have been big under normal circumstances, but it is bigger now … There is a recession and small businesses are going under. There are problems in the townships. The Australians' cricket tour is the only bright ray of hope in 1985 and 1986.[36]

Within the politics of international cricket, the tours ensured that the 'South African question' remained on the ICC's agenda; they also served to divide the international sports community on the question of the boycott. Moral principles were at stake: the right to ply one's trade against the attempt to isolate a pariah state in order to bring about peaceful change. The New Zealand government of Robert Muldoon, for instance, threatened to withdraw from the Gleneagles declaration because of the emphasis being placed on its wording by certain countries.[37] He also floated the idea of holding a referendum on New Zealand's sporting relationship with South

Africa. The Springbok Graeme Pollock argued, though, that 'The more disruptions we can make in world cricket the better it will be for us in the long term.'[38]

State involvement

So, what was the role of the South African government in promoting these tours? At the 1980 ICC conference, which discussed the delegation to South Africa, the SACU authorities presented a letter from P.W. Botha undertaking 'to introduce legislation to exclude sporting events from the application of the three laws considered to infringe the autonomy of sporting bodies to organise multi-racial sport'.[39] He also gave his assurance 'that any cricket team invited to South Africa by the SACU from any country abroad would be most welcome'.[40] Gerrit Viljoen, his minister of national education, reiterated in 1983 that international sports contacts should be encouraged.[41]

Support, though, went beyond the tinkering with petty-apartheid and encouragement of sporting links. Fundamentally, it was financial. There was significant discussion over the means of funding the tours. SACU always denied that they were being assisted by the state. Many sponsors also played down their role in the tours for fear of being boycotted. Likewise, the government denied direct involvement. So no-one picked up the bill! Initially the first England tour in 1981 was to be a commercial venture: the England side would be playing under their sponsor's name, the South African Breweries XI. By doing so, the cricketers would not be representing their country and so should avoid sanction. This changed when Alvin Kallicharan, who had qualified to play for England, was selected for the rebel squad. SACU were forced to step in and insist that a West Indian not be selected as they wanted to stage the contests as England versus South Africa.

All claims that the tours were mere festivals of cricket were invalidated. Whilst this may have satisfied SACU, who were becoming increasingly concerned by the withering of the sport in the Republic, international competition presented the regime with not only a propaganda coup and a morale boost but also with an important factor in its quest to secure the white hegemony. If South Africa could once again engage in international sporting competition it could convince itself that it had been restored to normality. In this case, the 'right kind' of cricket tour should certainly be encouraged. Viljoen had stated that government financial support to specific sporting events would be dependent upon 'international importance and overall publicity'.[42] He reiterated the significance of the West Indian visits when he stated that the regime would be 'sympathetic' towards requests for assistance with the West Indian tour.[43]

Ultimately, the government indirectly funded the contests through very generous rebates to companies who offered sponsorship. A section of the Income Tax Act – called Eleven Bis, section 11 – allowed companies to be reimbursed for costs if their products were promoted internationally. This was strengthened by the Income Tax Act of 1986. During the first Australian tour it was announced that tax rebates of 90 per cent would be granted to both National Panasonic and Yellow Pages, the official sponsors, who thus would only be contributing 10 per cent of the bill. This abuse of the taxation system meant that the two sponsors – who both put up about $1.5 million for the 'Tests' and one-day games respectively – would only be paying a combined total of about $270,000.[44] The remaining $2.7 million would be picked up by the state, allowing Mihir Bose to conclude that the rebel tours were government-funded operations which brought comfort to apartheid: 'Governments do not give such tax concessions unless they believe they are going to benefit from it.'[45]

Reaction

The rebel tours threatened to seriously damage the international game. There were many who advocated a split along racial lines,[46] there were even more who feared that this was a strong possibility. English administrators soon deduced that England could find itself isolated, with only South Africa for company. It was essential, then, if only for the preservation of the ICC, that the strongest acceptable sanctions be applied against any cricketer who defied the English cause for the Rand.

Measures to deal with rebel players fell under the jurisdiction of individual boards. Their severity and justification provide an insight into attitudes towards South Africa. Once again, it has to be emphasised that such decisions were not based on cricketing issues alone. The state of play in South African domestic politics and the prevailing opinions of respective cricket boards probably had a greater influence on opinion than gut reaction. It was initially claimed that the first English tour, sponsored by the South African Breweries, was neither international nor representative and so was not covered by the Gleneagles Agreement, despite the fact that caps were awarded to the South Africans for competing in the 'Tests' and that they were recognised by *Wisden* as first class.[47] Still, the players involved were banned from international cricket for three years. One might have felt that the Test and County Cricket Board (TCCB), which had replaced the Cricket Council as the leading authority in English cricket, were embarrassed by their retribution. George Mann, the chairman, stated that 'The players had broken no law, none of our rules. We are not trying to penalise them, merely taking the minimum steps needed to protect cricket.'[48] Mann further praised the South Africans for encouraging multiracial cricket, and reiterated that the TCCB wanted to help its sister organisation 'but not in such a way to drive a wedge among the other countries.'[49] He later cleared two 'rebels' – Gooch and Emburey – to play against the West Indians for their South African provincial sides.

This attitude was reflective of the Conservative government under Mrs Thatcher. The tourists had, in fact, received the official sanction of at least 50 Conservative MPs, who also claimed that the prime minister gave an 'expression of quiet support' for the players.[50] Along with the United States, Britain was increasingly condemned for abusing its status at the United Nations by preventing a hardening of sanctions against South Africa. A report issued by the United Nations Special Committee against Apartheid said that Britain, along with the US, had most sporting contacts with South Africa. The British authorities appeared to be doing the least to maintain pressure on the Republic. Britain formally opposed sporting exchanges but had not taken 'every practicable step to do so, as called for by the Gleneagles Agreement between Commonwealth countries in 1977.'[51]

Despite the secrecy and the deception, the players who went to South Africa in 1981/82 maintained that they were doing nothing wrong. The TCCB was probably sympathetic to this claim. Indeed, John Edrich, one of the England selectors, admitted that he had made 'one or two tentative inquiries' on behalf of SACU.[52] Derrick Robins recalled that the tours he organised to South Africa enjoyed the 'blessing of Lord's'.[53] John Woodcock claims that the TCCB had, in fact, been pushing South Africa towards breaking their isolation.[54] However, the greater concern rested with the financial repercussions if the game's authorities were seen not to condemn such actions. Tours by both Pakistan and India were expected in the summer, and the TCCB acknowledged potential monetary deficiencies if these visits were cancelled;[55] Peter Lush, TCCB spokesman, warned that some counties could 'go to the wall' if the summer's tours by India and Pakistan were cancelled.[56] The World Cup was scheduled for England in 1983 and the West Indies were expected the following season. Hence, the arguments of the English authorities rested on the potential damage any split in the international ranks could have on England. It was one purely motivated by self-interest. For all the praise for South Africa's advancement towards multiracial sport (which was still a very long way off), an official condemnation of apartheid was absent. This would have been to enter the arena where politics and sport meet.

In contrast, the Sri Lankan rebels were banned from playing, coaching or administering cricket in their homeland for 25 years. The West Indian tours had a similarly enormous impact back home in the Caribbean. Vivian Richards, the West Indian batsman and future captain, reminded his colleagues that in the West Indies 'you cannot evade the point that playing cricket is in itself a political action.'[57] The governments of the region, in common with Third World African states, had been emphatic in the campaign against South Africa. This wasn't simply about the politics of right and wrong: it went a lot deeper. The West Indies, as a geographical, economic and political entity, was the end product of racism and colonialism. Cricket came to reflect these attitudes. In Barbados, Vic Johnson, the minister of sport, stated that 'there is no price for which self-respect or human integrity can ever be bought.'[58] Lacking economic muscle, the West Indies relied on their 'influence and presence' as a sporting nation 'in the world political arena' for their contribution to the struggle against apartheid.[59] Consequently, the players were banned from international cricket for life,[60] and there was general disappointment in some quarters that the rebels were eventually granted an amnesty. In St. Lucia, for example, there were calls for a national poll on the question.[61]

The Australian authorities – political and cricketing – presented themselves as strong moral opponents of sporting relations with South Africa. The West Indian players were declared *personae non gratae* and banned from playing in Australia. This was significant, for Australia provided lucrative employment opportunities for an increasing number of West Indian cricketers at both state and club level. The Australian Cricket Board (ACB) immediately reacted to the news of an Australian rebel tour by taking legal action against the players. One by one the state boards banned the rebel cricketers from representing their clubs.[62] Bob Hawke, the prime minister (1983–91), threatened to ban the players for life and to relieve them of their earnings through thorough scrutiny of their tax returns; the immigration minister further proposed (though didn't carry out) to refuse the issue of visas to the players, making travel to and from Australia almost impossible. Pressure was also applied on the television stations resulting in a virtual blackout of the two tours and, by implication, denying SACU a lucrative source of revenue.

As with England, strong sentiments, but a sincerity that was questionable. In most states, players were quietly informed that it was unlikely that their bans would be endorsed.[63] A member of the Victorian Cricket Association complained that 'we don't really want to ban them [the rebel cricketers], but if we don't we could get into trouble with the stupid demonstrators again'.[64] The ACB publicly confirmed support for their government's position, but always with an endorsement of the 1981 ICC statement that cricket boards be the sole responsible party for the selection of cricket teams. After the tours had finished, Ali Bacher showed the journalist Chris Harte documentation from the ACB which suggested that they were willing accomplices in the operation: 'I saw faxes in which the Australian board even suggested players the South Africans could recruit.'[65] During the visit, 4 of the 14 members of the ACB flew to South Africa to watch some of the matches.[66]

By restricting actions to verbal condemnations, the Australian government could claim to champion the anti-apartheid cause whilst at the same time providing it with the very lifeline that ensured its survival: Australian exports to South Africa had risen by 80 per cent over the previous two years. According to Mike Proctor, it was apparently 'much easier to have a go at Kim Hughes' team.'[67]

A primary ambition of any governing authority is the maintenance of order, stability and control. In other words, the key objective is to perpetuate its existence and to remain the sovereign power. The South African question threatened to expose the ICC to major cleavages based, in the main, on the criteria of race. The organisation would not have been able to survive such a serious rift, and the future of international cricket would be prone to confusion and uncertainty (as has happened with boxing given its numerous boards of control). As a result of the fractiousness, politicians were increasingly becoming active in the administration of the game. That a schism was in sight 'persuaded' the major players to settle the problem, once and for all, on the provision that any decision be unanimous and binding on all parties. At stake was the future of international cricket.[68]

The ICC meeting of 23 January 1989 devised guidelines which provided minimum sanctions that each Test playing nation would adhere to. Any cricketers who went to coach or play in South Africa after 31 March 1989 would be banned from international cricket for 4 years (3 if under 19; 5 if a member of a touring team). All 25 countries voted for the measures, which included the following points and important clause:

- All countries should be at liberty to choose their sides without interference from others. Furthermore, they retained the right to cancel a tour if a player who is not on the banned register is refused entry by a national government.
- An amnesty would be granted for players who had previously visited South Africa.
- Those who felt strongly about the South African question were mollified by the clause: 'Nothing in this resolution shall affect the right of a member of the [International Cricket] Conference to continue a ban already imposed or to impose a ban in the future for a period longer than that provided for in this resolution on its own players.'[69]

The importance of the ICC's decision should not be disregarded. Sonny Ramphal, the Commonwealth secretary-general, was shown the draft document and stated his support, making himself available if the ICC felt the need for consultation. The statement was discussed at individual government level in the Caribbean,[70] and collectively by the Caribbean Community heads of government summit (CARICOM). Armon Adams, Guyana's first secretary, insisted that 'It is the governments of the cricket-playing countries who will determine whether cricket is played in these territories, not the Cricket Boards.'[71] However, the CARICOM leaders supported the settlement as a means of pressurising apartheid.

It appeared that if anyone would be reluctant to sign up to such a settlement it would be England, for long the purveyors of an ethos that was seriously under challenge. This was their game, exported to the colonies, only for these same 'dependencies' to dare to challenge their authority. In the House of Commons, 50 Conservative MPs signed a motion deploring 'the decision to prevent those cricketers who play and coach in South Africa gaining international representation'.[72] Clive Rice believed that 'England have backed down on those principles of freedom of choice which they hold dear.'[73] Were England wholeheartedly behind the measures or were they forced to concede ground in the interests of a greater cause? After South Africa, the greatest losers from the ICC's decision would be itself: between 70 and 80 cricketers spent the previous winter in South Africa.[74] These players, if they had international ambitions, would now experience a serious reduction in their annual income. Not only that, but commentators such as Jack Bannister, Christopher Martin-Jenkins and Tony Lewis provided their services for both South African broadcasting and the press. Clearly, the bonds were strong and ran deep. Following the ICC decision, the Gatting rebel tour was announced. 'An inescapable happening', was how E.W. Swanton described it.[75] E.M. Wellings actually believed that some of the members of the ICC were more concerned with inflicting harm on England rather than South Africa 'however they saccharine their campaign with anti-apartheid claptrap'.[76]

Economics probably dictated England's response in the end. The counties were dependent upon the income generated from international contests (at least 45 per cent of every county's income is supplied by the annual donation from the TCCB). Mike Turner, the chief executive of Leicestershire, admitted that 'We would have no chance of surviving without our share of the Test pool. We would quickly go to the wall, and we would be joined by most of the other counties.'[77] If countries refused to play England because of South African connections, it would mean isolation and the effects of this were open for all to see in South Africa. Australia could not be relied on to support England as they would surely have preferred the more attractive competition from the West Indies and Pakistan. Leadership of international cricket was also at stake. The MCC provided the president and the secretariat of the ICC. Any split would jeopardise their role as the guardian of the game. Colin Cowdrey turned down an invitation to attend the South African centenary celebrations for fear of jeopardising his appointment as the head of the ICC. The TCCB were, in effect, then, making a political decision, balancing the twin conceptions of the right of freedom of movement for its members and maintaining leadership of international cricket. Studying the history of the sport, it is no surprise that they chose the latter.

Protest

The later tours took place during a period of great unrest within South Africa. The townships revolted in September 1984 in defiance of the government's tricameral constitution. Three thousand people were to lose their lives and 30,000 their freedom in this latest phase of the struggle for political equality. From this disorder rose the UDF, an umbrella organisation that held together and linked trade unionists, liberation theologians, educators and members of the ANC. Sporting groups were included in this broadest of movements, which was formed to galvanise opposition to the new constitution.

Seen as a stimulant for South African morale, the cricket tours found themselves entwined in the broader political process. Cricket became a vehicle for anti-racist solidarity, and a central force for opposing the white hegemony. The Australians were threatened with violence. Ahmed Mangera, the secretary of SACB, warned that 'We may capitalise on the upsurge of violence in the country to dissuade them.'[78] Alfred Nzo, secretary-general of the ANC, commented at the Commonwealth Heads of Government meeting that 'the people of South Africa are capable of harming the cricketers. I give that warning.' He added that cricket grounds would become 'war-zones' and that the ANC would not be responsible if any of the Australian cricketers were hurt.[79] Nothing came of what amounted to intimidation, but the South African cricketing authorities were concerned enough to threaten the ANC with the force of the state in support of Bacher's project: 'We have intensive security arrangements, most undercover, linked through a senior government expert.'[80]

The English were snubbed throughout their visit. At two luxury hotels where they stayed, there were protest strikes by staff belonging to the South African Commercial, Catering and Allied Workers Union. Where they did play, demonstrations ensured that the tour remained on the front pages of the press. No opportunity was wasted to embarrass the team, showing sport to be an easy target for the promotion of political ideals. The level of protest against the Gatting visit dwarfed anything that had arisen during previous rebel tours. This perhaps highlights the better organisational skills of the ANC-aligned National Sports Congress (NSC), who were able to draw on their African supporters in the trade unions and wider political circles. Demonstrations had been illegal until the recent de Klerk liberalisation programme – and it was cricket which provided a focal-point for the first-ever legal protests allowed in South Africa.

The tour was carefully managed to show to the international community the measures that the Cricket Union had taken towards multiracial sport. As such, it proved a public-relations disaster. At the first 'Test' the South African Broadcasting Company commentators noted that nearly half of the exceptionally small crowd was made up of police officers.[81] The South African organisation 'Freedom in Sport' ferried in a number of black spectators who obviously knew little about cricket. Freedom in Sport had been set up by Afrikaans businessman Peter Celliers, who admitted to purchasing the tickets for the black audience. 'Yes I paid for their tickets. You know why? I wanted them to see how we whites enjoy an afternoon playing our kind of sport.'[82] The development programme was suspended in most of the townships. A number of black officials, such as Liaqat Nosarka, resigned from SACU, and a number of Asian businessmen severed links with the white-led organisation. Throughout the tour, the protests against the cricket actually received more international coverage than de Klerk's reform proposals (with the obvious exception of his speech on 2 February 1990). Thus, did this particular rebel tour prove to be totally counterproductive.

On Sunday, 11 February 1990, Nelson Mandela was released from 27 years of imprisonment. On the same day Ali Bacher completed a deal with the NSC – without the authority of the SACU – conceding the second 'Test' and the planned return of the English 'rebels' in favour of a stay of execution for the one day games, and an end to the demonstrations. Geoff Dakin, the SACU president, stated that in the present political climate tours run counter 'to the wider interests of South Africa as a whole'.[83] Bacher, moreover, later claimed that SACU had agreed to cut short the tour 'to show its support for the dramatic changes' announced by de Klerk on 2 February.[84] The deal incensed many, but as Mike Proctor expressed it, 'the release of Mandela and the unbanning of the ANC were more important to South Africa at that time than a cricket tour'.[85] Indeed, the tour actually complicated the environment for negotiations.[86] The government's primary purpose now with the release of Mandela and the unbanning of the ANC was to dampen down social unrest. The last thing it wanted was a central focus that could allow for the expression of discontent.

Conclusion

The key question refers to the game of cricket. The rebel cricketers were invited to South Africa, primarily, it has to be assumed, to engage in contest with a South African national XI. It was hoped that their visits would rejuvenate the game at large and encourage more black players to come forward. That it was political is beyond doubt: the government contributed financially to the tours to the extent that SACU would have been bankrupt without their support, and they allowed a number of exceptions to apartheid legislation in order to accommodate the sportsmen. This is because cricket, and sport in general, was viewed as a component of the 'total strategy'. So, although the sporting and political authorities claimed to be 'doing all that they can' to extend the game to the widest possible of populations, the opposition cried foul – for the reasons behind this attempted expansion had little to do with the furtherance of a non-racial society; quite the reverse, in fact.

Regarding the question of cricket, one has to be concerned with the properties of the sport. It may be considered just a game, but how does it fit into the wider picture with other sports and with guidelines that regulate them? All sport in South Africa was subject to the legislation of the Nationalist government. If sport was relieved of the worst aspects of apartheid, why was this the case? If it is because the regime wanted to promote an activity considered politically 'neutral', sought international recognition and aimed to provide an opiate to distract the mass population from engaging in political activity, then sport is political. The South African regime, under pressure from forces beyond its control, attempted to reinvent itself with a more liberal taint, its reason being quite simply survival. Visits from acknowledged and respected cricketers enabled the government's policies to be viewed in a more favourable light. Nonetheless, these visits were viewed as a component of the 'total strategy' meant that it would continue to be associated with apartheid and, as such, would invite condemnation.

Despite the claims that rebel tours were helping to break down apartheid by encouraging the game amongst black children, Bacher acknowledged that its purpose was to 'maintain standards at the highest level'. In reality, though, Bacher conceded at the end of the tour that 'They have not been arranged either to break down or support apartheid. At the end of the day they are cricket tours.'[87] That the visit of an England team ruptured the development programme suggested that the foundations laid in the townships were weak, and that politics was a more potent force for change than sport could ever be.

The ICC could not pretend that the political developments in South Africa were not taking place. It is inevitable that sport becomes embroiled in any widespread disturbance (see, for example, the problems for football in the Balkans following the fighting in Kosovo and the earlier disintegration of Yugoslavia). In this context, it is not surprising that South Africa was not welcomed back into the international fold. To do so would be seen as giving credence to the Nationalist regime. However, there was the real fear of splits and divisions among the cricketing fraternity over the question of how to deal with rebel tours. Any piecemeal resolution of the South African question would only lead to further disruption as cricketing authorities came increasingly under pressure from governments determined to sever all links with South Africa.

SACU appeared, at last, to accept that political developments and relationships shape the wider fabric of society when they commissioned Bacher to investigate all aspects of South African cricket and to redefine its goals following the monumental shift in South Africa's political fortunes.[88] Amongst Bacher's aims were:

- to create unity and an autonomous body for all cricketers in South Africa;
- to ensure that cricket is used as a medium for the complete eradication of apartheid;
- to prepare South Africa for international cricket in a post-apartheid society.[89]

A new hegemony was being forged in South Africa. Over ten years on, and the question of race is still primary to South African cricket (although this has been somewhat overshadowed by Hansie Cronje's match-fixing). Quotas seem to have dominated the questions relating to the selection of both provincial and national sides.

12

Conclusion: The Role of Sport in Influencing Change in South Africa

The primary aim of this book has been to examine the formal relationship between politics and sport. My approach to this problem has been through the definition of key concepts and then their examination in both an historical and contemporary context. In order to give some practical relevance to this theoretical structure, I have analysed the history of cricket in South Africa. This has been conducted through both a theoretical analysis and an examination of notable case histories. This exercise has been engaged for one overriding purpose – to explore the influence of what I perceive politics to be on the sport's development. Having established that the history of South African cricket has been intimately bound up with broader political developments, I now examine the sport's role in the downfall of apartheid. Finally, the book reverts to definition and seeks to place the 'no sport and politics' argument within a framework of conservative thought, concluding that such statements were themselves part of a wider structure which encompassed politics.

The perception that sport had the ability to influence political developments in South Africa is a long one. Dr Koornhof, the Sports Minister, for example, told an audience in 1977: 'Let us admit here this afternoon that play and sport are strong enough to cause political and economic relations to flourish or collapse.'[1] The Hertstigte Nasionale Party (HNP) attributed the watering down of petty-apartheid in the 1980s to the late 1960s when Vorster reacted to the international sports boycott by granting concessions toward multi-racial sports. If Vorster had not done this 'the present mixed constitution would not have been possible'.[2] The whole ethos of the bridge-building position was supposedly that maintaining relations with South Africa would undermine racial structures.[3]

The development programme introduced cricket into the troubled black townships, providing opportunities to those who lacked the resources to compete on a 'level playing field'. Black schools were encouraged to take up sport and compete against their white counterparts. Through such measures and by advancing multi-racial cricket, the sporting authorities claimed that they were undermining apartheid, highlighting that change was possible and could be both piecemeal and peaceful. By the 1980s the normative base of apartheid could decline no further and there no longer remained the need to prolong a racial system, so wrought with contradiction that it created the conditions for its own destruction.

So, how do we assess the role of cricket, within the wider format of sport, in the transformation from racial segregation to 'one person-one vote'? In order to assess its role as a force for change I have reverted to an analysis influenced by definition and sought an explanation that probes the theory of political change. This is then related to factors specific to South Africa, and is then finally applied to sport. I contend that it is only possible to determine the effect of sport on the reform and downfall of apartheid once one is aware of all other phenomena that influenced change. Therefore, this concluding chapter provides considerable detail.

Theories of political change

Guy Swanson defines 'change' as that which 'refers to a difference in a structure, the difference occurring over time and being initiated by factors outside that structure'.[4] There are two broad forms of change: 'developmental', in which minor reforms are enacted to alleviate difficulty or to advance a cause. Such piecemeal and evolutionary changes may result in a different political system being established on contrasting principles to the prevailing one. 'Radical' change involves a thorough overhaul of a political system to an extent so severe that from it emerges a new social structure, so distinct that it constitutes a turning point in a nation's history; the fundamentalist regimes in Iran (1979) and Afghanistan (1998) provide recent examples of this.

What distinguishes change from other processes is that the sources of adaptation lie outside the primary political framework. There are a number of variables associated with changes in social structures: sources of food, the presence or absence of private property, the existence and elaborateness of differences in wealth, the extent of religious/secular movements, urban development, and finally the form of the society's political system. It is the latter that is of primary concern here.

As with all issues that derive from political phenomena, there is no acknowledged and accepted scientific process whose end-result is political change. Marxists will stress the economic forces that ultimately influence the structures of all societies, and by association necessitate change. Others may well focus on the method of political leadership and assess its alienation from the mass as a fundamental cause of discontent. What we have to accept, in an exercise such as this, is that there are several interacting factors which singly and collectively influence change. It is the goal here to outline such explanations.

Crisis situations such as military defeats discredit authority by undermining national leadership. Wars can lead to material scarcities and a sense of injured national pride. Defeat could result in the imposition of a political apparatus, as experienced by Germany after the Second World War. Direct intervention, as experienced by Nicaragua, Panama and Grenada at the hands of the United States, can also result in political change. Economic crises can threaten an individual's prosperity and security. Change in neighbouring states can affect the domestic equilibrium – the 'Domino effect', as shown in Eastern Europe in 1989. When changes in society are so excessive that the structure of authoritative decision-making fails, the government may no longer be able to apply coercion successfully. When the systems of coercion fail for the government then the structures favoured by the existing elite come under pressure. These crisis situations permit radical ideas to acquire a sense of respectability and legitimacy. The established order, the 'norm', is undermined and new values are given the intellectual freedom to develop, enabling competition between different sets of beliefs.

The *resolve of the political regime* could ultimately affect its outcome. Plato argued that 'revolution always starts from the outbreak of internal dissension in the ruling class. The constitution cannot be upset so long as that class is of one mind, however small it may be'.[5] An established, ideologically dominant and unified hierarchy, determined at all costs to defend its grip on the reigns of power, will be more difficult to dislodge than one stricken by division and indecisiveness. The history of the failed French Third Republic is dominated by conflicts within the elites. In contrast, in Italy since the Second World War politics has been unstable due to the numerous turnover of governments. Yet the political system has remained solid because the same social elites have commanded power. Only when dominance becomes undermined does the cohesiveness of the social regime become psychologically threatened.

The *effectiveness of political structures* can be important in how governments deal with political conflict. Systems can collapse if the institutional structures and processes fail to settle contentious matters. If there is no agreement on the rules that govern how the political system operates; if there are no accepted forms of communication there can be no implementation of policies that could dampen hostility. Well-established procedures for the resolution of grievances work to channel disputes within a legalised format. It is a key feature of liberal political society, setting the parameters within which the opposition can operate. If there are no such mechanisms, political opposition may have to be restricted. Such weakened forms of political apparatus are exposed when confronted by a crisis situation.

Governments are weakened when they must *rule without the consent of vast sections of the population*. Governments become legitimised through contact with their electorate. In the absence of legitimacy, rule is maintained through fear and coercion. This is obvious in the case of dictatorship, but also prevails if, for example, there are tensions between different ethnic, tribal or national groups. The anthropologist A.R. Radcliffe-Brown noted that 'In order that a society may exist and continue to exist the groups that constitute it must possess a certain degree of cohesion. A people to maintain itself and its culture must possess a certain degree of social integration.'[6]

E. Allardt and Y. Lithunen argue that the most stable political conditions exist where numerous social divisions overlap and are forced into coalitions. All groups thereby feel that they can influence the political agenda.[7] Neglect of one or other group can render the political elite susceptible to external interference. This could come in the form of military intervention or in the introduction of new ideas or institutional models that derive from contact between societies of similar levels of complexity. In times of crisis such division could break out into internal warfare. The problem is exacerbated if an alternative authority, such as an Ayatollah or a government-in-exile, exists.

Political elites are susceptible to the wider social and economic currents within a modernising society. They have to adapt to changes in the natural environment, the demographic process and technological innovation. Institutions that fail to adapt to such phenomena will soon lose legitimacy in the minds of the populace. These flows give rise to the gestation of *ideas that can forge new social movements*. The pluralist approach to social change claims that trends evolve as the direct outcome of competition between ideas and interests. These, in turn, create and shape political consciousness. They provide overall guides to political action and other social behaviour. 'The issues on a political agenda may be rationally linked ... to some comprehensive political ideal or principle that transcends the agenda.'[8] Thus, politics is subject not only to the social and economic environment in which it sits, but also to a wider agenda that embraces more than simply the rule of a party.

Such forces for change can result in one of two scenarios: the removal of a political elite and its replacement by a new social, economic and political order (revolution), or the reform of existing political structures within the established social and economic framework. As the latter was the case in South Africa, it is the question of reform that concerns this chapter. An early definition of 'reform' was to literally re-form, to re-assess and re-establish a position. In this sense reform is viewed as a reactionary implement used to sustain the existing authority. The 'Reformation' in the sixteenth century, for example, described the establishment of Protestantism as a movement to restore an older form of spiritual experience. In contemporary language, however, reform is defined as to make anew and is linked to the notions of progress and improvement. However, despite these positive qualities, reform, whilst removing the more undesirable characteristics of a political structure, is enacted to maintain and ultimately strengthen the prevailing institution. Machiavelli described policy as an activity for *sustaining power*.[9] Reform is an endorsement, therefore, of the status quo; a set of measures that are preferable to the replacement of the existing order. In the Disraeli tradition it promotes the easing of inequality as being in the interests of the rich. It is criticised, as a concept, because by its nature reform perpetuates that which it appears to condemn. It instigates change within an established constitutional or socio-economic framework. It still, though, has to give the impression of progress if it is to satisfy the requirements of the developmental model. Ultimately, however, reform is a component of the ultimate political objective, power.

Factors in the defeat of apartheid

The preceding explanations can all to some extent be applied to the South African environment in the period under review. What I am constructing is not necessarily a series of laws that explain political reform, but rather a structure that will emphasise phenomena in a non-uniform manner depending on the subject under study. What is particularly relevant for this book is the contrasting roles of the different explanations of 'politics' in assessing political reform. If change comes about as a result of causes beyond the realm of institutional studies then it is only reasonable to assume that the study of politics embraces a much wider programme.

Crisis situations

History is invariably determined by issues that derive from economics. The process of racial segregation, for example, owed its force to the great gold- and diamond-mining corporations. Apartheid implanted further racial distinctions onto a structure already infected with the 'logic' of imperialism and white supremacy. Capitalism obviously benefited from a large supply of cheap labour, and helped to determine the nature of South African politics. Political change, therefore, does not simply devolve from the ideological preferences of a leader or of a party but is an end-result of the powerful forces shaping society.

It was the contradictory nature of apartheid itself that ultimately led to its collapse. So irrational had racial politics become that the regime would have had to bankrupt the country in order to preserve itself. The long-term structural economic problems, a direct consequence of apartheid philosophy, are outlined in Chapter 4. During the 1970s they could no longer be glossed over. The economy stagnated to the point where the rate of growth was insufficient to maintain a ceiling on unemployment. An estimated 40 per cent of the black population was permanently without work,[10] two-thirds of whom were under the age of 30.[11] A large number of these were matriculates who had benefited from the expansion in African education, only to be denied employment opportunities because of the restrictive economic conditions. Inflation had been in double figures since 1973,[12] and was exacerbated by the wage demands of the burgeoning black trade union movement. Domestic weaknesses were distorted by changes in the world economy leading to a reduced demand for South Africa's primary commodities. Gold prices, which had helped the economy through the oil crisis and recessions of the 1970s declined in the 1980s.[13]

South Africa no longer appeared so attractive a destination for foreign direct investment. *Business Week* estimated that the average return on foreign investment dropped from 20 per cent in 1980 to 5 per cent by 1985. There was virtually no new foreign investment in the early 1980s.[14] When exchange controls were relaxed in 1983 the four largest British investors (including the three biggest non-banking foreign companies listed on the Johannesburg stock exchange) withdrew their capital. By the summer of 1986, total debt had amassed to $23.2 billion,[15] of which 67 per cent of the $16.5bn foreign debt was made up of short-term loans.[16] This represented a staggering 50 per cent of GDP[17] and had to be paid out of whatever trade surpluses could be salvaged in the face of international sanctions and declining foreign reserves. Following P.W. Botha's Rubicon speech[18] in August 1985, which re-committed the NP to a racial political system, American banks called in their loans, quickly followed by British, German and Swiss. The Rand plunged 35 per cent in a fortnight, hitting an all-time low of 34.75 cents.[19] By 1987 over 250 foreign companies had withdrawn from South Africa.[20] The Republic was turned into a 'siege economy', starved of foreign exchange and development capital. A month after 'Rubicon' business leaders flew to Lusaka to hold 'cordial' talks with the ANC.

These grim indices provided a foundation for the rebellion that broke out in the townships in 1984. The ANC called on black South Africans to make the country 'ungovernable' and by the end of 1985, 155 townships had become affected. Amid this upheaval the government's resources became alarmingly over-stretched. Government spending increased by an annual average of 18.5 per cent during Botha's tenure, rising from 25.1 per cent to 27.3 per cent of GDP.[21] A large repressive force was required to protect the state from opposition to its policies. The defence budget increased from $60m in 1960 to $3bn in 1982.[22] Conscription for young white males further exacerbated the shortage of skilled labour. South Africa considered itself to be *the* African superpower and played up its role in the Cold War. It conducted military operations in Angola, occupied Namibia and armed dissident groups in neighbouring countries. The priority given to military expenditure eventually undermined its ability to fund social measures and repay the debt, which, in turn, meant further deprivation in the black communities and lack of access to the capital markets necessary to boost growth.

The authority of the political elite had clearly waned. Botha simply undermined parliament by elevating the role of the State Security Council, giving the military a greater influence in the decisions of government. At the same time as the President concentrated power into his own hands, a massive political apparatus was installed to administer his commands and give the impression of representation to all sections of South African society. By 1988 this political bureaucracy consisted of five 'presidents', nine chief ministers, 300 cabinet ministers, more than 1,500 members of legislative bodies and tens of thousands of local councillors. The wage bill consumed close to 60 per cent of the national budget, or approximately a quarter of South Africa's GNP.[23]

There was a series of external international events that further weakened the South African position. The independence of Mozambique (1975), Angola (1975), and Zimbabwe (1980) had given a boost to black South Africans, indicating the fallibility of the 'master race'. When the army was turned back in Angola in 1975, it showed that the military machine was not invincible. The Afrikaner revolution now entered a phase of crisis and decline.[24] The 1988 settlement with the US, Soviet Union and Cuba on the independence of Namibia was made from a position of relative weakness. This was in part because the growing co-operation between Moscow and Washington meant that the US was less willing to defend Pretoria, as its geopolitical significance waned. Finally, Soviet perestroika undermined the psychology of 'total onslaught', and with it the whole justification of military oppression.

Disunity of regime

What had maintained the Afrikaner *volk* as a political entity was its sense of unity and purpose in the face of a number of common enemies – the English, blacks, liberalism, communism. Verwoerd had always claimed that the NP was more than simply a political party, it was a movement, which was to become synonymous with the state.[25] This afforded the justification for excluding other groups from government, for advancing the interests of the state became the sole aim of policy. Racial segregation was sold as a norm, to be in the best interests of the black population. This position could not be intellectually sustained. During the 1980s the ruling establishment increasingly accepted that it could no longer be either morally or politically justified. The reforms of the 1980s[26] represented the demise of the notion of grand apartheid, and as such the *raison d'être* of the National Party. The 'total strategy' implicitly conceded that white supremacy was neither natural nor part of some divine plan. Thus the normative basis of apartheid was totally undermined and the fragile coalition that had sustained Afrikaner nationalism came to an end.

The business community, uneasy bedfellows with the regime in the 1970s, further distanced themselves from Pretoria. Following P.W. Botha's Rubicon speech, an advertisement in *The Sunday Times* placed by 100 leading industrialists issued a set of demands including the lifting of the State of Emergency, the abolition of statutory racial segregation, the granting of full citizenship to all South Africans, and negotiations with black leaders toward the aim of power sharing. A select few even engaged in dialogue with the ANC in an attempt to forge a pro-capitalist and anti-revolution consensus with the 'government-in-exile'. The government worried that due to decades of economic favouritism, Afrikaners were becoming influential captains of industry[27] and forming class structures similar to the English. They were unlikely to abandon their new-found position for some mystic call to the unity of the *volk*. Botha reacted to these concerns by embracing the cause of business interests to the detriment of those of the small farmer, the state bureaucrat and the Afrikaner worker, the traditional bedrock of Afrikaner nationalism.[28]

There were significant changes within Afrikaner society, themselves a result of the increased prosperity flowing from apartheid. David Welsh of the University of Cape Town pointed out that 'ninety per cent are urban – perhaps more than 50 per cent are middle class – and more than 30 per cent proceed from school to University or technikon'.[29] The expansion in higher education created a large intelligentsia who, influenced by European literature and philosophy, began to question the values of apartheid. Very few intellectuals remained loyal to either apartheid or the NP. An increasing number actually emigrated, depriving the economy of scores of accountants, doctors, lawyers and other professionals.

In 1985, 16 theologians of the Dutch Reformed Church signed a 'confession of guilt' recognising their church's compliance with apartheid. They now rejected the view that there was a Biblical justification for apartheid. This was significant for four out of five Cabinet ministers and a majority of NP MPs belonged to this church.

Botha's reforms were an attempt to consolidate his own position as *Hoofleier* and to isolate the *verkramptes* (hard-line reactionaries) in his party. He had manoeuvred himself through the 1977–78 Muldergate scandal[30] to enable the more liberal Cape NP to force through a series of measures which ultimately strengthened military and business interests. The effect of such a position was to dismay the hard right within the NP. In 1982 disgruntled right-wing MPs formed the Conservative Party. About a quarter of Transvaal NP district and branch committee members soon defected.[31] This had consequences for the Broederbond which distanced itself from the regime and even withdrew its exclusive support for the NP in September 1981, reversing its policy to expel any Broeder supporting the HNP.

Not only did Botha antagonise his right wing, he managed to isolate the more liberal elements within his party. The 'total strategy' envisaged the apparatus of policy in the hands of a single individual. It was far too important to be trusted to NP politicians. The State of Emergency, for example, proclaimed by the President on 12 June 1986, was made without approval from parliament. State policy became monopolised by the National Security Management System, which was dominated by the South African Defence Force. In 1987 the Nationalist MP Wynand Malan left the NP to fight his seat as an Independent. The Ambassador to Britain, Dr Dennis Worall, and Professor Ester Lategan joined him in founding the Independent Movement. An increasing number of academics and intellectuals also parted company, causing one commentator to remark that the National Party had become 'brain dead'.[32]

The NP's sole mission now appeared to be simply the maintenance of power. This lack of a big 'idea' and the ever crumbling unity was reflected at the ballot box. From 65 per cent of the vote at the 1977 general election, the NP's majority was cut to ten (48 per cent of the vote) by 1989. It was losing ground to both the Conservative Party, which had replaced the HNP as a more effective right-wing opposition, and the newly formed liberal Democratic Party. There was no longer a coherent Afrikaner ideology expressed through one political party. The lines of division now lay within Afrikanerism rather than between Afrikaners and non-Afrikaners. By 1989 the NP actually received the majority of its support from the English-speaking electorate.[33]

Effectiveness of political structures

Traditionally there were no structures through which to channel black opinion, except for the ramshackle homeland system. Political parties and trade unions were outlawed and the vote had long been a distant memory. Such systems of political rule bred alienation and discontent, creating future hazards for the regime. The business-inspired Lombard Report (1980) argued that effective government could not be provided by separate development, but only by 'the emergence of new, legitimate political institutions that allow the effective participation of the governed'.[34] The 'total strategy' envisaged that a legalised democratic apparatus could assist in creating conditions that would be more conducive to capitalism and thereby the white hegemony. Middle-class blacks would be given the political responsibility for administering difficult to manage territories, ensuring those issues such as housing, transport and medical provision became depoliticised. Political tensions between different class and tribal interests could then be exploited. NP reformists believed that this would eventually legitimise the apartheid state. In all reality it recycled United Party initiatives from 1948 and further alienated conservative Afrikaners.

Parliaments were established for the Indian and coloured communities, sitting alongside, but always subservient to, the white assembly. A form of local government was also concocted for the African townships. The structures that existed, however, could not claim meaningful independence from the government. Members of the African local governments could be appointed and removed by central government. The policy of granting 'independence' to the homelands was accompanied by the condition of cooperative government. Kwa Ndeble, for instance, was refused independence in 1986 until a stable leadership (that is, pro-Pretoria) was established. In effect, then, these institutions would become a vehicle for implementing government policy. Their function was to carry out the regime's 'dirty work', being primarily agents to whom the central state 'sub-contracted' responsibility for controlling black areas.

This experiment in black 'democracy' was rejected. The turnout for the 1983 township elections was officially recorded as 21 per cent of registered voters (because of out-dated voters lists, and the thousands who failed to register, the UDF could claim the actual figure to be much lower). In some townships the official figure was as low as 5.6 per cent.[35] In Soweto, for example, with a population of over one million the mayor was elected with a mere 1,115 votes.[36] In elections to the coloured House of Representatives in August 1984 only 29 per cent of *registered* coloureds and 19 per cent of *registered* Indians voted. In elections to municipal authorities in 1988, less than half the township wards were contested. In Soweto only 8,000 voted.[37]

The township insurrections pushed these fragile institutions aside. They were replaced by the UDF, who co-ordinated strikes and boycotts, organised funerals into great political rallies and administered their own systems of justice. In the Port Elizabeth townships the UDF even issued hawkers' licences and fixed the price of staple commodities in black-owned stores.[38] Even when the 1986 Emergency Regulations virtually strangled these infant democratic structures, the government could not succeed in crushing resistance to its rule. Calls for boycotts and work stoppages were met with very positive responses; elections in 1988 were once again snubbed.

Rule without the consent of the population

This, in effect, is an extension and a consequence of the lack of political structures to channel grievance. Authority is based on a perceived right to rule, and invokes a moral obligation on the part of the ruled to obey.[39] The National Party could not claim authority from among all the population groups within South Africa. As well as denying them a voice in the mechanisms of power, resources were unevenly distributed according to colour of skin. If politics is concerned with the allocation of such resources, then it is inevitable that inequalities breed discontent. Therefore, the regime was viewed as failing to satisfy its responsibilities as a ruling power. This may be considered as a theoretical argument, but it was increasingly adopted as an official stance by Western powers in their attempts to 'persuade' Pretoria to reform.

The basis of political 'legitimacy' was steadily shrinking. The white population, 21 per cent of all inhabitants in 1911 declined to 17 per cent in 1970 and to a projected 14 per cent by the early 2000s.[40] This real decline proved insufficient to spur growth and provide the expanding market for consumer goods that manufacturing interests demanded. The political environment ensured that immigration would fail to make up the shortfall. Between 1961 and 1968 South Africa welcomed an average annual influx of 40,000 whites; between 1980 and 1987 that average had fallen to 7,500.[41]

Botha sought the appeasement of the black middle class in order to bolster his claims to political legitimacy. However, he was forced to use repressive measures in order to maintain stability. This in turn alienated the black middle class. Here lies a further weakness of the regime, namely that it was dependent on the very people that it repressed. This imposed limits on the degrees of repression. It was not economically viable, for instance, to have thousands of the productive class under lock and key. An appearance of normality had to be restored. International opinion had to be mollified in order to stave off economic collapse. It was therefore imperative that sanctions be lifted and the flow of foreign capital switched back on. The regime could only achieve this through negotiations with legitimate representatives of the black majority.

New ideas

The liberation movement became far more focused and organised in the 1980s. The UDF was founded in 1983 as a protest movement that sought to place an irrevocable strain on the resources of the state. Its creation was in direct response to the creation of the tricameral (Indian, coloured and white) parliament. Allan Boesak declared that 'we need a united front ... There is no reason why churches, civic associations, trade unions, student organisations, and sports bodies should not unite on this issue.'[42] At its peak it claimed an affiliation of 700 groups representing two million people in all the major centres in South Africa.

Affiliation implied recognition of the ANC's claim to leadership of the liberation movement, socialism and expectations of revolutionary change.[43] Immediate objectives included the overthrow of black local government, consumer boycotts and the institution of 'people's power', whereby neighbourhood bodies would replace the state in the provision of education, justice and municipal administration. The UDF developed a political consciousness that flourished into a rival ideological structure that would challenge the white hegemony. It represented a distinct political culture, in which alternative values and discipline, replaced the traditional forces of social control and order such as the family and the church. It refused to permit the government breathing space for its 'concessions'. Its objectives though remained broad in order to create a sense of unease in the white communities by mobilising a diverse, vast constituency, which formulated an image of apartheid that was totally unreasonable, thereby undermining the normative basis of nationalist rule.

By the fall of 1984, the townships were engaged in open revolt against the state apparatus. Civil government collapsed and was being replaced by civic organisations and street committees who installed a popular mechanism of self-rule. Radical leaders used this form of proto-democracy to organise a meticulous campaign against apartheid through rent and consumer boycotts, strikes and rallies. A system of self-government posed an immediate threat to the Nationalist oligarchy, such that their rule was totally rejected, evident by the open display of ANC flags in the 'liberated' townships and black power salutes on the streets.

The relaxation of the labour laws permitting black trade unions resulted in a spiralling membership that grew from 808,053 in 1979 to 1,406,302 in 1984.[44] Out of the 'community unions' emerged in 1985, the Congress of South African Trade Unions (COSATU), which immediately adopted a political tone arguing that the struggle for rights in the workplace was synonymous with the campaign for political rights in the wider community. They became involved in struggles over rents, transportation and education.[45] Cyril Ramaphosa, Secretary-General of the National Union of Mineworkers, warned that 'Management should take heed that the NUM is prepared to take up any issue be it wages, be it political issues, be it safety, and it could mobilise workers around any issue, virtually.'[46]

Whilst the black community was defining a political consciousness for itself, the ANC, still maintaining a military presence,[47] adapted its strategy to further undermine white authority and to present itself as a government-in-waiting. By 1988 it had moved from a position in which it would only negotiate a transfer of power with a defeated white regime to one that called on the white population to support it in forming a coalition to establish a non-racial society based on multi-party democracy and a mixed economy. From making the country ungovernable, the ANC adopted the approach of focusing on those institutions that remained committed to segregation. Such was the movement's authority and status that no settlement could be negotiated without it. This was acknowledged by first businessmen and later church leaders and sports administrators who began to open dialogue with an organisation that was still officially categorised by the regime as 'terrorist'.

These three distinct arms of the liberation movement presented themselves as capable of government. They also gave the impression that they had the resources with which to seize power. Increasingly they were listened to, further undermining any residual white commitment to apartheid and to white minority rule.

Power

All the previous points indicate the pressures that the regime faced. These combined, it could be claimed, to force Pretoria into a position in which it sought first to reform and later to dismantle apartheid. This, I feel, leaves the picture incomplete. The state machine was both substantial and brutal; it could have engaged in protracted toe-to-toe combat with its opponents. This certainly would have been the position if the Conservative Party had come to power. The opening chapter, which debated the definition of 'politics', concluded that any stance, from the institutional to the hegemonic, is based on the question and nature of 'power'. Without power there is no political rule. The NP introduced its reform programme in order to maintain power, initially for itself and then predominantly for the economic interests that it increasingly came to represent. South African capitalism could no longer afford the reform process. It was sacrificed in order to maintain the prevailing economic relationships. This whole question underpins the nature of politics and its relationship to the wider structures that operate in any society.

Reform was always instigated in the interests of maintaining power. Botha's line of argument was that maintaining policies that did not work represented a danger to the Afrikaner people for it gave their opponents opportunities to attack the government. The 'total strategy' was a means to prolong apartheid. 'I will do everything that I deem necessary for our survival.'[48] Botha wanted to sweep away the obsolete socio-economic policies of previous NP governments, he *did not* anticipate the termination of white control. He stressed that 'as long as I am the leader of the NP, there will not be one person one vote in parliament'.[49]

Ruling elites have often assumed that they can buy time for themselves by placating the masses with a few token concessions. For three-quarters of the population, though, Botha's changes amounted to little. The promise of reform – then its limitations – sharpened sensitivity to discrimination, intensifying what Isaiah Berlin called 'social dissonance', caused by advances in some areas and a lack of progress in others. Because the regime refused to ditch central elements of Grand Apartheid theory (the vote, segregated structures, homelands policy) and that it still held to the principal ambition of separate development, meant that it could not legitimise its reforms. Therefore its solutions were doomed to failure. The ever-maturing and sophisticated opposition could not be bought off with an improvement or two in material conditions whilst being denied the vote. Verwoerd had acknowledged that concessions do not necessarily ease pressure and that piecemeal reform actually renders it more difficult to maintain one's position.[50] Alexis de Tocqueville remarked that 'The most perilous moment for a bad government is when it seeks to mend its ways ... Patiently endured so long as it seemed beyond redress, a grievance comes to appear intolerable once the possibility of removing it crosses men's minds ... '[51]

As President, de Klerk was forced to introduce measures that amounted to the death of apartheid. He stated that the government's aim was 'a totally new and just constitutional dispensation in which every inhabitant will enjoy equal rights, treatment and opportunity in every sphere of endeavour – constitutional, social and economic'.[52] This blueprint for a new South Africa promised the vote for all and a bill of rights with the condition that no racial group would dominate others. This was a further ploy to maintain some influence on the structures of power. Following the NP's poor showing at the 1989 election, his Minister of Law and Order, Adriaan Vlok, conceded that 'Everybody, including the police, the government and the country, realises that the status quo cannot continue.'[53] De Klerk was praised by Western leaders, and was even compared to the Soviet leader Mikhail Gorbachev. However, he had no grand political vision, just a desire to maintain white privilege.[54] At the state opening of parliament on 2 February 1990 he announced the end of the ban on the ANC, PAC and Communist Party. Nelson Mandela was released nine days later. Even now, this approach remained founded on self-preservation. De Klerk was buying time with which to lift sanctions and further raise the profiles of conservative blacks against the ANC. He remained reluctant to commit his party to one-person, one-vote. The Party's future now lay with people who shared its economic, as opposed to its previous racial, values.

The combined force of the liberation movement, especially COSATU, created panic within the business sector. Something had to be done to avoid the risk of facing a victorious black political machine that would throw the 'capitalist baby out with the apartheid bathwater'. Merle Lipton's thesis holds that the pressures for reform from business interests were ultimately responsible for the demise of apartheid. This would suggest, though it is not Lipton's argument, that this could only be if economic interests wielded political authority. The employers' organisation the Consultative Business Movement challenged the business community to 'define the real nature of their own power', and to see how this could be used 'to advance the society towards non-racial democracy'.[55] This organisation merged with the Progressive Federal Party and Malan's National Democratic Movement to form the Democratic Party in April 1989, with the financial backing of both Afrikaner and English capital. Botha also projected his administration as the government of a broad alliance of all sections of capital. Executives from the major monopolies were brought into the decision-making process to supervise the restructuring of the civil service. Provincial figures suggested that efforts for reform should now focus on the 'reasonable people' in the NP.[56] So, in an attempt at least to influence the new emerging power structure, the NP sought to reinvent itself as a traditional Western-style Christian Democratic party.

The reforming qualities of sport

The motivation for this discussion on the reform of apartheid has been to highlight the forces that influenced political reform. The changes afoot in South African sport and especially cricket could not take credit for these wider developments, they were part and parcel of the same process; reflective, as I have argued throughout this book, of the same social, economic and political environment. When this setting became subject to pressures that resulted in a thorough re-evaluation, it was inevitable that sport would be prey to the same changes. That cricket actually became embroiled in the reform process reinforces not only the centrality of the game in a nation's consciousness, but the bond that cultural phenomena enjoy with politics. This is borne out by an examination of the political developments in the game but located within the structure of political change outlined above.

The major reforms in cricket and sport came at times of particular strain for the government. The sporting policies of 1971, the autonomous sports policy of the 1980s, and the general relaxation of measures that affected sport were all reactions to internal and external pressures. Sport became associated with political change because of its centrality to white hegemony and because, on the international stage, it was clearly visible – it was important to project the image of change, and sport could help do this. The Broederbond Executive, who were responsible for drawing up the multinational sports policy in 1971, conceded that 'sport [is important] in international affairs, for the prestige of countries and the promotion of a cause'.[57] March Krotee remarked that 'it seemed that the South African government has been more sensitive to international pressures concerning sport policy than any other policy within its domain of over 200 racially repressive apartheid acts'.[58] Peter Lambley argued that concessions in sport served the same purpose at home as well. The government could make allowances on petty-apartheid, because these issues were unrelated to the power structure.

> While the authorities busied themselves with strategic supplies, building up armed forces, infiltrating its neighbouring countries, fermenting unrest in Angola, Zambia, Rhodesia, Mozambique and Zaire, we in Cape Town watched to see if black cricket teams would be allowed to play in white leagues.[59]

Fundamentally, sport became important because of the benefits that it presented to the regime. Following the 1986 New Zealand rugby tour to South Africa, Dannie Craven, the head of the white South African Rugby Board, declared that 'this tour has done wonders for the country. Rugby has changed the front pages of newspapers. We no longer see Mandela's name, he has been removed to page six so as to accommodate rugby.'[60] In periods of crisis, sport was promoted as a smokescreen to deflect attention away from the social turmoil gripping the nation. This created its own problems, for if the authorities could exploit sport, the opposition could also target it. Sport became a means to condemn South Africa. The African and other developing nations found they had influence in international organisations such as the IOC that were not determined by economic strength. The Western nations also used sport to pressurise Pretoria, as it offered an alternative to severing more traditional political and economic ties. The sporting boycott was without doubt the most successful (in terms of participation and observance) of all the sanctions against the apartheid regime. In times of crisis, then, sport found itself thrust to the forefront of the South African debate. Indeed, when de Klerk held a referendum in 1992 (held on the day that South Africa were playing England in the cricket World Cup semi-finals) for whites to approve the reform process, sport was ruthlessly exploited. The government threatened that a no vote would mean a return to isolation, which was backed up by the United Cricket Board of South Africa, who stated that a rejection would lead to the South Africans withdrawing from the World Cup.[61]

The extent that the resolve of the regime was undermined by criticism from cricketers is difficult to quantify. Following their casting into the wilderness in 1970, cricketers became more outspoken in favour of multi-racial cricket, whilst maintaining a silence against the racial policies of the government. This has to be viewed, to an extent, as an exercise in self-interest. There were no such demands before their isolation. In elections four-fifths of the white population continued to support parties that advocated racial segregation.

> Are we to believe that South Africa's white sportsmen and women, sports administrators and sports enthusiasts, who pretend to the world that they are for race integration, did not form part of the 80 per cent which wanted strict segregation?[62]

However, criticism does hurt and can help in undermining the collective consciousness. Take the example of Graeme Pollock. He was arguably one of South Africa's, if not international cricket's, finest ever batsmen; a player who was unable to display the extent of his true capabilities because of his country's politics; the stuff that legends are made of. In his final 'international' against the rebel Australians in 1987 he scored 144. This innings sparked widespread celebrations throughout the country providing welcome respite from the developing political crisis. Pollock used this sense of occasion to attack the NP:

> I can see the justice of our cricket isolation now, though it was hard at the time. The changes will have to be political because cricket itself has done a great deal. Pressure for change in South Africa will now have to come by way of international trade and political sanctions, rather than through sport.[63]

When a national sporting hero makes so explicit a political statement such as this it inevitably leaves an aftertaste. It is not so easy to dismiss as rhetoric, and becomes part of the incremental undermining of 'normality'.

The government of cricket reflected that of the state in that there was no provision for structures that represented the different races on an equal footing. Both the SACU and the SACB considered themselves to be the legitimate voice of cricketing interests. Membership of these bodies determined opportunities on the field of play. It was widely believed that the government was supporting the white organisation. Ignorance of black cricket meant that to be heard, SACB had to resort to non-sporting initiatives. How could two opposing camps project their interests and avoid politics?

A regime that imposes its authority without the consent of the mass of the population requires a 'something in common' to integrate its parts. It was claimed at the outset[64] that one of the factors that determines politics' association with sport is such a medium. The integrative qualities of sport could, of course, never replace the denial of political liberty; they could, however, assist in the creation of a less hostile population. Richard Evans wrote, when reporting on the Gatting rebel tour, that:

> Sport ... must be recognised as a serious contributor to education, self-confidence and an alternative lifestyle to crime, all three of which are

crucial to the development of healthy future generations ... what choice has a virile, unemployed teenager got in an underprivileged environment other than sport on one side or drugs, sex and rock and roll on the other?[65]

The values that sport promoted – adherence to the rules, 'fair play' and respect for authority – were fundamental to any social system. The notion that such values could help pacify a politically hostile population was, of course, firmly established.[66]

But what if the integrative qualities bypassed the political authority? The development programme, rebel tours and contact with South Africa were all cited by bridge-builders as examples of how cricket could help integrate South African society. A few months after the end of the 1983 West Indies tour, for example, over 100 sporting bodies in South Africa committed themselves to a philosophy of 'equal opportunities' in sport, from school to international level. Joe Pamensky believed that such measures led to a rethinking of government policy regarding segregation:

> These policies have been executed in so responsible a manner that the government has recognised a de facto situation and has amended all the relevant laws which affect sport ... the success of integration on the cricket field has led and will continue to lead to other changes in South African society.[67]

Cricket succeeded where the government failed in penetrating black communities. Such moves, the argument progressed, weakened the government's resolve to adhere to segregation, showing not only how it was possible for black and white to co-exist, but that success was not determined by the colour of skin; nor for that matter was it reliant on politics! Sport, more than any other factor of social life, was supposedly an opportunity for progression by merit. This is an interesting line, because those who supported cricketing relations with South Africa did so, initially, on the argument that politics and sport should not mix. The argument had now advanced to a claim that cricket could actually influence politics, the closest to an admission of the intimacy of the two subjects. Mike Gatting even claimed credit for the talks that eventually led to the UCBSA: 'I think just by being here we have forced people to face the issues and talk to each other.'[68] This approach reflects the Crick stance that politics is about arriving at decisions through a process of rational discussion.[69] It was nonsense. The South African regime closed off all channels for such dialogue and, as such, put itself outside of the realms of acceptable practice. It was only when this was challenged, through the pressure exerted by the black opposition, that the possibility of a unified cricket board, based on 'non-racial' principles, could be realised. Cricket's ability alone to integrate was minimal.

The view that cricket acted as a catalyst for the social and political trans-formations that developed in South Africa is absurd. If anything, the rebel tours acted as a counter-force to the political developments within South Africa. The NP had entered into secret and later formal discussions with the ANC over the future of South Africa. The cricket tour re-emphasised the past rather than what lay ahead, and, as such, provided the regime with negative publicity. The tour also forced the non-racial camp to reiterate its stance, providing the newly organised Mass Democratic Movement with a cause with which to inflict mortal injury on the government. This led to a further polarisation of polity, making negotiations difficult and threatening to undo all the work that was being covertly conducted.

Sport did not directly influence politics. Cricket was, as it has been throughout its 100-year history, at the whim of the dominant economic and political forces. The UCBSA was born out of an ANC strategy that not only appreciated the importance of sport in helping to heal the racial rifts in society, but also viewed moves towards multi-racialism as an implement to undermine racial segregation. By following a strategy of flexibility with white sporting organisations, the ANC were revealing that any blockages were the fault of white South Africa. It was a demonstration of their ability to exercise overwhelming power without having to resort to force. Even if sport were completely integrated at an administrative level, could that really affect the economic wellbeing of the majority population? This, once again, draws us back to the factors that influence political reform. A unified sport-ing structure is not one of them.

All the major concessions in South African sporting history were a reaction to the ensuing political and economic developments. Economic crisis, a direct consequence of apartheid policy, created the demands for social change. The business community began to embrace economic measures, if not always political initiatives, in order to win black workers over to stability and faith in the capitalist system. Sport became caught up in this process, because it was cheap, highly visible, and obviously enjoyable.

Whilst I accept that sport's ability to influence actual programmes of reform was marginal, it was able to promote a counter-culture to the dominant hegemony and should, therefore, be viewed as an integral part of the opposition to apartheid. Jasmat Dhiraj, a one-time South African 'non-racial' tennis champion explains how through sport he became politically conscious:

> What is non-racialism? It is equality in sport. I wasn't politically aware when I took up sport but through sport non-racialism becomes alive, you begin to breathe it and eat it, you come into contact with people and, although you are not talking politics but sport, you are all aware that you want equality and once that seeps into your mind you are willing to fight ... the fight for equality in sport is one with the fight for equality in Soweto, they go hand in hand to a certain extent.[70]

The Gramscian model argues that power is at its most stable when it assumes a broad-based support throughout civil society. Such an order is sustained 'through the ordinary experiences and relationships of everyday life'.[71] Herein lies the importance of culture to the political process. As South African sport was a reflection of racist values, it helped 'normalise' them, projecting them as 'common sense'. By challenging these norms, then, the opposition undermined the normative basis of apartheid. Sport was able to do this. The boycott, as a political tool, proved effective in dismissing the comfortable sense of 'normality' that white South Africa had allowed itself to relax into. The liberation movement was able to exploit popular, visible phenomena in the negotiations for a non-racial society, using sport to placate the anxiety of whites regarding democratic rule. The role of sport was at its most potent in the reform process through its ability to propagate new ideas. By doing so it shifted the notions of the 'common sense' ideals that formed the bedrock of the existing hegemony. This assisted the path to change for it made it more difficult to justify racist structures.

Richard Evans wrote above that sport offered the unemployed teenager an alternative to drugs, sex and rock and roll. He might have added revolt to his list. The developments in sport were part of a wider process of piecemeal reform instigated in order to preserve the power of the apartheid regime. Whilst sporting facilities for the black population remained poor, the sports stadium was one of the first public projects in the Bantustans. The development programme took cricket into the townships and taught the rudimentary basics of the game to African children. A process, so its advocates held, that assisted the erosion of the racial barriers that so dominated South Africa. This process, though, cannot be considered outside of the wider 'total strategy' designed to win over sections of the African population to middle-class ideals and by so doing entice them away from the maturing counter-hegemony of the liberation movement. It was the classic 'opiate': a means to divert the masses from a political agenda. The 'Low Intensity Conflict' tactic that succeeded the 'total strategy' took as its basis survival as the ultimate morality. It coupled repressive measures with a 'soft war' initiative that sought to alleviate the socio-economic conditions in the black townships. It focused on 34 townships –'oilspots' where 'sympathetic and helpful' state representatives would 'take the lead of all groups, classes, clubs and societies, with the organisation of social, career, *sport*, education, medical, religious and military activities' (my italics) and win over the population.[72] The revolutionary organisations had to be neutralised and replaced by groups that could obtain the confidence of the masses by satisfying their material needs. Sport became embroiled in this process. Surely the timing of the development programme was no coincidence.

In reality, below the highest professional level, very little had changed. In the schools and sports clubs sports remained segregated. Critics may have conceded that the development programme was aiding integration but questioned what SACU had actually 'achieved in terms of breaking down institutionalised racism'.[73] English players had been going to South Africa for the previous 15 years, their actions justified because they were coaching black players. Yet none of their 'benefactors' had forced themselves into the national squad.

What emerges from this study is that the South African authorities exploited sport to promote the impression that it was prepared to accept reform. The white cricketing fraternity in both South Africa and on the ICC happily endorsed such a strategy. Whilst the changes afoot in South African society appeared to be hinting at a new approach to racial politics they did so from the position of redefining and strengthening white capitalist rule. 'Reform' reverted to its original definition of re-establishing one's position in the light of contemporary events. Cricket inevitably became of assistance in this process.

Because the regime was prepared to engage politics in sport it presented the opposition with measures, such as the boycott, to undermine its initiatives. This is how politics is carried out. Two distinct self-interested groups adapt their embracing ideologies to accommodate phenomena that are considered to lie outside their traditional area of concern and so each can criticise the other for any association. The difference between ideologies of the left and right, though, is one of measurement. Socialists, who argue that politics is determined by the economic relations that invariably affect all societies, would claim that *all* social phenomena are at least influenced by the economic super-structure; conservatives who are primarily concerned with the analysis of the legislative apparatus would not. Because sport is not formally related to the institutions of government it is not an issue that should concern politics. What should be beyond doubt is that the position an individual assumes is an ideological one. The same can be said for the position taken on the sports boycott. Bridge-builders argued that only by breaking sanctions could South African cricket move towards a multi-racial future. However, without international pressure South Africa may have lacked the impetus to reform at all. It was in this reformist zeal that cricket became embroiled, and for its credit played a significant role. This immediately leads to speculation on the part played by the sports boycott in the demise of apartheid. I do not subscribe to it a leading role, but I believe the boycott to be important in helping to undermine the psychological will of the white South African population, not only depriving them of a favourite pastime, but also helping to condemn them in the eyes of an increasingly hostile international community. The international sporting community enjoyed a knowledge of South African politics that it rarely did of any other country.

As was said at the outset, political science does not subscribe to a set of laws or assumptions based on right or wrong. It is an area that demands interpretation of evidence structured around a set of theories. This chapter concludes by examining one such theory – conservatism – in order to seek an intellectual basis for excluding issues such as sport from the political arena.

A philosophy of conservatism

Conservative thought does not command the expansive literature that leftist philosophy does. A key explanation for this is that conservatism, primarily, is concerned with a preservation of the social and political equilibrium. Joseph de Maistre (1753–1821), the French monarchist and leading opponent of the 1789 Revolution, claimed that the possibility to perfect human nature by political and social change was a false optimism.[74] It inevitably follows that conservatism is opposed to change, but, more fundamentally, it is sceptical of political theory, and so logic suggests that it does not even consider itself to be a distinct political ideology.

Despite the claims that it is beyond the reaches of political philosophy, there are several themes that are salient within conservative thought. Initially, the conservative is concerned with tradition. The established customs and institutions of the past have been 'tested by time' and should be preserved and revered.

> Like any political being, a conservative is 'for' certain things: he is for them, not because he has arguments in their favour, but because he knows them, lives with them, and finds his identity threatened (often he knows not how) by the attempt to interfere with their operation.[75]

Such a position supports continuity in politics, such as the maintenance and nurturing of existing institutions and practices. Change is a journey into the unknown; it creates uncertainty. There are too many unintended consequences that emerge from change. The political system influences various aspects of life; therefore, where change is to be permitted it should be gradual in order to nullify any detrimental side effects.

Conservatives make several assumptions about the behaviour of humankind. One such presumption is that the world is too complex for intellectually limited human reason to grasp. The conservative rejects 'abstract' notions such as 'freedom' and 'political rights'. They are suspicious of theoretical ideas, political knowledge and thought that explain contemporary situations. There is no literal science of politics.

> That men are disposed to believe in the existence of natural rights is, of course, an all-important political fact. But that there *are* natural rights, existing objectively and independently of any positive law which might otherwise be held to have created them, is a disputed thesis of philosophy. It cannot be the task of policy to settle an undecided philosophical question.[76]

Management of public affairs is best left to those with extensive experience. Ideas should be steeped in history and evolved from experience, they help to understand, they should not be adapted in order to formulate laws. Political wisdom is therefore derived from an inherited collection of established legislation and institutions.

Natural forces have shaped the key structures and institutions. These would include, of course, the church. In South Africa, Calvinist belief held that God, to whom rulers were held responsible, ordained the state. 'God's hand was always clearly "visible" in the history of the nation, which had a task ... or calling.'[77] Nations are formed naturally by people who share the same language, history, culture and traditions. One has to acknowledge that society itself has a will, and that tradition, culture and prejudice have shaped this.[78] Suspicion of foreigners is a characteristic as people from alien cultures threaten social cohesion. Because of these distinct evolving characteristics political science should be conducted in a comparative rather than generalising way. Columbia and Uruguay may share common interests, it is doubtful whether Thailand and Spain do. It should also concern itself with questions of morality. Society should protect itself by upholding a set of shared beliefs and values. The function of law (the 'authorised part of custom')[79] then should be to uphold moral principles.

The conservative promotes society as an organism, comparing it to the functioning of the human body. As with a body each individual part is unique and of importance. Where something is wrong it is best to create the conditions in which it can get better rather than use force to cure it. Emergencies may require drastic measures, but they are rare. Such an analogy allows for a rejection of equality. Just as the heart, brain and liver perform different functions with the body, the various groups that make up society have their own specific roles.

Finally, the conservative believes in authority. This is necessary and beneficial, as individuals need guidance to know 'where they stand'. It reflects a basic need for leadership and guidance. Authority is provided from a ruling order that has emerged over time. Its moral essence derives from Paul's admonition in Romans 13:

> Everyone must submit himself to the governing authorities, for there is no authority except that which God has established. The authorities that exist have been established by God. Consequently, he who rebels against the authority is rebelling against what God has instituted, and those who do so will bring judgement on themselves.[80]

In one of the first political manifestos of the English Conservative Party, appeal was explicitly made to 'that great and intelligent class of society ... which is far less interested in the contentions of party, than in the maintenance of order and the cause of good government'.[81] Authority, thereby, becomes the *raison d'être* of politics. Citizens are taught awareness of duties and obligations, not merely their rights. No citizen is possessed of a natural right that transcends his or her obligation to be ruled. Freedom becomes an acceptance of social obligations, 'doing one's duty'. Similarly, government has responsibilities to the individual, namely not to encroach on issues that are considered private. Michael Oakeshott defined politics as a limited activity and suggested that government was 'not designed to make men good or even better'.[82] This leads us nicely onto the field of sport.

If you place the political baggage associated with conservatism to one side, it is remarkable to observe the similarities between conservative thought and the ethos of cricket, as first articulated by the English establishment. It is, in fact, difficult to envisage any other major sport that is so steeped in morality and tradition as cricket. Consider the thoughts of Abe Bailey, the Vice President of the South African Cricket Association, in 1915:

> Strive to win by all fair means, but make the winning of the game or rubber of secondary importance unless this can be accomplished through the channels of good sportsmanship, accompanied by gentlemanly behaviour worthy of a representative South Africa.[83]

Notions such as equality and democracy could not be allowed to taint such allegiances to the past. The black and the professional could not captain the national side, not because of ability but because of such tradition. It was to such leanings that we owe the standard bearer of cricketing ethos – the notion of 'fair play'. This taught the sportsman respect for the opposition, how to lose gracefully, 'knowing one's place', to abide by the rules at all time, and fundamentally to treat authority with the highest regard. In South Africa, the NP politician Dr Theophilus Donges alleged that 'justice and fair play' for the 'non-Europeans' could only be found through racial separation.[84] These values were at least as important as technical capability.

Likewise, for the conservative, the values that have been accumulated and passed down through the years are central to his or her vision of political life. Somehow they have become a mantra and are considered to be above politics. Such moral positions are to be celebrated for they represent what is good in society. Any threat to this value-system is to be resisted but not on the political battlefield. Cricket and sport in general cannot become an issue for politics because they fall outside of the parameters of traditional political study. 'There exists among [cricketers] a fellowship which transcends politics, and one that until now has helped to make such a politically vulnerable game so wonderfully resilient.'[85] To consider them political would be to threaten such traditions, an action that was certainly 'not cricket'. Quite simply, politics should be left to the politicians:

> the playing of cricket was not or should not be the concern of politicians unless legislation demanded that it should be so. Moral issues were for individuals and these beliefs should be respected; but ... the argument for retaining contact through the game, linked with an old-fashioned notion of not letting down those in South Africa who had

contributed so much to the game internationally, were principles to which the majority adhered.[86]

So when protestors resorted to extra-parliamentary measures to force the South Africans to cancel the 1970 tour to England, they actually threatened more than a series of Test cricket; they refused to abide by standards of 'fair play' and committed the cardinal sin of fusing two distinct sets of matter – politics and sport. When the ICC, in 1989, devised a resolution on the 'South African problem', which banned any future player who played or coached in South Africa, it was the first time that 'political interference' had tainted the game![87]

This book has attempted to demonstrate the total bankruptcy of the position that politics and sport do not mix. It concludes by arguing that this stance is actually intensely political in itself. Consider what the conservative ideology and the ethos of cricket both represent – self-interest. Moral values are held in greater esteem than the 'bread-and-butter' issues of political theory such as 'democracy', 'justice' and 'equality'. Why? Because these values represent a means of enforcing a set of intellectual beliefs, a conscious prescription of viewing what is 'normal' and 'acceptable' in society. They are Gramsci's notions of 'common sense', a method of enforcing hegemony in order to assert and maintain authority. By such standards of examination they are political. So it is easy for the conservative to dismiss the export of political systems from one nation to another, not though political values. So rather than share political apparatus or theories of government, imperialist Britain sent abroad the graduates from elitist educational establishments.

Conservatism, representing tradition, gradual evolution and social hierarchy imposed itself on cricket. That the large landowners became the sport's first patrons did not mean that they were the first to play it, for the game's history derives from more 'humble' origins, just as when it was exported to the colonies it was enjoyed by all social strata. What it gave the benefactors was an authority, from which they could impose their outlook on the sport, and by doing so create a means through which they could project such values into the wider environment. Thus does politics associate itself with sport and thus does it determine the criteria for acceptable behaviour ensuring that any challenge to its perspective can be dismissed as bringing politics into sport. Perhaps this authority can be viewed as traditional, but let us not pretend that it lies outside the scope of politics and that it is not the servant of self-interest. Power affords any ruling group an ability to legislate or to simply advise. It has the ability to create 'barriers to the public airing of policy conflicts', to ensure that 'some issues are organised into politics while others are organised out'.[88] Such authority meant that the Parsi cricketers in India and the blacks in South Africa were not acknowledged until it was politically beneficial for the authorities to do so. No wonder politics should remain outside the boundaries of the cricket field, for it represented a threat to the political order on it.

'And what do they know of cricket that only cricket knows?'[89] Where tradition thrives, where the ethos of the game is considered of greater merit than the task of victory, cricket has suffered. Nowhere is this more apparent than in England, less so, but still, in India. On the other hand, where such ideological standpoints have been challenged such as in Australia and the West Indies, the game has prospered. What of South Africa? If this book has expounded one thing it is the interrelationship of all social matter. By challenging x you are ultimately having an effect on y. The attitudes of segregation that were steeped in tradition, stripped of political value and justified as organic, dominated both the political apparatus and the cricket field. And what of those who throughout the 1970s and 1980s supported the maintenance of links with South African cricket, who constantly argued that sport and politics do not mix? Many, such as those organised as 'Freedom in Sport' and the 'Freedom Association', did not want to see an end to apartheid at all. Lord Chalfont, for example, a one time President of 'Freedom in Sport', was a member of the MCC, a former director of IBM in South Africa and a favourite of Margaret Thatcher. Alec Bedser, the chairman of the selection panel that initially rejected Basil D'Oliveira for the 1968–69 tour to South Africa, was a founding member of the 'Freedom Association'. John Carlisle, Tory MP and member of the MCC, had declared his belief that 'the system of apartheid in South Africa has worked in terms of government'.[90] Andrew Hunter MP, another who supported links with the Republic, had the triple allegiance of Conservative MP, member of MCC, and businessman with South African interests. Unlike visits to the sub-continent, there was never difficulty in assembling an English team to tour South Africa. Indeed, Trevor Bailey noted:

> From the social angle the most enjoyable of all cricket tours were those to South Africa. The hospitality was on a scale unequalled anywhere else in the world, the country varied and fascinating, the climate beautiful and the cricket excellent … their basic approach was very reminiscent of public-school sides … it all stemmed from a life-style which, though materially rewarding, is at the same time rather narrow and isolated.[91]

Only a concerted campaign against the whole philosophical structure of conservatism could bring about real change. This is where the refusal of black sportspeople to partake in any kind of 'normal' activity with their oppressors could assist the overall struggle to defeat apartheid. It also provided a platform for an international movement to counter conservatism on a wider scale. Thus did the sports boycott prove to be a very effective political strategy, not just in South Africa, but also in Britain, Australia and New Zealand, forcing regimes to re-evaluate their attitudes toward racial questions.

This, however, was not simply an ideological crusade, but embraced the academic stage, by accepting that politics is ultimately what participants want it to be about, not just those who are paid to practise it. The ANC's *Reconstruction and Development Programme* acknowledged that economic change was the prerequisite to success for the majority population on the sporting field.[92] In South Africa, ten years after de Klerk's famous speech, we still await Ali Bacher's vision of a South African XI dominated by black faces. There remains a long way to go.

Postscript:
Constructing the Rainbow Nation

Having established the role of sport in the political structures of apartheid South Africa, its function in the liberation movement, and its part in the contributing factors that explain social change, logic suggests some brief reflection of the progress cricket has made in the 'new' South Africa. The 2003 World Cup provides us with one of those key occasions from which historians can take stock and examine what has occurred. The arguments that have provided the foundation for this book, notably economic and racial inequity, continue to provide the indicators from which to measure and assess progress. During the post-apartheid era South African sport has experienced many high points, notably the Rugby World Cup in 1995, a great occasion from which it seemed possible that deep social scars could be healed. The African Cup of Nations, held in South Africa in 1996, showed the international community that the South Africans could compete with the round ball and they have since qualified for the last two World Cups. In cricket South Africa have tasted success, being bettered by only the almighty Australians. Yet amid this sporting optimism there remains a sense of unease. With the exception of the footballers, it is the white sportsmen who have carried South Africa back into the international arena. If sport, as has been argued throughout this book, is reflective of the economic and social environment, what does that have to say about the new country and the direction in which the ANC government is taking? To examine this, this brief postscript looks at the role assigned to sport by the new political elite, the progress made by the development programmes, and the all-important determinant of opportunity: inequality.

On 10 July 1991, South Africa was re-admitted to full membership of the International Cricket Council. The supporters of 'bridge-building' in England were amongst those who were overwhelmed. Richard Hutton, the editor of *The Cricketer*, wrote that 'South Africa's readmission … is probably the most significant development in cricket since the legislation of overarm bowling.'[1] 'Now it is time', wrote former Somerset captain and journalist Peter Roebuck, 'for renewal and growth, time for sport to resume its roles as a spectacle and an entertainment, as a vehicle giving everyone a chance to escape.'[2] Whilst maintaining the 'opiate' qualities that sport has historically assumed from religion, it would be naivety of the most absurd nature to assume that sport would now settle down in a post-apartheid age and become simply a means of entertainment. As political elites had in the past, firstly the new NP-ANC coalition, and then the dominant ANC had a role for sport in the political process. Whilst under apartheid sport served as a means to segregate, in the new 'rainbow' era sport was assigned the task of reconciliation. Its ability to eradicate the injustices of the past would inevitably be used as a measure in which both supporters and critics would evaluate the government's attempt to build a more egalitarian society. Whether the twin responsibilities of reconciliation and equality would prove contradictory has not really been satisfied today.

The new politics of cricket

Of all of the qualities that sports afforded political elites (see Chapter 2) integration was considered to be the most immediately pressing for the new ANC regime. A diverse population, that includes hard-line Afrikaners, Zulu nationalists, liberal whites, coloured communities, immigrants of South Asian descent, and both urban and traditional Africans, would prove difficult to unite around vague political notions such as 'democracy', 'equality' or 'nationalism'. Indeed, elections have divided the population largely along racial lines. Ideological differences will take generations to mould into any form of national identity free of racial issues. Symbols such as the flag and the national anthem have proved to be areas that have ignited passions and fashioned division, so whilst claiming to represent South Africa, they could not claim to be national. What could draw people from all walks of society together was sport. Cricket in particular enjoyed a tradition amongst the different ethnic groups, and so held the advantage over rugby and football in the potential numbers from which it could select players.

Despite the obvious integrative qualities sport had to be about more than a focus around which people could unite. It had to express the social changes necessary to create a society more at ease with itself. This society would be built on the notions of merit and equality of opportunity. Such concepts had become sacred to the non-racial sporting organisations. The UCB's initial statement of intent attempted to embrace these thoughts and included a number of points that set the tone for the political role cricket would play in the re-development of South Africa. Point A set it the task of endeavouring 'to achieve peace and harmony in cricket in our country'. The new body hoped to 'formulate strategies to redress urgently imbalances in regard to separate educational systems, sponsorships and facilities'. The most ambitious, and directly political, statement however, was the aspiration to 'contribute, through cricket, to the creation of a just society in South Africa where everybody democratically has a common say and a common destiny'.[3] Cricket was thus assigned a role in the reconstruction of the new democratic and non-racial South Africa. The relationship between politics and sport had become formal, and the progress of cricket would have to reflect the overall nature of wider societal change.

The development programmes

Ali Bacher had placed enormous faith in the development programmes. He claimed that South Africa would dominate world cricket within five years, primarily due to the influx of black players.[4] The development programme has indeed made notable progress since the days when it was viewed as a means to subvert revolt, and as such, an arm of the apartheid regime. It has provided mini-cricket for the under-10s. Young players such as Abraham Sinclair, Donald Letlhake and David Makopanele have been sent to Australia to improve their game. The same Makopanele had had to walk three kilometres to practise before.[5] The scheme can boast of many successes: the *1993 Protea Assurance Cricket Annual of South Africa* records the inclusion, on merit, of an African player in the South African Schools XI for 1992/93, together with a young coloured batsman from Cape Town, Herschelle Gibbs. At the same time an under-15 South African Schools XI which took part in a tournament against their English equivalents included five players of colour, 'all chosen on merit and all performing with skill'.[6] South African under-19 and South African Schools XIs have included players from the disadvantaged communities, providing opportunities for cricketers such as Walter Masemola, Tulani Ngxoweni, Makhaya Ntini, Ahmed Omar, Ashwell Prina and Linda Zondi – all graduates from the development programme.

International cricket was being taken to areas that have not experienced it before. The first round of the Under-19 World Cup in 1998, for example, saw contests taking place at club and school grounds in areas such as Soweto, Laudium and Lenasia. England's first tour to South Africa for 31 years began with a contest against a South African XI at Soweto.[7] The commentator, Gerald de Kock, enthused at how 'the audience for cricket is broadening all the time and has reached areas where no-one ever imagined it would'.[8]

Despite these advances, the development programme has still to fulfil Ali Bacher's vision of a national side representative of the country's racial groups. This has proven to be the issue that has dominated South African cricket over the last decade. Progress has to be gauged against a backdrop of impatience in which the black political class wants to see sport maintaining pace with the transformation of other areas of social life. It is evident that despite the improvements made within the disadvantaged communities the nurturing of cricket still takes place in a society characterised by inequality and disadvantage. Eddie Barlow, Director of the Western Cape Coaching Academy and former South African all-rounder, even argued in 1995 that ten years of the development programme had seen the emergence of 'little of quality'.[9] Lulu Xingwana, chairperson of the Parliamentary Sports and Recreation Committee, went further and suggested that the 'development programme has failed'.[10] 'We are running out of patience,' Duminsani Zulu, spokesman for the Department of Sports, complained in 1999. The 'development programmes have been in place for almost eight years and we are still not seeing the emergence of black players. We are dealing with legacies of the past and are meeting with pockets of resistance.'[11] Examination of provincial and national cricket suggests that the sport remains over-represented by the white communities. Things have to change. Cricket has been assigned a political role, and politics is a short-term business. The government addressed such concerns to the UCB and informed them that 'the [Sports] Ministry should look at ways of addressing the issue'.[12]

Targets

During apartheid the opposition pointed out that due to acute economic inequality black cricketers would never be able to compete on an equal footing with their white counterparts. Whites went to the best schools, were protected in skilled and higher paid employment, enjoyed decent accommodation, and having received coaching at school and club level (often from contemporary or ex-professionals) played their sports on the best grounds. Blacks were at best disadvantaged, at worst excluded, not only from the opportunities to play cricket at a high level, but from the avenues that formulated quality of life. The ANC was obviously committed to ending these disparities, and equality of opportunity became central to its blueprint for the future South Africa. The reconstruction of post-apartheid society insisted that positive discrimination be a prerequisite to a fair and egalitarian nation. Indeed, the constitution made references to 'redressing the imbalances of the past to achieve broad representation' in the public sphere.[13]

Targets would be employed to create a more representative workforce. They were not immediately introduced into sport. Though it was clear that the selectors were expected to pick players from the disadvantaged communities, this was non-arbitrary. The development programmes would eventually provide the talent to ensure a meritocratic side would also be a multi-racial one. When they failed to do so, the politicians became both anxious and impatient. In November 1998 an ANC statement described both the rugby and cricket teams as 'lily-white'. Whilst acknowledging that many young players of colour had demonstrated potential on the cricket field, the ANC questioned why 'nothing has been done by … cricket associations to help them develop to levels where they would be considered for selection in the national teams'.[14] An all-white XI for the first Test against, of all teams, the West Indies led to further condemnation about the racial imbalance of the national team. In order to avoid legislation the UCB introduced its Transformation Charter setting targets at all senior levels from September 1999. Black cricketers would now be given opportunities to experience cricket at provincial and national levels.

Targets have divided the cricketing community with players such as Rodney Ontong and Ashwell Prince being described as 'tokens', in the side because of their colour. The same was once said of Makhaya Ntini – as I write the number 8 ranked bowler in the world[15] – and Herschelle Gibbs, especially when he was quickly reintroduced to the side following his ban for involvement in match-fixing. Any player needs a run in a team if he is to adapt to cricket at a higher level. Ntini was infrequently chosen, and only following pressure did he become a regular and go on to become one of the best bowlers in the world. The coloured left-arm spinner Paul Adams has not been treated with the same level of patience, and must wonder if he has a future at Test level. If cricket is to take off in the disadvantaged communities it needs role models. Jonty Rhodes and Sean Pollock may well have got more recognition today than they could have hoped for 15 years ago, but how long will this last before the different ethnic populations start to demand their own heroes? If African role-models are to be found only in football then it will be to cricket's detriment.

The question of targets remains a principal one in cricket today. In the winter of 2002 Percy Sonn, President of the UCB, announced their abandonment. This was done in the face of a 5–1 drubbing by Australia.[16] The UCB's decision was immediately challenged by Ngconde Balfour, the Minister of Sport, who again reminded the cricket establishment of their responsibility to the wider issues that affected South Africa. A reiteration that five players of colour would be in the squad to represent South Africa at the forthcoming World Cup seemed more like a compromise than a commitment to further the cause of positive discrimination. The Proteas are about to embark on an era of rebuilding. They will have to assess their attitude to targets and possibly give more chances to players from the disadvantaged communities, as they attempt to take the sport to a wider audience. This may have to come at the expense of initial and immediate success. 'We are a proud sporting nation', said Ali Bacher, 'and we have to maintain the high standards that we have achieved since unity. But we must also make sure that we give the opportunity to those who were previously deprived of it.'[17] To the African National Congress, of course, a decade after the dismantling of apartheid and into their second term in office, they can see the vestiges of the old system still rooted in sport – in selection, coaching and administration. At the same meeting of the UCB that voted to scrap targets, the Easterns Cricket Union was condemned for not integrating players of colour. Both Gautland and Natal were similarly criticised. There is still some way to go.

Inequality

At the heart of the philosophical standpoint against 'normality' on the cricket field during apartheid was the belief that normal relations could not exist in an abnormal setting. Today it is argued that because the political apparatus of apartheid has been dismantled, 'merit will once again become the only criteria by which players will be judged and selected'.[18] This proposition assumes that South Africa has reinvented itself as a meritocracy. This presupposes a rather narrow definition for politics, associating equality with the right to vote. Here lies the crux of the problem: South Africa has never been a society in which merit was the sole criterion for the selection of professional sports teams. There have always been barriers preventing members of disadvantaged communities from competing on a level playing field. These were considered in some detail in Chapter 6. They require continuous scrutiny if we are to assess the progress being made towards the ideals of the non-racial sports movement.

Revisiting the education system, we know that South African schools cricket has always been of a high standard. Like in England, though, the best-serviced schools are the ones you have to pay for, taking, by nature, only those who can afford the high fees.[19] At Hilton College, for example (the 'Eton' of South Africa), the journalist Jonathan Rice wrote in 1993 of 3,200 acres for 470 boys – seven acres per boy.[20] These children have the chance to play in the three or four XIs that could be fielded at senior or colts level. Most black children are excluded from these institutions, if no longer legally because of their colour, then economically because of their standing on prosperity's ladder. On page one of a *Poverty and Inequality in South Africa* report (funded by a number of organisations, including the United Nations and the World Bank), the authors began by saying that 'the distribution of income and wealth in South Africa may be the most unequal in the world'.[21] A United Nations survey carried out in November 1996 placed South Africa's secondary schools at the bottom of a league table of 42 'developed' nations. It is these schools that most African children attend. I say most because a 1997 survey found that a staggering 57 per cent of young men said that they had been forced to abandon their education for financial reasons.[22]

The problems of poverty are the greatest impediment to the development of cricket within the disadvantaged communities. As well as the obvious difficulties associated with concentrations of people in urban townships there is a large rural population that the UCB has to address. Many are unable to access services due to long distances from facilities, poor quality of services, lack of information and the cost of using the service. If people have to walk long distances to reach facilities or incur significant transaction costs in the form of time, effort and transportation then they are at an obvious disadvantage. If essential items such as water, shelter and education are not catered for, then participation in sport is not going to be high on people's agendas.

For most whites, on the other hand, the new South Africa is little different to the old country. They have kept their maids, houses and cooks, and continue to enjoy a decent standard of living. They have had to sacrifice the vote, but in the main this has not been at the expense of their disproportionate share of the national income. Such a picture continues to exacerbate the belief that South Africa is not a single entity, but two distinct countries. The

United Nations Human Development Index,[23] for example, showed that whilst white South Africans enjoyed a level of human development similar to that of Israel or Canada, African standards were similar to those in countries such as Egypt or Swaziland.[24] Available statistics show that whites live on average ten years longer than Africans and that the infant mortality rate varies between 7 for whites and 54 for Africans.[25]

The ANC may have emphasised the importance of reducing inequality and poverty, but this has had to take place within an economic strategy of tight public expenditure control, falling budget deficits and high real interest rates. The ANC's primary constituency has proved to be the financial markets, the IMF and the US Treasury. Such policies have left the bulk of the nation's resources in white hands. Gone have been the historical promises of wealth distribution, but not the problems associated with a population of which 50 per cent live in poverty and one in three are without work.[26] The likelihood for equality of opportunity in such conditions is difficult. It is not possible for those at the bottom to have the same chances to succeed at cricket as those attending the well-funded schools. While the vast differences in income and wealth distribution remain determined by racial group, South Africa will not be a country at ease with itself, and will not be represented by a fully integrated national XI selected on merit.

Conclusion

By assigning cricket a political role in the construction of the future South Africa, the ANC was also acknowledging its responsibility to the sport. To some the ANC's role is seen as interference and is unwelcome. The manner in which Ngconde Balfour rejected the UCB's dismissal of targets may have been considered as a minister overstepping his mark. In all reality, though, the responsibility of the government is multi-faceted as it is ultimately the body that is accountable for motivating the direction of the infant nation. Ex-Sports Minister Steve Tshwete, for example, made it clear that the UCB was under obligation to replicate the wider changes taking place in society. As for the government, he told parliament that its 'responsibility is the creation of that environment in which sport and recreation will become the property of an entire nation'.[27] That does not just mean support and investment, it means creating the conditions whereby every citizen is given an opportunity to excel at what they do best, without the restrictions imposed by ethnic group membership or economic disadvantage. How far the regime can go in satisfying this challenge will determine not only its own place in history, but also the future of cricket in South Africa.

South African cricket will only satisfy the founders of the non-racial movement once they accept that talented players of colour have been provided with the means and opportunities to represent their schools, provinces and ultimately country. In order to realise such ambitions black cricketers require facilities and coaching. Moreover, they need time, space and a comfortable upbringing. If a child cannot concentrate at school or take part in strenuous activities due to hunger, or cannot study in the evenings due to lack of electricity, this child is being denied the necessities of life. The development programme will struggle to produce enthusiasts within such an environment. This raises the question of whether the selection of a team on merit, a principle strongly defended by the white liberal establishment, precludes the selection of a side by equality of opportunity. In a society where the economic means remain deeply skewered it surely does.

The relationship between the government and the UCB remains increasingly strained, and awaits the fallout from the World Cup. There is obvious impatience at the lack of transformation. Whilst the ANC claim that sport is behind the rest of society in eliminating the legacy of white rule, they have to acknowledge their responsibility. Politics determined the nature of cricket in South Africa during the 125 years of racial rule before the demise of apartheid. It will inevitably shape its future direction. If there remain obstacles to opportunities to play cricket at a high level, then critics will look beyond the cricketing authorities. The ANC's *Reconstruction and Development Programme*, for example, acknowledged that economic change was the prerequisite to success for the majority population on the sporting field.[28] The *CIA Factbook* (2002) described the South African economy:

> South Africa is a middle-income, developing country with an abundant supply of resources, well-developed financial, legal, communications, energy, and transport sectors, a stock exchange that ranks among the 10 largest in the world, and a modern infrastructure supporting an efficient distribution of goods to major urban centres throughout the region.[29]

Yet it cannot feed, look after or provide jobs for large sections of its population. South Africa is a country of two economies – one developed and the other developing. The ANC's political strategy relies on developmental rather than radical change, on transition rather than revolution. An economic approach that is built around privatisation, lay-offs, cuts in spending in the public sector, and corporate tax cuts will not be able to provide decent housing, health care and water to all of the population. 'Apartheid is not exactly *finish en klaar*', insists the academic John Matshikiza,

> if we still live with apartheid institutions like blacks-only townships, those blitzed-out, treeless, overcrowded areas reserved for the majority of the population, where life is cheap, infrastructure is non-existent, and anything goes — all this cheek-by-jowl with opulence and splendour for the lucky few just down the road.[30]

To suggest that equality of opportunity can exist amid such disparity is either patently absurd, or else driven by political ideology. Because of its occupation in the forefront of domestic and international life cricket will continue to reflect its environment, and be exploited in the ANC's ultimate goal which is to 'formulate strategies' to 'redress imbalances' as South Africa attempts to build the 'just society' in which everyone enjoys a 'common destiny' – a political role for a sport that has always known politics.

The early days of enthusiasm generated by the progress made in the World Cups of cricket, football and rugby, have given way to a more reflective air. Those involved in South African sports are considering the future direction of their relative activities. Cricket, symbolic of this reflection, now stands at a crossroads. The Proteas were unceremoniously dumped out of their own World Cup in the first round. Gone are the likes of Alan Donald, Jonty Rhodes, and possibly Gary Kirsten and Lance Klusener. Sean Pollock has been replaced as captain by the inexperienced Graeme Smith. Add to these the early departures of Hansie Cronje and Darrell Cullinan, and it becomes evident that the team is entering a new era. The next chapter in South African cricket will be the first to include a significant number of players from the disadvantaged communities. This is a consequence of the development programmes, but also because of targets and political pressure. Targets will remain in cricket, as they will in other walks of life. In reality they provide compensation both for the injustices of the past and the slow nature of reform of the present. But this situation cannot remain indefinitely. South African politics faces similar questions. The ANC may appear indestructible, but there are cracks appearing, especially among the Trade Union and Communist Party sections. President Mbeki has warned that if his government does not close the disparities (defined by colour) then people will rebel against democracy, 'Because it hasn't brought them anything.'[31] The next decade in the separate histories of both South African cricket and politics will be fascinating. What is certain will be their continued relationship, and the author of this history will be writing about the same issues and problems that have been raised in this book.

Notes

NOTES TO SERIES EDITOR'S FOREWORD

1. Jon Gemmell, *The Politics of South African Cricket* (London: Taylor & Francis, 2004), Introduction, p. 1.
2. J.A. Mangan, *The Games Ethic and Imperialism: Aspects of the Diffusion of an Ideal* (London: Frank Cass, 1998), Preface, p. 17.
3. Gemmell, *The Politics of South African Cricket*, p. 187.
4. In words inevitably rather more elegant than mine, Thomas Macaulay wrote of John Milton as having an 'independent mind, emancipated from the influence of authority and devoted to the search for the truth'. See *Macaulay's Essay on Milton* edited by John Dowie (London: Blackie & Son, 1900), p. 3.

NOTES TO INTRODUCTION

1. A full bibliography is included at the end of the book.
2. An exception to this allegation is Douglas Booth, who gives three references to a definition of politics in *The Race Game: Sport and Politics in South Africa* (London: Frank Cass, 1998) (pp. 2, 55 and 105). However, his study does not allow for a thorough analysis.
3. See, for example, Merle Lipton, *Capitalism and Apartheid* (Aldershot: Wildwood House, 1986).
4. Even the rebel tours were publicly condemned by national bodies.
5. Ernesto Laclau, 'Discourse', in Robert E. Goodin and Phillip Pettit (eds.), *A Companion to Contemporary Political Philosophy* (Oxford: Blackwell, 1997), p. 432.
6. I have not considered Andre Odendaal's *Cricket in Isolation: The Politics of Race & Cricket in South Africa* (Cape Town: published by the author, 1977 as academic because, although an excellent and valuable source, it is documentary rather than analysis.
7. Odendaal is the exception.

NOTES TO CHAPTER 1

1. David Easton, *The Political System: An Inquiry into the State of Political Science*, 2nd edn (New York: Alfred Knopf, 1971), p. 3.
2. Carlton Rodee, Totton Anderson, Carl Christol and Thomas Greene, *Introduction to Political Science* (New York: McGraw Hill, 1976), p. 5.
3. See George H. Sabine and Thomas L. Thorson, *A History of Political Theory*, 4th edn (Illinois: Dryden Press, 1973), Chapter 1 – 'The Context of Political Theory'.
4. Bernard Crick, *In Defence of Politics*, 4th edn (London: Penguin Books, 1993), p. 27.
5. Professor Seeley is recorded as saying that political science is the fruit of history and history is the root of political science. (A. Appadorai, *The Substance of Politics*, 10th edn (London: Oxford University Press, 1968), p. 7.)
6. Andrew Gamble, 'Theories of British Politics', *Political Studies*, Vol. 38, No. 3 (1990) p. 406.

7. Quoted in Gerry Stoker and David Marsh (eds.), *Theory and Methods in Political Science* (Basingstoke: Macmillan, 1995), p. 44.
8. Gamble, 'Theories of British Politics', p. 408.
9. R.A.W. Rhodes, 'The Institutional Approach', in Stoker and Marsh, *Theory and Methods in Political Science*, p. 42.
10. Nevil Johnson, 'The Place of Institutions in the Study of Politics', *Political Studies*, Vol.23, Nos 2–3 (1975), p. 154.
11. Ibid.
12. Daryl Glazer, 'Normative Theory', in Stoker and Marsh, *Theory and Methods in Political Science*, p.22.
13. D.D. Raphael, *Problems of Political Philosophy* (London: Macmillan, 1985), p. 27.
14. W.J.M. MacKenzie, *Politics and Social Change* (London: Penguin Books, 1967); see Part 2 – 'Political Science in the Universities', pp. 57–80.
15. W.T. Jones, *Masters of Political Thought*, Vol.2 (London: George Harrap & Co, 1964), p. 116.
16. Peter Nicholson, 'Politics and Force', in Adrian Leftwich (ed.), *What is Politics? The Activity and its Study* (Oxford: Blackwell, 1984), p. 43.
17. Bernard Crick and Tom Crick, *What is Politics?* (Great Britain: Edward Arnold, 1987), p. 1.
18. Nicholson, 'Politics and Force', in Leftwich, *What is Politics?*, p. 43.
19. Aristotle, 'The Politics' (translated by Ernest Barker) (Oxford: Oxford University Press, 1995), p.10. There is some dispute to the actual phraseology here. Herbert Spiro (*Politics as the Master Science: From Plato to Mao* (New York: Harper & Row, 1970), p. 7) contests that the term *zoon politikon* translates as 'political being' rather than 'political animal'.
20. Tony Bilton, Kevin Bonnett, Philip Jones, Michelle Stanworth, Ken Sheard and Andrew Webster, *Introductory Sociology* (Basingstoke: Macmillan, 1985), p. 171.
21. For an assessment of the African communal system of *ubuntu*, see Allister Sparks, *The Mind of South Africa* (London: Arrow Books, 1997).
22. William Welsh, *Studying Politics* (London: Nelson, 1973), p. 15.
23. David Held and Adrian Leftwich, 'A Discipline of Politics?', in Leftwich, *What is Politics?*, p. 145.
24. Thus, theology and ethics were a meaningless process of enquiry. (David Sanders, 'Behavioural Analysis', in Stoker and Marsh, *Theory and Methods in Political Science*, p. 59.)
25. Jean-François Lyotard, *The Post-Modern Condition, A Report on Knowledge* (Manchester: Manchester University Press, 1984), p. 75.
26. Geoffrey Ponton and Peter Gill, *Introduction to Politics* (Oxford: Martin Robertson, 1982), pp. 5–6.
27. Michael Laver, *Invitation to Politics* (Oxford: Martin Robertson, 1983), p. 1.
28. Adrian Leftwich, 'Politics: People, Resources and Power', in Leftwich, *What is Politics?*, p. 63.
29. J.D.B. Miller, *The Nature of Politics* (London: Gerald Duckworth, 1962), p. 15.
30. Bilton *et al.*, *Introductory Sociology*, p.171.
31. Jenny Chapman, 'The Feminist Perspective', in Stoker and Marsh, *Theory and Methods in Political Science*, p. 95.
32. John Dearlove and Peter Saunders, *Introduction to British Politics*, 2nd edn (Cambridge: Polity Press, 1991), p. 10.
33. MacKenzie, *Politics and Social Change*, p. 57.
34. Dearlove and Saunders, *Introduction to British Politics*, p. 9.
35. Ibid., pp. 64–5.
36. Laver, *Invitation to Politics*, p. 1.
37. Miller, *The Nature of Politics*, p. 19.
38. V.I. Lenin, *Collected Works* (Moscow: Foreign Languages Publishing House, 1965), Vol.XXXII, p. 32.
39. Karl Marx, *The German Ideology* (London: ElecBook CD Rom, 1998), p. 92.
40. See, for example: Ralph Miliband, *Parliamentary Socialism* (London: George Allen & Unwin, 1961); Ralph Miliband, *The State in Capitalist Society* (London: Weidenfeld & Nicolson, 1967); Ralph Miliband, *Capitalist Democracy in Britain* (Oxford: Oxford University Press, 1982).
41. Robert Bocock, *Hegemony* (Chichester: Ellis Horwood, 1986), p. 7.
42. George Taylor, 'Marxism', in Stoker and Marsh, *Theory and Methods in Political Science*, p. 253.

NOTES TO CHAPTER 2

1. Jay J. Coakley, *Sport in Society: Issues and Controversies* (St Louis: Times Mirror/Mosby College, 1990), p. 11.
2. See Johan Huizinga, *Homo Ludens: A Study of the Play Elements in Culture* (London: Routledge, 1949).
3. Lincoln Allison claims that the intensity of the debate in South Africa about abandoning the Springbok sporting symbol was greater in some quarters than the debate about constitutional reform. (Lincoln Allison (ed.), *The Changing Politics of Sport* (Manchester: Manchester University Press, 1993), p. 3.)
4. 'The Economic Impact and Importance of Sport in the United Kingdom,' a study prepared for the Sports Council by the Henley Centre for Forecasting. A summary of its findings was published in the *Times*, 16 Jan. 1987, p. 30.
5. Ibid.
6. A. Johnson, 'Government, Opposition and Sport: The Role of Domestic Sports Policy in Generating Political Support', *Journal of Sport and Social Issues*, 6, 2 (1982), pp. 22–34, quoted in Coakley, *Sport in Society*, p. 310.
7. By way of illustration, Ireland – at the risk of expulsion from the competition – cancelled one of its European football championship qualifying matches against Yugoslavia in 1999 in protest against Serbia's actions in Kosovo.
8. Martin Polley, *Moving the Goalposts* (London: Routledge, 1998), p. 12.
9. See Ken Foster, 'Developments in Sporting Law', in Allison, *The Changing Politics of Sport*, pp. 112–13.
10. Lawrence Donegan, 'Stumped by political games', *Guardian* (Internet version: www.guardian unlimited.co.uk), 24 Aug. 1999.
11. E. Grayson, *Sport and the Law*, 2nd edn (London: Butterworths, 1994), pp. 458–9.
12. C. Offe, 'The Theory of the Capitalist State and the Problems of Policy Formation', cited in David Whitson, 'Sport and Hegemony: On the Construction of the Dominant Culture', *Sociology of Sport Journal*, 1, 1 (1984), p. 66.
13. Eric Hobsbawm, *The Invention of Tradition* (Cambridge: Cambridge University Press, 1983), p. 143.
14. Quoted in Joseph Maguire, 'Sport, Identity, Politics and Globalisation', *Sociology of Sport Journal*, 11, 4 (1994), p. 408.
15. Quoted in Garry Whannel, *Blowing the Whistle: The Politics of Sport* (London: Pluto Press, 1983), p. 81.
16. J.A. Mangan, *Athleticism in the Victorian and Edwardian Public School: The Emergence and Consolidation of an Educational Ideology* (Cambridge: Cambridge University Press, 1983), p. 192.
17. Joint Association of Classical Teachers, *The World of Athens* (Cambridge: Cambridge University Press, 1988), p. 174.
18. N.I. Ponomaryov, 'Sport and Society' (Moscow: Progress Publishers, 1981), quoted in Coakley, *Sport in Society*, p. 307.
19. Kenneth Brody, 'Institutionalised Sport as Quasi-Religion; Preliminary Considerations', *Journal of Sport and Social Issues*, 3, 2 (1979), p. 23.
20. Ibid.
21. Howard Nixon, 'Idealised Functions of Sport: Religious and Political Socialisation through Sport', *Journal of Sport and Social Issues*, 6, 1 (1982), p. 4.
22. *Independent*, 12 April 1994, p. 15.
23. James A.R. Nafziger, 'Foreign Policy in the Sports Arena', quoted in D. Stanley Eitzen (ed.), *Sport in Contemporary Society: An Anthology* (New York: St. Martin's Press, 1989), p. 236.
24. Monique Belioux (ed.), *Olympism* (Lausanne: International Olympic Committee, 1972), p. 1, quoted in Eitzen, *Sport in Contemporary Society*, p. 247.
25. Christopher Lumer, 'Rules and Moral Norms in Sports', *International Review for the Sociology of Sport*, 30, 3–4 (1995), p. 265.
26. Harry Pearson, review of the book 'Football Cultures and Identities' by Gary Armstrong and Richard Giulianotti (eds.) (Basingstoke: Macmillan, 1999) in *When Saturday Comes*, Sept. 1999, p. 12.
27. Cited in Lincoln Allison (ed.), *The Politics of Sport* (Manchester: Manchester University Press, 1986), p. 16.

28. H. Meller, *Leisure and the Changing City* (London: Routledge & Kegan Paul, 1976), Chapter 6, quoted in John Hargreaves, *Sport, Power and Culture: A Social and Historical Analysis of Popular Sports in Britain* (Cambridge: Polity Press, 1986), p. 61. A number of today's professional football teams can also trace their origins to organised religion.

29. Report of the Wolfenden Committee on Sport, *Sport and the Community* (London: CCPR, 1960), p. 4, quoted in Hargreaves, *Sport, Power and Culture*, p. 183.

30. J. Sugden and A. Bairner, *Sport, Sectarianism and Society in a Divided Ireland* (Leicester: Leicester University Press, 1993), p. 115.

31. John F. Coghlan with Ida Webb, *Sport and British Politics since 1960* (London: The Falmer Press, 1990), p. 5.

32. See J. Walvin, *The People's Game* (Edinburgh: Mainstream Publishing, 1994), pp. 92–4.

33. Ponomaryov, 'Sport and Society', quoted in Coakley, *Sport in Society*, p. 305.

34. Amy Lawrence, 'Sukerman likes it hot', *Observer*, 7 Nov. 1999, p. 19.

35. Janet Lever, *Soccer Madness* (Chicago: The University of Chicago Press, 1983), p. 25.

36. Allen Guttmann, *Sports Spectators* (New York: Columbia University Press, 1986), p. 20.

37. Quoted in G. Green, *The Official History of the FA Cup* (London: Naldrett Press, 1949), p. 69.

38. Terry Monnington, 'Politicians and Sport: Uses and Abuses', in Allison, *The Changing Politics of Sport*, p. 134.

39. Report of the Wolfenden Committee, *Sport and the Community*, cited in Hargreaves, p. 183.

40. Lumer, 'Rules and Moral Norms in Sports', p. 276. Joseph Maguire ('Sport, Identity Politics and Globalisation', *Sociology of Sport Journal*, 11, 4 (1993), pp. 398–427) provides an excellent account of the development of organised sport in Britain, breaking down its progression into five distinct phases – all closely linked to the dominant social and political trends.

41. See Whitson, 'Sport and Hegemony', p. 65.

42. John Underwood, 'A Fan's Lament: The Commercialisation of Sport', in John Underwood, *Spoiled Sport* (Boston: Little, Brown, 1984), quoted in Eitzen, *Sport in Contemporary Society*, p. 213.

43. R. Chesshyre and C. Brasher, 'Sponsorship, Who Benefits?' *Observer*, 7 Oct. 1979, quoted in Hargreaves, *Sport, Power and Culture*, p. 120.

44. Quoted in Tony Mason, *Sport in Britain* (London: Faber & Faber, 1988), p. 347.

45. Quoted in Whitson, 'Sport and Hegemony', p. 65.

46. Ibid., p. 71.

47. N. Petryszak, 'Spectator Sports as an Aspect of Popular Culture – An Historical View', *Journal of Sport Behaviour*, 1, 1 (1978), pp. 14–27, quoted in Eitzen, *Sport in Contemporary Society*, p. 33.

48. P. Hoch, 'Rip off the Big Game' (New York: Doubleday, 1972), quoted in Eitzen, p. 33.

49. XXVIII, iv.28, quoted in H.A. Harris, *Sport in Greece and Rome* (Great Britain: Thames & Hudson, 1984), p. 222.

50. Quoted in Mason, *Sport in Britain*, p. 97.

51. Leon Trotsky, *Where is Britain Going?* (London: Communist Party of Great Britain, 1926), p. 175, quoted in Allison, *The Politics of Sport*, p. 4.

52. Quoted in Benjamin Lowe, David Kanin and Andrew Strenk (eds.), *Sport and International Relations* (Illinois: Stipes Publishing Company, 1978), p. 5.

53. Quoted in Alan Tomlinson and Garry Whannel (eds.), *Five Ring Circus* (London: Pluto, 1984), p. 28.

54. Quoted in James Riordan, 'Marx, Lenin and Physical Culture', *Journal of Sport History*, Vol.3 (1976), p. 159.

55. Karl Marx, 'Preface to a Critique of Political Economy' (London: Elecbook CD Rom, 1998), p. 8.

56. M. Tomlinson, 'State Intervention in Voluntary Sport: The Inner City Policy Context', *Leisure Studies*, Vol.6 (1987), p. 340.

57. Whitson, 'Sport and Hegemony', p. 73.

58. Nicholas Browne-Wilkinson, 'Conley v Heatley', quoted in Ken Foster, 'Developments in Sporting Law', in Allison, *The Changing Politics of Sport*, p. 105.

59. B. Houlihan, *The Government and Politics of Sport* (London: Routledge, 1991), p. 5.

60. Whannel, *Blowing the Whistle*, p. 21.

61. 'European Sport for All Charter', text and background, Council of Europe, Strasbourg, 1977, cited in Coghlan with Webb, *Sport and British Politics since 1960*, p. 237.

62. In the case of the West Indies, sport is actually *the* unifying force, far ahead of attempts at political and economic integration.

NOTES TO CHAPTER 3

1. P.F. Warner (ed.), *Imperial Cricket* (London: The London & Counties Press Association, 1912), editor's note.
2. Neville Cardus, *English Cricket* (London: Collins, 1945), p. 9.
3. Quoted in Malcolm Tozer, 'Cricket, School and Empire', *International Journal of the History of Sport*, Vol.16 (Sept. 1989), p. 159.
4. Quoted in Derek Birley, *The Willow Wand* (London: Sportspages, 1989), pp. 10–11.
5. J.D. Coldham, *Lord Harris* (London: The Crowood Press, 1983), p. 109.
6. Quoted in Mike Marqusee, *Anyone but England* (London: Verso, 1994), p. 57. 'Fair play' is first mentioned in the laws in 1774; the 1787 Laws stipulate that 'umpires are the judges of fair and unfair play' (ibid., p. 52).
7. Quoted in Tozer, 'Cricket, School and Empire', p. 162.
8. John Lester, 'Century of Philadelphia Cricket', pp. 136–8, in Thomas Jable, 'Cricket Clubs and Class in Philadelphia', *Journal of Sport History*, 18, 2 (1991), p. 220.
9. Quoted in Richard Cashman, *Patrons, Players and the Crowd* (New Delhi: Orient Longman, 1980), p. 11.
10. Quoted in J.T. Henderson, 'English Cricket in Natal', in M.W. Luckin (ed.), *The History of South African Cricket* (Johannesburg: W.E. Hortor & Co, 1915), p. 84.
11. Dr K. Elford, 'Sport in Australian Society: A Perspective', in T.D. Jaques and G.R. Pavia (eds.), *Sport in Australia* (Sydney: McGraw-Hill, 1976), p. 36.
12. Ibid., p. 39.
13. Quoted in Ramachandra Guha, 'Cricket, Caste, Community, Colonialism: The Politics of a Great Game', *International Journal of the History of Sport* Vol. 14., No. 1 (April 1997), p. 175.
14. One such example is the enclosure of cricket pitches within a formal setting, introducing the concept of boundaries – which were alien to earlier games.
15. F.W Farrar, 'In the Days of thy Youth' (London, 1889), p. 373, in B. Simon and I. Bradley, *The Victorian Public School* (London: Gill & Macmillan, 1975), p. 148.
16. Quoted in N.G. Annan, *Roxburgh of Stowe* (London: Longmans, 1965), p. 11.
17. H.S. Altham and E.W. Swanton, *History of Cricket* (London: George Allen & Unwin, 1948), p. 119.
18. *Wisden* (1877), p. 72.
19. Quoted in Richard Holt, *Sport and the British* (Oxford: Clarendon Press, 1989), p. 76.
20. Theodore Cook, *Character and Sportsmanship* (London: Williams & Norgate, 1927), p. 72.
21. 'Temple Bar', 1862, article 'Lords and Players', quoted in David Rayvern Allen (ed.), *Cricket's Silver Lining, 1864–1914* (London: Guild Publishing, 1987), p. 6.
22. Marqusee, *Anyone but England*, p. 69. See also Keith Sandiford, *Cricket and the Victorians* (Aldershot: Sugar Press, 1994), p. 37.
23. Quoted in Benny Green, *A History of Cricket* (London: Guild Publishing, 1988), p. 126.
24. P. Scott, 'Cricket and the Religious World in the Victorian Period', *Church Quarterly* (July 1970), pp. 134–44. This was probably a reference to the antagonisms between amateur and professional players that were inherent in the game. Professionals did not always adhere to the ethos of cricket; they also tended to be bowlers.
25. Cook, *Character and Sportsmanship*, p. 72
26. 'Temple Bar', 'Lords and Players', quoted in Rayvern Allen, *Cricket's Silver Lining*, p. 19.
27. Green, *A History of Cricket*, p. 193.
28. Tozer, 'Cricket, School and Empire', p. 157.
29. Michael Manley, *A History of West Indies Cricket* (London: Guild Publishing, 1988), p. 20.
30. Quoted in Guha, 'Cricket, Caste, Community, Colonialism', p. 176.
31. The process of installing favour for a particular set of policies using the apparatus of the state is one that is common throughout history. In South Africa the policy of 'Winning Hearts and Minds' is a contemporary example.
32. Green, *A History of Cricket*, p. 197.
33. Quoted in Holt, *Sport and the British*, p. 6.
34. B. Hemyng, *Jack Harkaway at Oxford* (London: Edwin J. Brett, 1872), p. 144.
35. F.S. Ashley-Cooper, 'Some Notes on Early Cricket Abroad', *Cricketer Annual* (1922/3), quoted in Rayvern Allen, *Cricket's Silver Lining*, p. 157.
36. P.A. Dunae, *Gentlemen Emigrants: From the British Public Schools to the Canadian Frontier* (Manchester: Manchester University Press, 1981), p. 8.

37. Quoted in L. O'Brien Thompson, 'How Cricket is West Indian Cricket? Class, Racial, and Colour Conflict', quoted in Hilary McD Beckles and Brian Stoddart (eds.), *Liberation Cricket: West Indies Cricket Culture* (Manchester: Manchester University Press, 1995), p. 169.

38. Quoted in Green, *A History of Cricket*, p. 143.

39. Sandiford, *Cricket and the Victorians*, p. 146.

40. F.A. Hoyos, 'Some Eminent Contemporaries' (Bridgetown, 1944), pp. 112–14, quoted in Beckles and Stoddart, *Liberation Cricket*, p. 52.

41. Owen Conway, 'Lord Hawke at Home', *Windsor Magazine* (1898), quoted in Rayvern Allen, *Cricket's Silver Lining*, p. 241.

42. K.S. Inglis, 'Imperial Cricket', in R. Cashman and M. McKernan, *Sport in History: The Making of Modern Sporting History* (Queensland: University of Queensland Press, 1979), p. 155.

43. J. Strutt, 'The Sports and Pastimes of the People of England' (London, 1801), quoted in Peter McIntosh, *Fair Play: Ethics in Sport and Education* (London: Heinemann, 1979), p. 1.

44. Peter Wynne-Thomas, 'Re-writing History: Where was the Game Really Born?' *Cricket Digest* (Spring 1997), pp. 2–3.

45. J. Nyren, *The Cricketers of My Time* (London: Robson Books, 1988), p. 67.

46. Marqusee, *Anyone but England*, p. 40

47. *All the Year Round* (conducted by Charles Dickens) (1877), quoted in Rayvern Allen, *Cricket's Silver Lining*, p. 372.

48. Tony Lewis, *Double Century: The Story of the MCC and Cricket* (London: Hodder & Stroughton, 1987).

49. Marqusee, *Anyone but England*, p. 74.

50. Holt, *Sport and the British*, p. 112.

51. Guha, 'Cricket, Caste, Community, Colonialism', p. 175.

52. Jable, 'Cricket Clubs and Class in Philadelphia', p. 216.

53. Ibid., p. 218.

54. *Bulletin*, 23 Nov. 1884, quoted in Dr W. Mandle, 'Cricket and Australian Nationalism in the Nineteenth Century', in Jaques and Pavia, *Sport in Australia*, p. 62.

55. S. Canynge Caple, *The Springboks at Cricket, 1888–1960* (Worcester: Littlebury & Company, 1960), pp. 65–6 (the italics are mine).

56. '[A]ll were outstanding quick bowlers of their time, all were no-balled into obscurity, all were black, all were destined never to play for Australia.' (Ashley Mallett, 'Lords of the Bush', *The Cricketer* (Dec. 1997), p. 39.)

57. Quoted in Christopher Brookes, *English Cricket: The Game and its Players through the Ages* (London: Weidenfeld & Nicolson, 1978), p. 142.

58. Jack Grant, *Jack Grant's Story* (London: Lutterworth Press, 1980), p. 31.

59. Frank Birbalsingh, *The Rise of West Indian Cricket: From Colony to Nation* (Antigua: Hansib, 1996), p. 23.

60. Frank Worrell, *Cricket Punch* (London: Stanley Paul, 1960), p. 73.

61. Chris Searle, 'Race before Cricket: Cricket, Empire, and the White Rose', *Race and Class*, 31, 3 (1990), pp. 343–5.

62. A political unit composed of Princes, which was given limited powers as a sop and designed to dampen enthusiasm for the emerging nationalist movement.

63. Ashis Nandy, *The Tao of Cricket* (New Delhi: Penguin Books, 1989), p. 90.

NOTES TO CHAPTER 4

1. 'Cypher', 'The History of Natal Cricket', in Luckin, *The History of South African Cricket*, p. 67.

2. Quoted in John Nauright, *Sport, Cultures and Identities in South Africa* (London: Leicester University Press, 1997), p. 30.

3. Abe Bailey, 'Cricket in South Africa', in Warner, *Imperial Cricket*, pp. 323–4.

4. J.T. Henderson, 'English Cricket in Natal', in Luckin, *The History of South African Cricket*, p. 86.

5. On 29 Dec. 1895, Sir Leander Jameson led a band of men into the Boer colony of Transvaal in an effort to support an impending rebellion by British settlers and to further Cecil Rhodes's ambition for a united South Africa.

6. H.S. Altham, *A History of Cricket: From the Beginnings to the First World War* (London: George Allen & Unwin, 1962), p. 295.

7. Canynge Caple, *The Springboks at Cricket*, p. 21.

8. Floris J.G. van der Merwe, 'Sport and Games in Boer Prisoner-of-War Camps during the Anglo-Boer War, 1899–1902', *International Journal of the History of Sport*, (Dec. 1992), pp. 439–54.

9. 'News in Brief', *Abantu Bathos*, Johannesburg, 5 March 1931, quoted in Alan Cobley, 'A Political History of Playing Fields: The Provision of Sporting Facilities for Africans in the Johannesburg Area to 1948', *The International Journal of the History of Sport*, 11, 2 (1994), p. 226.

10. Baruch Hirson, *Tuskagee: The Joint Councils and the All African Convention*, mimeograph, Institute of Commonwealth Studies, London University (May 1978), quoted in Robert Archer and Antoine Bouillon, *The South African Game: Sport and Racism* (London: Zed Press, 1982), p. 119.

11. Jack and Ray Simons, *Class and Colour in South Africa, 1850–1950* (London: International Defence & Aid Fund, 1983), p. 320.

12. Report of the National European–Bantu Conference, 1929, pp. 195–6 and 200, quoted in Archer and Bouillon, *The South African Game*, p. 120

13. Dorothy Maud, 'Ekutuleni – An Adventure in Peacemaking' (July 1929), quoted in Cobley, 'A Political History of Playing Fields', p. 219.

14. Ibid., pp. 222–3.

15. Ray Phillips, *The Bantu in the City: A Study of Cultural Adjustment on the Witwatersrand* (Lovedale: Lovedale Press, 1936), p. 304.

16. Jack and Ray Simons, *Class and Colour in South Africa*, pp. 466–7. The quotation is by Jameson G. Coka of the Communist Party, who wrote a number of articles on the ANC for the publication *Umsebenzi*.

17. Brian Bunting, *The Rise of the South African Reich* (London: Penguin, 1964), p. 88.

18. The vote to support the Allies against Germany was 80–67.

19. Dan O'Meara, *Forty Lost Years* (Randberg: Ravan Press, 1996), p. 24.

20. See Alex Callinicos and John Rogers, *Southern Africa after Soweto* (London: Pluto Press, 1977), p. 48.

21. The United Party took 51 per cent of the vote and the National Party only 41 per cent, some 103,000 votes less. It was not until 1958 that the National Party won a majority of votes (O'Meara, *Forty Lost Years*, p. 64).

22. Ibid., p. 41.

23. For an exploration of this position, see: H.I.J. Van der Sprug, 'The Psychology of South Africa', *New Society*, Vol.30 (1974), pp. 671–3; D. Archibald, 'The Afrikaners as an Emergent Minority', *British Journal of Sociology*, Vol. 4, 20 (1969), pp. 416–26.

24. Monica Wilson and Leonard Thompson (eds.), *The Oxford History of South Africa, Vol II – 1870–1966* (Oxford: Clarendon Press, 1971), pp. 406–7. Segregation of the races was also accepted as standard by the opposition United Party, whose *raison d'être* was rooted in economic rather than purely racial terms.

25. Lipton, *Capitalism and Apartheid*, pp. 15–16.

26. 'Mr Strijdom on the Senate', *Times*, 11 Sept. 1957, p. 8.

27. Dr A.L. Geyer, the High Commissioner for the Union of South Africa, to the South African Club, London. 'Racial problem in South Africa: Dr. Geyer's defence of apartheid', *Times*, 14, June 1950, p. 3.

28. 'Race problems in South Africa. Official attitude explained', *Times*, 5 Oct. 1956, p. 5.

29. Sparks, *The Mind of South Africa*, p. 153.

30. *The Holy Bible. New International Version* (London: Hodder and Stoughton, 1979), p. 1,140.

31. Rene de Villiers in Wilson and Thompson, *The Oxford History of South Africa*, p. 371.

32. Quoted in Bunting, *The Rise of the South African Reich*, p. 91.

33. Rene de Villiers, 'Afrikaner Nationalism' in Wilson and Thompson, *The Oxford History of South Africa*, p. 386.

34. Ibid., p. 366.

35. 'Racial problem in South Africa', *Times*, 14, June 1950.

36. Quoted in Gwendolen M. Carter, *The Politics of Inequality: South Africa since 1948* (London: Thames & Hudson, 1958), p. 87.

37. Harold Wolpe, *Race, Class and the Apartheid State* (London: UNESCO, 1988), Ch.1.

38. *Sunday Times*, London, 16 March 1965, quoted in Joan Brickhill, *Race Against Race: South Africa's 'Multinational' Sport Fraud*, (London: International Defence & Aid Fund, 1976), p. 7.

39. O'Meara, *Forty Lost Years*, p. 110.

40. 'Africans apart', *Times*, Editorial, 12 March 1957, p. 9.

41. 'Dr Malan's cable to All Blacks', *Times*, 24 Sept. 1948. The All-Blacks had just lost a series of Tests to the Springboks.
42. 'Dr Malan's message to Springboks', *Times*, Jan. 29 1952, p. 4.
43. *Die Transvaler*, 7 Sept. 1965, quoted in Archer and Bouillon, *The South African Game*, p. 194.
44. Indeed, passports were denied to representatives of the non-racial South African Soccer Federation in 1958 and to black table tennis players attending the world championships in 1959.
45. 'Apartheid in Sport', *Times*, 5 Feb. 1963, p. 9.
46. See Muriel Horrell (ed.), *A Survey of Race Relations in South Africa* (Johannesburg: South African Institute of Race Relations, 1962), p. 213.
47. Richard Lapchick, *The Politics of Race and International Sport: The Case of South Africa* (London: Greenwood Press, 1975), p. 45.
48. Quoted in Peter Hain, *Don't Play with Apartheid* (London: George Allen & Unwin, 1971), p. 35.
49. *Verwoerd Speaks*, p. 168, quoted in Lipton, *Capitalism and Apartheid*, p. 25.
50. See, for example, Verwoerd's rejection of the report of the Tomlinson Commission in 1956.
51. 'Dr Verwoerd, "Deeper friendship as republic"', *Times*, 6 March 1961, p. 9.
52. The Secretary for Native Affairs, de Wet Nel, explaining the philosophical basis of the 1959 Bantu Self-Government Bill. (Quoted in O'Meara, *Forty Lost Years*, p. 73.)
53. Sparks, *The Mind of South Africa*, p. 235.
54. 'Reserves fall by £9m', *Times*, 14 April 1960.
55. 'South African economy faces new crisis', *Times*, 26 May 1961, p. 20.
56. Lipton, *Capitalism and Apartheid*, p. 301.
57. 'Dr. Verwoerd rejects any apartheid concession', *Times*, 2 Dec. 1960, p. 10.
58. O'Meara, *Forty Lost Years*, p. 109.
59. Lipton, *Capitalism and Apartheid*, p. 143.
60. Hansard Report, 11 April 1967, quoted in Lapchick, *The Politics of Race and International Sport*, p. 87.
61. Ibid., p. 88.
62. Ibid.
63. 'Mr Vorster warns sportsmen', *Times*, 13 April 1967, p. 4.
64. 'South Africa may use secret fund to aid other countries', *Times*, 6 March 1967, p. 4.
65. Quoted in John Laurence, *The Seeds of Disaster* (London, Victor Gollancz, 1968), p. 241.
66. 'Multiracial sport for South Africa', *Times*, 12 April 1967, p. 4.
67. 'Mr Vorster warns sportsmen', *Times*, 13 April 1967, p. 4.
68. Quoted in Lapchick, *The Politics of Race and International Sport*, p. 91.
69. 'Cost of living lowest in the world', *Times*, 18 Feb 1965, p. 22.
70. Callinicos and Rogers, *Southern Africa after Soweto*, p. 70.
71. Sir Arthur Robinson of Johannesburg Consolidated Investments, quoted in ibid., pp. 72–3.
72. Lipton, *Capitalism and Apartheid*, pp. 87–8.
73. 'Band of Brothers' – a secret society established in 1918 by a group of clerks, clerics and policemen, which aimed to promote Afrikaner interests in all walks of life. Virtually all NP cabinet ministers had belonged to the Broederbond. In the 1970s it became dominated by businessmen and bankers, reflecting the changing socio-economic structure of Afrikaner employees.
74. 'Vorster and Hertzog clash at party rally', *Times*, 11 Sept 1969, p. 4.
75. Colin Legum and John Drysdale, *Africa Contemporary Record, Annual Survey and Documents, 1969–70* (Exeter: Africa Research, 1970), p. 273.
76. The South African government refused tennis player Arthur Ashe the visa he needed to enter the 1970 South African tennis championships. However, they were prepared to admit him as part of the US Davis Cup team.
77. *Rand Daily Mail*, 18 Aug. 1971, quoted in Brickhill, *Race Against Race*, p. 25.
78. Ivor Wilkins and Hans Strydom, *The Broederbond* (London, Paddington Press, 1979), p. 246.
79. Dr Koornhof, *Hansard*, 25 May 1973, quoted in Archer and Bouillon, *The South African Game*, p. 209.
80. 'South Africa adjusts its sports apartheid policy', *Times*, 29 May 1973, p. 5.
81. Michael Knipe, 'Minister defends petty apartheid measures', *Times*, 2 April 1973.
82. Wilkins and Strydom, *The Broederbond*, p. 250.
83. Minister of sport and recreation, *Hansard*, 18 May 1977, quoted in Grant Jarvie, *Class, Race and Sport in South Africa's Political Economy* (London: Routledge & Kegan Paul, 1985), p. 1.
84. Quoted in Brickhill, *Race Against Race*, p. 23.
85. 'Vorster pledge to resist multi-racialism', *Times*, 28 Aug. 1971, p. 4.

86. Sam Ramsamy, *Apartheid, The Real Hurdle* (London: International Defence & Aid Fund, 1982), p. 23.
87. Ray Kennedy, 'South African finance head in City talks', *Times*, 6 July 1976, p. 17.
88. O'Meara, *Forty Lost Years*, p. 177.
89. 'Gold slump expected to worsen decline in South African reserves', *Times*, 22 July 1976, p. 22.
90. According to the Johannesburg 'Rand Daily Mail' South Africa required an annual investment of R1,000 million simply to keep the economy moving. ('Business fears rise in black jobless', *Times*, 22 July 1976, p. 22.)
91. Lipton, *Capitalism and Apartheid*, p. 233.
92. Tom Lodge and Bill Nasson, *All, Here, and Now: Black Politics in South Africa in the 1980s* (London: Hurst & Company, 1992), p. 38.
93. J.D. Omer-Cooper, *History of Southern Africa*, 2nd edn (London: James Currey, 1994), p. 224.
94. Francis Meli, *South Africa Belongs to Us. A History of the ANC* (London: James Currey, 1988), p. 190.
95. Lipton, *Capitalism and Apartheid*, p. 230.
96. Sparks, *The Mind of South Africa*, p. 328.
97. Ibid., p. 308.
98. Callinicos and Rogers, *Southern Africa after Soweto*, p. 158.
99. Lipton, *Capitalism and Apartheid*, p. 243.
100. Ray Kennedy, 'South African finance head in City talks', *Times*, 6 July, 1976, p. 17.
101. Quoted in Jarvie, *Class, Race and Sport*, p. 3.
102. O'Meara, *Forty Lost Years*, p. 225.
103. Republic of South Africa, 'White Paper on Defence and Armaments Supply' (Pretoria: Government Printer, 1977), p. 5, quoted in Douglas Booth, 'South Africa's Autonomous Sport Strategy', *Sporting Traditions* Vol. 6, No. 2 (May 1990), p. 156.
104. Quoted in International Defence & Aid Fund *The Apartheid War Machine* (London: International Defence & Aid Fund 1980), p. 5.
105. Quoted in Lipton, *Capitalism and Apartheid*, p. 50.
106. Callinicos and Rogers, *Southern Africa after Soweto*, p. 166.
107. *Financial Mail*, Feb 1 and June 6 1980, quoted in John Saul and Stephen Gelb, *The Crisis in South Africa: Class Defence, Class Revolution* (London: Monthly Review Press, 1981), p. 2.
108. Ibid., p. 45.
109. Lipton, *Capitalism and Apartheid*, p. 109. The report was commissioned by the Natal business community.
110. The community councils held limited powers and were concerned with matters such as raising and collecting rents.
111. Quoted in Lipton, *Capitalism and Apartheid*, p. 55.
112. P.W. Botha, quoted in Deborah Posel, 'The Language of Domination', in Shula Marks and Stanley Trapido (eds.), *The Politics of Race, Class and Nationalism in Twentieth Century South Africa* (London: Longman, 1987), pp. 422–3.
113. Quoted in Saul and Gelb, *The Crisis in South Africa*, p. 56.
114. 'Connie Mulder allows a peak behind the veil', *Durban Times*, 26 Feb. 1978, p. 13, quoted in March Krotee, 'Apartheid and Sport: South Africa Revisited', *Sociology of Sport Journal*, 15, 2 (1988), p. 129.
115. Circular issued by the South African Department of Sport on 27 Oct. 1979, quoted in Ramsamy, *The Real Hurdle*, p. 38.
116. Quoted in Krotee, 'Apartheid and Sport', p. 130.
117. Odendaal, *Cricket in Isolation*, p. 80.
118. Quoted in ibid., pp. 123–4.
119. Nicholas Ashford, 'Blind eye turned on race in sport', *Times*, 16 Nov. 1976, p. 11.
120. Wilkins and Strydom, *The Broederbond*, p. 248.
121. Tony Koenderman, *Sanctions: The Threat to South Africa* (Johannesburg: Jonathan Ball Publishers, 1982), p. 239.
122. P. Hawthorne, 'A few Cracks in the Racial Barrier', *Sports Illustrated*, 22 Nov. 1976, quoted in Krotee, 'Apartheid and Sport', p. 130.
123. Bruce Kidd, 'From Quarantine to Cure: The New Phase of the Struggle against Apartheid Sport', *Sociology of Sport Journal*, 8, 1 (1991), p. 35.
124. Quoted in O'Meara, *Forty Lost Years*, p. 308.

NOTES TO CHAPTER 5

1. See Archer and Bouillon, *The South African Game*, Chapter 2.
2. Robert Morrell explains how the Natal gentry embraced rugby as a means of distancing themselves from football because of its associations with both the urbanised white working class and the black population. Sport offered an opportune means to encourage racial exclusivity – and soon became divided along racial rather than merely class lines. (Robert Morrell, 'Forging a Ruling Race: Rugby and White Mmasculinity in Colonial Natal, c.1879-1910', in John Nauright and Timothy Chandler (eds.), *Making Men: Rugby and Masculine Identity* (London: Frank Cass, 1996), pp. 91–120.)
3. C.W. de Kiewiet, *A History of South Africa, Social and Economic* (Oxford: Clarendon Press, 1941), p. 30.
4. Quoted in Louis Duffus, Michael Owen-Smith and Andre Odendaal, 'South Africa', in E.W. Swanton, George Plumtree and John Woodcock (eds.), *Barclays World of Cricket. The Game from A to Z* (London: Guild Publishing, 1986), p. 113.
5. W.H. Mars, 'The History of Cricket in the Western Province', in Luckin, *The History of South African Cricket*, p. 139.
6. Gerald Howat, *Cricket's Second Golden Age* (London: Hodder & Stoughton, 1989), p. 90.
7. Andre Odendaal, 'South Africa's Black Victorians: Sport and Society in South Africa in the Nineteenth Century', in J.A. Mangan (ed.), *Pleasure, Profit, Proselytism: British Culture and Sport at Home and Abroad, 1700–1914* (London: Frank Cass, 1988), p. 197.
8. 'Zonnebloem College', 'African Political Association', 24 Sept. 1910, ibid., p. 197.
9. In 1899 the Rand produced 27 per cent of the world's gold; by 1913 it was 40 per cent. (William Beinart, *Twentieth Century South Africa* (Oxford: Oxford University Press, 1993), p. 27.)
10. Quoted in Tim Couzens, '"Moralising Leisure Time": The Transatlantic Connection and Black Johannesburg, 1918–36', in Shula Marks and Richard Rathbone (eds.), *Industrialisation and Social Change in South Africa: African Class Formation, Culture, and Consciousness, 1870–1930* (London: Longman, 1982), p. 321.
11. W.H. Mars, 'The History of Cricket in Western Province', in Luckin, *The History of South African Cricket*, p. 148.
12. Indians were first brought to South Africa in the 1860s as a result of labour shortages in the Natal sugar plantations.
13. The Malays were introduced to the Cape as slaves by the Dutch East India Company.
14. Douglas Booth, *The Race Game*, p. 30.
15. John Buchan, 'The African Colony: Studies in Reconstruction', *Studies in Reconstruction* (London: William Blackwood & Sons, 1903), pp. 49–50.
16. G. Allsop, 'Reminiscences of Cricket' in Luckin, *The History of South African Cricket*, p. 128.
17. Mars, 'The History of Cricket in the Western Province', in ibid., p. 135.
18. A.W. Wells, *South Africa: A Planned Tour of the Country Today* (London: J.M. Dent & Sons, 1949), p. 131.
19. Nauright, *Sport, Cultures and Identities*, p. 27.
20. Quoted in Howat, *Cricket's Second Golden Age*, p. 111.
21. See Van der Merwe, 'Sport and Games in Boer Prisoner of War Camps', pp. 439–54.
22. Nauright, *Sport, Cultures and Identities*, p. 27.
23. *Amper Krieket Kampioene* (Almost Champion Cricketers) by Werner Barnard, 1956.
24. See M. Commaille (Western Province, Orange Free State and South Africa), 'The South African team in England – 1924', in M.W. Luckin (ed.), *South African Cricket, 1919–1927* (Johannesburg: published by the author, 1927), pp. 317–18.
25. G.A. Parker, *South African Sports: An Official Handbook* (London, 1897), p. 47.
26. Nauright, *Sport, Cultures and Identities*, p. 26.
27. Luckin, *South African Cricket, 1919–1927*, pp. 18–19.
28. In the same publication, H.W. Taylor (Natal, Transvaal and South Africa) suggested that Coloured boys, who already tended to the cricket pitches, be employed as ground bowlers. ('How South African Cricket Should be built up', ibid., p. 34.)
29. Throughout the 1960s South Africa's record in international cricket stood at 7 wins, 8 losses and 16 draws. All but 5 of these 31 contests were against England and Australia, and included series victories over each of the arch rivals. At the start of 1970 the Springboks whitewashed Australia

4–0 and proclaimed themselves to be world champions.

30. Archer and Bouillon, *The South African Game*, p. 44.
31. John Woodcock, 'South Africa on a sticky wicket', *Times*, 2 Feb. 1967, p. 12.
32. Michael Melford, 'Ups and downs of the Springboks', *Wisden* (1970), pp. 147–8.
33. Roland Bowen, *Cricket: A History of its Growth and Development Throughout the World* (London: Eyre & Spottiswoode, 1970), p. 216.
34. Christopher Warman, 'Most of Springboks wanted to go home by Christmas', *Times*, 29 Jan. 1970, p. 10.
35. Joshua 9:23.
36. Rene de Villiers, 'Afrikaner Nationalism', in Wilson and Thompson, *The Oxford History of South Africa, Vol II*, p. 371.
37. Sparks, *The Mind of South Africa*, p. xvii.
38. Bowen, *Cricket*, p. 277.
39. A.F. Hattersley (ed.), *John Sheddon Dobie South African Journal, 1862–6*, 1st series, No.26 (Cape Town: Van Riebeck Society, 1945).
40. Odendaal, *Cricket in Isolation*, p. 306.
41. Ibid., p. 324.
42. Ibid., p. 307.
43. Brian Willan, 'An African in Kimberley: Sol T. Plaatje, 1894–1898', quoted in Archer and Bouillon, *The South African Game*, p. 89.
44. Ibid., p. 27.
45. See, for example, the *Official Year Book of the Republic of South Africa* (Pretoria, 1974), p. 881.
46. Odendaal, *Cricket in Isolation*, p. 325.
47. Cited in Krish Reddy, 'SACB – A Historical Perspective', *1991 Protea Assurance Cricket Annual of South Africa*, Vol.38 (Cape Town: Protea Assurance, 1991), p. 27.
48. Quoted in 'Colour in cricket', *Times*, 28 Jan. 1967, p. 8.
49. Andre Odendaal, 'South Africa's Black Victorians: Sport and Society in South Africa in the Nineteenth Century', in Mangan, *Pleasure, Profit, Proselytism*, p. 199.
50. P.F. Warner, *The MCC in South Africa* (London: Chapman & Hall, 1906), p. 2.
51. Odendaal, *Cricket in Isolation*, p. 309.
52. Brian Crowley, 'South Africa's lost Generation', *The Cricketer*, Sept. 1990, p. 20.
53. Brian Crowley, *Cricket's Exiles: The Saga of South African Cricket* (London: Angus & Robertson, 1983), p. 11.
54. Quoted in Odendaal, *Cricket in Isolation*, p. 32.
55. Ibid., p. 326.
56. Bowen, *Cricket*, p. 150.
57. Lipton, *Capitalism and Apartheid*, p. 119.
58. African cash wages, as a proportion of working costs, declined from 16.4 per cent in 1911 to 8.8 per cent in 1969 (ibid., p. 121).
59. Ibid., p. 18.
60. Quoted in Lipton, *Capitalism and Apartheid*, p. 263.
61. Odendaal, 'South Africa's Black Victorians', in Mangan, *Pleasure, Profit, Proselytism,* p. 204.
62. Booth, *The Race Game*, p. 20.
63. Howat, *Cricket's Second Golden Age*, p. 112.
64. Quoted in Sparks, *The Mind of South Africa*, pp. 136–7.
65. Archer and Bouillon, *The South African Game*, p. 141.
66. Basil D'Oliveira, *D'Oliveira – An Autobiography* (London: Sportsmans Book Club, 1969), pp. 41–2.
67. Meli, *South Africa Belongs to Us*, p. 121.
68. Quoted in Lodge and Nasson, *All Here and Now*, p. 334.
69. See Chapter 3, pp. 71–2.
70. Bowen, *Cricket*, p. 214.
71. See Odendaal, *Cricket in Isolation*, pp. 117–18.
72. Quoted in Hain, *Don't Play with Apartheid*, p. 77.
73. Speech of Alan Paton at the opening ceremony of SASA, 10 Jan. 1959, quoted in Chris de Broglio, *South Africa: Racism in Sport* (London: International Defence & Aid Fund, 1970), p. 3.
74. The critics included Basil D'Oliveira, who argued that the cancellation denied blacks the opportunities of communicating with people from another country on the cricket field, and C.L.R. James.

75. Archer and Bouillon, *The South African Game*, p. 191.
76. Marqusee, *Anyone but England*, p. 186.
77. A key principle stated that 'no discrimination is allowed against any country or person on grounds of race, religion or political affiliation'. (Quoted in Douglas Booth, 'The South African Council on Sport and the Political Antinomies of the Sports Boycott', *Journal of Southern African Studies*, 23, 1 (March 1997), p. 53.) This had also been a key pillar of the South African Non-Racial Olympic Committee (SAN-ROC), which campaigned against all white sports teams representing South Africa in the Olympic Games. SAN-ROC became a potent and effective thorn in the side of the apartheid regime as the Olympics took on an increasingly political character.
78. Archer and Bouillon, *The South African Game*, p. 229.
79. Sam Ramsamy, 'Racial Discrimination and Sport in South Africa', quoted in ibid., pp. 232–3.
80. Brickhill, *Race Against Race*, p. 74.
81. The memorandum named eight foreign firms who donated between the years 1965 and 1972. They contributed about R457,750 to white sport, R30,000 to racial black unions and R6,300 to non-racial sport, a ratio of 1:15:73. (Ibid., p. 75.)
82. Ramsamy, *The Real Hurdle*, p. 78.
83. *Rand Daily Mail*, 6 April 1978, quoted in Jarvie, *Class, Race and Sport*, p. 60.
84. Dawie de Villiers, quoted in Archer and Bouillon, *The South African Game*, p. 8. De Villiers was ambassador to Britain 1979–80, Springbok rugby captain 1965–70 and an MP 1980–81.
85. Sports Council of Great Britain, 'Sport in South Africa, report of the Sports Council's fact-finding delegation' (London, 1980), quoted in ibid., p. 8.
86. Quoted in Chris Harte, *Two Tours and Pollock. The Australians in South Africa, 1985–87* (London: Sports Marketing, 1988), p. 133.
87. Tony Greig, *My Story* (London: Stanley Paul, 1980), p. 82. Greig is a South African-born former England captain.
88. 'Race problems in South Africa. Official attitude explained', *Times*, 5 Oct. 1956, p. 5.
89. Sparks, *The Mind of South Africa*, p. 210.
90. Nauright, *Sport, Cultures and Identities*, p. 36.
91. Mike Proctor, *South Africa, The Years of Isolation and the Return to International Cricket* (Durban: Bok Books International, 1994), p. 29.
92. Irving Rosenwater, 'The South African Tour Dispute', in Benny Green (ed.), *Wisden Anthology, 1963–1982* (London: Guild Publishing, 1984), p. 81.
93. Quoted in Ibid.
94. *'Not lightly done'*, Times, 12 April 1960. p. 12.
95. Proctor, *The Years of Isolation*, p. 27.
96. *Guardian*, 25 May 1970.
97. SACA president Jack Cheetham suggested that both Suleiman Abed and Owen Williams be the first blacks to be included in the South African side.
98. Barry Richards, *The Barry Richards Story* (Exeter: Readers Union, 1978), p. 120.
99. Ibid.
100. Lapchick, *The Politics of Race and International Sport* (London: Greenwood Press, 1975), p. 210.
101. Paper presented to United Nations Anti-Apartheid Seminar by SAN-ROC, April–May 1975, quoted in Brickhill, *Race Against Race*, p. 49.
102. Quoted in Brickhill, *Race Against Race*, p. 50.
103. David Frith, 'The Ultimate Museum Piece', *Wisden Cricket Monthly*, April 1989, p. 5.
104. David Frith, 'Hypocrites', *Wisden Cricket Monthly*, April 1989, p. 16.
105. Odendaal, *Cricket in Isolation*, p. 316.
106. In a referendum of the white soccer union, FASA, 70 per cent of players favoured mixed soccer, yet no progress could be made because of government policy – notably the Group Areas Act and the Reservation of Separate Amenities Act (Brickhill, *Race Against Race*, p. 47).
107. 'No Changes in Australian Test party', *Times*, 5 Dec. 1975; John Woodcock, 'Winter tours for 1975–76 open to offers', *Times*, 20 Feb. 1975, p. 11.
108. Quoted in Odendaal, *Cricket in Isolation*, p. 41.
109. Quoted in Proctor, *The Years of Isolation*, p. 63.
110. Quoted in Odendaal, *Cricket in Isolation*, p. 42.
111. Proctor, *The Years of Isolation*, p. 63.
112. The government approved the inclusion of two blacks, John Shepherd of the West Indies and Younis Ahmed of Pakistan, in the Derrick Robins' team.

113. Eric Marsden, 'New wave ripples English shore', *Times*, 19 Aug. 1977, p. 10.
114. 'Politics roar back into South African sport', *The Times*, 13 Oct. 1976, p. 10.
115. Quoted in Odendaal, *Cricket in Isolation*, pp. 266–7.
116. Heribert Adam, *Modernising Racial Domination: The Dynamics of South African Politics* (Berkeley, University of California Press, 1971), pp. 87 and 91.
117. Proctor, *The Years of Isolation*, p. 65.
118. Quoted in Lipton, *Capitalism and Apartheid*, pp. 345–6.
119. Memorandum submitted by SACOS to the International Tennis Federation, February 1978, quoted in Ramsamy, *The Real Hurdle*, p. 14.
120. Krish Reddy, 'SACB – A Historical Perspective', p. 35.
121. Ibid., p. 34.
122. Quoted in Crowley, *Cricket's Exiles*, p. 127.
123. Joe Pamensky (president of SACU), 'Cricket, not race, is our Concern', *The Cricketer*, March 1983, p. 28.
124. Joe Pamensky, 'The Principles of SACU', *The Cricketer*, July 1982, p. 30.
125. Quoted in *The Cricketer*, Jan. 1981, p. 33.
126. A securocrat quoted in Sparks, *The Mind of South Africa*, p. 357. Under former president P.W. Botha, the 'securocrats' – seconded personnel from the South African security establishment – exercised extensive influence over state decision-making and policy implementation. The key elements of the securocrat establishment were the State Security Council and the National Security Management System – its implementation instrument.
127. The new constitution proposed an executive president ruling over a tricameral parliament of three ethnic 'Houses' – white, coloured and Indian. Each parliament would deal with its 'own affairs', but the 'general affairs' of the whole population would be dealt with by all three. A majority was retained in the white parliament, and the president had the ultimate sanction over any dispute. Africans were 'encouraged' to see their natural residence as being in one of the homelands.
128. Robert Schrire, *Adapt or Die: The End of White Politics in South Africa* (London: Hurst & Company, 1992), p. 81.
129. Quoted in Omar Henry, *The Man in the Middle* (Herts: Queen Anne Press, 1994), p. 153.
130. Quoted in Booth, *The Race Game*, p. 178.
131. Ibid.
132. Booth, 'South Africa's Autonomous Sport Strategy', p. 171.
133. Mihir Bose, *Sporting Colours: Sport and Politics in South Africa* (London: Robson Books, 1994), p. 153.
134. The SACU constitution stated that any white school that refused to play against township sides would be expelled from the Primary Schools Association.
135. See Jack Bannister, 'Township Cricket', *Wisden Cricket Monthly*, Feb. 1989, p. 13.
136. Joe Pamensky, 'A Catalyst for Change', *Cricket Life International,* Oct. 1989, p. 14.
137. Quoted in Ashley Mallett, 'Bloodbath fear leads to Miracle', *Wisden Cricket Monthly*, June 1989, p. 35.
138. Douglas Booth, 'Accommodating Race to Play the Game', *Sporting Traditions* (May 1992), p. 202.
139. Peter Hain, *Sing the Beloved Country: The Struggle for the New South Africa* (London: Pluto Press, 1996), p. 169.
140. Muleleki George, quoted in Bose, *Sporting Colours*, p. 158.
141. Ibid., p. 160.
142. Ibid., p. 161.
143. Quoted in Hain, *Sing the Beloved Country*, p. 156.
144. Ibid., p. 157.
145. Interview with Sam Ramsamy, Booth, 'Accommodating Race to Play the Game', p. 188.
146. Membership of the ICC was proposed by India. This has a certain poignancy as India was the first country to impose sanctions on South Africa.
147. Quoted in Marqusee, *Anyone but England*, p. 212. A year earlier Mandela had attacked Margaret Thatcher: 'It is only those who support apartheid who say that the Pretoria government should be rewarded for the small steps it has taken.' (Ibid.)
148. Quoted in Jimmy Cook, *The Jimmy Cook Story* (London: Pelham Books, 1993), pp. 150–1.
149. Quoted in Marqusee, *Anyone but England*, p. 212.

NOTES TO CHAPTER 6

1. 'Cover-Point' and 'Eastern Province Cricket', from Luckin, *The History of South African Cricket*, p. 27
2. Quoted in J.T. Henderson, 'English cricket in Natal', in ibid., p. 85.
3. F. Reid, 'Cricket at the Diocesan College', in ibid., p. 791.
4. P.W.H. Kettlewell, 'Cricket at St. Andrews College, Grahamstown', in ibid., p. 800.
5. M.J. Susskind (Cambridge University, Middlesex, Transvaal and South Africa), 'A Survey of Transvaal Cricket Since the War', in Luckin, *South African Cricket, 1919-1927*, p. 117.
6. G.K. Clive Fuller, 'The History of Border Cricket', in Luckin, *The History of South African Cricket*, p. 25.
7. See 'Cover-Point' and 'Eastern Province Cricket', in ibid.
8. Dudley Nourse, *Cricket in the Blood* (London: Hodder & Stoughton, 1949), p. 16.
9. Ibid.
10. F.A. Morris, 'Cricket in the South-Western Districts', in Luckin, *The History of South African Cricket*, p. 121.
11. Archer and Bouillon, *The South African Game*, p. 26.
12. Ibid., p. 115.
13. Jack and Ray Simons, *Class and Colour in South Africa*, p. 29.
14. De Kiewiet, *A History of South Africa*, p. 234.
15. Other means included: the 1911 Mines and Works Act, which reserved positions of responsibility for whites only; the 1922 Apprenticeship Act, which imposed wage rates and educational qualifications for entry to industrial apprenticeships – having the effect of excluding blacks; and the 1923 Native Urban Areas Act, intended to secure hygienic conditions in native slum areas – which in practice restricted the rights of Africans to reside in the towns.
16. P.J. Meyer, 'Trek Verder: Die Afrikaner in Afrika', quoted in Wilson and Thompson, *The Oxford History of South Africa*, p. 399.
17. De Villiers, 'Afrikaner Nationalism', in ibid., p. 399.
18. Greig, *My Story*, p. 42.
19. 'Verwoerd speaks', quoted in Lipton, *Capitalism and Apartheid*, p. 24.
20. Archer and Bouillon, *The South African Game*, p. 47.
21. Bunting, *The Rise of the South African Reich*, p. 211.
22. Callinicos and Rogers, *Southern Africa after Soweto*, p. 161.
23. Bose, *Sporting Colours*, p. 149.
24. Behind the US, the second highest proportion in the world.
25. Booth, 'Accommodating Race to Play the Game', p. 203.
26. Archer and Bouillon, *The South African Game*, p. 164.
27. See Odendaal, *Cricket in Isolation*, pp. 128–9.
28. Booth, *The Race Game*, pp. 69–70. In 1982 the National Party allocated R14,700 to sport for African pupils, whilst providing R35,000 for tug-of-war visitors (ibid., footnote no.63).
29. Hassan Howa, quoted in Odendaal, *Cricket in Isolation*, pp. 269–70 and 276–7.
30. Booth, *The Race Game*, p. 70.
31. Quoted in Booth, 'South Africa's Autonomous Sport Strategy', p. 174.
32. Sparks, *The Mind of South Africa*, p. 135.
33. Archer and Bouillon, *The South African Game*, p. 159.
34. Booth, *The Race Game*, p. 64.
35. Ibid.
36. Henry, *The Man in the Middle*, p. 16.
37. E. Jokl in 'Report of the South African National Conference on the Post-War Planning of Social Work' (1944), quoted in Archer and Bouillon, *The South African Game*, p. 129.
38. Alan Cobley, *Class and Consciousness: The Black Petty-Bourgeoisie in South Africa, 1924–1950* (London: Greenwood, 1994), p. 215.
39. Quoted in Archer and Bouillon, *The South African Game*, p. 127.
40. Ibid., p. 168; Brickhill, *Race Against Race*, p. 71?]
41. Brickhill, *Race Against Race*, p. 19.
42. Ibid. p. 71.
43. Kidd, 'From Quarantine to Cure', p. 36.
44. Basil D'Oliveira, *Time to Declare: An Autobiography* (London: W.H. Allen & Co, 1980), pp. 2–3.

45. Sedrick Conrad, 'Crossing the Line', in Odendaal, *Cricket in Isolation*, p. 227.
46. H.L. Crockett (chairman, Natal Cricket Association), 'Turf Wickets in South Africa', in Luckin, *South African Cricket, 1919-1927*, p. 35. It was not until the 1926/27 season that first-class matches were played without matting. (H.E. Holmes, 'Natal Cricket', ibid., p. 109. See also Canynge Caple, *The Springboks at Cricket*, p. 107.) It was not until the second Test of the 1930–31 MCC tour to South Africa that Test cricket was played on a turf wicket. In 1935 the Springboks won their first Test in England.
47. Marshall Lee, 'Cricket on Corrugated Iron', in Odendaal, *Cricket in Isolation*, p. 233.
48. Christopher Merrett, letter to *The Cricketer*, April 1982.
49. Harte, *Two Tours and Pollock*, p. 25.
50. Quoted in ibid., p. 42.
51. Ellen Hellmann, 'Urban Areas', quoted in Booth, *The Race Game*, p. 65.
52. '£15 a month for an African family', *Times*, 29 Aug. 1958, p. 7.
53. M. Williams, 'An Analysis of South African Capitalism', *Bulletin of the Conference of Socialist Economists*, Feb. 1974, quoted in Lipton, *Capitalism and Apartheid*, p. 121.
54. Ibid. Tables 10 and 11, pp. 409–10.
55. 'Colour among doctors', editorial, *Times*, 15 May 1969, p. 9.
56. Archer and Bouillon, *The South African Game*, p. 162.
57. 'Are hungry children held back for life?', *Times*, 30 May 1973.
58. Francis Wilson and Mamphela Ramphele, *Uprooting Poverty: The South African Challenge* (Cape Town: David Philip, 1989), p. 4.
59. Hassan Howa, quoted in Odendaal, *Cricket in Isolation*, pp. 269–70 and 276–7.
60. Booth, *The Race Game*, pp. 71–2.
61. As early as 1927 M.W. Luckin argued that the 'spirit of cricket, with its ennobling and unifying influence' required grass wickets. (Luckin, *South African Cricket, 1919–1927*, p. 19.)
62. Hain, *Sing the Beloved Country*, p. 166.
63. Excerpt from a SACB pamphlet, quoted in Harte, *Two Tours and Pollock*, p. 52.
64. Ali Bacher quoted in Booth, *The Race Game*, p. 138.
65. 'Bacher seeks help for cricket's "boat people"', *The Star* (South Africa), 25 Feb. 1992, quoted in Booth, 'Accommodating Race to Play the Game', pp. 202–3.
66. Policy Statement of the South African Council on Sport, first published in 'Souvenir Brochure of the Natal Council of Sport', 13 Dec. 1980, quoted in Ramsamy, *The Real Hurdle*, p. 17.
67. Ibid., pp. 17–18.
68. Hassan Howa, quoted in Odendaal, *Cricket in Isolation*, pp. 269–70 and 276–7.

NOTES TO CHAPTER 7

1. Dr A.J.R. van Rhijn, South African high commissioner, quoted in 'Scope for UK in South Africa trade', *Times*, 10 Feb. 1959, p. 7.
2. 'UN call to South Africa', *Times*, 22 Jan. 1957, p. 7.
3. 'Vote in United Nations for South Africa arms ban', *Times*, 8 Aug. 1963, p. 8.
4. 'Blind pursuit', editorial, *Times*, 28 Dec. 1957, p. 7.
5. See Richard Thompson, *Retreat from Apartheid: New Zealand's Sporting Contacts with South Africa* (London: Oxford University Press, 1975), Chapter 11, 'The Protest Movement'.
6. Wilf Wooler, secretary of Glamorgan CCC, replied: 'As far as our guests, the South African cricketers, we shall welcome them with true Welsh hospitality.' ('Ban urged on South Africans fixtures', *The Times*, 6 April 1960, p. 10.)
7. '500 to demonstrate outside airport', *The Times*, 14 April 1960, p. 7.
8. John Arlott, 'The South Africans in England', in *Playfair Cricket Annual* (1961), quoted in David Rayvern Allen (ed.), *The Essential John Arlott: Forty Years of Classic Cricket Writing* (London: Guild Publishing, 1989), pp. 135–40. Whereas the South Africans took back a profit of £36,000 from their previous tour of England in 1955, this time their share of the gates did not quite cover their expenses of £35,000. (Norman Preston, 'South Africans in England, 1960', in *Wisden* (1961), pp. 264–7.)
9. Lapchick, *The Politics of Race and International Sport*, p. 56.
10. 'The problems still engulfing South Africa', editorial, *Playfair Cricket Monthly* (April 1962), p. 3.
11. '... I always supported the visiting country – after all, they weren't denying me the chance to play

in such a magnificent stadium' [Newlands]. (D'Oliveira, *Time to Declare*, p. 4.)

12. Marqusee, *Anyone but England*, p. 186.
13. See, for example, Carter, *The Politics of Inequality*, p. 99.
14. Quoted in Bunting, *The Rise of the South African Reich*, pp. 134–5. See also Booth, *The Race Game*, p. 102.
15. O'Meara, *Forty Lost Years*, p. 103.
16. 'Contact' (Cape Town), 8 August, 1959, p. 7, quoted in Tom Lodge 'Sanctions and Black Political Organisations' in Mark Orkin (ed.), *Sanctions Against Apartheid* (London: Catholic Institute for International Relations, 1989), p. 35.
17. Orkin, *Sanctions against Apartheid*, p. 6.
18. Quoted in Lapchick, *The Politics of Race and International Sport*, p. 199.
19. Tony Koenderman, *Sanctions*, p. 238.
20. Quoted in Bose, *Sporting Colours*, p. 104.
21. Greig, *My Story*, pp. 86–7.
22. Booth, *The Race Game*, p. 85.
23. Quoted in Hain, *Don't Play with Apartheid*, p. 216.
24. 'Rapport', Johannesburg, 12 Sept. 1971, quoted in Adrian Guelke, 'The Politicisation of South African Sport', in Allison, *The Politics of Sport*, p. 143.
25. *Sunday Times*, 13 May 1984, quoted in ibid.
26. See, for example, 'UN vote on South Africa. British Attitude', *The Times*, 5 Feb. 1957, p. 11.
27. Christopher Martin-Jenkins, 'Editorial', *The Cricketer*, April 1982, p. 9.
28. Proctor, *The Years of Isolation*, p. 71.
29. Speech to the 55th session of the IOC in Munich (May 23, 1959), from *The Speeches of President Avery Brundage 1952 to 1968* (Lausanne: IOC, 1969), p. 42.
30. Sparks, *The Mind of South Africa*, p. 185.
31. Hain, *Don't Play with Apartheid*, pp. 88–9.
32. Christopher Martin-Jenkins, 'Common sense prevails, but the problem remains', *The Cricketer*, Dec. 1981, p. 4; 'Editorial', *The Cricketer*, April 1982, p. 9.
33. Cricket had made advances into the Afrikaner community. Following the successes of the 1967 and 1970 Springboks, the game was increasingly entering Afrikaans schools and players from this community were pressing through to the higher echelons of the game. Kepler Wessells, who went on to represent both Australia and South Africa, was one of the first of a new generation of players.
34. Birley, *The Willow Wand*, p. 162.
35. Bob Woolmer, *Pirate and Rebel? An Autobiography* (London: Arthur Baker, 1984), p. 112.
36. De Villiers, 'Afrikaner Nationalism', in Wilson and Thompson, *The Oxford History of South Africa*, p. 418.
37. This was a line advanced in a Mobil Corporation advertisement, 'Sanctions: The Last Resort', which appeared in the *New York Times*, 15 Feb. 1996.
38. R. First, J. Steel and C. Gurney, *The South African Connection* (Harmondsworth: Penguin, 1973), pp. 26–7.
39. Dan van der Vat, 'Vorster sees plot by communists in sport boycott', *Times*, 2 June 1970, p. 7.
40. Peter Kirsten, 'No need for sympathy', *The Cricketer*, Oct. 1981, p. 21.
41. Thompson, *Retreat from Apartheid*, p. 58.
42. 'Barlow's doubts about re-entry into the fold', *Times*, 18 Aug. 1980, p. 6.
43. Muriel Horrell, *Survey of Race Relations, 1973* (Johannesburg: Institute of Race Relations, 1974), p. 46.
44. Tommie Campbell, '"Freedom in Sport" – the way forward', *The Cricketer*, Dec. 1981, p. 7. Campbell, a Dublin business executive, was a leading figure behind the formation of FIS.
45. Greg Chappell, 'Play with South Africa', in Odendaal, *Cricket in Isolation*, p. 168; 'Ashe sees "vast potential for good" in South Africa', *Times*, 26 Nov. 1974, p. 13.
46. Quoted in Irving Rosenwater, 'The South African Tour Dispute', in Green, *Wisden Anthology*, p. 75.
47. *Wisden* (1982), p. 88.
48. Quoted in Harte, *Two Tours and Pollock*, p. 125.
49. P.J. Badenhorst, 'Parliamentary Debate on Sport', 22 May 1980, quoted in Ramsamy, *The Real Hurdle*, p. 63.
50. Gordon Ross, *A History of Cricket* (London: Arthur Baker, 1972), p. 170.
51. Quoted in Lapchick, *The Politics of Race and International Sport*, p. 105.

52. Bill Hicks, 'Give South Africa a sporting chance', *Times*, 1 April 1981, p. 13.
53. R.A. Pape, 'Why Economic Sanctions Do Not Work', *International Security*, Vol. 22 (1997), pp. 106–7.
54. Michael Ellis, 'We have paid the price', *The Cricketer*, Jan. 1989, p. 8.
55. Quoted in Harte, *Two Tours and Pollock*, p. 134.
56. 'Greg Chappell calls for Australian tour of South Africa', *Times*, 9 Jan. 1976, p. 6.
57. De Broglio, *Racism in Sport*, pp. 2–3.
58. M.P. Naicker, 'Demolishing the bridge-building myth', *Times*, 8 Sept. 1976, p. 7.
59. Oliver Tambo, quoted in Allister Sparks, *Tomorrow is Another Country* (London: Arrow, 1995), p. 65.
60. Orkin, *Sanctions Against Apartheid*, p. 12. CASE described itself as an 'independent policy-research agency', which conducted a number of studies of black attitudes in South Africa in the mid 1980s. (Ibid., p. vii.)
61. 'Resolution passed in Canberra', *Times*, 29 April 1960, p. 10.
62. Robert Wolff, 'The Moral Dimensions of the Policy of Anti-Apartheid Sanctions', in Orkin, *Sanctions Against Apartheid*, p. 107.
63. 'Chappell is disappointed at South African decisions', *Times*, 16 Sept. 1975, p. 8.
64. Alex Bannister, 'England's hands are clean', *The Cricketer*, April 1981, p. 7.
65. Mike Brearley, 'Is the time right for an international tour?', *The Cricketer*, Oct. 1981, p. 20.
66. Martin-Jenkins, 'Common sense prevails, but the problem remains', p. 4; Christopher Martin-Jenkins, 'Bans despicable but MCC tour is no answer', editorial, *The Cricketer*, April 1983, p. 6.
67. 'Mr Kirk explains his order to cancel South African tour', *Times*, 11 Apr, 1973, p. 8.
68. Neil Macfarlane, minister of sport, interviewed by Christopher Martin-Jenkins, *The Cricketer*, Dec. 1981, p. 6.
69. Quoted in John Woodcock, 'Notes by the Editor', *Wisden* (1983), p. 80.
70. Quoted in Booth, *The Race Game*, p. 106.
71. Brian Stoddart, 'Caribbean Cricket: The Role of Sport in Emerging Small-Nation Politics', in Beckles and Stoddart, *Liberation Cricket*, p. 249.
72. D. Bernard, Guyana, letter to *Wisden Cricket Monthly*, April 1989, p. 2.
73. By which I am loosely referring to leading players, administrators and writers. The rebel 'Tests' were recorded in *Wisden*, for example, whereas the details of SACB were not.
74. Resolution to a special meeting of the MCC: 'That the members of MCC Committee implement the selection of a touring party to tour South Africa in 1983/4', quoted in *The Cricketer*, July 1983, p. 8.
75. Ibid.
76. Martin-Jenkins, 'Bans despicable but MCC tour is no answer', p. 6.
77. The same team was invested with informal diplomatic status; the team captain received an OBE and the vice-captain an MBE. (Thompson, *Retreat from Apartheid*, p. 55.)
78. Ibid.
79. 'Australia and Africa', Australian Foreign Affairs Record, Canberra, Nov. 1982, quoted in Keith D. Suter, *Australia's Changing Policies Towards Apartheid* (New York: UN Centre Against Apartheid, 1985), p. 12. Sport was used by the Australians to show their 'distaste' of apartheid. Annual trade with the country it refused to play cricket with was in 1984 four times that of 1970. (International Monetary Fund, 'Direction of Trade Statistics Yearbook, 1977, 1980, 1987.) The regime justified this on the grounds that the free flow of capital and goods would help erode those policies of which it disapproved.
80. O'Meara, *Forty Lost Years*, p. 341.
81. Hain, *Sing the Beloved Country*, p. 71.
82. Quoted in Odendaal, *Cricket in Isolation*, p. 142.
83. Ibid., p. 143.
84. Ibid.
85. Ibid., p. 144.
86. Ibid., p. 146.
87. Quoted in Ramsamy, *The Real Hurdle*, pp. 68–9.
88. Quoted in Koenderman, *Sanctions*, p. 236.
89. Quoted in Booth, *The Race Game*, p. 96.
90. 'Racial problems in South Africa. Pakistan memorandum', *Times*, 11, Aug. 1953.
91. 'Britain may face Olympics ban from Third World', *Daily Telegraph*, 22 Oct. 1979, p. 5; 'Threat of boycott recedes despite Britain's policy', *Times*, 14 Dec. 1979, p. 9.

92. Booth, *The Race Game*, p. 112.
93. Proctor, *The Years of Isolation*, p. 22.
94. Greig, *My Story*, p. 87.
95. Richard Streeton, 'Isolation has produced change, Craven says', *Times*, 18 Jan. 1980, p. 11.
96. Quoted in Hain, *Sing the Beloved Country*, pp. 61–2.
97. David Black, '"Not Cricket": The Effects and Effectiveness of the Sports Boycott', in Neta Crawford and Audie Klotz (eds.), *How Sanctions Work. Lessons from South Africa* (Basingstoke: Macmillan Press, 1999), p. 225.

NOTES TO CHAPTER 8

1. O'Meara, *Forty Lost Years*, pp. 61–2.
2. Leader-in-chief.
3. Quoted in A.N. Pelzer, *Verwoerd Speaks: Speeches 1948–1966* (Johannesburg: Afrikaanse Perboekhandel, 1966), p. 516.
4. De Villiers, 'Afrikaner Nationalism', in Wilson and Thompson, *The Oxford History of South Africa*, p. 394.
5. Quoted in Odendaal, *Cricket in Isolation*, p. 3.
6. 'The Gadarene Trek', editorial, *Times*, 8 Oct. 1960, p. 7.
7. 'South Africa decides to leave', *Times*, 16 March 1961, p. 14; 'World-wide reactions to South African decision', *Times*, 17 March 1961, p. 12; 'Prime Minister regrets the breach', *Times*, 17 March 1961, p. 17.
8. The Balfour Declaration of 1926, which formed part of the Statute of Westminster (1931), determined constitutional equality for all the dominions.
9. 'South Africa decides to leave', *Times*, 16 March 1961, p. 14; 'New strength for Commonwealth', *Times*, 18 March 1961, p. 7.
10. 'Disappointment overseas', *Times*, 21 July 1961, p. 4.
11. Norman Preston, 'Notes by the Editor', *Wisden* (1968), p. 93. When *Playfair* informed its readers of this decision, they received a letter asking them if, on occasion, they could also include some statistics in relation to black cricket in South Africa (letter from E.P. Newnham, Essex, January 1966 issue).
12. Roy Webber, 'The ICC', *Playfair Cricket Monthly*, Sept. 1961, p. 20.
13. C.O. Medworth, 'The future of South African cricket', *Playfair Cricket Monthly*, Sept. 1962, p. 15.
14. 'More arrests in South Africa', *Times*, 6 Nov. 1961, p. 10.
15. Medworth, 'The future of South African cricket', p. 15.

NOTES TO CHAPTER 9

1. John Arlott, 'Introduction' to D'Oliveira, *D'Oliveira*, pp. 11–12.
2. Lee, 'Cricket on Corrugated Iron', p. 234.
3. Greig, *My Story*, p. 43.
4. Peter Wynne-Thomas and Peter Arnold, *Cricket in Conflict* (Middlesex: Newnes Books, 1984), p. 114.
5. Quoted in Lapchick, *The Politics of Race and International Sport*, p. 82.
6. 'Barbados bans three South Africans', World News Briefs, *Playfair Cricket Monthly*, March 1967, p. 8.
7. 'Banning D'Oliveira Would Stop Tour', *Times*, 31 Jan. 1967, p. 1.
8. Jack Bailey, *Conflicts in Cricket* (London: The Kingswood Press, 1989), p. 47.
9. 'Banning D'Oliveira Would Stop Tour', *Times*, 31 Jan. 1967, p. 1.
10. Bailey, *Conflicts in Cricket*, pp. 49–50.
11. Quoted in Basil D'Oliveira, *The D'Oliveira Affair* (London: Collins, 1969), p. 84.
12. Bailey, *Conflicts in Cricket*, p. 49.
13. Michael Melford, 'Cancellation of South African Tour' (*Wisden* (1969)), in Green, *Wisden Anthology*, p. 73.
14. 'MCC omit Rhodesian matches', *Times*, 27 May 1968, p. 12. The white Rhodesian government, under the leadership of Ian Smith, had declared independence from Britain in 1965 – and was

subject to economic and social sanctions.

15. Quoted in Graeme Wright, *Betrayal. The Struggle for Cricket's Soul* (Great Britain: H.F. & G. Witherby, 1993), p. 141.
16. Ibid.
17. The South African Sports Foundation was established in 1964 by Anton Rupert, a Broeder businessman, 'to promote sport among all racial groups.' It offered finance to black sportsmen who collaborated with white federations.
18. Odendaal, *Cricket in Isolation*, p. 9.
19. Bailey, *Conflicts in Cricket*, p. 52.
20. D'Oliveira, *Time to Declare*, p. 69.
21. Melford, 'Cancellation of South African Tour', p. 71.
22. Quoted in C.L.R. James, *Cricket* (London: Allison & Busby, 1989), p. 212.
23. 'D'Oliveira left out of South Africa tour', *Times*, 29 Aug. 1968, p. 1.
24. Wright, *Betrayal*, p. 145.
25. Brickhill, *Race Against Race*, p. 12.
26. Quoted in Hain, *Don't Play with Apartheid*, p. 81.
27. Melford, 'Cancellation of South African Tour', p. 72.
28. Quoted in Odendaal, *Cricket in Isolation*, p. 10.
29. 'D'Oliveira threat by Vorster', *Times*, 12 Sept. 1968, p. 1.
30. Rex Alston, 'Talking points', *Playfair Cricket Monthly*, Nov. 1968, p. 4.
31. Cartwright later told Peter Hain that pressure from Lord's had forced him to accept a place on the tour even though he was injured. He also claimed that he pulled out of the tour out of conviction, not for the reason given publicly. (Hain, *Sing the Beloved Country*, p. 49.)
32. 'D'Oliveira picked to tour South Africa after all', *Times*, 17 Sept. 1968, p. 1.
33. 'D'Oliveira "political cricket ball"', *Times*, 18 Sept. 1968, p. 1.
34. Quoted in Odendaal, *Cricket in Isolation*, p. 10.
35. See, for example, D'Oliveira, *The D'Oliveira Affair*, pp. 85–6.
36. D'Oliveira's own captain, Colin Cowdrey, wrote in the foreword to his autobiography that 'whatever we might think about apartheid, at least it seems to work in their country; it is none of our business'. (Ibid., pp. 8–9.)
37. Wright, *Betrayal*, p. 148.
38. *Guardian*, 11 Sept. 1968, taken from Matthew Engel (ed.), *The Guardian Book of Cricket* (London: Pavilion Books, 1986), p. 169.
39. Quoted in Lapchick, *The Politics of Race and International Sport*, p. 129.
40. Bowen, *Cricket*, p. 212.
41. 'D'Oliveira "political cricket ball"', *Times*, 18 Sept. 1968, p. 1.
42. This was the view of Charles Barr, an associate member of the MCC. ('50 challenge MCC on D'Oliveira omission', *The Times*, 5 Sept. 1968.)
43. S.E.D. Brown, a leading Nationalist commentator, wrote in the right-wing *South African Observer* – of which he was editor – that Vorster had told a meeting of Nationalists many weeks ago that Basil D'Oliveira would not be allowed to enter South Africa.
44. Booth, *The Race Game*, p. 99.
45. John Hennessy, 'Year of destiny for Olympic movement', *Times*, 23 Feb. 1968, p. 9.
46. Melford, 'Cancellation of South African Tour', p. 73.

NOTES TO CHAPTER 10

1. In their election addresses, 26% of Conservative candidates advocated no further increase in immigration, whilst 12% proposed voluntary repatriation. Moreover, 60% of Conservative candidates and 15% of Labour mentioned the law and order problem as a social issue. (David Butler and Michael Pinto-Duschinsky, *British General Election of 1970* (London: Macmillan, 1971), pp. 438–9.)
2. John Arlott, *Cricket on Trial: John Arlott's Cricket Journal* (London: William Heinemann, 1960), p. 252.
3. Hain, *Don't Play with Apartheid*, p. 200.
4. Thompson, *Retreat from Apartheid*, p. 61.
5. Warman, 'Most of Springboks wanted to go home by Christmas', p. 10.
6. 'Plan to stop South African matches', *Times*, 11 Sept. 1969, p. 3.

7. *Sunday Times*, 26 April 1970.
8. Irving Rosenwater, 'The South African Tour Dispute', in Green, *Wisden Anthology*, p. 76
9. Television interview, April 16 1970, quoted in ibid.
10. 'Feel free to demonstrate says Wilson', *Times*, 17 April 1970, p. 1.
11. Quoted in Hain, *Don't Play with Apartheid*, p. 186.
12. Quoted in Rosenwater, 'The South African Tour Dispute', in Green, *Wisden Anthology*, p. 77.
13. James Callaghan, the Home Secretary, quoted in ibid., p. 78.
14. Bailey, *Conflicts in Cricket*, p. 57.
15. *Daily Sketch*, April 21 1969.
16. *Guardian*, 4 May 1970.
17. Lapchick, *The Politics of Race and International Sport*, p. 169.
18. 'Wilson asks Cricket Council to think again on Springbok tour', *Times*, 1 May 1970, p. 2.
19. Butler and Pinto-Duschinsky, *British General Election of 1970*, p. 77.
20. Quoted in Lapchick, *The Politics of Race and International Sport*, p. 172.
21. Ibid., p. 171.
22. Quoted in Marqusee, *Anyone but England*, p. 189.
23. Hain, *Sing the Beloved Country*, p. 80.
24. 'Error for government to interfere directly on tour', 'Parliament', *Times*, 15 May 1970, p. 9.
25. 'Weather permitting', editorial, *Times*, 13 Feb. 1970, p. 11.
26. 'Kenya calls off MCC tour', *Times*, 8 Jan. 1970, p. 1.
27. Quoted in Hain, *Don't Play with Apartheid*, p. 176.
28. A referendum by the Cricketers' Association in January 1970 showed that 81 per cent of English first-class players were in favour of the tour.
29. Bailey, *Conflicts in Cricket*, p. 60.
30. The Cricket Council statement, 18 May 1970, quoted in Rosenwater, 'The South African Tour Dispute', in Green, *Wisden Anthology*, pp. 79–80; Wynne-Thomas and Arnold, *Cricket in Conflict*, pp. 119–20.
31. Gordon Ross, 'Cricket, it seems, is irretrievably caught in the web of politics', *Playfair Cricket Monthly*, Aug. 1969, p. 1.
32. Ibid.
33. Ibid.
34. See article by E.W. Swanton in the *Daily Telegraph*, 16 May 1970.
35. Quoted in Rosenwater, 'The South African Tour Dispute', in Green, *Wisden Anthology*, p. 82; Wynne-Thomas and Arnold, *Cricket in Conflict*, p. 122.
36. *Guardian*, 23 May 1970.
37. Quoted in Wynne-Thomas and Arnold, *Cricket in Conflict*, p. 123.
38. Christopher Martin-Jenkins, *Twenty Years On: Cricket's Years of Change, 1963–1983* (London: Willow Books, 1984), p. 96.
39. *Sunday Times*, 24 May 1970.
40. Quoted in Hain, *Don't Play with Apartheid*, p. 193.
41. John Wood (ed.), *Powell and the 1970 Election* (Kingswood: Elliot Right Way Books, 1970), p. 106.
42. Bailey, *Conflicts in Cricket*, p. 66.
43. Peter Evans, 'Hogg's charge of weakness', *Times*, 23 May 1970, p. 1.
44. Bailey, *Conflicts in Cricket*, p. 66.
45. Peter Evans, 'Students prepare for Springbok protest', *Times*, 4 Nov. 1969, p. 1.
46. Bose, *Sporting Colours*, p. 95.
47. 'Cricketer's race plea', *Times*, 20 Aug. 1970, p. 4.

NOTES TO CHAPTER 11

1. Much has been made of this delegation's recommendations. In fact, only representatives of the three white members plus Bermuda and the US were represented. At the 1978 ICC annual meeting the following countries requested that they be publicly disassociated from the visit: West Indies, India, Pakistan, East Africa, Bangladesh, Sri Lanka and Malaysia. Canada and Singapore abstained. (*Wisden* (1979), p. 1,122.)
2. Peter Kirsten, 'No need for sympathy', *The Cricketer*, Oct. 1981, p. 21. So 'minor' were Sri Lanka that in the space of only 15 years they would become one-day world champions – being,

in 1996, the only country to win on 'home soil' (the tournament was shared between Sri Lanka, India and Pakistan). There was definitely a sense among the English establishment that South Africa was more deserving of its old seat than Sri Lanka. Consider these remarks from Christopher Martin-Jenkins on Sri Lanka becoming the seventh member of the ICC: 'But it is not the same seven who played more or less harmoniously together until South Africa's automatic expulsion from the Imperial Cricket Conference after the new Republic had left the Commonwealth in 1961.' (Ibid.) South Africa had only ever played three of the other six teams!

3. Eric Marsden, 'Taking the slow revolution road back', *Times*, 19 Nov. 1981, p. 20.
4. Cook, *The Jimmy Cook Story*, pp. 6–7.
5. Michael Owen-Smith, 'Go it alone plea', *The Cricketer*, Jan. 1981, p. 29.
6. Quoted in Bose, *Sporting Colours*, p. 135.
7. Tony Cozier, 'The Cream stays in the Caribbean', *The Cricketer*, March 1983, p. 10.
8. Kallicharan went on to play for Orange Free State, the 'spiritual home of the National government', where he was granted special permission to live – a requirement for Indians. (Proctor, *The Years of Isolation*, pp. 85–6.)
9. Michael Owen-Smith, 'Open verdict in South Africa', *The Cricketer*, Feb. p. 35.
10. Letter from Joe Pamensky, president of SACU, to *The Cricketer*, June 1983, p. 50.
11. Harte, *Two Tours and Pollock*, p. 263.
12. Michael Owen-Smith, 'Overtaken by events', *The Cricketer*, April 1990, p. 50.
13. Proctor, *The Years of Isolation*, p. 84.
14. *Encyclopaedia Britannica*, 'Political ideology', CD Rom.
15. Quoted in Crowley, *Cricket's Exiles*, p. 138.
16. Quoted in Booth, *The Race Game*, p. 93.
17. Bruce Francis, '"Guilty": Bob Hawke or Kim Hughes?' (Victoria: Roger Page, 1989), book review, *Wisden Cricket Monthly*, Jan. 1990, p. 41.
18. Hain, *Sing the Beloved Country*, p. 153.
19. Christopher Merrett, letter to *The Cricketer*, April 1982.
20. Quoted in Crowley, *Cricket's Exiles*, p. 144.
21. Harte, *Two Tours and Pollock,* p. 235.
22. Quoted in Bose, *Sporting Colours*, p. 132.
23. Ibid., p. 133.
24. Geoff Boycott, *The Autobiography* (London: Guild Publishing, 1987), p. 221.
25. Geoff Cook, 'Why I said no', *The Cricketer*, April 1982, p. 10.
26. 'Profit hath no honour in its own country', *Times*, 18 Jan. 1983, p. 24.
27. Booth, *The Race Game*, p. 147.
28. Imran Khan, 'Rebels without a cause', *Cricket Life International*, Sept. 1989, p. 9.
29. John Woodcock, 'Only Taylor and Gooch relieve the gloom', *The Cricketer*, May 1982, p. 12.
30. Ali Bacher, 'More Action, less Admiration', *The Cricketer*, Oct. 1982, p. 23.
31. The transcript of the speech can be found in the 1989 *Protea Cricket Annual of South Africa*, Vol.36 (Cape Town: Protea Assurance, 1989), pp. 12–17.
32. Quoted in Booth, *The Race Game*, p. 145.
33. Geoff Hewitt, letter to *The Cricketer*, June 1982, p. 30.
34. Joe Pamensky, former SACU president, 'A Catalyst for change', *Cricket Life International*, Oct. 1989, p. 14.
35. Beinart, *Twentieth Century South Africa*, p. 234.
36. Quoted in Harte, *Two Tours and Pollock*, pp. 21–22.
37. 'Commonwealth gets out the stocks', editorial, *The Times*, 30 July 1981, p. 13.
38. 'South Africa needs rebel tours, says Pollock', '*The Age*' (Melbourne), 20 Dec. 1985, quoted in Booth, 'South Africa's Autonomous Sport Strategy', p. 161.
39. The three laws were the Liquor Act, the Group Areas Act and the Group Urban Areas Consolidation Act. This was part of the process of autonomy for sports (see Chapter 4).
40. John Woodcock, 'ICC respect governmental wishes and keep South Africa out', *The Times*, 24 July 1981, p. 17.
41. Ray Kennedy, 'West Indies "to play in South Africa"', *The Times*, 5 Jan. 1983, p. 16.
42. Republic of South Africa, *Hansard* (1983), Col.6149, quoted in Booth, 'South Africa's Autonomous Sport Strategy', p. 162.
43. Ibid.
44. Harte, *Two Tours and Pollock,* p. 163.
45. Bose, *Sporting Colours*, pp. 143–4.
46. Advocates of this position included Lord Chalfont and the journalist E.M. Wellings. The *Times*

journalist John Woodcock thought that the black nations would feel the financial pressure of any such split, and by implication, would seek a return to 'normality'. ('South Africa could return to the fold next year', *Times*, 19 Oct. 1981, p. 19.)

47. The pretence of awarding caps was reversed by statisticians who were in uproar when a Gooch 100 was deemed ineligible for official records.

48. Quoted in Marqusee, *Anyone but England*, p. 197.

49. John Hennessy, 'Board more to avoid split', *Times*, 20 March 1982, p. 18.

50. Philip Webster and John Witherow, 'Thatcher lukewarm over cricketers', *Times*, 3 March 1982, p. 1.

51. Simon Scott Plummer, 'Britain and US top the blacklist', *Times*, 2 March 1982, p. 19.

52. Eric Marsden, 'South African ruling body deny association with proposed tour', *Times*, 12 Aug. 1981, p. 12. Mike Brearley, the former England captain, later confirmed that Edrich, while a selector, had approached him about his availability for an illegal tour to South Africa. (Michael Hornsby and John Withero, 'Tour of South Africa was first mooted 17 months ago', *Times*, 3 March 1982, p. 17.)

53. Derrick Robins, 'A cowardly agreement', *The Cricketer*, June 1982, p. 12.

54. John Woodcock, 'Only Taylor and Gooch relieve the gloom', *The Cricketer*, May 1982, p. 12.

55. Geoff Cooke gave the impending tours as part reason for his refusing a contract to tour South Africa. He anticipated that the poor fortunes of the counties from cancellations would inevitably trickle down to the players. (Geoff Cook, 'Why I said no', *The Cricketer*, April 1982, p. 10.)

56. 'TCCB consider plan for a ban', *Times*, 10 Mar, 1982, p. 26.

57. Viv Richards, *Hitting Across the Line* (London: BCA, 1991), p. 186. Richards was formally thanked by the ANC for his position.

58. Quoted in Hilary McD Beckles, 'West Indian Cricket and Anti-Apartheid Struggles', in Beckles (ed.), *A Spirit of Dominance. Cricket & Nationalism in the West Indies* (University of the West Indies: Canoe Press, 1998), p. 117.

59. Brian Stoddart, 'Caribbean Cricket: the Role of Sport in Emerging Small-Nation Politics', in Beckles and Stoddart, *Liberation Cricket*, p. 250.

60. Some of the governments sought the severest retribution possible. For example, Forbes Burnham, the prime minister of Guyana, banned the English cricketers who had competed in South Africa from Guyana, even after their suspensions were lifted.

61. 'West Indies Amnesty', *Cricket Life International*, July 1989, p. 4.

62. In Australia you have to represent your club side before you can be considered for state cricket, which in turn makes you eligible for the national team.

63. Harte, *Two Tours and Pollock*, p. 127.

64. Ibid., p. 53.

65. Harte quoted in Bose, *Sporting Colours*, p. 142.

66. Ibid.

67. Proctor, *The Years of Isolation*, p. 91.

68. Christopher Martin-Jenkins, 'South Africa and the ICC', editorial, *The Cricketer*, Jan. 1989, p. 3.

69. Keith Holder and R. Mathias, 'West Indies rebels face uncertain future', *Cricket Life International*, Aug. 1989, p. 8. The Sri Lankan Board lifted the lifetime ban on 12 of the 14 players who went to the Republic in 1982. However, they were informed that they would not be welcome to represent their country, having already turned their backs on it. The ban on Bandula Warnapura, Sri Lanka's first captain, and Tony Opatha, the organiser of the tour, remained.

70. For a detailed outline of the various stands of the Caribbean governments, see Tony Cozier, 'The hopes for England's Tour', *The Cricketer*, May 1989, p. 77.

71. *The Cricketer*, March 1989, p. 5.

72. Ibid.

73. *Wisden Cricket Monthly*, March 1989, p. 10.

74. Geoff Cook, chairman of the Cricketers' Association, 'Our young players must be protected', *The Cricketer*, Jan. 1989, p. 5.

75. Quoted in the *1989 Protea Cricket Annual of South Africa*, p. 25.

76. E.M. Wellings, 'Always on the Defensive', *Wisden Cricket Monthly*, March 1989, p. 13.

77. 'ICC implications assessed', *The Cricketer*, March 1989, p. 7.

78. Quoted in Harte, *Two Tours and Pollock*, p. 12.

79. Ibid., p. 13.

80. Ibid.

81. Ameen Akhalwaya, Johannesburg, 'SACU's game', *Cricket Life International*, April 1990, p. 42.

82. Richard Evans, *The Ultimate Test* (London: Partridge Press, 1990), p. 49.

83. Quoted in Booth, *The Race Game*, p. 179.
84. Quoted in Carole Cooper, *Race Relations Survey 1989/90* (Johannesburg: South African Institute of Race Relations, 1990), p. 25.
85. Proctor, *The Years of Isolation*, p. 99.
86. A fact conceded by Dr Bacher in his address in the 1990 *Protea Cricket Annual of South Africa* (Vol.37 (Cape Town: Protea Assurance, 1990), p. 12.)
87. Ali Bacher in interview with John Bishop, 'English Press vilified Gatting', *Wisden Cricket Monthly*, March 1990, p. 10.
88. John Bishop, 'Season of discontent', *Wisden Cricket Monthly*, June 1990, p. 20.
89. 'Unofficial tours to end?', *The Cricketer*, May 1990, p. 5.

NOTES TO CHAPTER 12

1. 'Hansard', 18 May 1977. Quoted in Grant Jarvie, *Class, Race & Sport in South Africa's Political Economy* (London: Routledge & Kegan Paul, 1985), p. 5.
2. *Die Afrikaner*, 26 Nov. 1986, quoted in Shaun Johnson (ed.), *South Africa: No Turning Back* (Basingstoke: Macmillan, 1988), p. 212.
3. See Chapter 7.
4. Guy Swanson, *Social Change* (London: Scott, Foresman & Company, 1971), p. 3.
5. Quoted in Alan Ball and Guy Peters, *Modern Politics and Government* (Sixth Edition) (Basingstoke: Macmillan, 2000), p. 300.
6. Quoted in H. Ian Hogbin, *Social Change* (London: Watts, 1958), p. 25.
7. E. Allardt and Y. Lithunen (eds), *Cleavages, Ideologies and Party Systems* (Helsinki: The Westermarck Society, 1964).
8. Matthew Crenson, *The Unpolitics of Air Pollution: a Study of Non-Decision Making in the Cities* (Baltimore: John Hopkins University Press, 1971), p. 173.
9. Wayne Parsons, *Public Policy* (Cheltenham: Edward Elgar, 1995), p. 44.
10. C. Coker, 'Disinvestment and the South African "Siege Economy": A Business Perspective' in Shaun Johnson (ed.), *South Africa: No Turning Back*, p. 286.
11. Tom Lodge and Bill Nasson, *All, Here, and Now: Black Politics in South Africa in the 1980s* (London: Hurst & Company, 1992), p. 31.
12. Ibid., pp. 285–6.
13. The opening up of new gold streams in Canada, Australia and the US saw South Africa's share of world gold production fall from 52 % to 32.5 % between 1980 and 1986 (Commonwealth Foreign Ministers Committee, *South Africa's Relationship with the International Financial System: Report of the Intergovernmental Group* (London, 1988), p. 12).
14. Dan O'Meara, *Forty Lost Years* (Randberg: Ravan Press, 1996), p. 329.
15. Coker, 'Disinvestment and the South African "Siege Economy"', p. 290.
16. Allister Sparks, *The Mind of South Africa* (London: Arrow Books, 1997), p. 350.
17. Douglas Booth, *The Race Game: Sport and Politics in South Africa* (London: Frank Cass, 1998), p. 153.
18. Botha's speech was supposed to present a package of reforms that would satisfy the international and business communities, thereby buying time for the debt-ridden regime. Instead Botha announced to his audience that his government had already crossed the 'Rubicon' of reform and was in no mood for further change.
19. Ibid., p. 351. Only a few years before it had been trading at between $1.30 and $1.40.
20. O'Meara, *Forty Lost Years*, p. 330.
21. *South Africa Barometer*, 24 March 1989, p. 354.
22. Sparks, *The Mind of South Africa*, p. 308.
23. O'Meara, *Forty Lost Years*, pp. 351–2.
24. Sparks, *The Mind of South Africa*, p. 300.
25. 'It is a nation on the move'. Brochure issued by Transvaal National Party on its 50th birthday, 8 Sept. 1964. Quoted in Monica Wilson and Leonard Thompson (eds), *The Oxford History of South Africa, Vol II – 1870-1966* (Oxford: Clarendon Press, 1971), p. 370.
26. See Chapter 4, pp. 118–20.
27. Afrikaans share of ownership of the private sector rose from 3% of manufacturing and construction before World War II to 15% in 1975; from 5 to 21% of finance; and from 1 to 30% of mining. Merle Lipton, *Capitalism and Apartheid* (Aldershot: Wildwood House, 1986), p. 307.

28. The (white) Mine Workers Union openly opposed the NP government at the end of the 1970s and practically aligned itself with the HNP. The South African Confederation of Labour denounced the abolition of job reservation and the recognition of black trade unions.

29. D. Welsh, *Sunday Times* (Johannesburg), 29 March 1987. Quoted in Johnson, *South Africa: No Turning Back*, p. 226.

30. Public funds (about R64m) had been illegally appropriated in attempts to buy or set up English newspapers in South Africa and abroad. Connie Mulder, the Information Minister was the chief victim. He was driven out of the NP and formed the National Conservative Party to contest the 1981 election.

31. O'Meara, *Forty Lost Years*, p. 312.

32. Robert Schrire, *Adapt or Die: The End of White Politics in South Africa* (London: Hurst & Company, 1992), p. 113.

33. O'Meara, *Forty Lost Years*, p. 400.

34. Merle Lipton, *Capitalism and Apartheid*, p. 109.

35. Schrire, *Adapt or Die*, p. 79.

36. 'Survey of Race Relations in South Africa', 1983, p. 261. Cited in Tom Lodge and Bill Nasson, *All, Here, and Now*, p. 58.

37. Schrire, *Adapt or Die*, p. 103.

38. Sparks, *The Mind of South Africa*, p. 338.

39. Andrew Heywood, *Political Ideologies* (Second Edition) (Basingstoke: Macmillan Press, 1988), p. 86.

40. Lipton, *Capitalism and Apartheid*, p. 349.

41. Schrire, *Adapt or Die*, p. 12.

42. Lodge and Nasson, *All, Here, and Now*, p. 48.

43. Ibid., p. 35.

44. Ibid., p. 38.

45. See Jon Lewis, 'The Trade Unions', *Monthly Review*, Vol.37, No.11 (April 1986), pp. 84–5.

46. Quoted in Johnson, *South Africa: No Turning Back*, p. 40.

47. Its armed wing carried out 231 attacks in 1986, 235 in 1987 and 245 in 1988. Lodge and Nasson Lodge, *All, Here, and Now*, p. 114. Spectacular operations such as the rocket attack on the military headquarters in Voortrekkerhoogte and the disabling of the Koeberg nuclear plant displayed an ability to strike at any time.

48. Quoted in O'Meara, *Forty Lost Years*, p. 256.

49. Quoted in Schrire, *Adapt or Die*, p. 47.

50. Sparks, *The Mind of South Africa*, pp. 201–2 and p. 329.

51. A. de Tocqueville, 'The Old Regime and The French Revolution', quoted in Lipton, *Capitalism and Apartheid*, p. 350.

52. Quoted in Schrire, *Adapt or Die*, p. 132.

53. *Financial Mail*, 10 Feb 1989. Quoted in Dan O'Meara, *Forty Lost Years*, p. 402.

54. Booth, *The Race Game*, p. 167.

55. Quoted in O'Meara, *Forty Lost Years*, p. 387.

56. Ibid., p. 295.

57. I. Wilkins and H. Strydom, *The Super-Afrikaners* (Johannesburg: Jonathan Ball, 1978), p. 240.

58. March Krotee, 'Apartheid and Sport: South Africa Revisited', *Sociology of Sport Journal*, Vol.15, pt.2 (1988), p. 132.

59. Peter Lambley, *The Psychology of Apartheid* (London: Secker & Warburg, 1980), p. 31.

60. Quoted in Mihir Bose, *Sporting Colours. Sport and politics in South Africa* (London: Robson Books, 1994), pp. 184–5.

61. Adrian Guelke, 'Sport and the End of Apartheid', in Lincoln Allison (ed.), *The Changing Politics of Sport* (Manchester: Manchester University Press, 1993), p. 151.

62. Sam Ramsamy, Chairman of SANROC, 'Normal cricket – but only for a day', article in *The Cricketer* (March 1983), p. 26.

63. Quoted in Mike Proctor, *South Africa, The Years of Isolation and the Return to International Cricket* (Durban: Bok Books International, 1994), p. 90.

64. Chapter 2, pp. 37–40.

65. Richard Evans, *The Ultimate Test* (London: Partridge Press, 1990), p. 84.

66. See Chapter 2, pp. 41–2.

67. Joe Pamensky, 'Cricket, Not Race, is our Concern', *The Cricketer* (March 1983), p. 28.

68. Richard Evans, *The Ultimate Test*, p. 59.
69. Bernard Crick, *In Defence of Politics* (Fourth Edition) (Harmondsworth: Penguin Books, 1993), p. 167.
70. Jasmat Dhiraj, South African non-racial tennis champion, interview in Archer and Bouillon, *The South African Game: Sport and Racism* (London: Zed Press, 1982), vi–viii.
71. J. Hargreaves, 'Theorising Sport: An Introduction', in Jennifer Hargreaves (ed.), *Sport, Culture, and Ideology* (London: Routledge and Kegan Paul, 1982), p. 14.
72. *Weekly Mail*, 23 June 1988. Quoted in O'Meara, *Forty Lost Years*, p. 347.
73. Imran Khan, 'Comment', *Cricket Life International*, September 1989, p. 1.
74. Joseph de Maistre, *Considerations on France*, chapter VII, 'Signs of Nullity in the French Government' (Writing of Joseph de Maistre in English Translation (www.geocities.com/Capitol Hill/2125/de_Maistre/).
75. Roger Scruton, *The Meaning of Conservatism* (Second Edition) (London: Macmillan, 1984), pp. 12–13.
76. Ibid., p. 8.
77. Rene de Villiers, 'Afrikaner Nationalism', in Wilson and Thompson, *The Oxford History of South Africa*, p. 371.
78. Scruton, *The Meaning of Conservatism*, p. 24.
79. Anthony Quinton, 'Conservatism', in Robert E. Goodin and Philip Pettit (eds.), *A Companion to Contemporary Political Philosophy* (Oxford: Blackwell, 1997), p. 259.
80. 'Romans 13', verses 1 and 2. *The Holy Bible (New International Version)* (London: Hodder & Stoughton, 1985), p. 1140.
81. Peel, *The Tamworth Manifesto*, 1834. Quoted in Roger Scruton, *The Meaning of Conservatism*, p. 15.
82. Andrew Heywood, *Political Ideologies*, p. 80.
83. Abe Bailey, Foreword to M.W. Luckin (ed.), *The History of South African Cricket* (Johannesburg: W.E. Hortor & Co, 1915).
84. Gwendolen M. Carter, *The Politics of Inequality. South Africa since 1948* (London: Thames & Hudson, 1958), p. 87.
85. John Woodock, 'Notes by the Editor', *Wisden* (1986), p. 56.
86. Jack Bailey, *Conflicts in Cricket* (London: The Kingswood Press, 1989), p. 56.
87. Jack Bailey, 'ICC and South Africa', *Wisden* (1990), p. 53.
88. P. Bachrach and M. Baratz, 'The Two Faces of Power', in F.G. Castles, D.J. Murray and D.C. Potter (eds.), *Decisions, Organisations and Society* (Harmondsworth: Penguin, 1981), pp. 380–2.
89. Apologies to C.L.R. James.
90. Mike Marqusee, *Anyone but England* (London: Verso, 1995), p. 199.
91. Quoted ibid., p. 187.
92. The Reconstruction and Development Programme, 1994, p. 9.

NOTES TO POSTSCRIPT

1. Richard Hutton, 'Taking Guard', *The Cricketer*, Aug. 1991, p. 2.
2. Peter Roebuck, *The Cricketer*, January 1992, p. 6.
3. Statement of Intent, quoted in 'A Breakthrough in South Africa', *The Cricketer*, Feb. 1991, p. 4.
4. Eddie Barlow, '25-year development', *The Cricketer*, April 1995, p. 6.
5. Peter Roebuck, 'Teenybopper quartet', *The Cricketer*, Feb. 1994, p. 12.
6. Brian Crowley, 'History of South African cricket', *The Cricketer*, May 1994, p. 21.
7. England had played two warm-up contests before this game, but neither of them was first-class.
8. Tanya Aldred, 'The man behind the voice', *Wisden Cricket Monthly*, Aug. 1998, p. 7.
9. Eddie Barlow, '25-year development', p. 6.
10. Ian Hawkey, 'Mandela and Beyond', in Rob Steen (ed.), *The New Ball (Universal Stories)*, Vol. 2 (London: Mainstream Publishing, 1999), p. 43.
11. Vivek Chaudhary, 'End of the Lilywhite Rainbow', *Guardian*, 26 Feb. 1999.
12. Ian Hawkey, 'Mandela and Beyond', p. 48.
13. *Constitution of the Republic of South Africa 1996*, [28 Nov. 2002].
14. ANC Statement On Transformation in Sport, Issued by ANC department of Information and Publicity, 30 Nov. 1998. [1 Dec. 2002].
15. The PriceWaterhouseCoopers Ratings. [25 Feb. 2003].

16. The two series (home and away) were supposed to represent the 'World Championship' of Test cricket. In the three contests in Australia the Aussies won by 246 runs, nine wickets and ten wickets. In South Africa they won the first Test by an innings and 360 runs (South Africa's worst ever defeat), the second by only four wickets before losing the third. It was awesome cricket, and left the South Africans humiliated.
17. 'South Africa – lily-white cloud hanging over', *The Cricketer*, Jan. 1999.
18. Mark Smit, 'Which is it, Kicking the ladder away or a giant leap of faith?', *Business Day*, 12 July 2002.
19. Michael Owen-Smith estimated in 1992 that there were at least 25 outstanding schools in South Africa ('The Nuffield Contribution', *The Cricketer*, April 1992, p. 37).
20. Jonathan Rice, 'A successful winter tour', *Wisden Cricket Monthly*, May 1993, p. 59.
21. *Poverty and Inequality in South Africa*, Report prepared for the Office of the Executive Deputy President and the Inter-Ministerial Committee for Poverty and Inequality, May 1998, p. 1. [1 March, 2003].
22. D. Everatt and R. Jennings, *Educated for Servitude? A National Survey of 'Out-of-school' Youth in South Africa* (Braamfontein: Community Agency for Social Enquiry 1995).
23. The HDI was devised to determine how nations compare three factors are taken into consideration: longevity (as measured by life expectancy at birth); educational attainment (as measured by a combination of adult literacy and enrolment rates); and standard of living (as measured by real GDP per capita).
24. UNDP, Human Development Report. United Nations Development Program (New York: Oxford University Press, 1994).
25. *Poverty and Inequality in South Africa*, p.105.
26. CIA, *The World Factbook 2002, South Africa* (http://www.odci.gov/cia/publications/factbook/geos/sf.html#Geo).
27. Emma Thomasson, 'South African sports bodies address "lily-white" criticisms', *Reuters*, 5 April 1999.
28. The Reconstruction and Development Programme, 1994, p. 9 (http://www.polity.org.za/html/govdocs/rdp/rdp3.html#3.5).
29. CIA, *The World Factbook 2002, South Africa*.
30. John Matshikiza, 'A state of permanent transition', *Mail and Guardian*, 3 Feb. 2003.
31. Hugo Young, 'The Legacy of Apartheid is still with us; it seeps into all levels of society', *Guardian*, 29 May 2001.

Bibliography

Adam, Heribert, *Modernising Racial Domination: The Dynamics of South African Politics* (Berkeley, University of California Press, 1971)

Allardt, E. and Lithunen, Y. (eds), *Cleavages, Ideologies and Party Systems* (Helsinki: The Westermarck Society, 1964)

Allison, Lincoln (ed.), *The Politics of Sport* (Manchester: Manchester University Press, 1986).

Allison, Lincoln (ed.), *The Changing Politics of Sport* (Manchester: Manchester University Press, 1993).

Altham, H.S., *A History of Cricket: From the Beginnings to the First World War* (London: George Allen & Unwin Ltd, 1962).

Altham, H.S. and Swanton, E.W., *History of Cricket* (London: George Allen & Unwin, 1948).

Annan, N.G., *Roxburgh of Stowe* (London: Longmans, 1965).

Appadorai, A., *The Substance of Politics*, 10th edn (London: Oxford University Press, 1968).

Apter, David, *Political Change* (London: Frank Cass, 1973).

Archer, Robert and Antoine Bouillon, *The South African Game: Sport and Racism* (London: Zed Press, 1982).

Aristotle, *The Politics* (translated by Ernest Barker) (Oxford: Oxford University Press, 1995)

Arlott, John, *John Arlott's Cricket Journal* (London: William Heinemann Ltd, 1960).

Bailey, Jack, *Conflicts in Cricket* (London: The Kingswood Press, 1989).

Ball, Alan and B. Guy Peters, *Modern Politics and Government*, 6th edn (Basingstoke: Macmillan, 2000).

Barry, Norman P., *An Introduction to Modern Political Theory*, 2nd edn (Basingstoke: Macmillan, 1989).

Beckles, Hilary McD (ed.), *A Spirit of Dominance. Cricket and Nationalism in the West Indies* (University of the West Indies: Canoe Press, 1998).

Beckles, Hilary McD and Brian Stoddart (eds.), *Liberation Cricket: West Indies Cricket Culture* (Manchester: Manchester University Press, 1995).

Beinart, William, *Twentieth-Century South Africa* (Oxford: Oxford University Press, 1993).

Beinart, William and Saul Dubow (eds), *The Historiography of Segregation and Apartheid in Twentieth-Century South Africa* (London: Routledge, 1995).

Berry, Scyld, *Cricket Wallah: with England in India, 1981–2* (London: Hodder & Stoughton, 1982).

Bilton, Tony, Kevin Bonnett, Philip Jones, Michelle Stanworth, Ken Sheard and Andrew Webster, *Introductory Sociology* (Basingstoke: Macmillan, 1985).

Birbalsingh, Frank, *The Rise of West Indian Cricket: From Colony to Nation* (Antigua: Hansib, 1996).

Birley, Derek, *The Willow Wand* (London: Sportspages, 1989).

Birley, Derek, *Land of Sport and Glory. Sport and the British Society, 1887–1910* (Manchester: Manchester University Press, 1995).

Birley, Derek, *Playing the Game: Sport and the British Society, 1910–45* (Manchester: Manchester University Press, 1995).

Boardman, John, Jasper Griffin and Oswyn Murray (eds), *Greece and the Hellenistic World* (Oxford: Oxford University Press, 1989).

Bocock, Robert, *Hegemony* (Chichester: Ellis Horwood Ltd, 1986).

Booth, Douglas, 'South Africa's Autonomous Sport Strategy', *Sporting Traditions* (May 1990).

Booth, Douglas, 'Accommodating Race to Play the Game', *Sporting Traditions* (May 1992).

Booth, Douglas, 'The South African Council on Sport and the Political Antinomies of the Sports Boycott', *Journal of Southern African Studies* 23, 1 (March 1997).

Booth, Douglas, *The Race Game. Sport and Politics in South Africa* (London: Frank Cass, 1998).

Bose, Mihir, *A Maiden View: The Magic of Indian Cricket* (London: George Allen & Unwin, 1986).

Bose, Mihir, *A History of Indian Cricket* (London: Andre Deutsch, 1990).

Bose, Mihir, *Sporting Colours. Sport and Politics in South Africa* (London: Robson Books, 1994).

Bowen, Rowland, *Cricket: A History of Its Growth and Development throughout the World* (London: Eyre & Spottiswoode, 1970).

Boycott, Geoff, *The Autobiography* (London: Guild Publishing, 1987).

Bradley, James, 'The MCC: Society and Empire', *International Journal of the History of Sport*, Vol.17 (1990).

Brickhill, Joan, *Race Against Race: South Africa's 'Multinational' Sport Fraud* (London: International Defence & Aid Fund, 1976).

Brody, Kenneth, 'Institutionalised sport as quasi-religion; preliminary considerations', *Journal of Sport and Social Issues*, 3,2 (1979).

Brohm, Jean-Marie, *Sport – A Prison of Measured Time* (London: Ink Links, 1978).

Brookes, Christopher, *English Cricket. The Game and Its Players through the Ages* (London: Weidenfeld & Nicolson, 1978).

Buchan, John, *The African Colony: Studies in Reconstruction* (London: William Blackwood & Sons, 1903).

Bunting, Brian, *The Rise of the South African Reich* (London: Penguin, 1964).

Butler, David and Michael Pinto-Duschinsky, *British General Election of 1970* (London: Macmillan, 1971).

Callinicos, Alex, 'Can South Africa be Reformed?', *International Socialism* (Spring 1990).

Callinicos, Alex, 'South Africa after Apartheid', *International Socialism* (Spring 1996).

Callinicos, Alex and John Rogers, *Southern Africa after Soweto* (London: Pluto Press, 1977).

Canynge Caple, S., *The Springboks at Cricket, 1888–1960* (Worcester: Littlebury & Company, 1960).

Cardus, Neville, *English Cricket* (London: Collins, 1945).

Carter, Gwendolen M., *The Politics of Inequality. South Africa since 1948* (London: Thames & Hudson, 1958).

Cashman, Richard, *Patrons, Players and the Crowd* (New Delhi: Orient Longman, 1980).

Cashman, R., and McKernan, M., *Sport in History: The Making of Modern Sporting History* (Queensland: University of Queensland Press, 1979).

Castles, F.G., Murray D.J. and Potter D.C. (eds), *Decisions, Organisations and Society* (Harmondsworth: Penguin, 1981).

Coakley, Jay J., *Sport in Society. Issues and Controversies*, 4th edn (St. Louis: Times Mirror/Mosby, 1990).

Coghlan, John F. with Ida Webb, *Sport and British Politics since 1960* (London: The Falmer Press, 1990).

Coldham, J.D., *Lord Harris* (London: The Crowood Press, 1983).

Cook, Jimmy, *The Jimmy Cook Story* (London: Pelham Books, 1993).

Cook, Theodore, *Character and Sportsmanship* (London: Williams & Norgate, 1927).

Cooper, Carole, *Race Relations Survey 1989/90* (Johannesburg: South African Institute of Race Relations, 1990).

Crawford, Neta and Audie Klotz (eds), *How Sanctions Work. Lessons from South Africa* (Basingstoke: Macmillan Press, 1999).

Crenson, Matthew, *The Unpolitics of Air Pollution: A Study of Non-Decision Making in the Cities* (Baltimore: Johns Hopkins University Press, 1971).

Crick, Bernard, *In Defence of Politics*, 4th edn (London: Penguin Books, 1993).

Crick, Bernard and Tom Crick, *What is Politics?* (Great Britain: Edward Arnold, 1987).

Crowley, Brian, *Cricket's Exiles. The Saga of South African Cricket* (London: Angus & Robertson, 1983).

D'Oliveira, Basil, *D'Oliveira – An Autobiography* (London: Sportsmans Book Club, 1969).

D'Oliveira, Basil, *The D'Oliveira Affair* (London: Collins, 1969).

D'Oliveira, Basil, *Time to Declare: An Autobiography* (London: W.H. Allen & Co., 1980).

De Broglio, Chris, *South Africa: Racism in Sport* (London: International Defence & Aid Fund, 1970).

De Kiewiet, C.W., *A History of South Africa, Social and Economic* (Oxford: Clarendon Press, 1941).

Dearlove, John and Peter Saunders, *Introduction to British Politics*, 2nd edn (Cambridge: Polity Press, 1991).

Docker, Edward, *History of Indian Cricket* (Delhi: Macmillan, 1976).

Dunae, P.A., *Gentlemen Emigrants: From the British Public Schools to the Canadian Frontier* (Manchester: Manchester University Press, 1981).

Dunning, Eric (ed.), *The Sociology of Sport* (London: Frank Cass, 1971).

Easton, David, *The Political System: An Inquiry into the State of Political Science*, 2nd edn (New York: Alfred Knopf, 1971).

Eatwell, Roger and Anthony Wright (eds), *Contemporary Political Ideologies* (London: Pinter Publishers, London, 1993).

Eitzen, D. Stanley (ed.), *Sport in Contemporary Society. An Anthology* (New York: St. Martin's Press, New York, 1989).

Engel, Matthew (ed.), *The Guardian Book of Cricket* (London: Pavilion Books, 1986).

Evans, Richard, *The Ultimate Test* (London: Partridge Press, 1990).

Fieldhouse, D.K., *Economics and Empire, 1830–1914* (London: Macmillan, 1984).

First, R., Steel, J., and Gurney C., *The South African Connection* (Harmondsworth: Penguin, 1973).

Gamble, Andrew, 'Theories of British Politics', *Political Studies*, Vol. 38. No.3 (1990).

Goodin, Robert E. and Philip Pettit (eds), *A Companion to Contemporary Political Philosophy* (Oxford: Blackwell, 1997).

Goodwin, Clayton, *West Indians at the Wicket* (London: Macmillan, 1986).

Grant, Jack, *Jack Grant's Story* (London: Lutterworth Press, 1980).

Green, Benny (ed.), *Wisden Anthology, 1963–1982* (London: Guild Publishing, 1984).

Green, Benny, *A History of Cricket* (London: Guild Publishing, 1988).

Green, G., *The Official History of the FA Cup* (London: Naldrett Press, 1949).

Greig, Tony, *My Story* (London: Stanley Paul, 1980).

Guha, Ramachandra, *Spin and Other Turns – Indian Cricket's Coming of Age* (New Delhi: Penguin Books, 1994).

Guha, Ramachandra, 'Cricket, Caste, Community, Colonialism: The Politics of a Great Game', *International Journal of the History of Sport*, Vol.14 (April 1997).

Guttmann, Allen, *Sports Spectators* (New York: Columbia University Press, 1986).

Hain, Peter, *Don't Play with Apartheid* (London: George Allen & Unwin Ltd, 1971).

Hain, Peter, *Sing the Beloved Country: The Struggle for the New South Africa* (London: Pluto Press, 1996).

Haralambos, M. and M. Holborn, *Sociology – Themes and Perspectives*, 3rd edn (London: Collins Educational, 1991).

Hargreaves, Jennifer (ed.), *Sport, Culture and Ideology* (London: Routledge & Kegan Paul, 1982).

Hargreaves, John, *Sport, Power and Culture: A Social and Historical Analysis of Popular Sports in Britain* (Cambridge: Polity Press, 1986).

Harris, H.A., *Sport in Greece and Rome* (Great Britain: Thames & Hudson, 1984).

Harris, Peter, *Foundations of Political Science* (London: Hutchinson, 1976).

Harte, Chris, *Two Tours and Pollock. The Australians in South Africa, 1985–87* (Adelaide: Sports Marketing, 1988).

Harte, Chris, *A History of Australian Cricket* (London: Andre Deutsch, 1993).

Hattersley, A.F. (ed.), *John Sheddon Dobie South African Journal, 1862–6*, 1st series, No.26 (Cape Town: Van Riebeck Society, 1945).

Hemyng, B., *Jack Harkaway at Oxford* (London: Edwin J. Brett, 1872).

Henry, Omar, *The Man in the Middle* (Herts: Queen Anne Press, 1994).

Heywood, Andrew, *Political Ideas and Concepts – an Introduction* (Basingstoke: Macmillan, 1994).

Heywood, Andrew, *Political Ideologies*, 2nd edn (Basingstoke: Macmillan Press, 1998).

Hobsbawn, Eric, *The Invention of Tradition* (Cambridge: Cambridge University Press, 1983).

Hogbin, H. Ian, *Social Change* (London: Watts, 1958).

Holt, Richard, *Sport and the British* (Oxford: Clarendon Press, 1989).

Horrell, Muriel, *Survey of Race Relations, 1973* (Johannesburg: Institute of Race Relations, 1974).

Houlihan, B., *The Government and Politics of Sport* (London: Routledge, 1991).

Howat, Gerald, *Cricket's Second Golden Age* (London: Hodder & Stoughton, 1989).

Huizinga, Johan, *Homo Ludens. A Study of the Play Element in Culture* (London: Temple Smith, 1949).

Jable, Thomas, 'Cricket Clubs and Class in Philadelphia', *Journal of Sport History*, 18, 2 (1991).

James, C.L.R., *Beyond a Boundary* (London: The Sportsmans Book Club, 1964).

James, C.L.R., *Cricket* (London: Allison & Busby, 1989).

Jarvie, Grant, *Class, Race and Sport in South Africa's Political Economy* (London: Routledge & Kegan Paul, 1985).

Jaques, T.D. and G.R. Pavia (eds.), *Sport in Australia* (Sydney: McGraw-Hill, 1976).

Johnson, Shaun, *South Africa: No Turning Back* (Basingstoke: Macmillan, 1988).

Joint Association of Classical Teachers, *The World of Athens* (Cambridge: Cambridge University Press, 1988).

Jones, W.T., *Masters of Political Thought*, Volume Two (London: George Harrap & Co Ltd, 1964).

Judd, Denis, *The British Imperial Experience* (Hammersmith: Harper Collins, 1996).

Kidd, Bruce, 'From Quarantine to Cure: The New Phase of the Struggle Against Apartheid Sport', *Sociology of Sport Journal*, 8, 1 (1991).

Koenderman, Tony, *Sanctions. The Threat to South Africa* (Johannesburg: Jonathan Ball Publishers, 1982).

Krotee, March, 'Apartheid and Sport: South Africa Revisited', *Sociology of Sport Journal*, 15, 2 (1988).

Lambley, Peter, *The Psychology of Apartheid* (London: Secker & Warburg, 1980).

Lapchick, Richard, *The Politics of Race and International Sport: The Case of South Africa* (London: Greenwood Press, 1975).

Laurence, John, *The Seeds of Disaster* (London, Victor Gollancz Ltd, 1968).

Laver, Michael, *Invitation to Politics* (Oxford: Martin Robertson, 1983).

Leftwich, Adrian (ed.), *What is Politics? The Activity and Its Study* (Oxford: Blackwell, 1984).

Legum, Colin, and Drysdale, John, *Africa Contemporary Record, Annual Survey and Documents, 1969–70* (Exeter: Africa Research Ltd, 1970).

Lenin, V.I., *Collected Works* (Moscow: Foreign Languages Publishing House, 1965), Vol. XXXII.

Lever, Janet, *Soccer Madness* (Chicago: The University of Chicago Press, 1983).

Lewis, Tony, *Double Century: The Story of the MCC and Cricket* (London: Hodder & Stoughton, 1987).

Lipton, Merle, *Capitalism and Apartheid* (Aldershot: Wildwood House, 1986).

Lively, Jack, *Democracy* (Oxford: Basil Blackwell, 1975).

Lodge, Tom, and Bill Nasson, *All, Here, and Now: Black Politics in South Africa in the 1980s* (London: Hurst & Company, 1992).

Lowe, Benjamin, David Kanin and Andrew Strenk (eds), *Sport and International Relations* (Illinois: Stipes Publishing Company, 1978).

Luckin, M.W. (ed.), *The History of South African Cricket* (Johannesburg: W.E. Hortor & Co, 1915).

Luckin, M.W. (ed.), *South African Cricket, 1919–1927* (Johannesburg: published by the author, 1927).

Lumer, Christopher, 'Rules and Moral Norms in Sports', *International Review for the Sociology of Sport*, vol. 30, Parts 3–4 (1995).

Lyotard, Jean-François, *The Post-modern Condition, a Report on Knowledge* (Manchester: Manchester University Press, 1984).

MacKenzie, W.J.M., *Politics and Social Science* (Middlesex: Penguin Books, 1967).

Maguire, Joseph, 'Sport, Identity, Politics and Globalisation', *Sociology of Sport Journal*, 11, 4 (1994).

Mangan, J.A., *Athleticism in the Victorian and Edwardian Public School: The Emergence and Consolidation of an Educational Ideology* (Cambridge: Cambridge University Press, 1983).

Mangan, J.A., *Pleasure, Profit, Proselytism: British Culture and Sport at Home and Abroad, 1700–1914* (London: Frank Cass, 1988).

Manley, Michael, *A History of West Indies Cricket* (London: Guild Publishing, 1988).

Marks, Shula, and Rathbone, Richard (eds), *Industrialisation and Social Change in South Africa: African Class Formation, Culture, and Consciousness, 1870–1930* (London: Longman, 1982).

Marks, Shula and Trapido, Stanley (eds), *The Politics of Race, Class and Nationalism in Twentieth Century South Africa* (London: Longman, 1987).

Marqusee, Mike, *Anyone but England* (London: Verso, 1994).

Marshall, Michael, *Gentlemen and Players* (London: Grafton Books, 1987).

Marx, Karl, *The German Ideology* (London: ElecBook CD Rom, 1998).

Martin-Jenkins, Christopher, *Twenty Years On: Cricket's Years of Change, 1963–1983* (London: Willow Books, 1984).

Mason, Tony, *Sport in Britain* (London: Faber & Faber, 1988).

McIntosh, Peter, *Fair Play: Ethics in Sport and Education* (London: Heinemann, 1979).

Meli, Francis, *South Africa Belongs to Us. A History of the ANC* (London: James Currey, 1988).

Miliband, Ralph, *Parliamentary Socialism* (London: George Allen & Unwin, 1961).

Miliband, Ralph, *The State in Capitalist Society* (London: Weidenfeld & Nicolson, 1967).

Miliband, Ralph, *Capitalist Democracy in Britain* (Oxford: Oxford University Press, 1982).

Miller, J.D.B., *The Nature of Politics* (London: Gerald Duckworth, 1962).

Moorhouse, Geoffrey, *Lord's* (London: Hodder & Stoughton, 1983).

Morrah, Patrick, *The Golden Age of Cricket* (London: Eyre & Spottiswoode, 1967).

Nandy, Ashis, *The Tao of Cricket* (New Delhi: Penguin Books, 1989).

Nauright, John, *Sport, Cultures and Identities in South Africa* (London: Leicester University Press, 1997).

Nauright, John and Chandler, Timothy (eds), *Making Men: Rugby and Masculine Identity* (London: Frank Cass, 1996).

Nixon, Howard, 'Idealised Functions of Sport: Religious and Political Socialisation through Sport', *Journal of Sport and Social Issues*, 6, 1 (1982).

Nourse, Dudley, *Cricket in the Blood* (London: Hodder & Stoughton Ltd, 1949).

Nyren, J., *The Cricketers of My Time* (London: Robson Books, 1988).

O'Meara, Dan, *Forty Lost Years* (Randberg: Ravan Press, 1996).

Odendaal, Andre, *Cricket in Isolation: The Politics of Race and Cricket in South Africa* (Cape Town: published by the author, 1977).

Omer-Cooper, J.D., *History of Southern Africa*, 2nd edn (London: James Currey Publishers, 1994).

Orkin, Mark (ed.), *Sanctions against Apartheid* (London: Catholic Institute for International Relations, 1989).

Parker, G.A., *South African Sports: An Official Handbook* (London, 1897).

Pape, R.A., 'Why Economic Sanctions Do Not Work', *International Security*, Vol.22 (1997).

Parsons, Wayne, *Public Policy* (Cheltenham: Edward Elgar, 1995).

Pelzer, A.N., *Verwoerd Speaks: Speeches 1948–1966* (Johannesburg: Afrikaanse Perboekhandel, 1966).

Pollard, Jack, *The Formative Years of Australian Cricket, 1803–93* (London: Angus & Robertson, 1987).

Pollard, Jack, *The Complete Illustrated History of Australian Cricket* (Ringwood Victoria: Pelham Books, 1992).

Polley, Martin, *Moving the Goalposts* (London: Routledge, 1998).

Ponton, Geoffrey and Gill, Peter, *Introduction to Politics* (Oxford: Martin Robertson, 1982).

Porter, Bernard, *The Lion's Share. A Short History of British Imperialism, 1850–1983*, 2nd edn (London: Longman, 1984).

Pounds, N.J.G., *The Culture of the English People. Iron Age to Industrial Revolution* (Cambridge: Cambridge University Press, 1994).

Proctor, Mike, *South Africa: The Years of Isolation and the Return to International Cricket* (Durban: Bok Books International, 1994).

Protea Cricket Annual of South Africa, vol.37 (Cape Town: Protea Assurance, 1990)

Ramachandra, Guha, 'Cricket, Caste, Community, Colonialism', *International Journal of the History of Sport*, Vol.14 (1997).

Ramsamy, Sam, *Apartheid, The Real Hurdle* (London: International Defence & Aid Fund, 1982).

Raphael, D.D., *Problems of Political Philosophy* (London: Macmillan, 1976).

Rayvern Allen, David (ed.), *Cricket's Silver Lining, 1864–1914* (London: Guild Publishing, 1987).

Rayvern Allen, David (ed.), *The Essential John Arlott* (London: Guild Publishing, 1989).

Richards, Barry, *The Barry Richards Story* (Exeter: Readers Union, 1978).

Richards, Vivian, *Hitting Across the Line* (London: BCA, 1991).

Riordan, James, 'Marx, Lenin and Physical Culture', *Journal of Sport History*, Vol.3 (1976).

Rodee, Carlton, Anderson Totton, Carl Christol and Thomas Greene,

Introduction to Political Science (New York: McGraw Hill, 1976).

Ross, Gordon, *A History of Cricket* (London: Arthur Baker, 1972).

Sabine, George H. and Thomas L. Thorson, *A History of Political Theory*, 4th edn (Illinois: Dryden Press, 1973).

Sage, George H. (ed.), *Sport and American Society: Selected Readings* (Massachusetts: Addison-Wesley Publishing Company, 1974).

Sandiford, Keith, *Cricket and the Victorians* (Aldershot: Sugar Press, 1994).

Saul, John and Stephen Gelb, *The Crisis in South Africa: Class Defence, Class Revolution* (London: Monthly Review Press, 1981).

Schrire, Robert, *Adapt or Die: The End of White Politics in South Africa* (London: Hurst & Company, 1992).

Scruton, Roger, *The Meaning of Conservatism,* 2nd edn, (London, Macmillan, 1984).

Searle, Chris, 'Race before Cricket: Cricket, Empire, and the White Rose', *Race and Class*, 31, 3 (1990).

Simon, B. and Bradley, I., *The Victorian Public School* (London: Gill & Macmillan, 1991).

Simons, Jack and Ray Simons, *Class and Colour in South Africa, 1850–1950* (International Defence & Aid Fund for Southern Africa, 1983).

Soltau, Roger, *An Introduction to Politics* (London: Longmans, Green & Co, 1951).

Sparks, Allister, *Tomorrow is Another Country*, (London: Arrow Books, 1995).

Sparks, Allister, *The Mind of South Africa* (London: Arrow Books, 1997).

Spiro, Herbert, *Politics as the Master Science: From Plato to Mao* (New York: Harper & Row, 1970).

Stoker, Gerry and Marsh, David (eds), *Theory and Methods in Political Science* (Basingstoke: Macmillan, 1995).

Suter, Keith D., *Australia's Changing Policies towards Apartheid* (New York: UN Centre against Apartheid, 1985).

Swanson, Guy, *Social Change* (London: Scott, Foresman & Company, 1971).

Swanton, E.W., George Plumptre and John Woodcock (eds), *Barclays World of Cricket. The Game from A to Z* (London: Guild Publishing, 1986).

Tansey, Stephen D., *Politics: The Basics*, 2nd edn (London: Routledge, 2000).

Thompson, Richard, *Retreat from Apartheid: New Zealand's Sporting Contacts with South Africa* (London: Oxford University Press, 1975).

Tomlinson, Alan and Whannel, Garry (eds), *Five Ring Circus* (London: Pluto, 1984).

Tomlinson, M., 'State Intervention in Voluntary Sport: The Inner city Policy Context', *Leisure Studies*, vol.6 (1987).

Tozer, Malcolm, 'Cricket, School and Empire', *International Journal of the History of Sport*, Vol.16 (1989).

Van der Merwe and J.G. Floris, 'Sport and Games in Boer Prisoner of War

Camps During the Anglo-Boer War', *International Journal of the History of Sport* (Dec. 1992).

Walvin, J., *The People's Game* (Edinburgh: Mainstream Publishing, 1994).

Warner, P.F., *The MCC in South Africa* (London: Chapman & Hall, 1906).

Warner, P.F. (ed.), *Imperial Cricket* (London: The London & Counties Press Association Ltd, 1912).

Wells, A.W., *South Africa: A Planned Tour of the Country Today* (London: J.M. Dent & Sons, 1949).

Welsh, William, *Studying Politics* (London: Nelson, 1973).

Whannel, Garry, *Blowing the Whistle: The Politics of Sport* (London: Pluto Press, 1983).

Whitson, David, 'Sport and Hegemony: On the Construction of the Dominant Culture', *Sociology of Sport Journal*, vol. 1 part 1 (1984).

Wilkins, Ivor and Strydom, Hans, *The Broederbond* (London: Paddington Press, 1979).

Wilson, Francis and Ramphele, Mamphela, *Uprooting Poverty: The South African Challenge* (Cape Town: David Philip, 1989).

Wilson, Monica and Leonard Thompson (eds), *The Oxford History of South Africa, Vol II – 1870–1966* (Oxford: Clarendon Press, 1971).

Wolpe, Harold, *Race, Class and the Apartheid State* (London: UNESCO, 1988).

Wood, John (ed.), *Powell and the 1970 Election* (Kingswood: Elliot Right Way Books, 1970).

Woolmer, Bob, *Pirate and Rebel? An Autobiography* (London: Arthur Baker, 1984).

Worden, Nigel, *The Making of Modern South Africa. Conquest, Segregation and Apartheid* (Oxford: Blackwell, 1994).

Worrell, Frank, *Cricket Punch* (London: Stanley Paul, 1960).

Wright, Graeme, *Betrayal. The Struggle for Cricket's Soul* (Great Britain: H.F. & G. Witherby, 1993).

Wynne-Thomas, Peter and Peter Arnold, *Cricket in Conflict* (Middlesex: Newnes Books, 1984).

List of Publications

Cricket Life
The Cricketer
The Guardian
The Independent
The Observer
Third Man
The Times
The Sunday Times
Wisden Cricket Monthly

Index

9 780714 682846